FEDERAL TAXATION OF CAPITAL ASSETS

ıd how they may be
e contributions, and
are affected by cor-
ons.

ion is needed on the
capital assets, it can
ok — short sales, puts,
ıins and losses, tax-
ınts, special situation

Robert S. Holzman's new book will prove invaluable to an expanding circle of investors and their advisors. It will serve the casual investor with questions of basis, holding period, and allocation. It will serve the sophisticated professional who is involved in straddle options, when-issued stocks, and flat bonds. The book is intended not only for those who sell or exchange capital assets; but for those who merely hold such assets.

Federal Taxation of Capital Assets is planned for corporate officials concerned with mergers and acquisitions. It is designed also for those who must appraise the consequences of capital transactions, such as securities brokers. It is intended for those who lend on securities and therefore must understand the valuation of collateral, such as bankers. Most importantly, it is meant for advisors — accountants, attorneys, and security analysts.

Capital assets can often be a tricky and exasperating area, requiring specialized knowledge and experience. Robert Holzman's new book gives the reader that knowledge, by providing an up-to-the-minute analysis of what capital assets are, how they are taxed, when they are taxed, how they are valued for tax purposes, how capital assets figure in

THE AUTHOR

n, Ph.D., is Professor
e Graduate School of
ıstration, New York

ıook to be published.
ıclude **Tax-Free Reor-**
to Pension and Profit
ınd **Business Purpose,**
r's **Problem of Proof.**
s tax articles have
counting, business,
ınanagement, and tax

past president of The
ın and is a member of
cutives Institute and of
ıing Council of New
as editor of The Tax
ary, and is a member
ooard of **Taxation for**

FEDERAL TAXATION
OF
CAPITAL ASSETS

by
Robert S. Holzman, Ph.D.

FARNSWORTH PUBLISHING COMPANY, INC.

Lynbrook, New York • 1969

Library of Congress
Catalog Card No. 69–17094

TO B₁

IN APPRECIATION

Preface

There is a vast difference between the capital gains tax and the taxation of capital assets. The former is only one phase of the latter. This book is concerned with the taxation of capital assets: what they are, how they are taxed, when they are taxed, how they are valued for tax purposes, how they figure in estate planning, how they are affected by corporate reorganizations, how they may be used for charitable contributions, what happens when a Governmental agency orders a divestiture of stock, the extent to which taxation is determined by the names on a stock certificate, how the language of a bond indenture shapes the tax consequences, and a whole host of other subjects mentioned in the detailed Table of Contents.

The seriousness of the problem may be masqueraded by the fact that many financially sophisticated persons cannot refer to capital gains taxation without a smirk. "Confronted with the continuance of extremely high surtax rates . . . the economically fortunate have supplemented golf and polo with a new pastime—the conversion of ordinary income into capital gains."* To play this game, it is necessary to know what a capital asset is for purposes of Federal taxation. The game is made difficult because the rules constantly are changing. There are many "complex, intricate, and sometimes technically significant factors which Congress, the weaver, evaluates as it weaves and unweaves the seamy web men call tax law." *United States v. Bond et al.,* 258 F.2d 577 (5th Cir., 1958). And in the manner of Penelope, the most famous of all weavers, Congress sometimes seems to unravel at night what it wove that very day.

The taxation of capital assets is a far more troublesome matter than one might suspect. Capital assets are not always given capital asset treatment. Non-capital assets are sometimes given capital asset treatment. Property may be a capital asset in the hands of one person but not in the hands

---

* Allan A. Bakst, "Does Dissolution Followed By Reincorporation Constitute a Reorganization?" *TAXES—The Tax Magazine,* November 1965, Volume 33, Number 11, Page 815.

of another. The capital characterization of an asset may change. Property passing to a parent corporation from its wholly owned subsidiary may lose its status as a capital asset.

Because of the advantages that (usually) are accorded to capital assets for tax purposes, many transactions are cast laboriously into the *manner* of capital assets or are made to resemble situations where capital treatment is available. In a case involving payments received by José Ferrer for portraying the dwarfed Toulouse-Lautrec in the motion picture "Moulin Rouge," the court observed: "The difficulties Mr. Ferrer must have had in fitting himself into the shape of the artist can hardly have been greater than ours in determining whether the transaction here at issue fits the rubric 'gain from the sale or exchange of a capital asset held for more than 6 months' . . . or constitutes ordinary income. . . ." *Commissioner v. Ferrer,* 304 F.2d 125 (2d Cir., 1962).

One of the difficulties of classification of capital assets is that the litigants shift roles with charming nonchalance. As one court noted: "If the situation here had been the other way around, that is to say, if the transactions had resulted in gains instead of losses, it would not be surprising to find the Commissioner occupying the position now championed by the taxpayer, and vice versa. So things are apt to go in the domain of tax litigation." *United States v. Chinook Investment Company,* 136 F.2d 984 (9th Cir., 1943).

The problem is complicated by the fact that many of the specific rules as to the taxation of capital assets are rendered inoperative by other provisions in the Internal Revenue Code. A transaction, even if unquestionably *bona fide,* may not be recognized for tax purposes if it is between persons of specified degrees of relationship. In many areas, the granting of specified tax treatment by one section of the Code is cancelled by another section, in recognition of the fact that "[s]ecurities transactions have been the most common vehicle for the creation of intra-family losses." *McWilliams et al. v. Commissioner,* 331 U.S. 694 (1947). Tax treatment varies as between United States and foreign parties; the number of shareholders of a corporation may affect taxability.

Ordinarily, a transaction with the primary or sole purpose of obtaining a tax advantage may be disregarded for tax purposes by the Internal Revenue Service. But the preferential treatment so often afforded to capital assets continues to be preferential in this area. "That the taxpayer's purpose was to achieve capital gains treatment," declared one court, "does not destroy the bona fides of the sale." *Harry Roff et al.,* 36 T.C. 818 (1961).

The frequent partiality of the tax laws towards capital assets takes many forms. But, to coin a *cliché,* there is no rose without a thorn. A function of this book is the pointing out of various traps for the unwary—even the sophisticated unwary. For example, it is widely believed that a corporate distribution cannot be taxed as a dividend unless the payor corporation has earnings and profits; the statutory definition of a dividend so states. But earnings and profits may be imputed to the corporation because, thirty years ago, this company had participated in a tax-free reorganization involving a corporation which *did* have earnings and profits. That the books of account gave no hint of this is irrelevant. "For some purposes," one court pointed out, "it may be entirely true that general financial statements do not always reflect all information pertinent to tax liability." *Dunning et al. v. United States,* 353 F.2d 940 (8th Cir., 1965).

Another definitional trap pointed out in this book is the chameleon-like meaning of certain key terms, where the statutory language varies with the particular section of the Internal Revenue Code involved. Terms such as "securities," "control," and "constructive ownership of stock" have no definition of universal application.

The problem of valuation is important in the case of the estate tax and the gift tax, and also in basis problems involving the income tax. There are tax traps here. It is believed in most quarters that for a listed stock, actual New York Stock Exchange (or other market) prices on the critical date are controlling. This book shows the highly important exceptions to this supposed "rule." Stock of closely-held corporations, shares with restrictions, and minority interests present other problems which are discussed here.

This book will serve the casual investor with questions of basis, holding period, and allocation. It will serve the sophisticated professional who is involved in straddle options, when-issued stocks, and flat bonds. The book is intended not only for those who sell or exchange capital assets or give them away, but for those who merely hold much assets: for example, there may be assessments, split-ups, partial liquidations, redemptions, etc., without affirmative action on the part of the taxpayer.

The book is planned for corporate officials concerned with mergers and acquisitions. It is designed also for those who must appraise the consequences of capital transactions (*e.g.,* corporate reorganizations), such as securities brokers. It is intended for those parties who lend on securities and therefore must understand the valuation of collateral, such as bankers. Most importantly (because variations on these problems constantly recur), it is meant for those who advise the persons that have been mentioned: accountants, attorneys, and security analysts.

ROBERT S. HOLZMAN

New York University.
March 1969

Table of Contents

ix

Chapter 1

What is a Capital Asset?

Introduction

The term "capital asset" as used for Federal income tax purposes differs from the meaning used by economists, accountants, and others. The tax meaning of the term is best understood by noting that the words were selected to implement the philosophy of preferential capital gains taxation.

"The capital gains provisions are remedial provisions. Congress intended to alleviate the burden on a taxpayer whose property had increased in value over a long period of time from having the profits from sales taxed at graduated tax rates designed for a single year's income. The purpose is to protect 'investment property' as distinguished from 'stock in trade,' or property bought and sold for a profit. It is our view that this policy was not meant to apply to a situation where one of the essential purposes in holding the property is *sale." Rollingwood Corp. v. Commissioner,* 190 F.2d 263 (9th Cir., 1951). Thus, "the 'capital asset' which is accorded favored treatment by the statute is commonly associated with a 'going concern.' . . . This favored treatment is given for the purpose of facilitating ready transfer of going enterprises by reducing the incidence of taxation on increments in value built up over a long period, such as might be attributable to good will and the like." *Haggard, Jr. et al. v. Wood,* 298 F.2d 94 (9th Cir., 1961). "It is therefore basic that to qualify as a capital asset, the property must represent an investment capable of appreciating in value over a period of time." *Lozoff et al. v. United States,* 266 F. Supp. 966 (D.C., E.D. Wis., 1967).

Not everything which can be called property in the ordinary sense, and which is outside the statutory exclusion, qualifies as a capital asset. A capital asset is something in which the taxpayer has an investment and hence a basis. *Ralph Bellamy et al.,* 43 T.C. 487 (1965). "One common characteristic of the group held to come within the capital gain provision is that the taxpayer had either what might be called an 'estate' in . . . or an 'encumbrance' on . . . or an option to acquire an interest in . . . property which, if itself held, would be a capital asset." *Commissioner v. Ferrer,* 304 F.2d 125 (2d Cir., 1962).

The courts interpret the definition of "capital assets" strictly. "The definition of 'capital asset' is considerably broader than is justified by the rationale for capital gains and if read literally would encompass income which Congress did not intend to give the benefit of the lower capital gains tax rate. Consequently, the courts have narrowly interpreted the definition of capital assets." *Jaglom et al. v. Commissioner,* 303 F.2d 874 (2d Cir., 1962).

The Capital Asset Definition

All property is to be treated as capital assets, unless this property can be brought within one of the stated exceptions in the definition of capital assets. *Achille O. Van Suetendael et al.,* T.C. Memo., Docket Nos. 107681, 109703, and 108929, entered September 25, 1944, *aff'd,* 152 F.2d 654 (2d Cir., 1945).

For Federal income tax purposes, the term "capital asset" means property held by the taxpayer (whether or not connected with his trade or business), except for:

(1) Stock in trade of the taxpayer or any other property which would properly be included in his inventory if on hand at the close of the taxable year, or property held by him primarily for sale to customers in the ordinary course of his trade or business.

(2) Property, used in his trade or business, which is subject to the depreciation allowance, or real property used in his trade or business.

(3) A copyright, a literary, musical, or artistic composition, or similar property, held by:

    (a) a taxpayer whose personal efforts created such property; or

    (b) a taxpayer in whose hands the basis of this property is determined in whole or in part by reference to the basis of the property in the hands of the person whose personal efforts created the property.

(4) Accounts or notes receivable acquired in the ordinary course of trade or business for services rendered or from the sale of property described in (1), above.

(5) An obligation of the United States or any of its possessions, or of

a state or territory, or any political subdivision thereof, or of the District of Columbia, issued on or after March 1, 1941, on a discount basis and payable without interest at a fixed maturity not exceeding one year from the date of issue. Internal Revenue Code Section 1221.

Any asset not excluded by one of these five exceptions is a capital asset. "In determining whether property is a 'capital asset,' the period for which held is immaterial." Regulations Section 1.1221-1(a).

In summary, to qualify as other than capital assets in the hands of a taxpayer, these assets must be: (1) Accounts receivable *acquired by* the taxpayer in carrying on *its* business; (2) inventories *of* the taxpayer used in carrying on *its* business; and (3) real estate and depreciable property *used* by the taxpayer in *its* business. *The Acro Manufacturing Company,* 39 T.C. 377 (1962), *aff'd,* 334 F.2d 40 (6th Cir., 1964).

The term "capital asset" in Section 1221 is to be applied narrowly, although its exclusions are to be interpreted broadly. Everyday operations of a business are directed to ordinary income rather than to capital gain and loss. *Corn Products Refining Co. v. Commissioner,* 350 U.S. 46 (1955). Taxpayers have not fared well by arguing that the sale of various rights did not beget ordinary income on the ground that these rights met the literal language of the statutory definition in Section 1221. "The federal courts have not felt bound by the literal words of the statutory definition." *Hallcraft Homes, Inc. v. Commissioner,* 336 F.2d 701 (9th Cir., 1964).

Section 1221 provides that the term "capital asset" does not include "property held by the taxpayer primarily for sale to customers in the ordinary course of his trade or business." "The critical language here is—*in the ordinary course of the taxpayer's trade or business." The Acro Manufacturing Company,* 39 T.C. 377 (1962), *aff'd,* 334 F.2d 40 (6th Cir., 1964). In ascertaining whether the assets acquired for sale were so acquired in the ordinary course of the taxpayer's trade or business, "the test normally applied . . . is the frequency and continuity of the transactions claimed to result in a trade or business." *Rollingwood v. Commissioner,* 190 F.2d 263 (9th Cir., 1951).

To the vast majority of persons, "capital assets" means stock or securities. But "Corporate stock is not invariably classified as a capital asset. To ascertain whether stock is bought and kept not for investment purposes, but only as an incident to the conduct of the taxpayer's business, all the surrounding circumstances must be considered. The substance, as distinguished from the form, of the taxpayer's actions determines whether the sale of the stock results in ordinary gain or loss in this particular case." *John J. Grier Co. v. United States,* 328 F.2d 163 (7th Cir., 1963). "The tax treatment of the loss on the sale of . . . stock depends on the purpose for which the [taxpayer] acquired the stock. Stock purchased as an investment is a capital asset; when sold, it creates a capital gain or loss. But stock purchased in the ordinary course of business where the only purpose is to insure a vital source of inventory is not a capital asset, and the loss upon its sale is deductible from ordinary income." *Electrical Fittings Corp.,* 33 T.C. 1026 (1960).

"As a general proposition, of course, capital stock does not constitute 'property' and, aside from stock sold by dealers in the usual course of their business, does not fall within any of the express exclusions of section 1221. . . . But the term 'property' as used in section 1221 is an elastic concept and not all-inclusive. . . . This flexible approach to the concept of 'capital asset' has been applied and developed in a number of . . . cases." *Booth Newspapers, Inc. et al. v. United States,* 303 F.2d 916 (Ct. Cl., 1962).

In the case of a bank, stock in another bank is not treated as a capital asset under certain circumstances. I.R.C. Section 582(b). See Chapter 13, "Special Situation Issues."

Other Forms Of Capital Asset

The following forms of property have been held to be capital assets:

Stock purchase warrants bought by an individual. *Commissioner v. Lauson Stone Estate,* 210 F.2d 33 (3d Cir., 1954).

A stockholder's right under a buy-sell agreement. *Turzillo v. Commissioner,* 346 F.2d 884 (6th Cir., 1965).

The right to buy or to sell stock on a "when issued" basis. I.T. 3721, 1945 CB 164.

Investment in stock of a co-operative apartment house. The investment was not in a lease but in stock. *Junius B. Peake et al.,* T.C. Memo., Docket No. 27636, entered June 15, 1951. The reputed tax advantages of being a stockholder in a co-operative apartment house corporation may be lost without the taxpayer's awareness. The statute requires that the corporation meet four tests: (1) one class of stock is to be outstanding, (2) each shareholder is entitled to an apartment solely by reason of his stockholding, (3) no stockholder is entitled to receive distributions not out of earnings except upon the complete or partial liquidation of the corporation, and (4) 80% or more of the gross income for the year must be derived from tenant shareholders. I.R.C. Section 216(b)(1). But one or more of these conditions may be forfeited without action or knowledge by the taxpayer.

Stock exchange membership. *Munson v. Commissioner,* 100 F.2d 363 (2d Cir., 1938).

A business name. *Rainier Brewing Company v. Commissioner,* 165 F.2d 217 (9th Cir., 1948). The right to the use of a corporate name under a state's corporation laws. Revenue Ruling 55–694, 1955–2 CB 299.

Good will. *Ensey Bank and Trust Company v. United States,* 154 F.2d 968 (5th Cir., 1946). Good will "is the sum total of those imponderable qualities which attract the custom of a business,—what brings patronage to the business." *Grace Bros., Inc. v. Commissioner,* 173 F.2d 170 (9th Cir., 1949).

A franchise, where the holder did not intend to use it in his trade or business; he intended to sell the franchise and in fact did so. *Arthur F. Brooks et al.,* T.C. Memo. 1964–285, filed October 30, 1964.

The sale of a partner's interest in a partnership constitutes the sale of a capital asset, except as otherwise provided in Section 751 with respect to unrealized receivables and inventory items which have appreciated substantially in value. Revenue Ruling 59–109, 1959–1 CB 168.

Asset Characterization Depends Upon Who Holds It

Certain assets are capital in the hands of one person but not in the hands of another person. Typical of this phenomenon is a warehouse receipt. In one case, a taxpayer was engaged in the wholesale and retail sale of groceries, cigars, perfumes, and alcoholic beverages. Although it was not a distiller, the taxpayer had its own rectifying and bottling plant, for which it had the necessary permits. It purchased barreled whiskey, some of which was stored in warehouses, the proprietors of which issued warehouse receipts to the taxpayer. In the taxable years, the taxpayer purchased warehouse receipts in excess of its requirements, in the belief that wartime shortages would lead to profitable sale of these receipts. There was no segregation of this whiskey from the taxpayer's other whiskey in warehouses; there was no differentiation on the books or in accounting procedures. All of the gain from warehouse receipts was taxable in full as being from the sale of a non-capital asset. *S. S. Pierce Company v. United States,* D.C., Mass., 1957.

But a contrary result was found in the case of another taxpayer, a wholesale liquor dealer, who purchased case goods from distillers and importers for re-sale to retail liquor dealers. This taxpayer never had engaged in buying and selling warehouse receipts as a broker. During the taxable period, the taxpayer obtained warehouse receipts from two sources: (1) as a dividend in kind on a minority interest (2½ %) on a distilling company's stock and (2) on a quota basis made by another distiller to all of its regular distributors, as this distiller wished to dispose of a particular brand and lacked the means of financing a regular sales program. The taxpayer argued that (1) was an investment and (2) was a means of obtaining the case goods it *did* need and want. "[T]hat the warehouse receipts could be converted into stock in trade," declared the court, "does not render inimicable their primary acquisition for investment purposes." This taxpayer had no way of using the whiskey covered by the warehouse receipts in the absence of a bottling permit, which it never had owned. The receipts were capital in the taxpayer's hands. *Continental Distributing Co., Inc. v. United States,* 143 F. Supp. 652 (D.C., N.D. Ill., 1956).

Demonstration cars of an automobile distributor were capital assets, where records showed that the vehicles were not used as inventory. *Latimer-Looney Chevrolet, Inc.,* 19 T.C. 120 (1952). Ordinary income was found where the taxpayer could not establish that the cars in question were not inventory items. *W. R. Stephens Co. v. Commissioner,* 199 F.2d 665 (8th Cir., 1952).

An endowment insurance policy upon his life was a capital asset in the hands of the insured. But when, twenty-seven years after the contract date and thirty-five days before the policy matured, he sold it, the entire amount of the gain realized was ordinary. One "may not convert what would otherwise have been received by him as ordinary income by casting the transaction as a sale of a capital asset." *Bolling Jones, Jr. et al.,* 39 T.C. 404 (1962).

Inventory assets are not capital assets if held by a taxpayer primarily for sale to customers in the ordinary course of his trade or business. I.R.C. Section 1221(1). But an asset of a type ordinarily regarded as an inventory item *is* a capital asset if it would not be included in the taxpayer's closing inventory were it on hand at year-end nor was it held for sale to customers in the ordinary course of the trade or business. Such was the finding in the case of a broker who sold malting barley, when he purchased on an experimental basis a quantity of an utterly different type of grain. His regular inventory was for sale to brewers for malting purposes; the new grain was for sale as seed to farmers who agreed to experiment with it. *Hufford et al. v. United States,* 254 F. Supp. 272 (D.C., E.D. Wash., 1966).

Commodity futures contracts, not acquired for hedging purposes, nor as a gambling transaction, are capital assets. But such is not the case where a taxpayer buys this commodity, owns it, and sells the same commodity. *Patterson v. Hightower, Jr. et al.,* 245 F.2d 765 (5th Cir., 1957). See Chapter 6.

The taxability of a sum received in settlement of a lawsuit depends for capital characterization upon the nature of the claim and the actual basis of recovery. *Ione Thompson et al.*, T.C. Memo. 1965–237, filed August 30, 1965.

The overwhelming weight of authority is that contracts for the performance of services are not capital assets, and the proceeds from their transfer will not be accorded capital gains treatment. For the citations *pro* and *contra*, see *Maryland Coal and Coke Company v. McGinnes,* 225 F. Supp. 854 (D.C., E.D. Pa., 1964). The right to earn ordinary income is not "property" for capital gain purposes under Section 1221. *Commissioner v. Gillette Motor Co.,* 364 U.S. 130 (1960). The consideration so received has been described as a lump sum substitute for future ordinary income. *Commissioner v. P. G. Lake, Inc.,* 356 U.S. 260 (1958). "[I]t was not the purpose of Congress to permit taxpayers to convert ordinary income into a capital gain by assigning the right to receive it to a third party." *Pridemark, Inc. v. Commissioner,* 345 F.2d 35 (4th Cir., 1965). "The ground rule is that a right to receive ordinary income, produced by a capital asset, is not transmuted into a capital asset by the sale or assignment of the capital asset together with the right to receive the ordinary income." *Tunnell v. United States,* 259 F.2d 916 (3d Cir., 1958).

"A distinction has arisen between an income-producing capital asset and the income which it produces. Gains arising from the sale of such an asset which has appreciated in value are capital gains, but gains flowing from the sale of an accrued right to collect the income from such an asset are not. Thus, the right to collect ordinary income is not transmuted into capital gain by its sale. . . . If both the income-producing asset and the right to accrued income from the asset are sold together, the purchase price must be allocated between the two, only the former being a capital asset." *Jaglom et al. v. Commissioner,* 303 F.2d 874 (2d Cir., 1962). Thus, if a taxpayer who owns common stock upon which a dividend has accrued sells the stock and the right to the dividend, that part of the sales proceeds allocable to the sale of the right to the dividend is ordinary income. *Brundage v. United States,* 275 F.2d 424 (7th Cir., 1960). If a taxpayer sells his interest in motion picture rights including accrued royalties, those proceeds which represent the accrued royalties are ordinary income. *Bessie Lasky et al.,* 22 T.C. 13 (1954), *appeal dismissed,* 235 F.2d 97 (9th Cir., 1956), *aff'd,* 352 U.S. 1027 (1957).

Capital gain was realized upon the sale of a life interest in a trust. "The question here is whether the taxpayer merely assigned future income or parted with title to the corpus of the estate from which income was expected to be produced." *Allen v. First National Bank & Trust Co.,* 157 F.2d 592 (5th Cir., 1946). A taxpayer purchased remainder interests in trusts. After the deaths of the tenants but prior to the distribution of the estate remainders to the trusts, he transferred his interests therein. His motivation was to obtain capital gain treatment for income tax purposes. To the extent that the gain realized was in fact the realization of interest discount, it was ordinary income. Thus, an allocation of the proceeds between ordinary income and capital gain components was necessary. *Jones et al. v. Commissioner,* 330 F.2d 302 (3d Cir., 1964).

Where property is sold for a stipulated percentage interest in the possible net profit to be realized from the ultimate resale of this property by the buyer, any receipts obtained by the original seller are not capital gain. The percentage interest is not a capital asset. *Pounds et al. v. United States,* D.C., S.D. Texas, 1965, *aff'd,* 372 F.2d 342 (5th Cir., 1967).

In a so-called "bootstrap" operation, it was held that ordinary income may be converted into capital gain if the owners of a business sell the venture to outside parties with payments to be made out of future earnings of the business. *Commissioner v. Brown et al.,* 380 U.S. 563 (1965). The Internal Revenue Service has announced that it will not follow this Supreme Court decision in any other situation, stating: "The *Clay Brown* decision does not extend to cases where the amount payable to the 'sellers' for their stock is in excess of the fair market value of the stock. In cases of this type the Service will continue to resist what is in substance an attempt to convert future business profits to capital gains." Revenue Ruling 66–153, 1966–1 CB 187.

"Held By The Taxpayer Primarily For Sale To Customers In The Ordinary Course Of His Trade Or Business"

An asset is non-capital if held for sale in the ordinary course of the taxpayer's trade or business. But "trade or business" is subject to various interpretations. *Fackler v. Commissioner,* 133 F.2d 509 (6th Cir., 1943). So is the term "ordinary course." *Thompson Lumber Co.,* 43 B.T.A. 726 (1941).

" '[C]arrying on any trade or business,' . . . involves holding one's self out to others as engaged in the selling of goods or services." Mr. Justice Frankfurter, concurring, in *Deputy v. DuPont,* 308 U.S. 498 (1940). " '[T]rade or business' presupposes an existing business with which the taxpayer is directly connected. . . ." *John F. Koons,* 35 T.C. 1092 (1961). " 'Used in the trade or business' means 'devoted to the trade or business,' and includes all such property, whether actually in use during the taxable year or not." *Carter-Colton Cigar Company,* 9 T.C. 219 (1947).

In one case, securities held by a broker were deemed to be capital assets. His contention that he might or would have sold them if he could have gotten "his price" for them did not make them securities for sale in the ordinary course of his business. *Franklin Q. Brown et al.,* 9 B.T.A. 965 (1927).

The term "held for sale to customers in the ordinary course of the business" includes a situation where there is only one large customer as well as the more common situation where there are many customers. *Nielsen et al. v. United States et al.,* 333 F.2d 615 (6th Cir., 1964).

Assets are not held for sale in the ordinary course of the business if they cannot in fact be sold in the ordinary course of this business. Thus, a corporation which sustained losses in securities after it had disposed of its manufacturing business could not treat these losses as ordinary. Neither the corporation nor any of its officers were members of a stock exchange, nor were they licensed either by the Securities and Exchange Commission or by the State of California to sell securities to the public. Any securities bought and sold, therefore, must have been for the corporation's own account, inasmuch as it could not have had customers. *Mirro-Dynamics Corporation v. United States,* 374 F.2d 14 (9th Cir., 1967).

The statute denies capital gain treatment to profits reaped from the sale of property held by the taxpayer *primarily* for sale to customers in the ordinary course of the trade or business. The purpose of the statutory provision is to differentiate between the "profits arising from the everyday operations of a business" on the one hand (*Corn Products Company v. Commissioner,* 350 U.S. 46 (1955)) and "the realization of appreciation in value accrued over a substantial period of time" on the other (*Commissioner v. Gillette Motor Company,* 364 U.S. 130 (1960)). As used in this connection, "primarily" means "of first importance" or "principally." *Malat et al. v. Commissioner,* 383 U.S. 569 (1966).

"Most of the cases dealing with the problem of whether property is held primarily for sale to customers in the ordinary course of the trade or business involve situations where the taxpayer is engaged in some activity apart from his usual occupation and the question is whether this activity amounts to a business." *Rollingwood Corp. v. Commissioner,* 190 F.2d 263 (9th Cir., 1951). If property at the time of sale was being held primarily for sale to customers in the ordinary course of the trade or business, capital treatment is denied, irrespective of the motive or cause. Thus, under a consent decree with the United States Department of Justice, a corporation sold assets which it held solely for leasing purposes. The income thus derived was ordinary, even though the taxpayer made the sale under compulsion against its own preference. *American Can Company et al. v. Commissioner et al.,* 317 F.2d 604 (2d Cir., 1963). But a sale of a corporation's assets did not result in ordinary income even though there had been two "forced" sales in the past fifteen years, where the property had not been held for the production of income. *Desilu Productions, Inc.,* T.C. Memo. 1965–307, filed November 20, 1965.

Stock or securities will not be capital assets where acquired primarily for reasons of business necessity and not for investment purposes. *Weather-Seal, Inc.,* T.C. Memo. 1963–102, filed April 8, 1963. If a taxpayer holds property for the dual purpose of rental or sale, whichever proves to be more profitable, capital gain treatment is not allowed. *Desilu Productions, Inc.,* T.C. Memo. 1965–307, filed November 20, 1965.

There is no fixed formula for resolving the issue of whether assets were held primarily for sale by the taxpayer in the ordinary course of his trade or business. "Rather, a congerie of factors is to be considered and weighed, no one factor being necessarily decisive." *Tidwell et al. v. Commissioner,* 298 F.2d 864 (4th Cir., 1962).

Real Estate.—Whether real estate has been held primarily for sale to customers in the ordinary course of the trade or business is determined by such factors as: (1) the purpose for which the property was acquired, (2) the making of improvements on the property, (3) the advertising of it to attract purchasers, and (4) the continuity and frequency of sales as distinguished from isolated transactions. *DeLisio v. Vidal,* 233 F.2d 909 (10th Cir., 1956). Other factors are:

The holding of a real estate license, telephone listing as a realtor, personal solicitations as opposed to sales to persons who initiated the negotiations. *Real Estate Corporation v. Commissioner,* 301 F.2d 423 (10th Cir., 1962).

Whether the property was listed for sale directly or through brokers. *Fishback, Jr. et al. v. United States,* 215 F. Supp. 621 (D.C., S.D., 1963).

Was the acquisition that of land adjoining the taxpayer's existing property? *Ralph J. Oace et al.,* 39 T.C. 743 (1963).

The length of period the property was held. *Lloyd E. Mitchell, Incorporated v. United States,* 259 F. Supp. 345 (D.C., Md., 1966).

Whether the property had been obtained by devise or gift. Where a person has inherited or unwanted property which cannot be disposed of in the form of unimproved acreage, subdivision and sale of the property in the form of individual lots may beget capital gain treatment, especially if this person is himself inactive and all sales activities are handled by an independent broker. *Gordon v. United States,* 159 F. Supp. 360 (Ct. Cl., 1958). This result may follow even though the heirs liquidate their inheritance themselves, without the aid of a real estate broker or developer. *Garrett v. United States,* 120 F. Supp. 193 (Ct. Cl., 1954).

"What was the vocation of the taxpayer at the time of the sale and prior thereto, whether a real estate broker or engaged in some similar or allied business, having in mind that he may have more than one business; and considering whether the taxpayer maintained only one office and that for his main vocation, and whether his engagement in the additional business was separable from his investment in the property?" *Smith et al. v. Dunn,* 224 F.2d 353 (5th Cir., 1955).

Securities.—The effect of the taxpayer's efforts is significant. *Frank, Jr. et al. v. Commissioner,* 321 F.2d 143 (8th Cir., 1963). Thus, where a dealer acquired securities from a corporation and established a substantial market in this security, it would appear that the dealer achieved what he might have been expected to try to achieve in the ordinary course of his trade or business.

Capital gain resulted where sales were to persons who initially contacted the taxpayer and who were unknown to the taxpayer prior to these contacts. *Goldberg et al. v. United States,* D.C., N.D. Ill., 1963.

The relation of the income realized from the sale in question to the taxpayer's total income is significant in ascertaining whether the transaction was in the ordinary course of the trade or business: that is, non-capital. *Harmon v. United States,* D.C., W.D. Mo., 1965.

"The taxpayers' purpose at the time of acquisition has evidentiary weight, but the end question is the purpose of the 'holding' at the time of the sale or sales." *S. O. Bynum et al.,* 46 T.C. 295 (1966). "That the taxpayer's purpose was to achieve capital gains treatment does not destroy the bona fides of the sale." *Harry Roff et al.,* 36 T.C. 818 (1961). In one case, conversion of ordinary income into capital gain was held to be proper, for "There was evidence that the reinvestment plan was conceived as a logical tax saving project in order to avoid incurring a heavy income tax in favor of a less severe capital gain." *Nasser et al. v. United States,* 257 F. Supp. 443 (D.C., N.D. Cal., 1966).

"It is axiomatic that nobody sells without an intent to sell, but it is the nature of the impetus to sell and the degree of sales activity that control." *Desilu Productions, Inc.,* T.C. Memo. 1965–307, filed November 20, 1965.

Change Of Capital Characterization

Where assets are received by a parent corporation upon the tax-free liquidation of a subsidiary company, it does not follow that the assets which were non-capital in the hands of the subsidiary will continue in that category in the hands of the parent. Thus, where the parent was not in the same business as the subsidiary and did not continue the subsidiary's business, the subsidiary's assets (despite a continuity of basis) did not have the characterization of non-capital in the parent's hands. *The Acro Manufacturing Company v. Commissioner,* 334 F.2d 40 (6th Cir., 1964).

A taxpayer purchased unimproved real estate with the intention of erecting thereon a business building which it would occupy. Plans and specifications were prepared, but the original purpose subsequently was changed and the property was sold at the first opportunity. It was held that the property was acquired for use in the trade or business and hence as a Section 1231 asset (property used in the trade or business) was still entitled to capital asset treatment. The property did not lose its character as property used in the trade or business (entitled to capital gain treatment) merely because it ceased to be used actively in the business. *Carter-Colton Cigar Company,* 9 T.C. 219 (1947). Nor does property acquired for use in the trade or business lose that character merely because it was not so used during the taxable year. *Graves Brothers Co.,* 17 T.C. 1499 (1952).

Where a corporation changed its business because of constant losses, assets which were non-capital in the original business were not converted into capital assets of the changed business. Assets do not lose their non-capital character merely because they cease to be used actively in the business. *Wofac Corporation v. United States,* 269 F. Supp. 654 (D.C., N.J., 1967).

Land left over after a rental house was destroyed by a hurricane did not lose its character as property used in business (renting)—a Section 1231 asset—where property was sold in minimizing the loss. *Solomon Wright, Jr.,* 9 T.C. 173 (1947).

Where property used in the trade or business (a building) was sold on a mortgage foreclosure, the loss was ordinary, as the Section 1231 assets had not changed in character because of the involuntary proceeding. *Alfred Kruse et al.,* 29 T.C. 463 (1957).

But in a different kind of involuntary conversion, property held by a real estate developer for improvement and sale was condemned by a state authority. This converted the property into a capital asset, for upon condemnation it ceased to be an asset held primarily for sale in the ordinary course of the trade or business. *Tri-S Corporation,* 48 T.C. 316 (1967).

Liquidation of an inheritance of land by persons who were not dealers in real estate received capital gain treatment. Despite the fact that 115 lots were sold in four years, the taxpayers were not holding the property primarily for sale to customers in the ordinary course of their trade or business. *Clark et al. v. United States,* 200 F. Supp. 668 (D.C., E.D. Tenn., 1961).

If property is acquired in the ordinary course of the trade or business for resale, it cannot be converted into a capital asset by a mere switch of intention. "The taxpayer cannot change the situation by making ·a determination, after he has acquired the property but before selling it, that the property is no longer necessary for his business. To hold otherwise would permit a taxpayer at will to transmute ordinary income into capital income; and thus to defeat the broad Congressional purpose of taxing net receivables at the higher rate." *S. S. Pierce Company v. United States,* D.C., Mass., 1957. Similarly, a mere desire by taxpayers to regard certain securities as no longer inventory but investments, and themselves as no longer dealers, cannot suffice to meet the requirements of the statute. *Vance Lauderdale et al.,* 9 T.C. 751 (1947).

Chapter 2

What is a Capital Asset?
(Continued)

Dealers In Securities

Gain realized by a dealer in securities from the sale or exchange of a security (to be defined in the following paragraph) will not be considered as gain from the sale or exchange of a capital asset unless:

(1) The security is, before the expiration of the thirtieth day after the date of its acquisition, clearly identified in the dealer's records as a security held for investment, or if acquired before October 20, 1951, was so identified before November 20, 1951; and

(2) The security is not held by the dealer primarily for sale to customers in the ordinary course of his trade or business at any time before the identification referred to in (1) has been made. "Unless both of these requirements are met, the gain is considered as gain from the sale of assets held by the dealer primarily for sale to customers in the course of his business." Regulations Section 1.1236–1(a).

For this purpose, the term "security" means any share of stock in any corporation, certificates of stock or interest in any corporation, note, bond, debenture, or evidence of indebtedness, or any evidence of an interest in or right to subscribe or to purchase any of the items listed. I.R.C. Section 1236(c).

A loss sustained by a dealer in securities from the sale or exchange of a security will not be considered an ordinary loss if at any time after November 19, 1951, the security has been clearly identified in the dealer's records as a security held for investment. Once a security has been identified after that date as being held by the dealer for investment, it will retain that character for purposes of determining loss on its ultimate disposition, even though at the time of its disposition the dealer holds it primarily for sale to customers in the ordinary course of business. But this rule does not apply to banks. I.R.C. Section 1236(b).

"The meaning of 'dealer in securities,' as defined in the controlling regulation, . . . is limited to one who, as a merchant, buys and sells securities to customers for the profit thereon." *Algernon S. Schafter et al.,* 39 B.T.A. 289 (1939), *aff'd,* 83 F.2d 317 (App. D.C.), *aff'd,* 299 U.S. 171 (1936). One who holds securities in the nature of stock in trade primarily for re-sale to customers is regularly engaged in the purchase of securities at wholesale. *Francis Shelton Farr,* 44 B.T.A. 683 (1941). He is a middleman in distributing the securities and he does not re-sell to the same class of persons from whom he buys. *Seeley v. Helvering,* 77 F.2d 323 (2d Cir., 1935).

"There is an element of investment as well as an unavoidable element of speculation in every business in which property, whether tangible or intangible, is regularly bought and sold. The 'in-and-out' market hanger-on who buys and sells through brokers on margin is a typical example of the pure speculator in stocks. . . . On the other hand, an investor is ordinarily thought to be a person who acquires property for the income it will yield rather than for the profit he hopes to obtain on a resale. Appellee appears to belong less in either of these categories than in the category of a dealer. While it dealt in intangibles associated in the popular mind with speculation or investment, nevertheless it carried on a regular business roughly comparable with that of a dealer in hogs or cattle or town lots, finding its customers where it could." *United States v. Chinook Investment Company,* 136 F.2d 984 (9th Cir., 1943).

Infrequent and isolated transactions are not sufficient to constitute a taxpayer a dealer in securities. *Pan-American Bank & Trust Co.,* 5 B.T.A. 839 (1926).

A financial and investment company acquired stocks, according to the president's testimony, for the purpose of holding them while the issuing companies were in the formative stage, for ultimate distribution when these companies were going concerns with earnings and assets. This financial and investment company was held not to be a dealer in securities: "It is true that plaintiff intended to resell securities purchased by it, but not as a merchant sells his goods to those who come to his place of business to buy. On the contrary, the plan was to buy and then hold securities until there was opportunity to sell at a profit. . . . That is not merchandising, that is investment or speculation. Neither were the activities of plaintiff in attempting to put all the aircraft business of the country in one company, whose securities would later be offered to the public, merchandising. It was pure speculation. Plaintiff's business was not that of a dealer in securities." *The Leach Corporation v. Blacklidge,* 23 F. Supp. 622 (D.C., N.D. Ill., 1938).

A company was engaged in the brokerage business and sold certain issues of unlisted stocks which it had underwritten. A trading account was set up through which the company could reduce its excessive underwritings when desirable. The trading business was conducted from the company's regular offices, and there was nothing to indicate on the office doors that it was transacting business as a dealer. It was not listed either in the telephone directory or in any commercial paper. It had a city license as a banker but it had no broker's permit. The company was not a dealer in securities. *Wilson et al. v. Commissioner,* 76 F.2d 476 (10th Cir., 1935).

A taxpayer's alleged status as a dealer is not proven by the fact that he had registered with the Securities and Exchange Commission and with the State of New York as a security dealer. Nor is this status proven by the fact that he had a teletype machine, four telephones, and statistical and financial publications in his office. *Achille O. Van Suetendael et al.,* T.C. Memo., Docket Nos. 107681, 109703, and 108929, entered September 25, 1944, *aff'd,* 152 F.2d 654 (2d Cir., 1945).

A company was organized for the purpose of buying and selling securities, participating in underwriting syndicates, and engaging in other investment activities. Purchases and sales were made through brokers or an affiliate. The company was not a dealer in securities. It had no place of business to which customers could come to buy; it was a customer of brokers, not they of it, as in the case of a specialist. Nor does a company become a dealer merely by acquiring bonds with an intention to sell them to the public sometime in the future when the company's executive committee should decide that the time was ripe. *Securities Allied Corporation v. Commissioner,* 95 F.2d 384 (2d Cir., 1938).

The Internal Revenue Service claimed that a dealer in securities must have acquired certain securities as an investment rather than for re-sale, for this dealer did not register them with the Securities and Exchange Commission; and lack of such registration imposed such limitations on the sale of the stock as to negate the idea that the shares were purchased for resale in the ordinary course of the business. But that allegation by the Service was not deemed to be dispositive of the intent and purpose of the dealer in acquiring the stock. He testified that there was an available intrastate market for the stock, which could thus have been sold lawfully. Hence, he properly included the stock in inventory for re-sale in the ordinary course of business. *Raney Investment Co., Inc. v. United States, . . .* F. Supp. . . . (D.C., E.D. Ark., 1967).

A taxpayer may be a dealer as to some securities and he may hold similar or other securities on his own account for purposes other than for resale to customers. As to the latter, he is not a dealer, and securities so purchased are capital assets. *E. Everett Van Tuyl et al.,* 12 T.C. 900 (1949).

A dealer in securities may acquire securities for the purpose of sale to customers and later change his purpose and hold them for investment. *Carl Marks & Co.,* 12 T.C. 1196 (1949). But a dealer's expressed intent to hold securities for other than sale must be supported by conduct on his part in regard to such securities which clearly is consistent with that intent. His treatment of securities held on his own account for investment must differ materially from his treatment of securities held for sale to customers. This may be accomplished by some form of segregation, on the books or physically or both. *Stern Brothers & Co.,* 16 T.C. 295 (1951).

For a discussion of the identification of co-mingled securities, see Revenue Ruling 64–160, 1964–1 (Part 1) CB 306 in Appendix 1.

A dealer may transfer securities actually held for investment out of inventory into a separate account without obtaining permission from the Internal Revenue Service to do so. *Stifel Nicholaus & Co.,* 13 T.C. 755 (1949).

A dealer in securities invested its surplus funds in securities solely for the purpose of making an investment of these funds. The securities thus acquired were segregated physically and on the books from securities held for sale to customers. The securities were not included in the dealer's inventory, were not sold to customers, and were not of a type ordinarily sold to customers. It was held that these securities were capital assets. "The same rule is applicable even though the securities acquired for investment are of the same type or of a similar nature as those ordinarily sold to the dealer's customers." I.T. 3891, 1948–1 CB 69.

A bank which has a separate department for the buying and selling of securities may be deemed to be a dealer in securities. *Harriman National Bank v. Commissioner,* 43 F.2d 950 (2d Cir., 1930).

A specialist on the New York Stock Exchange was held to be a dealer or merchant in transactions in those shares for which it was a specialist. "A 'Specialist' is a qualified member who accepts orders in selected securities from other members for execution." *Helvering v. Fried et al.,* 299 U.S. 175 (1936). "A specialist is one who, having a position at a designated 'post' on the floor of the Exchange, maintains a book in which he enters all offers and bids for the stocks in which he specializes, thus indicating the 'market' for the stocks. The offers and bids are ordinarily made by other members of the Exchange. But the specialist is required to be ready at the demand of other brokers to quote the market price and to buy and sell at the closest fluctuations possible. Where the 'bid' and 'asked' prices furnished by the brokers coincide and the transaction is thereby effected, the specialist acts as a broker in the transaction. But where there is too wide a 'spread' between the 'bid' and 'asked' prices, in order to create a market, he either buys or sells the stock for his own account." *Vaughan et al. v. Commissioner et al.,* 85 F.2d 497 (2d Cir., 1936).

A New York Stock Exchange member firm traded for others; it also bought and sold securities for itself, which transactions were carried on its books in a so-called "Error Account." The firm was not a specialist in the stocks carried in its "Error Account." These stocks were purchased in the expectation of a rise in the market. The transactions thus were of a capital nature, not being for sale in the ordinary course of the trade or business. *Schafer et al. v. Helvering,* 299 U.S. 171 (1936).

A dealer in securities who in his books of account regularly inventories unsold securities on hand at cost, at market, or at the lower of cost or market, may make his Federal income tax return upon the basis upon which the books are kept, provided that a description of the method employed is made a part of the tax return. All the securities must be inventoried by the same method. "A dealer in securities in whose books of account separate computations of the gain or loss from the sale of the various lots of securities sold are made on the basis of the cost of each lot shall be regarded, for the purpose of this section, as regularly inventorying his securities at cost. For the purposes of this section, a dealer in securities is a merchant of securities, whether an individual, partnership, or corporation, with an established place of business, regularly engaged in the purchase of securities and their resale to customers: that is, one who as a merchant buys securities and sells them to customers with a view to the gains and profits that may be derived therefrom. If such business is simply a branch of the activities carried on by such persons, the securities inventoried as provided in this section may include only those held for purposes of resale and not for investment. Taxpayers who buy and sell or hold securities for investment or speculation, irrespective of whether such buying or selling constitutes the carrying on of a trade or business, and officers of corporations and members of partnerships who in their individual capacities buy and sell securities, are not dealers in securities within the meaning of this section." Regulations Section 1.471–5.

Traders in securities receive capital gain and loss treatment. *Commissioner v. Burnett,* 118 F.2d 659 (5th Cir., 1941). Thus, losses are subject to the capital loss limitations of Section 1211. *Frank B. Polachek,* 22 T.C. 858 (1954). "Contrasted to 'dealers' are those sellers of securities who perform no such merchandising functions and whose status as to the source of supply is not significantly different from that of those to whom they sell. That is, the securities are as easily accessible to one as to the other and the seller performs no services that need be compensated for by a mark-up of the price of the securities he sells. The sellers depend upon such circumstances as a rise in value or an advantageous purchase to enable them to sell at a price in excess of cost. Such sellers are known as 'traders.' " *George R. Kemon*, 16 T.C. 1026 (1951).

Section 1231 Assets

Section 1221 defines capital assets, a definition which excludes depreciable property and real estate. Section 1231 specifically deals with part of such property as used in the taxpayer's trade or business.

Section 1231 embraces the best of both taxable worlds. If Section 1231 assets (to be defined below) which have been held for more than six months are sold at a gain, this is long-term capital gain. If the sale is at a loss, there is a fully deductible loss. The only hitch is that a taxpayer cannot receive favorable Section 1231 treatment both for gains and losses in one taxable year. The transactions must be aggregated and the tax treatment applies to the net result. It was said of the predecessor of the present Section 1231: "The avowed purpose was to allow taxpayers, whose property had been seized in furtherance of the war effort, a capital gain rather than an increase in ordinary income. This is so because not infrequently the taxpayer received much more for his seized property than his depreciated cost, and it seemed unjust to tax him at wartime's exceptionally high income tax rates. Conversely, the legislation provided in the event a net loss was sustained, the taxpayer should be entitled to an ordinary deduction. Thus, the effect of Section 1231 is twofold. If the gains exceed the losses, there is a capital gain treatment, and if the losses are greater they are ordinary deductions." *Maurer et al. v. United States,* 284 F.2d 122 (10th Cir., 1960).

This section provides that a taxpayer's gains and losses from the disposition (including involuntary conversion) of assets described in Section 1231 as "property used in the trade or business" and from the involuntary conversion of capital assets held for more than six months will be treated as long-term capital gains and losses if the total gains exceed the total losses. If the total gains do not exceed the total losses, all such gains and losses are treated as ordinary gains and losses. Therefore, if the taxpayer has no gains subject to Section 1231, a recognized loss from the condemnation (or from a sale or exchange under threat of condemnation) of even a capital asset held for more than six months is an ordinary loss. Capital assets subject to Section 1231 treatment include only capital assets which are involuntarily converted. The non-capital assets subject to Section 1231 treatment are:

(1) Depreciable business property and business real property held for

more than six months, other than stock in trade and certain copyrights and artistic property.

(2) Timber, coal, and iron ore, but only to the extent that Section 631 applies thereto. That section applies to an election as to gain or loss in the case of timber or coal.

(3) Certain livestock and unharvested crops. Regulations Section 1.1231–1(a).

Section 1231 applies to recognized gains and losses from the following:

(1) The sale, exchange, or involuntary conversion of property held for more than six months and used in the taxpayer's trade or business, which is either real property or is of a character subject to the depreciation allowance of Section 167 (even though fully depreciated), and which is not—

(a) Property of a kind which would properly be includible in the taxpayer's inventory if on hand at the close of the taxable year, or property held by the taxpayer primarily for sale to customers in the ordinary course of business;

(b) A copyright, a literary, musical, or artistic composition, or similar property, held by a taxpayer whose personal efforts created the property or who has the creator's basis; or

(c) Livestock held for draft, breeding, or dairy purposes (except to the extent included under (4), below), or poultry.

(2) The involuntary conversion of capital assets held for more than six months.

(3) The cutting or disposal of timber, or the disposal of coal or iron ore, to the extent considered arising from a sale or exchange by reason of the provisions of Section 631 and the regulations thereunder.

(4) The sale, exchange, or involuntary conversion of livestock if the requirements of Regulations Section 1.1231–2 are met (to be discussed below).

(5) The sale, exchange, or involuntary conversion of unharvested crops on land which is (a) used in the taxpayer's trade or business and held for more than six months and (b) sold at the same time and to the same person.

For purposes of Section 1231, the phrase "property used in the trade or business" means Items (1), (3), (4), and (5), above. But the rule of Section 1231 does not apply to certain uninsured losses, to be mentioned below.

Section 1231 does not apply to a sale, exchange, or involuntary conversion of an unharvested crop if the taxpayer retains any right or option to re-acquire the land on which the crop is, directly or indirectly (other than a right customarily incident to a mortgage or other security transaction).

The length of time for which the crop (as distinguished from the land) is held is immaterial. A leasehold or an estate for years is not "land" for the purposes of Section 1231.

Section 1231 applies to the sale, exchange, or involuntary conversion of livestock, regardless of age, held by the taxpayer for draft, breeding, or dairy purposes, and held by him for twelve months or more from the date of acquisition. For the purposes of this section, the term "livestock" is given a broad interpretation and includes cattle, hogs, horses, mules, donkeys, sheep, goats, fur-bearing animals, and other mammals. It does not include poultry, turkeys, pigeons, geese, other birds, fish, frogs, reptiles, etc.

"Whether or not livestock is held by the taxpayer for draft, breeding, or dairy purposes depends upon all of the facts and circumstances in each case. The purpose for which the animal is held is ordinarily shown by the taxpayer's actual use of the animal. However, a draft, breeding, or dairy purpose may be present if an animal is disposed of within a reasonable time after its intended use for such purpose is prevented or made undesirable by reason of accident, disease, drought, unfitness of the animal for such purpose, or a similar factual circumstance. Under certain circumstances, an animal held for ultimate sale to customers in the ordinary course of the taxpayer's trade or business may be considered as held for draft, breeding, or dairy purposes merely because it is suitable for such purposes or merely because it is held by the taxpayer for sale to other persons for use by them for such purposes. Furthermore, an animal held by the taxpayer for other purposes is not considered as held for draft, breeding, or dairy purposes merely because of a negligible use of the animal for such purposes or merely because of the use of the animal for such purposes as an ordinary or necessary incident to the other purposes for which the animal is held." Regulations Section 1.1231–2(b).

A patent right, because it is depreciable property, probably would be considered to be a Section 1231 asset. *C. A. Norgren Co. v. United States,* 268 F. Supp. 816 (D.C., Colo., 1967).

Inventory is not a Section 1231 asset; but the inventory which is excluded is that from which the taxpayer gets his normal sales profits. *Grant Oil Tool Company v. United States,* 381 F.2d 389 (Ct. Cl., 1967).

All gains and losses to which Section 1231 applies must be taken into account in determining whether and to what extent the gains exceed the losses. For the purpose of this computation, the provisions of Section 1211 limiting the deduction of capital losses do not apply, and no losses are excluded by that section. With that exception, gains are included in the computations under Section 1231 only to the extent that they are taken into account in computing gross income, and losses are included only to the extent that they are taken into account in computing taxable income.

The regulations supply these examples of gains and losses which are not included in the computations under Section 1231:

(1) Losses of a personal nature which are not deductible by reason of Section 165(c) or (d), such as losses from the sale of property held for personal use.

(2) Losses which are not deductible under Section 267 (relating to losses with respect to transactions between related taxpayers) or Section 1091 (losses from wash sales). Sections 267 and 1091 are discussed in Chapter 7.

(3) Gains on the sale of property (to which Section 1231 applies) reported for any taxable year on the installment method under Section 453, except to the extent the gain is to be reported under that section for the taxable year, that is, collections times the gross profit ratio for the year of sale.

(4) Gains and losses which are not recognized under Section 1002, such as those to which Sections 1031 through 1036 (relating to common nontaxable exchanges) apply. Regulations Section 1.1231–1(d).

Involuntary Conversions.—For purposes of Section 1231, the terms "compulsory or involuntary conversion" or "involuntary conversion" of property mean the conversion of property into money or other property as a result of complete or partial destruction, theft, or seizure, or an exercise of the power of requisition or condemnation, or the threat or imminence thereof. Losses upon the complete or partial destruction, theft, seizure, requisition, or condemnation of property are treated as losses upon an involuntary conversion whether or not there is a conversion of the property into other property or money, except in the case of certain uninsured losses mentioned in the following paragraph. "For example, if a capital asset held for more than 6 months, with an adjusted basis of $400, but not held for the production of income, is stolen, and the loss is not compensated for by insurance or otherwise, section 1231 applies to the $400 loss." Regulations Section 1.1231–1(e)(1).

Despite the provisions of the previous paragraph, losses sustained during a taxable year beginning after December 31, 1957, with respect to both property used in the trade or business and any capital asset held for more than six months and held for the production of income, which losses arise from fire, storm, shipwreck, or other casualty, or from theft, and which are not compensated for by insurance in any amount, are not losses to which Section 1231 applies. "Such losses shall not be taken into account in applying the provisions of this section." Regulations Section 1.1231–1(e)(2).

Section 1231 is aimed at involuntary conversions where there is compensation by insurance or otherwise, leaving Section 165 applicable to uncompensated losses. An *uninsured* casualty loss is fully deductible under Section 165 and does not have to be applied first against capital gains under Section 1231. *Maurer et al. v. United States,* 284 F.2d 122 (10th Cir., 1960). The Internal Revenue Service has announced that it will not follow this decision. Revenue Ruling 61–54, 1961–1 CB 398. In the case of a casualty loss not compensated for by insurance or otherwise, the Tax Court has held that, despite the *Maurer* decision, there must be a netting of this loss and Section 1231 gains, rather than a deductible loss. *E. Taylor Chewning et al.,* 44 T.C. 678 (1965). The Tax Court pointed out that *Maurer* was decided upon facts taking place prior to the 1958 amendments to Section 1231, Subsection (a) of which now states: "In the case of any property used in the trade or business and of any capital asset held for more than 6 months and held for the production of income, this subsection shall not apply to any loss, in respect of which the taxpayer is not compensated for by insurance in any amount, arising from fire, storm, shipwreck, or other casualty, or from theft."

Where a taxpayer's property is lost as a result of a statutory involuntary conversion, gain resulting from payment by means of insurance, Governmental award, etc., is not recognized for tax purposes to the extent that this award is fully utilized in the acquisition of property similar or related in service or use to the property so converted. I.R.C. Section 1033(a)(1). The definition of "involuntary conversion" and the time of replacement are set forth in Section 1033.

In lieu of purchasing replacement property, the taxpayer may purchase stock in the acquisition of control of a corporation owning the proper replacement property. I.R.C. Section 1033(a)(3)(A). For this purpose, "control" means the ownership of stock possessing at least 80% of the total combined voting power of all classes of stock entitled to vote and at least 80% of the total number of shares of all other classes of stock of the corporation. Regulations Section 1.1033(a)–2(c).

Replacement of lost property through the purchase of stock of a corporation owning such property was proper, even though the property was purchased by this corporation after its stock had been acquired. *John Richard Corp.,* 46 T.C. 41 (1966). The purchase of stock of a corporation owning replacement assets must be genuine. Non-recognition of gain is not possible where the so-called purchase price actually is a sham transaction with a related party. *American Truck Rental Corp.,* T.C. Memo. 1965–9, filed January 22, 1965, *aff'd,* 355 F.2d 928 (3d Cir., 1966).

Subdivided Real Estate

"[S]ection 1237 . . . is intended as an effort on the part of Congress to straighten out the Commissioner of Internal Revenue because he has gone so far afield from the intentions of Congress as to capital assets and capital gain treatment for the income derived from the sale of such capital assets." *Temple v. United States,* 229 F. Supp. 687 (D.C., S.D. Miss., 1964), *aff'd,* 355 F.2d 67 (5th Cir., 1966).

If Section 1237 applies to a transaction, a taxpayer may sell lots from a single tract held for investment without having gain taxed as ordinary income by virtue of the fact that the tract was subdivided or that he participated actively in the sale. But these tests must be satisfied:

(1) The taxpayer must have held the property for at least five years, unless he had acquired it by inheritance or devise.

(2) The taxpayer may not previously have held any part of the tract primarily for sale in the ordinary course of his trade or business, nor may he hold any other real property for that purpose in the year of sale.

(3) The taxpayer may not make any substantial improvement on the tract which would substantially enhance the value of lots sold. I.R.C. Section 1237(a).

"[W]here a taxpayer subdivides his property and offers it for sale shortly after he has purchased it, the courts have understandably rejected his claim that he bought it for purposes of investment." *Tidwell et al. v. Commissioner,* 298 F.2d 864 (4th Cir., 1962).

Sale Or Exchange Of Capital Assets

Not every disposition of a capital asset produces capital gain or capital loss. "Even though this was a capital asset, there is still the question . . . whether this was a 'sale or exchange.'" *Harold Becher et al.,* T.C. Memo. 1963–250, filed September 13, 1963. For capital treatment, the taxpayer must show an element essential to such treatment: namely, that the gain was on a "sale or exchange" of "property used in the trade or business." *Kurlan et al. v. Commissioner et al.,* 343 F.2d 625 (2d Cir., 1965).

"The essence of a capital transaction within the tax statutes and decided cases is that the sale or exchange of an asset results in a return of a capital investment coupled with realized gain or loss (as the case might be) which accrues to the investment over a certain period of time." *Holt v. Commissioner,* 303 F.2d 687 (9th Cir., 1962). "The particular statutory requirement of 'sale or exchange' has existed since 1921 when capital gain provisions were first inserted into the income tax structure. Despite this history, complications arise in applying the phrase 'sale or exchange' to the myriad transactions that occur in our free and remarkably flexible economy." *du Pont de Nemours and Company v. United States,* 288 F.2d 904 (Ct. Cl., 1961).

"For there to be a sale or exchange there must be a receipt of something valuable." *Ackerman et al. v. United States,* 335 F.2d 521 (5th Cir., 1964). "As applied to income derived from the sale or exchange of capital assets, it would be observed that the definition contains two elements: (1) a gain produced by or derived from capital, (2) a severance of such gain from the capital and receipt thereof by the taxpayer for his separate use, benefit and disposal." *O'Meara v. Commissioner,* 34 F.2d 390 (10th Cir., 1939).

Even though a sale is a transfer back to the original vendor, there is a "sale or exchange" and hence a capital transaction. *Harold Becher et al.,* T.C. Memo, 1963–250, filed September 13, 1963. A sale or exchange for capital gains purposes is not produced by the mere transfer of legal title. *Palmer v. Bender,* 287 U.S. 551 (1933). Rather, at the very least, there must be a meaningful economic transfer in addition to a change in legal title. *Corliss v. Bowers,* 281 U.S. 376 (1930).

A sound business purpose is not required to legitimize a sale for tax recognition. "No cases require that a *sale* have any business purpose beyond that of realizing a . . . gain." *Sun Properties, Inc. v. United States,* 220 F.2d 171 (5th Cir., 1955). "[T]he mere desire to sell, even if its sole purpose was to realize capital gains, should be a sufficient business purpose (assuming always that the substance complies with the form)." *Charles E. Curry et al.,* 43 T.C. 667 (1965). But in many cases that is a big assumption to have to make.

Where all of the stock is purchased in a corporation the only asset of which is cash, at a price less than the net cash, with a view to liquidating the corporation, any gain resulting from the transaction is denied capital gains treatment, for there has been no gain from the sale or exchange of a capital asset. *Lowndes et al. v. United States,* 384 F.2d 635 (4th Cir., 1967).

For a transaction to be recognized as capital, the taxpayer need not have set out to achieve this result. "[R]ecognition of capital gain or loss does not depend upon the existence of usual or stereotyped forms of conveyance. It may rest upon involuntary sales . . . or upon loss of property through condemnation proceedings . . ." *Margery K. Megargel,* 3 T.C. 238 (1944). A forced or tax sale produces a capital loss in the same manner as a voluntary sale. *Helvering v. Hammel et al.,* 311 U.S. 504 (1941). This includes a foreclosure. *Electro-Chemical Engraving Co., Inc. v. Commissioner,* 311 U.S. 513 (1941).

Abandonment of an option to acquire a partnership interest was regarded as equivalent to a sale or exchange of capital assets. *Dorman v. United States,* 296 F.2d 27 (9th Cir., 1961). In another case, the majority stockholder of a corporation transferred about one-quarter of his stock to a new executive to induce him to keep his position. The majority stockholder was permitted to take a capital loss in that his proportionate interest in the stock had been reduced as the result of an exchange, the loss being the difference between the adjusted basis of his stock and the fair market value of the stock at the time of the transfer. *J. K. Downer et al.,* 48 T.C. 86 (1967).

There was no sale or exchange of capital assets in the following situations:

The temporary taking of a taxpayer's right to use his own transportation assets. *Commissioner v. Gillette Motor Transport, Inc.,* 364 U.S. 130 (1960).

Surrender of an exclusive contract to purchase coal. *Commissioner v. Pittston Company,* 252 F.2d 344 (2d Cir., 1958).

Receipt of a lump sum in liquidation of a percentage of the gross receipts of motion pictures otherwise payable to a producer solely in return for personal services not yet performed. *Holt v. Commissioner,* 303 F.2d 687 (9th Cir., 1962).

Abandonment of land. *Richard E. Beck et al.,* T.C. Memo., Docket Nos. 15285–6, entered February 9, 1949.

Surrender of a single premium annuity contract to the insurance company which had issued it for a consideration. *Bodine v. Commissioner,* 103 F.2d 982 (3d Cir., 1939).

A compromise by the taxpayer with the maker of promissory notes (who was able to pay them) for less than their face value. *Hale v. Helvering,* 85 F.2d 819 (App. D.C., 1936).

Cancellation by a taxpayer of a franchise which it owned without consideration. *King Broadcasting Company,* 48 T.C. 542 (1967).

Disclosure of a secret process for a consideration. *du Pont de Nemours and Company v. United States,* 288 F.2d 904 (Ct. Cl., 1961).

Receipt of a lump-sum consideration for what otherwise would be received at a future time as ordinary income. *Commissioner et al. v. P. G. Lake, Inc. et al.,* 356 U.S. 260 (1958).

In order to have a loss deduction on a sale or other disposition, there must be a prior basis, cost or otherwise. *United States v. Lattimore,* 353 F.2d 379 (9th Cir., 1965).

For disallowances of capital losses, see Chapter 7.

Chapter 3

Tax Distinctions Between Stocks and Bonds

Areas Of Difference

There may be important tax distinctions both to the stockholder (or bond-holder) and to the corporation issuing the instruments if the characterization of the issue is "stock" or "bond." In Federal tax matters, unlike ordinary Wall Street parlance, the term "securities" does not indiscriminately bracket stocks and bonds. The term refers to the latter.

If the issue is a stock, the corporate payor does not get a tax deduction for payments to the distributees (dividends).

If a corporation redeems stock at a time when there are earnings and profits, this redemption will be treated as a dividend unless it falls within one of the specific exceptions of the statute, such as the complete elimination of a shareholder from any further participation in the company in any capacity. I.R.C. Section 302. But if bonds are redeemed by a corporation, even out of earnings, the result is capital. Retention of earnings in order to meet fixed maturities of bonds is a good defense against the accumulated earnings tax. *Gazette Telegraph Co.,* 19 T.C. 692 (1953).

Should a corporation expect to redeem its obligations if successful (that is, out of earnings), the security holders are in a better position than share-holders in that bond indentures may provide that a premium of (assume) 2% will be payable on face value for each year that maturity is accelerated. *Haskel Engineering & Supply Co. v. United States,* D.C., S.D. Cal., 1966, aff'd, 380 F.2d 786 (9th Cir., 1967).

The treatment of a redemption of stock as a dividend is not limited to common stock. Thus, redemption of preferred shares may be treated as a dividend. *Commissioner v. Berenbaum,* 369 F.2d 337 (10th Cir., 1966).

A tax advantage which may accrue to investors from having bonds rather

27

than stock relates to the consequences of corporate insolvency. Money that stockholders give to the corporation for shares is deemed to be the cost of the stock or a capital contribution; in case of default, there is a capital loss, the deduction of which is severely limited for tax purposes. But if the shareholder has part of his investment in the form of bonds which are accepted by the Internal Revenue Service as such, he may be entitled to a worthless bond or bad debt deduction. I.R.C. Section 165(c). "It is settled that loans by a controlling shareholder to his closely held corporation generally give rise to nonbusiness debts. This is because an investor is not engaged in a trade or business. An exception is made where the shareholder can establish his business as being that of promoting, managing and financing corporations." *Kelly v. Patterson,* 331 F.2d 753 (5th Cir., 1964).

If a corporation has little stock but a large amount of bonds, the company may be insulated against the accumulated earnings tax for a longer period. That is, the corporation may have so little in the way of capital funds that earnings will have to be accumulated for a longer period of time to take care of the normal requirements of the business for expansion, development, or other valid purposes. The corporation may save accumulated earnings tax. The stockholders' share of the corporation's "after tax" earnings will be larger; and many shareholders prefer not to receive dividends.

Where an investor has debt securities of a corporation, he is in position to participate subsequently in a tax-free recapitalization of the corporation. "Down-grading" of capitalization (*e.g.,* from bonds to stock) may be a tax-free recapitalization under Section 368(a)(1)(E). "Up-grading" (*e.g.,* from stock to bonds) is not.

If so-called "bonds" are not recognized as securities for tax purposes (for example, because of very short maturities), the transaction may lose characterization as a tax-free reorganization. Certain sections of the Internal Revenue Code (such as Sections 351 and 361) require a transaction to be solely for stock and securities. Where the alleged "bonds" are not securities or stock (they might be regarded as the equivalent of cash if the maturity is very short), the transaction loses its tax-free character. *Turner Construction Company et al. v. United States,* 364 F.2d 525 (2d Cir., 1966).

One of the tests of a small business corporation is that there be but a single class of stock. If so-called bonds are deemed to be stock, there is a question of whether small business corporation status is lost. "Obligations which purport to represent debt but which actually represent equity capital will generally constitute a second class of stock. However, if such purported debt obligations are owned solely by the owners of the nominal stock of the corporation in substantially the same proportion as they own such nominal stock, such purported debt obligations will be treated as contributions to capital rather than a second class of stock. But, if an issuance, redemption, sale, or other transfer of nominal stock, or of purported debt obligations which actually represent equity capital, results in a change in a shareholder's proportionate share of nominal stock or his proportionate share of such purported debt, a new determination shall be made as to whether the corporation has more than one class of stock as of the time of such change." Regulations Section 1.1371–1(g).

In order to ascertain whether the tax advantages of a small business corporation will be lost by the characterization of a second class of stock, the question is: did the alleged bond really constitute a second class of stock, so that the corporation did not qualify as a Subchapter S corporation under Section 1371? *Lewis Building and Supplies, Inc.,* T.C. Memo. 1966–159, filed June 30, 1966.

If bonds are issued in a recapitalization to stockholders or bondholders, the receipt of any greater principal amount of bonds than is surrendered to the corporation will be taxed as boot or "other income." I.R.C. Section 355(a)(3)(A). Thus, if what is received by a stockholder is deemed to be a bond, he will have taxable boot.

If a so-called "bond" is deemed to be a stock, the advantages of a tax-free reorganization may be lost and a corporation might sustain tax, to the end that there will be less left for the shareholders after a corporate liquidation. Section 337 permits a corporation to exclude from gross income the proceeds of a sale of assets (within certain limitations) if the corporation adopts a plan of complete liquidation and distributes all of its assets within the following twelve months, except for assets retained to meet claims. But amounts retained to meet claims of *stockholders* with respect to their stock do not qualify. Thus, if a corporation distributes all assets except those retained to pay off the bonds, and the bonds are deemed to be stock, the corporation has not been completely liquidated within the required twelve months and it will be taxed upon sales within that period. *John Town, Inc.,* 46 T.C. 107 (1966), *aff'd,* . . . F.2d . . . (7th Cir., 1967).

A difficulty is that the vital word "securities" is not defined in the Internal Revenue Code. Revenue Ruling 59–98, 1959–1 CB 76. "[T]he test as to whether notes are securities is not a mechanical determination of the time period of the note. Though time is an important factor, the controlling consideration is an overall evaluation of the nature of the debt, degree of participation and continuing interest in the business, the extent of proprietary interest compared with the similarity of the note to a cash payment, the purpose of the advances, etc." *Camp Wolters Enterprises, Inc.,* 22 T.C. 737 (1954), *aff'd,* 230 F.2d 555 (5th Cir., 1956).

Although the Code has not supplied a definition of "securities," the courts have stepped into the breach. "The question of the meaning of the term 'securities' as used in the various revenue statutes, has been considered by the courts in a number of cases. The rule appears to be settled that, when an act does not define the term, it denotes an obligation of a character giving the creditor some assured participation in the business of the debtor, or, in other words, an investment in the business, and that the term does not include evidences of indebtedness for short term loans representing temporary advances for current corporate needs." *Wellington Fund, Inc.,* 4 T.C. 185 (1944).

If bonds are of short maturity and there is virtual certainty because of the obligor's strong financial position that redemption in cash shortly will take place, the "bonds" are deemed to be the equivalent of the cash into which they soon will be metamorphosized. *Pinellas Ice and Cold Storage Company v. Commissioner,* 287 U.S. 462 (1933). Unfortunately, this case has been misconstrued widely to mean that no short-term bonds are to be recognized as bonds, even where there exists genuine doubt as to whether they will in fact be paid off in the near future in cash.

Tax Distinction Between Stockholders And Bond Holders

"The essential difference between a stockholder and a creditor is that the stockholder's intention is to embark upon the corporate adventure, taking the risks of loss attendant upon it, so that he may enjoy the chances of profit. The creditor, on the other hand, does not intend to take such risks so far as they may be avoided, but merely to lend his capital to others who do intend to take them." *United States v. Title Guarantee & Trust Co.,* 133 F.2d 990 (6th Cir., 1943). Stated somewhat differently, "The distinction between indebtedness and risk capital is that a loan is made upon the reasonable assumption that it will be repaid no matter whether the business venture is successful or not, while capital is put to the risk of the business." *Cuyuna Realty Company v. United States,* 382 F.2d 298 (Ct. Cl., 1967).

Nature of Indebtedness

Whether an issue is a stock or a bond is not for the management of a corporation to say once the capitalization has been set up. "The assets of a corporation are a trust fund, and the directors may not arbitrarily change the status of stockholders into that of general creditors." *Elko Lamoille Power Company v. Commissioner,* 50 F.2d 595 (9th Cir., 1931).

The essence of an equity interest is "a participation in the pot luck of the enterprise." *Aqualane Shores, Inc. v. Commissioner,* 269 F.2d 116 (5th Cir., 1959). On the other hand: "The classic debt is an unqualified obligation to pay a sum certain at a reasonably close fixed maturity date along with a fixed percentage in interest payable regardless of the debtor's income or lack thereof." *Gilbert v. Commissioner,* 248 F.2d 399 (2d Cir., 1957). All debt need not conform to this concept of "classic debt." But the risk of non-recognition of debt characterization increases to the extent of any variation.

"In most situations, interest is considered to be the cost of the use of the amounts owing a creditor and an incentive to prompt repayment and, thus, an integral part of a continuing debt." *Bruning v. United States,* 376 U.S. 358 (1964). Payments were not deductible as interest where they were not for the forbearance of money. *Merrill Stubbs et al.,* T.C. Memo. 1965–177, filed June 28, 1965.

Intent to create a debt is not requisite to the existence of valid indebtedness. "A debt can arise by operation of law without proof of specific intent to create a debtor-creditor relationship." *Iowa Southern Utilities Company v. United States,* 348 F.2d 492 (Ct. Cl., 1965).

Advances to a related corporation may be treated as capital rather than indebtedness despite the sincerity of the parties. "All were made in good faith, but the whole was risk capital." *Jewell Ridge Coal Corporation v. Commissioner,* 318 F.2d 695 (4th Cir., 1963).

The Guidelines

"Generally speaking, those securities which we have come to consider as typical stocks and typical bonds are readily distinguishable. But with the increasing complexity of business organization has come an ever growing number of securities which fall between the extremes represented by the typical stocks and bonds. These issues have features common to both stocks and bonds and virtually defy positive classification." *The Jordan Company v. Allen,* 85 F. Supp. 437 (D.C., M.D. Ga., 1949).

The real question in a bond versus stock (or interest versus dividend) situation is: was there in substance a debtor-creditor relationship? "What we must decide is not whether the individual steps necessary to establish a formalistic debtor-creditor relationship were undertaken but whether, when the transaction is considered as a whole and realistically, there was in substance a debtor-creditor relationship." *Rubin v. United States,* 304 F.2d 766 (7th Cir., 1962). Where there was no reality to an alleged debtor-creditor relationship, it was not recognized for tax purposes. *Goldstein et al. v. Commissioner,* 364 F.2d 734 (2d Cir., 1966).

The more important criteria set up by the court are the following:

Fixed maturity. "[T]he existence of a fixed maturity for the principal sum, together with a right to enforce payment of said sum as a debt in case of default, is the most significant, if not the essential feature of a debtor and creditor as opposed to a stockholder relationship." *The Jordan Company v. Allen,* 85 F. Supp. 437 (D.C., M.D. Ga., 1949). Indebtedness was not found where there was no fixed or ascertainable maturity date. *Wood Preserving Corporation of Baltimore, Inc. v. United States,* D.C., Md., 1964, *aff'd,* 347 F.2d 111 (4th Cir., 1965).

Interest was not recognized where the maturity date of a so-called bond was too distant. *John W. Walter, Inc.,* 23 T.C. 550 (1954). An issue without a realistic maturity date suggests a stock issue. Where there is no stated maturity date and the instrument is payable upon demand, there is a strong inference that this is not a security at all. *Peter Raich et al.,* 46 T.C. 604 (1966).

An inordinately postponed due date might indicate that there was no intention that the instrument be paid off and hence it is not a bond. *J. S. Biritz Construction Co. et al.,* T.C. Memo. 1966–227, filed October 18, 1966. A reasonable extension of time for payment of a "bond" is not fatal to recognition of debt. *Wilshire & Western Sandwiches, Inc. v. Commissioner,* 175 F.2d 718 (9th Cir., 1949). But an extension for an unreasonable period gravitates against the presence of a debt. *Sayles Finishing Plants. Inc. v. United States,* . . . F.2d . . . (Ct. Cl., 1968).

Lack of Ascertainable Principal Amount. Debt was not recognized for tax purposes where there was no principal amount ascertainable and payable in any event. *Sherwood Memorial Gardens, Inc. v. Commissioner,* 350 F.2d 225 (7th Cir., 1965).

What Indebtedness Represented. Indebtedness was not recognized where debentures did not come into being as promises to repay a borrowing or as a means of providing needed financing of the corporation. *R. C. Owen Company v. Commissioner,* 351 F.2d 410 (6th Cir., 1965).

Was it considered "whether the initial capital was adequate to begin the corporate life"? *Byerlite Corp. v. Williams,* 170 F. Supp. 48 (D.C., N.D. Ohio, 1958), *rev'd on another issue,* 286 F.2d 285 (6th Cir., 1961). Interest was allowed where the initial capital was found not to have been inadequate. *Turner Advertising of Kentucky, Inc.,* T.C. Memo. 1966–101, filed May 17, 1966.

There may be an inference that constantly increasing stockholder "borrowing" represents permanent capital. *L. D. Lansdale, Jr. et al.,* T. C. Memo. 1965–133, filed May 19, 1965.

Was the equity capital contributed for shares of stock adequate for the reasonable needs of the corporation? *McSorley's, Inc. v. United States,* 323 F.2d 900 (10th Cir., 1963).

Thinness of Capitalization. There is "no rule which permits the Commissioner to dictate what portion of a corporation's operations shall be provided for by equity financing rather than by debt." *Herbert B. Miller Estate v. Commissioner,* 239 F.2d 729 (9th Cir., 1956).

If a corporation's capitalization consists of a small amount of stock and an inordinately large amount of bonds, this capitalization (or the corporation) is said to be "thin." The implication is almost inevitable that the overpowering debt issue was created in order that the corporation get an interest deduction. There is no mathematical yardstick to determine how thin a corporation legitimately may be for tax purposes.

In order to justify its so-called bonds, a corporation must prove that its capitalization is adequate. *Oak Hill Finance Company,* 40 T.C. 419 (1963). Stockholder advances to a corporation were recognized as such and were not an incident of a thin capital situation where "a business need arose because of change in tax laws." *Campbell, Jr. v. Carter Foundation Production Company,* 322 F.2d 827 (5th Cir., 1963).

Although one corporation's bond : stock ratio was 9:1 in the taxable year, the bonds held by the stockholders were recognized for tax purposes. Here, the need for capital was of a short-term nature, and within three years this ratio had changed to 4:5. *Sherry Park, Inc. v. United States,* D.C., S.D. Fla., 1964. And a 700:1 ratio between bonds and stocks was accepted where a corporation operated a well-established business which had good prior earnings and indicated continuance of such earnings; the court felt that moneys advanced to the corporation were not in the nature of a capital investment with uncertainty as to repayment. *Baker Commodities, Inc. et al.,* 48 T.C. 374 (1967).

Where bank loans are guaranteed by stockholders, this may be attacked by the Internal Revenue Service as an indication of a thin corporation. See *Fors Farms, Inc., v. United States,* D.C., Wash., 1965.

Proportionate Stock And "Bond" Holdings. Notes given on a *pro rata* basis to stockholders in return for advances are likely to be treated as additional stock. *W. C. Gamman et al.,* 46 T.C. 1 (1966). Such also is the case where stockholder advances are made in proportion to stockholdings. *Bodsky et al. v. Commisisoner,* 321 F.2d 331 (5th Cir., 1963). Interest was recognized where notes were not held in proportion to the stock interest owned by the shareholders. *Turner Advertising of Kentucky, Inc.,* T.C. Memo. 1966–101, filed May 17, 1966.

"[T]he relationship of the financier to the financed objectively throws doubt upon these funds as loans." *Jewell Ridge Coal Corporation v. Commissioner,* 318 F.2d 695 (4th Cir., 1963).

Package Financing. "Could a stockholder ever buy stock in the corporation without buying a debenture? If he could this may indicate a true loan. However, if he has to buy a debenture to buy stock this may indicate a risk-capital investment." *815 Riverside Company v. United States,* D.C., M.D. Ga., 1965. Where bonds and stock were issued in the first instance as a package, this was deemed to be an investment entirely in stock. *Fellinger v. United States,* 363 F.2d 826 (6th Cir., 1966).

Significant also is the question of whether the so-called evidences of indebtedness are assignable without regard to any interest upon the part of the stockholders or upon the part of the assignee in stock or other securities of the corporation. *Intermountain Furniture Manufacturing Company, Inc. v. United States,* . . . (D.C., Utah, 1967).

If property was transferred to a corporation for stock and bonds, was the portion transferred for each type of instrument identified? *1432 Broadway Corporation,* 4 T.C. 1158 (1945), *aff'd,* 160 F.2d 885 (2d Cir., 1947).

Outsider Acceptability. Would the so-called notes have been acceptable to an outside investor? The answer was deemed to be No, where only 2% was payable. *John Town, Inc.,* 46 T.C. 107 (1966), *aff'd,* . . . F.2d . . . (7th Cir., 1967).

Stockholder advances to a corporation are far more likely to be recognized as indebtedness if it can be established that efforts had been made to borrow from outsiders before stockholder advances were made. *The Motel Company,* T.C. Memo. 1963–174, filed June 25, 1963, *aff'd,* 340 F.2d 445 (2d Cir., 1965).

Expectancy Of Repayment. One indication of indebtedness is the reasonable expectancy of re-payment. *Albert W. Petersen et al.,* T.C. Memo. 1965–145, filed May 26, 1965. "When the payment to the transferors is dependent on the success of an untried undercapitalized business with uncertain prospects, a strong inference arises that the transfer is an equity contribution." *Burr Oaks Corporation v. Commissioner,* 365 F.2d 24 (7th Cir., 1966).

A significant factor is whether the indicated corporate income was sufficient to retire the indebtedness so-called at maturity. *McSorley's, Inc. v. United States,* 323 F.2d 900 (10th Cir., 1963).

If there is no provision for retiring bonds periodically, as by a sinking fund, it might appear that re-payment is dependent upon corporate earnings exclusively, as in the case of stock. *Fellinger et al. v. United States et al.,* 363 F.2d 826 (6th Cir., 1966).

Independence Of Interest. Likeness to stock is lessened if interest on the alleged bonds is payable in any event, not only as determined by the board of directors. *Haguet Real Estate Corporation,* 30 T.C. 580 (1958). Income bonds pay interest only out of earnings, and hence such bonds are dangerous if the issue lacks the other positive characteristics of a bond. That is especially true if interest is payable out of earnings only as and to the extent declared by the board of directors.

"It is not essential that interest be computed at a stated rate but only that a sum definitely ascertainable shall be paid for the use of borrowed money, pursuant to the agreement of the lender and borrower." *Kena, Inc.,* 44 B.T.A. 217 (1941).

Indebtedness was not recognized where interest was non-cumulative in the event it was not paid in any given year. *The Gregg Company of Delaware v. Commissioner,* 239 F.2d 498 (2d Cir., 1956).

If interest is waived or is subject to unilateral modification by the corporation, there is grave doubt as to the reality of the indebtedness. *The Motel Company v. Commissioner,* 340 F.2d 445 (2d Cir., 1965). Interest was allowed where two payments had not been made but the plausible reason for this non-payment was oversight. *Air-Vent Aluminum Awning Manufacturing Co. v. United States,* D.C., S.D. Cal., 1965.

Where the so-called creditor fails to make claim for unpaid interest, this will be regarded as "scarcely the attitude of a money lender. . . ." *Jewell Ridge Coal Corporation v. Commissioner,* 318 F.2d 695 (4th Cir., 1963). Steps should be taken by the bondholder to foreclose if there is a default. *The Motel Company,* T.C. Memo. 1963–174, filed June 25, 1963, *aff'd,* 340 F.2d 445 (2d Cir., 1965). A bond issue was not accepted as such for tax purposes where action by 75% of the debenture holders was necessary to accelerate maturity upon default. *R. C. Owen Company v. Commissioner,* 351 F.2d 410 (6th Cir., 1965).

Failure to act upon default can be fatal if this inaction is by either corporation or bondholder. The corporation's failure to make principal payments on a purported debt was a very significant indication that there was not an indebtedness. *Foresun, Inc. v. Commissioner,* 348 F.2d 1006 (6th Cir., 1965). A debtor-creditor relationship was not recognized where other creditors were paid but not an affiliate. *Ludwig Baumann & Co. v. Commissioner,* 312 557 (2d Cir., 1963). Indebtedness was not recognized where the payment schedule to the transferring shareholders was ignored. *Aronov Construction Company, Inc. v. United States,* 223 F. Supp. 175 (D.C., M.D. Ala., 1963), *aff'd,* 338 F.2d 337 (5th Cir., 1964).

Participation In Management. Stockholders may participate in the management of a corporation; bondholders do not. Thus, it is pertinent to inquire: Do the bondholders possess control over the management? *R.C. Owen Co. v. United States,* 180 F. Supp. 369 (Ct. Cl., 1960). Did the person making the purported loan participate in the management of the considered." *Foresun, Inc.,* 41 T.C. 707 (1964), *aff'd,* 348 F.2d 1006 (6th Cir., 1960).

Subordination Of The "Indebtedness." "[S]ubordination alone is not sufficient to convert debt into capital. . . . However, it is a factor to be considered." *Foresun, Inc.,* 41 T.C. 707 (1964), *aff'd,* 348 F.2d 1006 (6th Cir., 1965).

Bonds were recognized as such where, upon liquidation, the preference of this security over the stock but its inferiority to the claims of other creditors was spelled out. *S. Glaser & Sons, Inc.,* T.C. Memo., Docket No. 2897, entered May 22, 1944. Here there was limited subordination.

Indebtedness was not recognized where "[i]n fact, [the sole stockholder] did not enforce the notes or the payment of interest thereon when and as they became due, but subordinated them to the claims of unsecured creditors." *Castle Heights, Inc. et al. v. United States,* 242 F. Supp. 350 (D.C., E.D. Tenn., 1965).

Interest could not be deducted by a corporation on its subordinated debentures. Here, the rights of the holders did not vary significantly from the rights of the preferred stockholders. There was no limitation upon the amount of dividends that could be paid, nor was there a sinking fund or reserve out of which payment after all other obligations could be assured. *United States v. Snyder Brothers Company,* 367 F.2d 990 (3d Cir., 1966).

Cyclical Repayments. Were stockholder "advances" repaid just before the end of each year with borrowed funds and then renewed early in the following year? *Atlanta Biltmore Hotel Corporation v. Commissioner,* 349 F.2d 677 (5th Cir., 1965). Such a course would indicate that the money was permanently invested in the corporation, in the manner of stock.

Use of A Standard Format. Was the method and form of capitalization in accordance with the customary pattern in the industry? *Sherwood Memorial Gardens, Inc. v. Commissioner,* 350 F.2d 225 (7th Cir., 1965). Where the form and amount of capitalization may be justified by financial considerations, "the entrepreneurs' choice of financing arrangements would appear to have been pre-eminently sound, and is not to be set aside by the dogma of an Internal Revenue theoretician." *Sherry Park, Inc. v. United States,* D.C., S.D. Fla., 1964.

Unpersuasiveness Of Label. So-called certificates of indebtedness were found to evidence a proprietary equity interest in the form of preferred stock. *Knollwood Memorial Gardens,* 46 T.C. 764 (1966). In another case, "preferred debentures" were not recognized as indebtedness. *Beaver Pipe Tools, Inc. v. Carey,* 139 F. Supp. 470 (D.C., N.D. Ohio, 1955), *aff'd,* 240 F.2d 843 (6th Cir., 1957). "Certificate notes" were deemed to be stock. *Anderson et al. v. Healy,* D.C., Mont., 1965. But "surplus contribution notes" were recognized as indebtedness. *Peter Theodore et al.,* 38 T.C. 1011 (1962).

In one case, the court made purposeful inquiry as to whether the language used deviated from standard phraseology. *Intermountain Furniture Manufacturing Company, Inc. v. United States,* . . . F. Supp. . . . (D.C., Utah, 1967).

Debentures or other notes should be unambiguous obligations. *McSorley's, Inc. v. United States,* 323 F.2d 900 (10th Cir., 1963). "[T]he application of the appropriate label to these hybrid securities has assumed an unusual significance." *The Jordan Company v. Allen,* 85 F. Supp. 437 (D.C., M.D. Ga., 1949).

Corroborative Evidence. Charter provisions describing the characteristics of a security issue may be a determining factor. *Choctaw, Inc.,* T.C. Memo., Docket No. 36173, entered December 9, 1953.

The reality of so-called indebtedness has been assayed by such factors as:
Book entries. *Ortmayer et al. v. Commissioner,* 265 F.2d 848 (7th Cir., 1959).
Financial statements. *Kennickell Printing Company v. United States,* D.C., S.D. Ga., 1966.
Tax return treatment. *Intermountain Furniture Manufacturing Company, Inc. v. United States,* . . . F. Supp. . . . (D.C., Utah, 1967).

Convertible Bonds

Where the owner of a bond exercises the right, *provided for in the bond,* of converting it into stock *in the same corporation,* the transaction does not result in a realization of profit or loss, the transaction not being closed for income tax purposes until the stock is sold. G.C.M. 18436, 1937–1 CB 101.

In the case of a small business investing company that operates under the Small Business Investment Act of 1958, an ordinary loss deduction rather than a capital loss is permitted on losses from convertible debentures (including stock acquired pursuant to the conversion privilege). I.R.C. Section 1243.

Stock Purchase Warrants

Stock purchase warrants are securities, not stock. *E. P. Raymond,* 37 B.T.A. 423 (1938).

Where an individual, in return for services, receives stock that is subject to so many restrictions that it has no fair market value, and subsequently the restrictions are eliminated without prior arrangement that this would be done, the increase in value of the stock does not constitute a taxable event. When ultimately he disposes of the stock, he will have capital gain: the excess of realization over zero. *Robert Lehman,* 17 T.C. 652 (1951).

Warrants to purchase voting stock were held not to be voting stock. *Helvering v. Southwest Corp.,* 315 U.S. 194 (1942).

Stock Rights

Stock rights do not constitute stock but represent a contractual right to purchase stock. *Goodhue v. United States,* 17 F. Supp. 86 (Ct. Cl., 1936).

Distinction Between Common And Preferred Stocks

The distinction between common stock and preferred stock was brought out in the following ruling, which contrasted the attributes of each of these classes with those of a special class of stock:

A corporation's articles of incorporation authorized the issuance of common and of special shares. The special stock was ruled not to be common stock "since the holders thereof do not share ratably either in the earnings of the corporation or in its assets on liquidation, it being specifically provided that the holders of shares of any designated series have no interest in the assets or income of any other series. Furthermore, the certificate of incorporation provides for the issuance of common stock, which stock has the normal characteristics of common stock and is entirely separate and distinct from any of the classes of special stock therein considered. Neither is the special stock a preferred stock since the holders thereof are not preferred as to dividends out of the entire earnings of the corporation and are restricted to the earnings of the segregated assets representing his [*sic*] particular class of special stock. Likewise the holder of special stock has no preference in the general assets of the corporation, excepting the right to share ratably with other members· of his class in the segregated assets representing that particular class of special stock." Revenue Ruling 54–65, 1954–1 CB 101.

More generally: "The distinction between common stockholders and preferred stockholders may be said to be that the common stockholder is an owner of the enterprise in the proportion that his stock bears to the entire stock, and entitled to participate in the management, profit, and ultimate assets of the corporation. . . . A preferred stockholder is a mode by which a corporation obtains funds without borrowing money or contracting a debt, the stockholder being preferred as to principal and interest, but having no voice in the management. . . . It differs only from other stocks in that it is given preference and has no voting right. A preferred stockholder is not a creditor of the company." *Elko Lamoille Power Company v. Commissioner,* 50 F.2nd 595 (9th Cir., 1931).

Chapter 4

When is a Transaction Taxed?

Time Of Sale

A sale takes place when the broker executes it, not when the taxpayer receives his money. The broker serves as the taxpayer's agent and receipt by an agent is receipt by the principal. *Huntington National Bank v. Commissioner,* 90 F.2d 876 (6th Cir., 1937).

Under the rules of most of the registered security exchanges, delivery and payment (upon either a purchase or a sale of a security) are not required to be made until the second full business day after the date on which the purchase or sale is executed. See I.T. 3705, 1945 CB 174.

When a contract to sell stock on a stock exchange was entered into on December 31 and delivery was made in the regular way on January 2 following, the resultant loss on the transaction was incurred in the year of the contract to sell rather than in the year of delivery. G.C.M. 21503, 1939–2 CB 205. This rule applies equally to a similar transaction involving a sale of bearer bonds on which interest is computed to the date of delivery. The loss is deductible for Federal income tax purposes for the year in which the transaction was consummated except for delivery of the bonds. I.T. 3442, 1941–1 CB 212.

A sale of stock is not necessarily completely closed as of the date of the sale, for right of action by virtue of fraudulent representations still might be open. *James N. Collins Estate,* 46 B.T.A. 765 (1942).

"Registration of a transfer of shares on the books of the corporation is not necessary to the validity of the transfer. Even where the charter or by-laws of a corporation, or the general law under which it is organized, provide that stock shall be transferable only on the books of the corporation, it is well settled that as between the parties, an unregistered transfer is valid." *Rule et al. v. Commissioner,* 127 F.2d 979 (10th Cir., 1942).

On December 30, an individual requested her broker to sell certain shares, stating that the certificates were in her safe deposit box and would be delivered right after the holidays. The broker sold the stock on December 30. The Commissioner claimed that the transaction did not take place for tax purposes in December, as what had taken place by year-end was merely a short sale, to be closed out when the seller supplied the stock in January. The court disagreed, pointing out that the taxpayer owned the shares and that they were within her control and available for delivery. She intended to sell the shares that she owned, and it was stipulated that they were in fact sold. Mere failure to deliver certificates is not enough to establish a short sale. *Dee Furey Mott,* 35 B.T.A. 195 (1936).

A short sale is completed on the date the sale is *covered,* not at the time the order for the sale was entered into. *Doyle et al. v. Commissioner,* 286 F.2d 654 (7th Cir., 1961). The time of delivery for a short sale is the taxable year within which the covering transaction is closed, and gain or loss is recognized at that time. *Richardson v. Commissioner,* 121 F.2d 1 (2d Cir., 1941).

A contract to sell can put gain or loss in a different taxable year, or it can extend the holding period. A sale that passes title to specified securities at a set price at a named future date is not a taxable event until that date is reached. *Doyle v. Commissioner,* 110 F.2d 157 (2d Cir., 1940).

Loss

"A loss upon the sale of stock is sustained by a taxpayer on the date a contract for the sale of such stock was entered into and not at a later date when he delivers the stock to the purchaser." Revenue Ruling 59–418, 1959–2 CB 184.

Loss on the sale of stock is realized when "obligation to deliver is so fixed that the loss is reasonably certain in fact and ascertainable in amount." *Lucas v. American Code Company, Inc.,* 280 U.S. 445 (1930). This is so even if, under the Uniform Sales Act, gain or loss is to be recognized when shares of stock are delivered. *Commissioner v. Robinson,* 103 F.2d 1009 (6th Cir., 1939).

"If a sale furnishes conclusive evidence that a loss has been sustained in a particular taxable year, it is not material to the establishing of the right to deduction that all technical details of the transaction relating to the sale be contemplated within the taxable year." *Commissioner v. Dashiel,* 100

F.2d 625 (7th Cir., 1938). Thus, loss took place at that time when the transaction was so far advanced that the taxpayer was bound to deliver the stock to his broker at a price which was then determined by the sale the broker made. *Ruml v. Commissioner,* 83 F.2d 257 (2d Cir., 1936).

A taxpayer sold shares on the New York Stock Exchange for cash on December 31, his broker borrowing stock for delivery. The taxpayer delivered his certificates to his broker on the following January 30. No short sale was contemplated or found, the parties having intended the sale to be completed on December 31, as it was. Loss was established on December 31, the transaction being so far advanced on that date that the taxpayer was obliged to go through with it at a price which was then determined by the sale the broker made. From and after December 31, the taxpayer was not legally free to do anything in respect to these shares which would destroy the legal consequences of the acts performed on and prior to December 31. *Commissioner v. Dashiel,* 100 F.2d 625 (7th Cir., 1938).

A stockholder's loss upon liquidation may be recognized prior to the final liquidation of the corporation, if the amount retained by the corporation is only for the expenses of dissolution. *Commissioner v. Winthrop,* 98 F.2d 74 (2d Cir., 1938).

Installment And Deferred Sales

The installment method of reporting for tax purposes may be used by dealers in personal property and in the case of sales of realty and casual sales of personalty. I.R.C. Section 453(a), (b). Thus, if the realty or personalty qualifies for capital gain treatment under Section 1231, the installment method may be used to spread the reporting of long-term capital gain over plural years.

Where the consideration for the sale of a capital asset was in the form of a percentage of the gross sales made during the year, the taxpayer was entitled to a capital gain limitation on the sums received each year. *Carl G. Dreymann,* 11 T.C. 153 (1948).

When-Issued Stock

Where there is a sale of stock on a "when-issued" basis, no actual sale can take place until the new stock is issued. "[D]ealings in stock on a 'when issued' basis are not sales of stock, but merely sales of contracts to sell stock which are made on the express condition that no delivery and payment are required unless and until the stock is issued." *Lewis K. Walker,* 35 B.T.A. 640 (1937).

"[W]here buy and sell contracts of 'when issued' securities are not sold or exchanged prior to their maturity but are retained until the final settlement date and cleared through the stock clearing corporation . . . there is a sale and exchange of the securities involved on the settlement date and a short term capital transaction follows as a consequence." *Morris Shanis*, 19 T.C. 641 (1953).

"The usual situation in which trading in securities on a 'when issued' basis takes place is one in which there is submitted a plan of reorganization of a corporation providing for the issuance, in exchange for its outstanding securities, of securities of a new corporation or of new securities of the old corporation. The time between submission of the plan and the actual exchange of old securities for new securities may be several years. After submission of the plan, trading may be commenced in the new securities which are to be issued. Inasmuch as these new securities are not in existence, the trading is on the basis of 'when issued.' " I.T. 3721, 1945 CB 164.

Contributions In Capital Assets

"Ordinarily a contribution is made at the time delivery is effected. . . . If a taxpayer unconditionally delivers (or mails) a properly endorsed stock certificate to a charitable donee or the donee's agent, the gift is completed on the date of delivery (or mailing), provided that such certificate is received in the ordinary course of the mails. If the donor delivers the certificates to his bank or broker as the donor's agent, or to the issuing corporation or its agent, for transfer into the name of the donee, the gift is completed on the date the stock is transferred on the books of the corporation." I.R.C. Section 170(b).

No charitable contribution was allowed for securities in the year that the donor wrote a letter to the charitable organization announcing his gift, where in fact the certificates remained in the custody of a broker until the following year. *William B. Neville et al.,* T. C. Memo. 1967–95, filed May 3, 1967. In the case of a gift of stock, the gift customarily is not regarded as complete until the names on the certificates are changed. *Ralph Owen Howard Estate,* 9 T.C. 1192 (1947). A gift of stock was not made when certificates, endorsed in blank, were delivered to the corporate secretary with instructions to issue a specified number of shares to a designated charity. The gift was not made until the transfer actually was effected. *Jack Winston Londen et al.,* 45 T.C. 106 (1965).

No gift of stock is recognized for tax purposes when the donor merely makes a verbal assignment. Transfer of stock by a form of assignment or on the transfer agent's books is necessary. There must be constructive or symbolic delivery, "a delivery as perfect as the nature of the property and surroundings of the parties reasonably permitted." *Lunsford Richardson et al.,* 39 B.T.A. 927 (1939), *aff'd,* 126 F.2d 562 (2d Cir., 1942).

An individual endorsed his stock certificate in a closely-held corporation to his wife; his signature was witnessed. He gave the certificate to his wife in an envelope stating: "Property of [the husband]." He then placed the envelope in a vault to which both he and his wife had access. After his death, it was held that the stock had passed to his wife by reason of his death, not as a gift. He never had indicated an intent to make a gift. When originally he handed the certificate to his wife, his words were: "Guard this with your life." He never during his lifetime had divested himself of absolute control and dominion of the shares. *Gorski v. United States,* D.C., N.D. Ill., 1964.

An *inter vivos* gift to charity, subject to a condition which may prevent actual payment of the gift to charity, is not deductible until such time as the condition in question is satisfied and the charitable destination of the gift becomes certain. *Jones, Jr. et al v. United States,* 252 F. Supp. 256 (D.C., N.D. Ohio, 1966).

Where an individual clipped unmatured coupons from bonds which he retained, and gave these coupons to another party, it was the donor who was taxed upon the interest income when received. In the horticultural words of the court, the fruit must be attributed to the tree upon which it grew. *Helvering v. Horst,* 311 U.S. 112 (1940).

The Holding Period

At first blush, determination of the holding period of capital assets would seem to be a simple matter that a person can solve with one hand, or, more precisely, inasmuch as the magic number is "more than six," with two hands. But the number of litigated cases on this subject indicates that the matter is not so disarmingly simple after all. When does the holding period start? When does it end? What about substituted basis, "tacking on," assets which fictionally are the same (at least in part) as assets long since departed?

The taxpayer's accounting period is not a factor to be considered. "[T]he length of the seller's holding period . . . must be determined *as of the time of the sale,* irrespective of whether the seller is on the cash or the accrual basis. . ." *Floyd R. Clodfelter et al.,* 48 T.C. 694 (1967).

The problem starts with acquisition. "To 'hold' property within the meaning of . . . the Internal Revenue Code is to own it." *Marian L. Bloxom et al.,* T.C. Memo., Docket Nos. 16968–9, entered February 20, 1950. "In order to own or hold one must acquire. The date of acquisition is, then, that from which to compute the duration of ownership or the length of holding." *McFeely et al. v. Commissioner,* 296 U.S. 102 (1935).

It is, then, the passage of title which starts the holding period of assets. *Commissioner v. Segall et al.,* 114 F.2d 706 (6th Cir., 1940). Passage of legal title is not required; rather, a transfer of the benefits and burdens of ownership is sufficient to start the holding period. *Ted F. Merrill,* 40 T.C. 66 (1963), *aff'd,* 336 F.2d 771 (9th Cir., 1964). "[I]t is the holding of an owner, as distinguished from the holding of a bailee or trustee, that is contemplated by the statute." *Howell v. Commissioner,* 140 F.2d 765 (5th Cir., 1944). "The cases considering the holding period have not required the actual issuance of stock or the transfer thereof upon the corporate books to start or end the holding period. It has been held frequently that the holding period of corporate stock begins or ends when a purchaser acquires substantial contractual rights which will ripen into full ownership unless defeated by a breach of contract by the other contracting party." *Swenson et al. v. Commissioner,* 309 F.2d 672 (8th Cir., 1962).

The holding period of an asset sold under an executory contract does not terminate until the performance date set in the contract. *Lucas v. North Texas Lumber Company,* 281 U.S. 11 (1930). Where a seller retains title under a conditional sales contract until all deferred payments have been received, the holding period dates back to the time of sale as if he had made the sale at that point and simultaneously had re-acquired this property through a mortgage from the purchaser. *Floyd R. Clodfelter et al.,* 48 T.C. 694 (1967).

The taxpayer has the burden of establishing how long property has been held. *Taylor v. Commissioner,* 76 F.2d 904 (2d Cir., 1935).

Starting And Ending Dates. There are two relevant dates in connection with security transactions: (1) the "trade date" (the date on which the contract to buy or to sell the security is made) and (2) the "settlement date" (the date on which the security is delivered and payment is tendered). Often settlement takes place a fixed number of days after the trade. In transactions involving bonds or other evidences of indebtedness, the buyer pays the interest accrued in the security to the date of settlement as part of the consideration for the transfer. Bonds as well as stock are considered to be acquired or sold on the respective "trade dates." Revenue Ruling 66–97, 1966–1 CB 190.

In determining the holding period for capital gain and loss purposes, the date the property is acquired is excluded, and the date the property is disposed of is included. I.T. 3287, 1939–1 CB (Part 1) 138. This rule is not affected by the intervention of holidays or less than full business days between the date of purchase or sale of a security and the date of delivery and payment. I.T. 3705, 1945 CB 174.

Inasmuch as the holding period of a capital asset begins to run on the day following the acquisition of the asset involved, a capital asset acquired on the last day of any month (regardless of whether the month has thirty-one days or fewer) must not be disposed of until on or after the first day of the seventh succeeding month of the calendar in order to have been "held for more than 6 months" within the meaning of Sections 1222(3) and (4) of the Code. For example, an asset acquired on April 30 must not have been disposed of before November 1 in order to have been held for more than six months. Revenue Ruling 66–7, 1966–1 CB 188.

Fractional Periods. The determination of the holding period of capital assets must be made with reference to calendar months and fractions thereof rather than with reference to days. In the computation of a holding period which is less than a calendar month and includes parts of two different months of the calendar, the fraction of a "month" should be formed by using as the numerator the number of days in the entire fractional-month period (less one) and using as the denominator the number of days in the month (of the calendar) immediately preceding the month in which the holding period ends. See Examples (1) and (2), below.

Similarly, where a holding period includes, in addition to one or more whole (calendar) "months," a fraction of a "month" which includes parts of two different months of the calendar, the fraction should be formed by using as the numerator the number of days remaining of the entire holding period after first computing the part which consists of a whole "month" or "months" and using the month in which the entire holding period ends. See Examples (3) and (4), below.

Where a holding period of less than a (calendar) "month" is included in only one month of the calendar, the fraction of a month should be formed by using as the denominator the number of days in the particular month of the calendar in which the period is included. That rule also is applicable in computing the fraction of a "month" involved where this fractional-month period is included in a holding period which also includes one or more whole (calendar) "months."

Example (1). Where a security was acquired on January 15 and sold on February 14 of the same year, the entire (fractional-month) holding period consists of sixteen days in January and fourteen days in February, or thirty days. That figure, thirty, should be used as the numerator. January, the month immediately preceding the month (of the calendar) in which the holding period ends (February), has thirty-one days. That figure, thirty-one, should be used as the denominator. Thus, the security was held for 30/31 of a "month."

Example (2). Similarly, a security acquired on February 14 and sold on March 13 of the same year was held for 28/29 of a "month."

Example (3). Where a security was acquired on November 15 and sold on the following February 14, the period it was held includes two whole (calendar) "months" (November 15 to January 15). The number of days included in the entire period, in addition to those two "months" (sixteen days in January and fourteen days in February) is thirty. That figure, thirty, should be used as the numerator of the fraction of a "month" included in the holding period. January, the month immediately preceding the month (of the calendar) in which the holding period ends (February), has thirty-one days. That figure, thirty-one, should be used as the denominator of the fraction. The security, accordingly, was held for two 30/31 "months."

Example (4). Similarly, a security acquired on November 15 and sold on March 14 of the following year was held for three 27/28 "months."

Example (5). A security acquired on March 1 and sold on March 31 was held for 30/31 of a "month."

Example (6). Similarly, a security acquired on November 15 and sold on February 28 of the following year was held for three 13/28 "months." I.T. 3985, 1949–2 CB 51.

The fractional parts of a day are to be disregarded. *Harriet M. Hooper,* 26 B.T.A. 758 (1932).

Co-mingled Stocks. If shares of stock in a corporation are sold from lots purchased at different dates or at different prices and the identity of the lots cannot be determined, the cost or other basis rules of the regulations under Section 1012 will be applied to determine the holding period. Regulations Section 1.1223–1(i).

Under those regulations, the first-in, first-out rule will be applied if there is no adequate identification. But the "FIFO" rule does not apply if the lot from which the stock is sold or transferred can be adequately identified. Such identification may be effected by identification of stock certificates or on a confirmation document. Regulations Section 1.1012–1(c).

Stock Dividends and Rights. The period for which a taxpayer has held stock, or stock subscription rights, received on a distribution is determined as though the stock dividend or right were the stock in respect of which the dividend was issued, if the basis for determining gain or loss on the sale or other disposition of the stock dividend or right is determined under Section 307, that is, receipt is tax-free unless received in lieu of cash. I.R.C. Section 1223(5).

Stock Acquired Through Rights. The period for which a taxpayer has held stock or securities issued to him by a corporation pursuant to the exercise by him of rights to acquire such stock or securities begins with and includes the day upon which the rights were exercised. This is so whether or not the receipt of taxable gain was.recognized in connection with the distribution of the rights. A taxpayer will be deemed to have exercised rights received from a corporation where there is an expression of assent to the terms of these rights made by the taxpayer in the manner requested or authorized by the corporation. I.R.C. Section 1223(6).

The holding period of stock acquired by the exercise of a stock right is limited to the time during which the stock itself has been held. *Weir v. Commissioner,* 173 F.2d 222 (3d Cir., 1949).

When one subscribes to stock in a corporation, the holding period is from the date of stock subscription and not the time the stock certificates were issued. "The issuance of a certificate of stock is not necessary to make one a stockholder in a corporation." *Edward R. Bacon Company et al.,* T.C. Memo., Docket Nos. 4043–4, entered September 10, 1945, *aff'd,* 158 F.2d 981 (9th Cir., 1947).

Options. When an option to purchase property is acquired, the holding period dates back to the time when the option is exercised. *Helvering v. San Joaquin Fruit & Investment Company,* 297 U.S. 496 (1936). Inasmuch as an option to purchase stock does not constitute a present interest therein, the period during which the option was held unexercised cannot be added to the period subsequent to its exercise in determining the holding period. *Winthrop Crane III et al.,* 45 T.C. 397 (1966), *aff'd,* 368 F.2d 800 (1st Cir., 1966).

In the case of stock obtained by exercise of an employee stock option, the holding period is measured as of the time the options were unexercised and not the time they were granted. *Commissioner v. LoBue,* 351 U.S. 243 (1956).

In computing the period during which stock, obtained as the result of a restricted stock option agreement, was held, the day upon which it was acquired by the taxpayer is to be excluded, and the day on which it was sold is to be included. A taxpayer "acquires" the stock when his acceptance becomes binding upon the company. *Becker et al. v. Commissioner,* 378 F.2d 767 (3rd Cir., 1967).

The call option contract and the shares of stock subject to call thereunder are not "substantially identical property" within the meaning of Section 1233 and, therefore, the holding period of the call option contract is not affected by the provisions of that section. Thus, gain or loss resulting from a sale of the call option would be long-term if the time between the purchase date of the call and its sale were more than six months. Revenue Ruling 58–384, 1958–2 CB 410.

If a taxpayer accepts delivery of a commodity in satisfaction of a commodities futures contract, the holding period of the commodity includes the period for which he held the commodity futures contract, provided the contract was a capital asset in his hands. I.R.C. Section 1223(8). In ascertaining the holding period for commodity calls, only the time between the date of purchase of the commodity and the date of its disposition by transfer of possession is considered, and the further period prior to the determination of the price by exercising the call cannot be added. *Patterson et al. v. Hightower, Jr. et al.,* 245 F.2d 765 (5th Cir., 1957).

Corporate Reorganizations and Tax-Free Exchanges. Where there is a reorganization that is *not* tax-free, there is no tacking on of the time the original and the replacement shares were held. There is a tacking on of holding periods if the reorganization is tax-free. I.T. 3721, 1945 CB 164.

The holding period of property received in an exchange by a taxpayer includes the period for which the property which he exchanged was held by him, if the property received has the same basis in whole or in part for determining gain or loss in his hands as the property exchanged. But this rule applies only if the property exchanged was at the time of the exchange a capital asset in the taxpayer's hands or property used in his trade or business as defined in Section 1231(b). For this purpose, "exchange" includes the following transactions:

(1) An involuntary conversion described in Section 1033.

(2) A distribution to which Section 355 (or so much of Section 356 as relates to Section 355) applies. This refers to the distribution of stock or securities of a controlled corporation, that is, a divisive reorganization or corporate separation. I.R.C. Section 1223(1).

Thus, stock of a controlled corporation received from the distributing corporation dates back to the date of acquisition by the distributor. Regulations Section 1.1223–1.

In computing the holding period of assets transferred to one corporation by another corporation which controlled its stock, the holding period of the transferor was tacked on to that of the transferee. *Frederick Steel Co.,* 42 T.C. 13 (1964).

In the case of the redemption of stock through a related corporation which is governed by Section 304, the holding period of the stock which is considered to have been redeemed is treated the same as the holding period of the stock actually surrendered. Regulations Section 1.304–2(a).

In a tax-free exchange, there is tacked on to the holding period of a capital asset the holding period of the asset for which it had been received in exchange, even though the asset surrendered had not been a capital asset. *Commissioner v. Gracey,* 159 F.2d 325 (5th Cir., 1947).

The owner of a convertible debenture that may be converted into common stock has a holding period for this stock that dates back to the date he acquired the debentures. Revenue Ruling 62–153, 1962–2 CB 186. But the determination can become quite complicated. An individual purchased rights entitling him to subscribe to a convertible debenture, which debenture was convertible into stock upon surrender of the bond and payment of $50. Each share of stock thus acquired had a split holding period: (1) that part of his investment in the stock which was attributable to his ownership of the debenture had a holding period which began with the date on which the right to acquire the debenture was acquired and (2) that part of his investment in the stock which was attributable to the additional cash required for the acquisition of the stock had a holding period beginning with the date following the date of acquisition. Revenue Ruling 62–140, 1962–2 CB 181.

When-Issued Stock. If a taxpayer sells stock of a reorganized corporation "when-issued," at a certain price, and he holds the stock in the old corporation until he receives the new stock, when he delivers the new stock in completion of his sale, the holding period depends upon whether the reorganization was taxable. If the reorganization is taxable, there is no tacking of the time the old stock was held to the time the new stock was held in determining whether the sale of the new stock gives rise to a long-term or a short-term capital gain or loss. If the reorganization is tax-free, the time the old stock was held is tacked on to the time the new stock was held in making the determination. Where an individual, who has contracted to buy (or to sell) stock "when-issued" sells his right to buy (or to sell), he sells a capital asset. The holding period depends upon the time he held the contract. I.T. 3721, 1945 CB 164, as modified by Revenue Ruling 57–29, 1957–1 CB 519.

Wash Sales. If the acquisition of stock or securities resulted in the non-deductibility under the wash sales provisions of the loss from the sale or other disposition of substantially identical stock or securities, the holding period of the newly acquired securities will include the period for which the taxpayer held the securities with respect to which the loss was not allowed. I.R.C. Section 1223(4).

Disallowed Losses and S.E.C.-Ordered Dispositions. Where a transferor is not permitted to deduct a loss on a transaction with a related party by virtue of Section 267 (see Chapter 7), the transferee is not permitted to tack on the transferor's holding period. But the transferee may include the time during which he held the property which he exchanged where, for example, he exchanged a capital asset in a transaction which was non-taxable to him under Section 1031 (property held for productive use or investment) and the property received in the exchange has the same basis as the property exchanged. Regulations Section 1.267(d)–1(c)(3).

In determining the period for which a taxpayer has held stock or securities received upon a distribution which was tax-free as having been made in accordance with an order of the Securities and Exchange Commission, there is included the period for which he held the stock or securities in the distributing corporation before the receipt of the stock or securities on the distribution. I.R.C. Section 1223(3).

Gift and Inheritance. A legatee's holding period dates from the decedent's death in spite of the fact that the legatee's basis was valued at the time of distribution to him by the executor. *McFeely v. Commissioner,* 296 U.S. 102 (1936).

If property in the hands of a taxpayer has the same basis as it had in the hands of another person (such as in the case of a gift after December 31, 1920), the holding period of this property in the taxpayer's hands includes the holding period of this other person. I.R.C. Section 1223(2).

Where the donee does not use the donor's basis (as in the case of a gift in contemplation of death), the holding period of the donee commences on the date of the gift. Revenue Ruling 59–86, 1959–1 CB 209.

Trust. A remainderman's interest dates back to the date of the decedent's death for property then owned and to the date of purchase for property bought by the trustee. "[W]e look to the time when the taxpayer first acquired the interest which later ripened into full ownership." *Helvering v. Gambrill,* 313 U.S. 11 (1941).

Where a trust agreement provided that the grantor would furnish funds to the trustee to purchase shares of a certain stock at no more than a stipulated ceiling price for the benefit of named beneficiaries, who, under certain circumstances, could obtain this stock from the trustee at its average cost, the holding period of the trustee could not be tacked on to the holding period of the beneficiaries. "For the beneficiaries to claim the 'same basis' as the trustee . . . it is necessary to find that the stock was held for them from the outset by the trustee. . . ." But such was not the case where the stock never would become the beneficiaries' unless they elected to pay for it. *Crane III et al. v. Commissioner,* 368 F.2d 800 (1st Cir., 1966).

Partnership and Community Property. In the case of assets distributed by a partnership to a partner, he may tack on to his own holding period the holding period of the partnership. I.R.C. Section 735(b). But where, under a buy-sell agreement, the surviving partner acquires the interest of a deceased partner for a stipulated price, the partnership thus terminating, the partnership assets are deemed to have been acquired by purchase rather than by distribution, and there is no tacking on of the holding periods. *Edwin E. McCauslen et al.,* 45 T.C. 588 (1966).

The holding period of property, in the case of the surviving spouse's share in the community, dates from the time of acquisition by the com-

munity. In the case of property acquired by inheritance from the deceased spouse's share of the community, the holding period dates from the time of the decedent's death. Revenue Ruling 59–220, 1959–1 CB 210.

Holding Period For Property Other Than Securities

In determining a taxpayer's holding period for real estate for purposes of Section 1231 (property used in the trade or business and involuntary conversions), consideration must be given not only to the dates on which bare legal title passes but also the dates on which the burdens and benefits of ownership are transferred in closed transactions. *Ted F. Merrill,* 40 T.C. 66 (1963), *aff'd,* 336 F.2d 771 (9th Cir., 1964). Where the real estate is the subject of an unconditional contract of sale, the holding period begins on the day following that on which title passes, or on the day following that on which title passes, or on the day following that on which delivery of possession is made and the burdens and privileges of ownership are assumed, whichever occurs first. I.T. 1378, I–2 CB 26. A delivery of possession under a mere option agreement, however, is without significance until a contract of sale comes into being through exercise of the option, so that the holding period of the seller cannot end prior to that date. Revenue Ruling 54–607, 1954–2 CB 177.

In the case of parts of a building, the holding period dates back to the completion of each part. *Paul v. Commissioner,* 206 F.2d 763 (3d Cir., 1953). Where an undivided half-interest in a certain property is purchased at one time and the other half-interest is purchased at another time, a subsequent sale of an undivided half-interest in the entire property involves two elements. The holding period for the interest sold out of each undivided half is determined by referring to the acquisition date of the particular part out of which the interest was sold. Revenue Ruling 67–309, I.R.B. 1967–38, 12.

Where a taxpayer has acquired a principal residence in a transaction which is to any extent not subject to gain upon disposition of his former residence, the holding period includes the holding period of the original residence. I.R.C. Section 1223(7).

Where a municipality condemned real estate owned by a taxpayer, he no longer "held" the property after the date of authorization of seizure by the city, for under this particular condemnation act, fee title of the property vested in the city at that time. *Commissioner v. Kieselbach et al.,* 127 F.2d 359 (2d Cir., 1942), *aff'd on other grounds,* 317 U.S. 399 (1943). All condemnation acts, however, are not worded in the same manner as that of New York City, which was involved in this case. The holding period of property requisitioned by the United States Maritime Commission did not terminate until a negotiated sale for an agreed price was effected. Here, the statute did not provide for automatic vesting of title in the Commission upon a taking. *R. O'Brien & Co., Inc. v. United States,* D.C., Mass., 1956. The date of destruction of a capital asset is the significant date in fixing the termination of the holding period. *Rose v. United States,* 229 F. Supp. 298 (D.C., S.D. Cal., 1964).

The holding period of timber, acquired by a corporation (transferee) in a non-taxable exchange under Section 351 (transfer to a controlled corporation) and subsequently cut by such corporation under the elective treatment accorded the cutting of timber, includes the period during which the timber was held by the transferor. Revenue Ruling 55–352, 1955–1 CB 372.

The holding period for a patent begins when it is "reduced to practice." *Lamar v. Granger,* 99 F. Supp. 17 (D.C., W.D. Pa., 1951). The quoted words have been incorporated into the tax law. *Samuel E. Diescher et al.,* 36 B.T.A. 732 (1937), *aff'd on other grounds,* 110 F.2d 90 (3d Cir., 1940). Reduction to practice "does not mean that whatever is being worked upon has to be in shape to be commercially marketable. On the other hand, it must be a demonstration that the inventor's idea works." *Farrand Optical Co. v. United States,* 325 F.2d 328 (2d Cir., 1963).

The holding period of an invention begins when the invention is completely conceived and drawings made sufficient to make its manufacture possible, and not when a patent is issued. *Edward C. Myers,* 6 T.C. 258 (1946).

In the case of a seat on the New York Stock Exchange, the holding period starts with the date of approval by the governing committee. *Herman Krech,* B.T.A. Memo., Docket No. 62866, entered July 26, 1933.

Composite Holding Periods

Sometimes property will be transferred in part as a gift and in part as a sale. For example, property might be sold at less than its fair market value, with the intention of making a gift to the vendee to the extent of the differential. "In determining the holding period for which the taxpayer has held property, however acquired, there shall be included the period for which such property was held by any other person, if under this chapter such property has, for the purpose of determining gain or loss from a sale or exchange, the same basis in whole or in part in his hands as it would have had in the hands of such other person." I.R.C. Section 1223(2).

Where property was transferred in part as a gift and in part as a sale, one court noted: "If they were acquired in whole or in part by gift, this is a transfer of basis under Section 1015 and there is a 'tacking' of the holding period under Section 1223(2)." *Winthrop M. Crane III,* 45 T.C. 397 (1966), *aff'd on other grounds,* 368 F.2d 800 (1st Cir., 1966).

Impact Of State Law

The holding period for Federal income tax purposes may be determined by state law, inasmuch as state law frequently defines the property rights which then are subjected to Federal taxation.

For holding purposes, acquisition occurs when ownership of the property in question is obtained. *Howell v. Commissioner,* 140 F.2d 765 (5th Cir., 1944). "The concept of ownership employed is found in applicable state law." Revenue Ruling 59–220, 1959–1 CB 210. Normally, under state law, ownership is obtained from the passage of title. *Patterson et al. v. Hightower et al.,* 245 F.2d 765 (5th Cir., 1957). Thus, the holding period ordinarily is to be computed from that date. But, in stated circumstances, Section 1223 requires the tacking on of the holding period of a prior holder.

"At what point did the taxpayer cease to 'own' the property, so that holding period ended? . . . When Congress determines a tax by reason of the period during which a taxpayer 'owns' a certain piece of property, the necessary implication is that the period of ownership is determined by state law." *R. O'Brien & Co., Inc. v. United States,* D.C., Mass., 1956.

Chapter 5

How is a Transaction Taxed?

Short- And Long-Term Capital
Gain And Loss

Gross income includes income from whatever sources derived, including "[g]ains derived from dealings in property. . . ." I.R.C. Section 61(a). Capital gains are income for Federal income tax purposes. *Merchants' Loan & Trust Company v. Smietanka,* 255 U.S. 509 (1921). But to the extent that the alternative tax provided in Section 1201 applies, capital gains are not taxed in the same manner as other income.

The term "short-term capital gain" or "short-term capital loss" means gain or loss from the sale or exchange of a capital asset held for *not more* than six months, if and to the extent that this gain or loss is taken into account in computing gross income. If the asset has been held for *more* than six months, there is "long-term capital gain" or "long-term capital loss." I.R.C. Section 1222(1)–(4).

After all capital assets which were sold or exchanged during the taxable year are classified as short-term or long-term, gain or loss on each transaction is to be determined. Short-term capital gains and losses are merged with each other by adding the gains and losses separately and subtracting one total from the other to obtain the net short-term capital gain or loss. Capital loss carryovers are short-term capital losses in the year to which they are brought forward, except that in the case of a taxpayer other than a corporation that has a net capital loss for any taxable year beginning after December 31, 1963, the excess of the net long-term capital loss over the net short-term capital gain for that year will be a long-term capital loss in the succeeding taxable year. Regulations Section 1.1222–1(b) (1).

In the case of a corporation, losses from sales or exchanges of capital

55

assets are allowed as deductions only to the extent of gains from such sales or exchanges. I.R.C. Section 1211(a). In the case of a taxpayer other than a corporation, losses from sales or exchanges of capital assets are allowed as a deduction only to the extent of the gains from such transactions, plus the taxable income of the taxpayer or $1,000, whichever is smaller. I.R.C. Section 1211(b). For purposes of this subsection, taxable income is to be computed without regard to gains or losses from sales or exchanges of capital assets and without regard to the deductions for personal exemptions or any deductions in lieu thereof. For example, the deductions available to estates and trusts under Section 642(b) are in lieu of the deductions for personal exemptions to individuals and are to be added back to taxable income for the purposes of Section 1211(b). Regulations Section 1.1211–1(a).

In the case of a joint Federal income tax return for husband and wife, the capital losses of one spouse may be deducted from the capital gains of the other. *Helvering v. Janney et al.,* 311 U.S. 189 (1940).

The fact that some part of a loss from the sale or exchange of a capital asset may finally be disallowed does not mean that this loss is not "taken into account in computing taxable income" within the meaning of that phrase as used in Sections 1222(2) and 1222(4). Regulations Section 1.1222–1(a).

In computing the adjusted gross income or the taxable income of a taxpayer other than a corporation, if for any taxable year the net long-term capital gain exceeds the net short-term capital loss, 50% of the amount of the excess is allowable as a deduction from gross income. I.R.C. Section 1202.

In the case of an estate or trust, for the purpose of computing this deduction, any long-term or short-term capital gains which, under Sections 652 and 662, are includible in the gross income of its income beneficiaries as gain derived from the sale or exchange of capital assets must be excluded in determining whether, for the taxable year of the estate or trust, its net long-term capital gain exceeds its net short-term capital loss. Regulations Section 1.1202–1(b).

The Alternative Tax

Corporations. In case the net long-term capital gain of any corporation exceeds the net short-term capital loss, an alternative tax is available in lieu of the regular income tax. The alternative tax is not in lieu of the personal holding company tax.

Other taxpayers. In case the net long-term capital gain of a taxpayer other than a corporation exceeds the net short-term capital loss, an alternative tax is available only if it is less than the regular income tax.

The alternative tax is the sum of—
   (1) A partial tax, computed at regular income tax rates, on the taxable income reduced by an amount equal to 50% of the excess of the net long-term capital gain over the net short-term capital loss, plus
   (2) 25% of the excess of the net long-term capital gain over the net short-term capital loss. I.R.C. Section 1201.

In the case of a joint return, the excess of any net long-term capital gain over any net short-term capital loss is determined by combining the long-term capital gains and losses and the short-term capital gains and losses of the spouses. Regulations Section 1.1201–1(d).

In general, an individual should use the alternative method when his taxable income (including capital gains) reaches a bracket in excess of 50%. He should then compute his tax under each of the methods and file on the basis of the one producing the lower tax.

Capital Loss Carryovers

The limitations upon the deductibility of capital losses in the year of incurrence have been mentioned. Unused capital losses may be carried forward, as discussed below.

A corporation sustaining a net capital loss will carry over this loss to each of the five succeeding taxable years. In each of these years, this loss is treated as a short-term capital loss to the extent that it had not been allowed as a deduction against any net capital gains of taxable years intervening between the taxable year in which the loss was sustained and the taxable year to which it was carried. The carryover thus is applied in each succeeding taxable year to offset any net capital gain in that year. The amount of the capital loss carryover may not be included in computing a new net capital loss of a taxable year which can be carried forward to the next five succeeding taxable years. For this purpose, a net capital gain will be computed without regard to capital loss carryovers. A net capital loss for a taxable year beginning before October 20, 1951 will be determined under the applicable law relating to the computation of capital gains and losses in effect before that date. "Thus, where the applicable law for a taxable year beginning before October 20, 1951, provided that only certain percentages of the gain or loss recognized upon the sale or exchange of a capital asset should be taken into account in computing net capital loss, such percentages are to be taken into account in computing net capital loss for any such taxable year under this subparagraph." Regulations Section 1.1212–1(a).

There is a 10-year carryover to the extent that the capital loss is attributable to a foreign expropriation capital loss: that is, losses sustained directly by reason of the expropriation, intervention, seizure, or similar taking of property by the government of any foreign country, any political subdivision thereof, or any of its agencies or instrumentalities.

This same treatment applies in the case of a taxpayer other than a corporation for taxable years beginning before January 1, 1964.

If a taxpayer other than a corporation sustains a net capital loss for any taxable year beginning after December 31, 1963, the portion which constitutes a short-term capital loss carryover may be carried over to the succeeding taxable year without limitation and treated as a short-term capital loss in that year; the portion which constitutes a long-term capital loss may be carried over to the succeeding taxable year and treated as a long-term capital loss incurred in that year. The carryovers are included in the succeeding taxable year in the determination of the amount of the short-term capital loss, the net short-term capital gain or loss, the long-term capital loss, and the net long-term capital gain or loss in that year, and the capital loss carryovers from that year.

In determining a net short-term capital gain or loss of a taxable year, for purposes of computing a short-term or long-term capital loss carryover to the succeeding taxable year, an amount equal to the excess of the capital losses allowable as a deduction for the taxable year over the capital gains for that year is treated as a short-term capital gain occurring in that year. A taxpayer other than a corporation sustaining a net capital loss for any taxable year beginning before January 1, 1964 must treat as a short-term capital loss in the first taxable year beginning after December 31, 1963 any amount which would be treated as a short-term capital loss in that year under the statute as in effect immediately before the enactment of the Revenue Act in 1964.

Husband And Wife. For computing the net capital loss carryovers by husband and wife, these rules apply:

(1) If a husband and wife making a joint return for any taxable year made separate returns for the preceding year, any capital loss carryovers of each spouse from that preceding taxable year may be carried forward to the taxable year.

(2) If a joint return was made for the preceding taxable year, any capital loss carryover from that preceding taxable year may be carried forward to the taxable year.

(3) If a husband and wife make separate returns for the first taxable year beginning after December 31, 1963, or for any prior taxable year, and they made a joint return for the preceding taxable year, any capital loss

carryover from that preceding taxable year must be allocated to the spouses on the basis of their individual net capital loss which gave rise to the capital loss carryover. The capital loss carryover so allocated to each spouse may be carried forward by the spouse to the taxable year.

(4) If a husband and wife making separate returns for any taxable year following the first taxable year beginning after December 31, 1963 made a joint return for the preceding taxable year, any long-term or short-term capital loss carryovers will be allocated to the spouses on the basis of their individual net long-term and net short-term capital losses for the preceding taxable year which gave rise to such capital loss carryovers, and the portions of the long-term or short-term capital loss carryovers so allocated to each spouse may be carried forward by each to the taxable year.

(5) If separate returns are made both for the taxable year and the preceding taxable year, any capital loss carryover of each spouse may be carried forward by such spouse. Regulations Section 1.1212–1(c).

Estates and Trusts. An unused capital loss carryover of a decedent dies with him. Revenue Ruling 54–207, 1954–1 CB 147.

But if, upon its termination, an estate or trust has an unused capital loss carryover, the beneficiaries succeeding to the property are allowed the deduction. I.R.C. Section 642(h).

The capital loss carryover is the same in the hands of the beneficiary as in the estate or trust, except that the capital loss carryover in the hands of a beneficiary which is a corporation, is a short-term loss irrespective of whether it would have been a long-term or short-term loss in the hands of the estate or trust. The capital loss carryover is taken into account in computing both taxable income and adjusted gross income. The first taxable year of the beneficiary to which the loss is carried over is the taxable year of the beneficiary in which or with which the estate or trust terminates. But for the purpose of determining the number of years to which a capital loss may be carried over by a beneficiary, the last taxable year of the estate or trust (whether or not a short taxable year) and the first taxable year of the beneficiary to which a loss is carried over each constitutes a taxable year, and, in the case of a beneficiary of an estate or trust that is a corporation, capital losses carried over by the estate or trust to any taxable year of the estate or trust beginning after December 31, 1963 are treated as if they were incurred in the last taxable year of the estate or trust (whether or not a short taxable year). Regulations Section 1.642(h)–1(b).

The term "beneficiaries succeeding to the property of the estate or trust" means those beneficiaries upon termination of the estate or trust who bear the burden of any loss for which a carryover is allowed. With reference to an intestate estate, the term means the heirs and next of kin to whom the estate is distributed; or, if the estate is insolvent, to whom it would have been distributed if it had not been insolvent. In the case of a testate estate, the term normally means the residuary beneficiaries (including a residuary trust), and not specific legatees or devisees, pecuniary legatees, or other non-residuary beneficiaries. But the term does not include the recipient of a specific sum of money even though it is payable out of the residue, except to the extent that it is not payable in full. On the other hand, the term includes a beneficiary (including a trust) who is not strictly a beneficiary, but whose devise or bequest is determined by the value of the decedent's estate as reduced by the loss or deductions in question. Thus, the phrase includes:

(1) A beneficiary of a fraction of a decedent's net estate after payment of debts, expenses, etc.

(2) A non-residuary legatee or devisee, to the extent of any deficiency in his legacy or devise resulting from the insufficiency of the estate to satisfy it in full.

(3) A surviving spouse receiving a fractional share of an estate in fee under a statutory right of election, to the extent that the loss or deductions are taken into account in determining the share. But the term does not include a recipient of dower or curtesy, or any income beneficiary of the estate or trust from which the loss is carried over.

These principles are equally applicable to trust beneficiaries. A remainderman who receives all or a fractional share of the property of a trust as a result of the final termination of the trust is a beneficiary succeeding to its property. "For example, if property is transferred to pay the income to A for life and then to pay $10,000 to B and distribute the balance of the trust corpus to C, C and not B is considered to be the succeeding beneficiary except to the extent that the trust corpus is insufficient to pay B $10,000." Regulations Section 1.642(h)–3(d).

The carryovers are allocated among the beneficiaries succeeding to the property of an estate or trust proportionately according to the share of each in the burden of the loss.

Corporate Reorganizations. In the case of certain types of tax-free reorganization, the unused capital loss carryover of another corporation may be utilized. This refers to:

(1) The complete liquidation of a subsidiary corporation (unless the subsidiary's stock had been purchased within two years in order to get the subsidiary's assets in liquidation).

(2) A tax-free acquisition of property solely for the transferor's voting stock in a reorganization, such as a statutory merger, consolidation, or mere change in identity, form, or place of organization.

(3) A transfer to a corporation which is controlled by the transferor immediately thereafter.

The capital loss carryover of the acquired corporation is subject to these conditions:

(1) The taxable year of the acquiring corporation to which the capital loss carryover of the acquired corporation is first carried over will be the first taxable year ending after the date of the acquisition.

(2) The capital loss carryover will be a short-term loss in the taxable year determined under (1) but will be limited to an amount which bears the same ratio to the net capital gain (determined without regard to a short-term capital loss attributable to capital loss carryover), if any, of the acquiring corporation in that taxable year as the number of days in the taxable year after the date of acquisition bears to the total number of days in the taxable year. I.R.C. Section 381(c)(3).

Basis

When an asset is sold or otherwise disposed of in a transaction where gain or loss is recognized, it is necessary to establish the cost or other basis of this asset. If the asset is the only one of its kind that the taxpayer possesses, there is no problem. If he has several assets of this type, there is the question of which was sold.

"[T]he 'First In First Out' rule applies only where there is neither identification by a certificate, nor by designation of the taxpayer." *Miller v. Commissioner,* 80 F.2d 219 (2d Cir., 1935). In one case, a taxpayer designated the securities to be sold as those purchased on a particular date and at a particular price. "It is only when such a designation was not made at the time of the sale, or is not shown, that the 'First-in, first-out' rule is to be applied." *Helvering v. Rankin,* 295 U.S. 123 (1935). But "If the particular shares cannot be identified, a first-in, first-out presumption is usually applied." *Eugene H. Walet, Jr. et al.,* 31 T.C. 461 (1958), *aff'd,* 272 F.2d 694 (5th Cir., 1960).

Where a taxpayer disposes of two blocks of stock having different bases, each block must be treated separately. It is not proper to total the bases of the various blocks and to subtract this total from the amount received. Revenue Ruling 68–23, I.R.B. 1968–3, 14.

There is a special rule for the identification of a "book-entry Treasury security" directed to be disposed of by the owner who holds securities of precisely the same description which were acquired on different dates or at different prices. This special rule permits the "serially-numbered advice of transactions" prescribed by the Fiscal Service of the Treasury Department to satisfy the requirements if made pursuant to a written instruction by the seller or transferor. In such a case, if the written instruction identifies the book-entry Treasury security to be sold either by purchase date and cost, or by reference to the serially-numbered advice of the transaction relating to the acquisition, the identification requirement is satisfied. For details as to this, see Revenue Ruling 67–419, I.R.B.

Where a shareholder acquires new stock in exchange for old stock obtained at different times (as in a recapitalization), the tax consequences to him on a sale of the new stock are the same as those on a sale of the old stock. *Leonard Osrow et al.,* 49 T.C. 333 (1968). That is, a shareholder may relate his sales to actual lots purchased so as to obtain the most advantageous basis.

Basis of property is deemed to be zero if the taxpayer cannot prove another figure. *Pasquale Colabella et al.,* T.C. Memo. 1958–136, filed July 15, 1958. There is no loss deduction until basis is established. *Anthony Delsanter et al.,* 28 T.C. 845 (1957).

Tax-Free Exchanges

Section 1031 provides that no gain or loss is recognized if property held for productive use in trade or business or for investment is exchanged solely for property of a like kind to be held either for productive use in trade or business or for investment. Property held for productive use in trade or business or for investment does not cover property held primarily for sale, nor stocks, bonds, notes, choses in action, certificates of trust or beneficial interest, or other securities or evidences of indebtedness or interest. But a dealer in securities may have a tax-free exchange of securities. Thus, a dealer could exchange defaulted municipal bonds, par for par, for here there was an exchange of property held for productive use in his trade or business for property of a like kind. *Wright v. Fahs,* D.C., S.D. Fla., 1952.

"As used in section 1031(a), the words 'like kind' have reference to the nature or character of the property and not to its grade or quality. One kind or class of property may not, under that section, be exchanged for property of a different kind or class. The fact that any real estate involved is improved or unimproved is not material, for that fact relates only to the grade or quality of the property and not to its kind or class. Unproductive real estate held by one other than a dealer for future use or future realization of the increment in value is held for investment and not primarily for sale." Regulations Section 1.1031(a)–1(b).

Gain or loss is recognized if a taxpayer exchanges United States Treasury bonds for an issue maturing ten years later, or if he exchanges a real estate mortgage for a consolidated farm loan bond. Regulations Section 1.1031(a)–1(d).

" 'Exchange' is a word of precise import meaning the giving of one thing for another, requiring the transfers to be in kind and excluding transactions into which money enters either as the consideration or as a basis of measure. . . . The term is almost synonymous with 'barter.' . . . The sale of property and the immediate re-purchase of like property is not an exchange, because the basis of the transaction is measured in money." *Trenton Cotton Oil Company v. Commissioner*, 147 F.2d 33 (6th Cir., 1945).

Boot. If a taxpayer receives other property (in addition to property which may be received without recognition of gain) or money in—

(1) an exchange of property held for productive use in trade or business for property of like kind to be held either for productive use or investment;

(2) an exchange of certain insurance policies or contracts as described in Section 1035(a);

(3) an exchange of common stock for common stock or preferred stock for preferred stock in the same corporation, not in connection with a corporate reorganization; or

(4) an exchange of United States obligations issued under the Second Liberty Bond Act for other such obligations (Section 1037)

the gain (if any) to the taxpayer will be recognized in an amount not in excess of the sum of the other property. Loss to the taxpayer from such an exchange will not be recognized in any amount. Regulations Section 1.1031(b)–1(a).

Consideration received in the form of an assumption of liabilities (or a transfer subject to a liability) is treated as "other property" for this purpose.

Basis. If, in an exchange in one of the four categories mentioned above, no part of the gain or loss was recognized under the law applicable to the year in which the exchange was made, the basis of the property acquired is the same as the basis of the property transferred by the taxpayer, with proper adjustments to the date of the exchange. If gain was recognized, the basis of the property acquired is the basis of the property transferred (adjusted to the date of the exchange), decreased by the amount of money received and increased by the amount of gain recognized on the exchange. I.R.C. Section 1031(d).

Loss. Just as gain is not recognized on a tax-free exchange, neither is loss. If real estate held for productive use or investment is exchanged for other such real estate and the property received has a fair market value which is less than the adjusted basis of the property surrendered, there is a loss that will not be recognized for tax purposes, even if the parties had not deliberately planned a tax-free exchange and might even have been unfamiliar with the procedure. *W. D. Haden Company,* T.C. Memo., Docket No. 5789, entered April 9, 1946, *aff'd on this issue,* 161 F.2d 588 (5th Cir., 1948).

Discount Obligations

Section 1232 applies to any bond, debenture, note, or certificate or other evidence of indebtedness (referred to here as an "obligation") (1) which is a capital asset in the hands of the taxpayer and (2) which is issued by any corporation, or by any government or political subdivision thereof.

In general, Section 1232(a)(1) provides that the retirement of an obligation, other than certain obligations issued before January 1, 1955, is considered to be an exchange and, therefore, is usually subject to capital gain or loss treatment. Section 1232(a)(2) provides that in the case of a gain realized on the sale or exchange of certain obligations issued at a discount after December 31, 1954, the amount of gain equal to this discount or, under certain circumstances, the amount of gain equal to a specified portion of the discount, constitutes ordinary income. Section 1232(c) treats as ordinary income a portion of any gain realized upon the disposition of (1) coupon obligations which were acquired after August 16, 1954 and before January 1, 1958, without all coupons maturing more than twelve months after purchase attached, and (2) coupon obligations which were acquired after December 31, 1957, without all coupons maturing after the date of purchase attached.

In order for Section 1232 to apply, an obligation must be a capital asset in the hands of the taxpayer. Obligations held by a dealer in securities (except as provided in Section 1236, which is concerned with such dealers), or obligations arising from the sale of inventory or personal services by the holder, are not capital assets.

The taxability of amounts received under "face-amount" certificates (as defined in the Investment Company Act of 1940) which are issued after December 31, 1954 is governed by Section 72 of the Code rather than by Section 1232 and is, therefore, subject to the limit on tax provided by Section 72(e)(3). Regulations Section 1.1232–1(c).

Any amount received by the holder upon the retirement of an obligation is considered as an amount received in exchange therefor. But this rule does not apply to obligations issued before January 1, 1955, which were not issued with interest coupons or in registered form, or which were not in registered form on March 1, 1954.

Gain realized upon the sale or exchange before January 1, 1958 of an obligation issued at a discount after December 31, 1954 and held by the taxpayer for more than six months is considered to be ordinary income to the extent it equals a specified portion of the "original issue discount," and the balance, if any, of the gain is considered to be long-term capital gain.

Gain realized upon the sale or exchange after December 31, 1957 of such an obligation is considered to be ordinary income to the extent that it does not exceed—

(1) An amount equal to the entire "original issue discount" or
(2) If at the time of the original issue there was no intention to call the bond or other evidence of indebtedness before maturity, a portion of the "original issue discount," and the balance, if any, of the gain is considered to be long-term capital gain.

Whether gain representing original issue discount realized upon the sale or exchange of obligations issued at a discount before January 1, 1955 is capital gain or ordinary income is determined without reference to Section 1232.

The term "original issue discount" means the difference between the issue price and the stated redemption price at maturity. The stated redemption price is determined without regard to optional call dates. If the original issue discount is less than one-fourth of 1% of the stated redemption price at maturity, multiplied by the number of full years from the date of original issue to maturity, then the discount is considered to be zero. The term "stated redemption price at maturity" means the amount fixed by the last modification of the purchase agreement, including dividends payable at that time. "Thus, in the case of face-amount certificates, the redemption price at maturity is the price as modified through changes such as extensions of the purchase agreement and includes any dividends which are payable at maturity." Regulations Section 1.1232–3(b).

The term "issue price" in the case of obligations registered with the Securities and Exchange Commission means the initial offering price to the public at which price a substantial amount of these obligations was sold. For this purpose, the term "the public" does not include bond houses and brokers, or similar persons or organizations acting in the capacity of underwriters or wholesalers. Ordinarily, the issue price is the first price at which the obligations were sold to the public; and the issue price will not change if, by reason of market developments, part of the issue must be sold at a different price. When obligations are privately placed, the issue price of each obligation is the price paid by the first buyer of the particular obligation, irrespective of the issue price of the remainder of the issue. The terms "initial offering price" and "price paid by the first buyer" include the aggregate payments made by the purchaser under the purchase agreement, including modifications thereof. Thus, all amounts paid by the purchaser under the purchase agreement or a modification of it are included in the issue price.

In the case of issues of obligations which are registered with the Securities and Exchange Commission, the term "date of original issue" means the date on which the issue first was sold to the public at the issue price. In the case of issues which are privately placed, the term means the date on which each obligation was sold to the original purchaser.

The term "intention to call the bond or other evidence of indebtedness before maturity" means an understanding between (1) the issuing corporation (the issuer) and (2) the original purchaser of the obligation (or, in the case of obligations constituting part of an issue, any of the original purchasers of such obligations) that the issuer will redeem the obligation before maturity. The term "original purchaser" does not include persons or organizations acting in the capacity of underwriters or dealers, who purchased the obligations for re-sale in the ordinary course of their trade or business. "It is not necessary that the issuer's intention to call the obligation before maturity be communicated directly to the original purchaser by the issuer. The understanding to call before maturity need not be unconditional; it may, for example, be dependent upon the financial condition of the issuer on the proposed early call date." Regulations Section 1.1232–3(b)(4).

Where part of the amount of gain is treated as ordinary income under Section 1232, that part is computed by multiplying the original issue discount by a fraction, the numerator of which is the number of full months the obligation was held by the holder and the denominator of which is the number of full months from the date of original issue to the date specified as the redemption date at maturity.

The general rule of Section 1232 does not apply to—

(1) Obligations the interest on which is excluded from gross income under Section 103 (relating to certain government obligations) or

(2) Any holder who purchased the obligation at a premium.

If an obligation which is issued at any time with interest coupons—

(1) Is purchased after August 16, 1954 and before January 1, 1958, and the purchaser does not receive all the coupons which first become payable more than twelve months after the date of purchase, or

(2) Is purchased after December 31, 1957, and the purchaser does not receive all the coupons which first become payable after the date of pur-

chase, any gain on the later sale or other disposition of the obligation by the purchaser (or by a transferee using the purchaser's basis) will be treated as ordinary income to the extent that the fair market value of the obligation (determined as of the time of the purchase) with coupons attached exceeds the purchase price. If both the preceding sentence and the general rule of Section 1232 apply with respect to the gain realized on the retirement or other disposition of an obligation, then the regular rule applies only with respect to that part of the gain to which the preceding sentence does not apply.

Obligations Issued At A Discount

Non-Interest-Bearing Obligations Issued At A Discount. If a taxpayer—
   (1) Owns any non-interest-bearing obligation issued at a discount and redeemable for fixed amounts increasing at stated intervals, or
   (2) Retains his investment in the maturity value of a Series E United States savings bond, in the manner described in Section 454(c) (2), below, and
if the increase in redemption price of this obligation occurring in the taxable year does not constitute income for that year under the method of accounting used in computing his taxable income, then the taxpayer may, at his election, treat the increase as constituting income for the year in which this increase occurs, rather than for the year in which the obligation is disposed of, or converted into a current income obligation of the United States (such as a bond of Series G or K). Any such election must be made in the taxpayer's return and may be made for any taxable year. If an election is made with respect to any such obligation, it will apply also to all other obligations of this type owned by the taxpayer at the beginning of the first taxable year to which the election applies and to those thereafter acquired by him. The election is binding for the taxable year for which the return is filed and for all subsequent taxable years, unless the Commissioner permits the taxpayer to change to a different method of reporting income from these obligations. Although the election once made is binding upon the taxpayer, it does not apply to a transferee of his. I.R.C. Section 454(a).

In any case in which this election is made, the amount which accrues in any taxable year to which the election applies is measured by the actual increase in the redemption price occurring in that year. This amount does not accrue ratably between the dates on which the redemption price changes. "For example, if two dates on which the redemption price increases (February 1 and August 1) fall within a taxable year and if the redemption price increases in the amount of 50 cents on each such date, the amount accruing in that year would be $1.00 ($0.50 on February 1 and $0.50 on August 1). If the taxpayer owns a non-interest-bearing obligation of the character described in subparagraph (1) of this paragraph [the preceding paragraph] acquired prior to the first taxable year to which his election applies, he must also include in gross income for such first taxable year the increase in the redemption price of such obligation occurring between the date of acquisition of the obligation (or the series E bond involved in the case of a matured United States savings bond), and the first day of this first taxable year." Regulations Section 1.454–1(a)(2). The regulations then provide this example:

"Throughout the calendar year 1954, a taxpayer who computes his taxable income under the cash receipts and disbursements method holds series E United States savings bonds having a maturity value of $5,000 and a redemption value at the beginning of the year 1954 of $4,050 and at the end of the year 1954 of $4,150. He purchased the bonds on January 1, 1949, for $3,750, and holds no other such obligation of the type described in this section. If the taxpayer exercises the election in his return for the calendar year 1954, he is required to include $400 in taxable income with respect to such bonds. Of this amount, $300 represents the increase in the redemption price before 1954 and $100 represents the increase in the redemption price in 1954. The increases in redemption value occurring in subsequent taxable years are includible in gross income for such taxable years."

The election for a taxpayer to treat as income in a taxable year the increases at stated intervals in the redemption price of non-interest-bearing obligations (such as Series E bonds), where this income does not otherwise constitute income to him in that year, may not be exercised by the taxpayer in an amended return filed after the statutory period for filing the original return, nor may the election be exercised by a taxpayer in a return which is not timely filed. Revenue Ruling 55–655, 1955–2 CB 253.

Where a taxpayer, at the end of his taxable year, owns Series H bonds which he had received in exchange for Series E, F, or J bonds pursuant to Treasury Department Circular No. 1036, the privilege of treating past increases in the redemption prices of the latter as income in that taxable year is available to him by making an election under Section 454(a). The election applies with respect to the reporting of all increases in redemption price of all obligations described in Section 454(a) owned by him during or prior to the first taxable year to which it applies, to the extent that these increases have not been included previously in his income and are reflected in the present value of bonds presently owned by him. It also applies to the increase in redemption price of all such obligations thereafter acquired by him and is binding for all subsequent taxable years unless the Commissioner permits him to change to a different method of reporting from these obligations. Revenue Ruling 64–89, 1964–1 CB (Part 1) 172.

A Series E bond, registered in the name of a father, payable on his death to his son, was redeemed by the father before maturity and a new bond was issued at his request in the sole name of his son. It was held that interest (increment in value) earned on the original bond was taxable to the father in the year he redeemed the bond and had the new bond issued in the son's name, unless the increment in value previously was properly reported on the accrual basis or pursuant to an election to report the increment currently. Revenue Ruling 54–327, 1954–2 CB 50.

A father purchased Series E bonds with his own funds and had them registered in the names of himself and his son as co-owners. Later he had the bonds re-issued solely in the son's name in order to effect a gift of the father's co-ownership. The value of the bonds for Federal gift tax purposes was their redemption value at the time they were re-issued. The interest (increment in value) that had accrued (as earned) on the bonds before their re-issue was includible in the father's gross income for his taxable year when he made the gift, except interest he had returned properly as income previously. Revenue Ruling 55–278, 1955–1 CB 471.

Where an individual used his own funds to purchase Series E bonds in the name of himself and a co-owner, and subsequently had them re-issued in his own name, this was not a disposition or redemption for Federal income tax purposes. The re-issuance of the bonds in his sole name was not a taxable transaction. Revenue Ruling 68–61, I.R.B. 1968–6, 17.

Short-Term Obligations Issued On A Discount Basis. In the case of obligations of the United States or any of its possessions, or of a state, or territory, or any political subdivision thereof, or of the District of Columbia, which are issued on a discount basis and are payable without interest at a fixed maturity date not exceeding one year from the date of issue, the amount of discount at which this obligation originally sold does not accrue until the date on which the obligation is redeemed, sold, or otherwise disposed of. This method applies regardless of the method of accounting used by the taxpayer. I.R.C. Section 454(b).

Matured United States Savings Bonds. In the case of a taxpayer who—

(1) Holds a Series E United States Savings Bond at the date of maturity and

(2) Pursuant to regulations prescribed under the Second Liberty Loan Act (a) retains his investment in an obligation of the United States, other than a current income obligation, or (b) exchanges this Series E bond for another non-transferable obli-

gation of the United States in an exchange upon which no gain or loss is recogniz d because of Section 1037 (which deals with certain exchanges of United States obligations),

the increase in redemption value (to the extent not previously includible in gross income) in excess of the amount paid for this Series E bond must be included in gross income in the taxable year in which the obligation finally is redeemed or in the taxable year of final maturity, whichever is earlier. This provision does not apply to a corporation, nor does it apply in the case of any taxable year for which the taxpayer's taxable income is computed under an accrual method of accounting or for which an election made by the taxpayer under Section 454(a) applies. I.R.C. Section 454(c).

Growth Savings Certificates. Growth savings certificates issued by a bank have face amounts greater than the amounts with respect to which they are issued and are redeemable at any time for amounts equal to the issue price plus increments which accrue regularly up to their maturity date. Thus, these certificates are in the nature of deposits. The increment in value of these certificates must be included in the gross income of a taxpayer on the cash basis in each taxable year in which the increase occurs, inasmuch as he (the certificate holder) has a right to redeem the certificate in that taxable year. Revenue Ruling 66–44, 1966–1 CB 94.

Certain Exchanges Of United States Obligations

When so provided by regulations issued by the Secretary of the Treasury in connection with the issue of obligations of the United States, no gain or loss is recognized on the surrender to the United States of obligations of the United States issued under the Second Liberty Bond Act in exchange solely for other obligations issued under that act. I.R.C. Section 1037(a).

If a bond, the gain on which is subject to the first sentence of Section 1232(a)(2)(A) (dealing with bonds and other evidences of indebtedness) because the bond was issued at a discount, is exchanged for another bond and the gain realized is not recognized because of the provisions of Sections 1037(a) or 1031(b) (gain from exchanges not solely in kind), the portion of the gain recognized upon the disposition or redemption of the bonds received in the exchange which is equal to the gain to which such first sentence would have applied at the time of the exchange (if gain then had been recognized) will be ordinary income.

Where the obligation surrendered in the exchange is a non-transferable obligation as described in Section 454(a) or (c) (that is, in general, a non-interest-bearing obligation issued at a discount and redeemable for fixed amounts increasing at stated intervals, an obligation in which the taxpayer has retained his interest in a matured Series E bond, or an obligation which was received by the taxpayer on his surrender of a Series E bond), the aggregate amount considered, with respect to the obligation surrendered, as ordinary income, is not to exceed the difference between the issue price and the stated redemption price of the obligation surrendered which applies at the time of the exchange. The issue price of the obligation received in the exchange is the stated redemption price of the obligation surrendered, increased by the amount of the consideration (if any) paid to the United States as part of the exchange. I.R.C. Section 1037(b)(1).

If a marketable obligation which was issued at not less than par is exchanged for another marketable obligation, the issue price of the latter will, for purposes of Section 1232 (bonds and other evidences of indebtedness) be considered to be the same as the issue price of the original bond, increased by the amount of the consideration (if any) paid to the United States as a part of the exchange. I.R.C. Section 1037(b)(2).

To the extent not affected by the special provisions of Section 1037(b), gain realized and recognized with respect to a bond received in an exchange to which Section 1037 applies will be characterized, under Section 1232, in accordance with the facts and circumstances relating to its acquisition and redemption or disposition.

Non-Recognition Of Gain Or Loss On Exchanges Or Distributions In Obedience To Orders Of The S.E.C.

Section 1081 is a re-enactment of earlier legislation to provide for non-recognition of gain or loss in the case of the disposition of property upon certain distributions ordered by the Securities and Exchange Commission in furtherance of policies of the Public Utility Holding Company Act of 1935. That act directed the S.E.C. to effect the simplification and geographical integration of public utility holding systems. In implementing this directive, the S.E.C. causes various properties to be re-grouped; corporations are completely or partially liquidated; stock and securities are shifted. Inasmuch as the exchanges and distributions for the achieving of these ends are compulsory transactions (whether initiated by the S.E.C. or in the form of a plan initiated by the corporations affected and submitted to the commission for its approval), Congress has decided to postpone recognition of gain or loss (wherever possible) until a voluntary realization occurs.

Sections 1081 through 1083 cover:

(1) Cases in which a holder of stock or securities in a registered holding company or a majority-owned subsidiary disposes of his stock or

securities by transferring them to this company or to another registered holding company or majority-owned subsidiary which is in the same holding company system in exchange for other stock or securities. I.R.C. Section 1081(a).

(2) The disposition of property by a member of a holding company system in exchange for other property. I.R.C. Section 1081(b).

(3) Distribution of stock or securities by registered holding companies or majority-owned subsidiaries to their shareholders. I.R.C. Section 1081(c).

(4) Disposition of property in a transaction between members of a limited class of closely related corporations. I.R.C. Section 1081(d).

The specialized meanings of "registered holding company," "majority-owned subsidiary," etc., are supplied in Section 1083.

Sections 1081 through 1083 create new exceptions to the rule that the entire amount of the gain or loss from the disposition of property is recognized. These exceptions are restricted by their own terms to the gain or loss attributable to the disposition as such of property in one of the exchanges directly attributable to the receipt as such of property in a distribution specifically described. It is the intent of these sections to postpone the recognition of gain or loss until a disposition of property is made which is not covered by the provisions. The continuation of the basis as provided in Section 1082 was designed to effect this result.

Section 1081(a) prescribes the prerequisites for the non-recognition of gain or loss resulting from the disposition by a holder of stock or securities in a registered holding company or a majority-owned subsidiary company, where the holder disposes of such stock or securities in exchange for stock or securities. In order that there be no recognition of gain or loss to such holder upon this disposition, it is required that:

(1) The exchange be made with the company which issued the stock or securities disposed of, or with a registered holding company or a majority-owned subsidiary which is in the same holding company system with the issuing company.

(2) None of the stock or securities received by the holder be non-exempt property.

(3) The exchange be made with a transferee corporation which is acting in obedience to an order of the S.E.C. directed to that corporation.

The term "non-exempt property" means:
(1) Any consideration on the form of evidences of indebtedness owned by the transferor or a cancellation or assumption of debts or other liabilities of the transferor (including a continuity of encumbrances subject to which the property was transferred).

(2) Short-term obligations (including notes, drafts, bills of exchange, and bankers' acceptances) having a maturity at the time of issuance of not exceeding twenty-four months, exclusive of days of grace.

(3) Securities issued or guaranteed as to principal or interest by a government or subdivision thereof (including those issued by a corporation which is an instrumentality of a government or subdivision thereof).

(4) Stock or securities which were acquired from a registered holding company or an associate company of a registered holding company which acquired such stock or securities after February 28, 1938, unless such stock or securities (other than obligations described as non-exempt property in (1), (2), or (3), above) were acquired in obedience to an order of the S.E.C. or were acquired with the authorization or approval of the S.E.C. under any section of the Public Utility Holding Company Act of 1935. I.R.C. Section 1083(e).

Section 1081(b) provides for non-recognition of gain or loss to a corporation which is a registered holding company or an associate company, if this corporation—

(1) disposes of property by transferring it in exchange solely for property (other than non-exempt property);

(2) is acting in obedience to an order of the S.E.C.; and

(3) this order recites that the exchange is necessary or appropriate to the simplification or integration of the holding company system of which the corporation is a member.

Section 1081(c) provides for the non-recognition of gain to a shareholder in a corporation which is a registered holding company or a majority-owned subsidiary company, if this corporation, acting in obedience to an order of the S.E.C., distributes to the shareholder stock or securities other than those which are non-exempt property. The gain not recognized in any such case is only that from the distribution as such. But this subsection applies only in cases where the distributions are made without the surrender by the shareholders of stock or securities. Distributions involving such a surrender are governed by the rules relating to exchanges.

Section 1081(d) provides for non-recognition of gain or loss to a corporation which is a member of a system group, as defined, if the corporation disposes of property by transferring it to another corporation which is a member of the same system group in exchange for other property (including money). Non-recognition also is afforded for gain to a corporation which is a member of a system group if property or money is distributed to the corporation as a shareholder in a corporation which is a member of the same system group, without the surrender by the shareholder of stock or securities in the distributing corporation. An exchange or distribution will be covered by this subsection only if all the corporations which are parties to the exchange or distribution are acting in obedience to an order of the S.E.C.

Section 1081(d) provides that if a corporation which is a member of a system group transfers property to another corporation which is a member of the same system group and receives in exchange stock or securities issued by this other corporation, the stock or securities, to the extent that they are preferred as to both dividends and assets, may be sold to any party outside of the system, without the recognition of gain or loss, if:

(1) The proceeds thereof are applied in retirement or cancellation of stock or securities of the corporation making the sale which were outstanding at the time the corporation received the stock or securities sold by it; and

(2) Both the sale of the stock or securities and the application of the proceeds thereof were made in obedience to an order of the S.E.C.

If any part of the proceeds are not applied as required, any gain realized is recognized to the extent of the proceeds not so applied. In any event, if the proceeds from the stock or securities sold exceed the fair market value of such stock or securities when received, any gain realized is recognized to the extent of this excess.

Section 1081(e) provides that any property received in addition to what may be received tax-free is treated as boot, but in an amount not in excess of the sum of the money and fair market value of what is received. Loss is not recognized.

Section 1081(f) provides that in order that gain or loss not be recognized upon these exchanges and distributions—

(1) The S.E.C. order must recite that the exchange or distribution is necessary or appropriate to effectuate the Public Utility Holding Company Act of 1935;

(2) The order must specify and itemize the stock and securities and other property and money which are ordered to be transferred and received upon the exchange or distribution; and

(3) The exchange or distribution must be made in obedience to the order and must be completed within the time prescribed in the order.

Section 1081(g) provides that an exchange, sale, or distribution which is within Section 1081 will, with respect to the non-recognition of gain or loss and the determination of basis, be governed only by Section 1081 and its correlative sections, to prevent overlapping the provisions of these and other Code sections.

Basis For Determining Gain Or Loss. Section 1082(a) prescribes the basis of property acquired upon exchanges described in Sections 1081(a), (b), and (c), above. The parties to the exchange who were wholly exempt from the recognition of gain or loss must carry as their basis for the newly acquired property a figure equal to the basis (adjusted to the date of the exchange) at which they had theretofore carried the property transferred upon the exchange. This may require a proper apportionment of this substituted basis over several items of property received upon the exchange.

If some portion of the gain realized in the exchange is recognized by reason of the receipt of non-exempt property (including money) as a part of the consideration for the transfer, a proper adjustment must be made with respect to the substituted basis. Section 1082(a) also provides that the basis of the newly acquired property will be the same as that of the property transferred, reduced in the amount of any money received and increased in the amount of any gain recognized in the transaction. The substituted basis so adjusted must be apportioned among the items of property received other than money, allocating to the non-exempt property (other than money) from the receipt of which gain is recognized an amount equal to the fair market value thereof as of the date of the exchange.

Section 1082(a) does not apply in the case of a corporation acquiring property in an exchange in which the consideration for the transfer consisted, in whole or in part, of stock or securities issued by that corporation.

Section 1082(b) provides that in the case of property acquired by a corporation as paid-in surplus or as a contribution to capital, or in exchange for stock or securities issued by it, including those cases in which a part of the consideration for the acquisition consisted of property or money in addition to such stock or securities, the basis of the property acquired will be the basis of the property transferred with adjustment to the date of the exchange and adjustment for the amount of any gain to the transferor recognized in the exchange.

Section 1082(c) prescribes the basis of stock or securities acquired in a distribution, the gain from which is not recognized under Section 1081(c). The taxpayer's basis of the stock with respect to which the distribution is made must be apportioned (under the regulations) between the newly acquired property and the stock with respect to which this newly acquired property was distributed.

Section 1082(d) prescribes the basis of property acquired in certain transactions between corporations both of which are members of the same system group. The basis for determining gain or loss, depreciation, and depletion, as well as the basis for determining the earnings and profits of the corporation available for distribution insofar as that question depends upon a particular asset, will be the same in the hands of the transferee as it was in the hands of the transferor. This rule applies equally to cases involving tangible property, stock or securities, money, and other property, or any of them.

Gain From Sale Or Exchange
To Effectuate Policies Of The F.C.C.

If the sale or exchange of property (including stock in a corporation) is certified by the Federal Communications Commission to be necessary or appropriate to effectuate a change in the policy of, or the adoption of a new policy by, the F.C.C. with respect to the ownership and control of radio broadcasting stations, this sale or exchange may (at the taxpayer's election) be treated as an involuntary conversion of the property within the meaning of Section 1033. I.R.C. Section 1071.

Section 1071 applies only in the case of a sale or exchange made necessary by reasons of the F.C.C.'s policies as to ownership of radio facilities (including television). The section does not apply in the case of a sale or exchange made necessary as a result of other matters, such as the operation of a broadcasting station in a manner determined by the commission not to be in the public interest or in violation of Federal or state law. Regulations Section 1.1071–1(b), (d).

For the purpose of this section, stock of a corporation operating a radio broadcasting or telecasting station will be treated as property similar or related in service or use to the property sold or exchanged. Securities of such a corporation other than stock, or securities of a corporation not operating a radio broadcasting station, do not constitute property similar or related in service or use to the property sold or exchanged. If the taxpayer makes the election, the gain realized upon the sale or exchange will be recognized to the extent of that part of the money received upon the sale or exchange which is not expended in the manner prescribed in Section 1033 (involuntary conversions). The taxpayer also may make another election to the effect that the amount of the gain that would be recognized will not be recognized but, instead, will be used to reduce the basis of depreciable property remaining in his hands after the sale or exchange or which was acquired by him in the same taxable year. Regulations Section 1.1071–2(b). With the consent of the Commissioner, the taxpayer may instead reduce the basis of other assets. Regulations Section 1.1071–3(b).

Section 1071 applies to the non-recognition of both gain and loss.

The purchase by the taxpayer of stock of a corporation which does not operate broadcasting stations, but which owns all the stock of a subsidiary corporation which owns and operates such stations, is not a purchase of stock of a corporation operating a radio broadcasting station. Thus, the transaction cannot be treated as a replacement of property involuntarily converted which qualifies for non-recognition of gain under Sections 1033 and 1071. Revenue Ruling 66–33, 1966–1 CB 183.

Distributions Pursuant To Orders Enforcing The Anti-Trust Laws

Where stock is received in an anti-trust distribution by—
(1) An individual shareholder or
(2) A corporation which is not entitled to the dividends received deduction (that is, regulated investment companies, real estate investment trusts, tax-option corporations, and non-resident foreign corporations),

the distribution is treated as a return of capital, and its full fair market value reduces the basis of the stock with respect to which it was made. If, however, the fair market value of the stock distributed exceeds the basis of the stock with respect to which the distribution was made, then gain is recognized to the extent of the excess and is taxable as any other gain would be. I.R.C. Section 1111(a). This is the same as the income tax treatment of distributions made by corporations which have no earnings and profits.

An anti-trust distribution is a distribution made in pursuance of a court order enforcing the Federal anti-trust laws under the Sherman or Clayton Acts. I.R.C. Section 1111(d). The rule applies only if the order, pursuant to which the distribution is made, requires the divestiture to be completed within three years or less from the date the order became final.

Involuntary Conversions

Where property is compulsorily or involuntarily converted as a result of destruction, theft, seizure, or requisition or condemnation or threat or imminence thereof, gain is not recognized if the property or the proceeds of the involuntary conversion are converted into similar property by the last day of the taxable year following the year in which the conversion took place. This rule does not refer to losses. I.R.C. Section 1033.

If, because of friction between shareholders, stock is sold under what amounts to compulsion and the proceeds are invested in stock of another corporation, there has not been an involuntary conversion coming under the rule of non-recognition of gain. I.T. 2247, IV–2 CB 19.

A sale of corporate stock pursuant to a state "deadlock" statute providing for its dissolution in the event of a stalemate between equally divided directors and stockholders does not qualify for involuntary conversion treatment. *Dear Publication & Radio, Inc. v. Commissioner,* 274 F.2d 656 (3d Cir., 1960).

The calling of a bond is not an involuntary conversion, even if it took place at a time when a replacement security would cost far more money. "By becoming a purchaser [of a callable bond], a taxpayer voluntarily agrees to such condition and under no reasonable construction can it be held that the redemption or retirement so provided is involuntary." I.T. 1354, I–1 CB 190.

Where the Securities and Exchange Commission ordered a taxpayer to dispose of a certain stock, this did not qualify as an involuntary conversion; for the United States did not take the property, for public use or otherwise. *American Natural Gas Company et al. v. United States,* 279 F.2d 220 (Ct. Cl., 1960).

Sale of rights was not an involuntary conversion where shares could not be issued because the issuing corporation had not complied with S.E.C. regulations. Revenue Ruling 57–517, 1957–2 CB 524.

A state statute provided that any stock life insurance company of that state could adopt a plan of mutualization and to that end acquire all of its stock. A shareholder who thus had to dispose of his stock could not claim the benefits of an involuntary conversion within the meaning of Section 1033. Revenue Ruling 55–717, 1955–2 CB 298.

In an anti-trust suit under the Sherman Act, a corporation was directed to dispose of shares in a stipulated company. This was not a compulsory or involuntary conversion. There was no "taking" by the Government. *Behr-Manning Corporation v. United States,* 196 F. Supp. 129 (D.C., Mass., 1961).

Stock For Stock Of Same Corporation

There is no gain or loss on the exchange of common stock for common stock, or preferred stock for preferred stock, of the same corporation. I.R.C. Section 1036. This is true even where voting stock is exchanged for non-voting stock, or vice versa. It is not limited to an exchange between two individual shareholders; it includes a transaction between a stockholder and the issuing corporation. A transaction between a stockholder and the corporation may qualify not only under Section 1036 but also under Section 368(a)(1)(E) (recapitalization) or under Section 305(a) (distribution of stock and stock rights). Regulations Section 1.1036–1.

The provisions of Section 1036 do not apply if stock is exchanged for bonds, or if preferred stock is exchanged for common stock, or common stock in one corporation is exchanged for common stock in another corporation.

Common stock in a foreign corporation may be exchanged tax-free for common stock in the same corporation, and preferred may be exchanged for preferred. Section 1036 permits such an exchange, even without the prior approval of the Secretary of the Treasury, which would be required for a recapitalization of a foreign corporation under Section 368(a)(1)(E), which this transaction also happens to be. Revenue Ruling 64–156, 1964–1 CB (Part 1) 139.

A special class of stock which is neither a common stock nor a preferred stock may not be exchanged tax-free for common or for preferred shares. Revenue Ruling 54–65, 1954–1 CB 101.

Flat Bonds

A special rule applies to the interest on flat bonds. "The term 'flat' . . . simply means that a purchase was made at a stated price for bonds that had unpaid coupons attached, but without any specified allocation as to how the price was computed as between principal and interest." *United States v. Langston,* 331 F.2d 879 (5th Cir., 1962).

According to the "flat purchase rule," "if the owner acquires bonds or notes with defaulted payments due thereon at a flat rate, the interest which has accrued thereupon up to the time of purchase constitutes a return of capital when collected; whereas, if the interest accrued thereon after purchase, it constitutes ordinary income when collected." *McDonald v. Commissioner,* 217 F.2d 475 (6th Cir., 1954).

Payments of defaulted interest, accrued before the taxpayer purchased flat bonds, are considered as amounts received in exchange therefor for the purpose of the capital gain treatment of Section 1232, regardless of any expectancy that the principal or face amount of the bonds ultimately will be collected. Interest accrued after acquisition of such bonds by the taxpayer represents interest taxable as ordinary income. *Hamilton C. Rickaby Estate et al.,* 27 T.C. 886 (1957).

Upon the sale of a bond, which presumably is not in default, between interest dates, that part of the selling price which represents interest accrued to the date of the sale is interest income. Regulations Section 1.61–7(d).

Those who purchase flat bonds with defaulted interest coupons are not required to treat later interest payments as ordinary income. The payments are but partial returns of the investment in the securities. *Horst et al. v. United States,* 331 F.2d 879 (Ct. Cl., 1964).

Securities Received For An Annuity

An individual sold certain securities to her children in return for their unsecured promise to pay her life annuities. She realized no taxable gain on the ground that annuity contracts undertaken by individual obligors do not have an ascertainable fair market value. *Commissioner v. Bertha F. Kann Estate,* 174 F.2d 357 (3d Cir., 1949). Where both the annuitant's life span and the obligor's ability to pay are uncertain, no fair market value should be ascribed to the contract or obligation. *J. Darsie Lloyd,* 33 B.T.A. 903 (1936). But it does not follow that an annuitant may not be liable for a capital gains tax when the amount received under an annuity contract exceeds the annuitant's adjusted basis for the property transferred therefor. Thus, where the decedent had transferred shares of stock to a syndicate organized by her sons in return for a down payment and an annuity, it was held that the payments received to the extent of the cost of the shares to the decedent constituted a return of capital, but that the excess of the amounts received (up to the value of the stock) over such cost was subject to tax as capital gain. The amounts received in the form of annuity payments (the amounts received after the down payment) were subject to tax as annuities. *C. V. Hill Estate v. Maloney,* 58 F. Supp. 164 (D.C., N.J., 1944).

An individual received certain stock, the consideration in part being his agreement to pay $500 per month to his father for life, thereafter to his mother for life. They both died before the taxable year; hence, his capital outlay was known and it was unnecessary to apply a theoretical method to ascertain his entire cost. The cost basis of the stock was in part the actual amount spent in such payments and not the cost of an annuity which would have produced the same payments. *D. Bruce Forrester,* 4 T.C. 907 (1945).

Two individuals agreed to pay their mother an annuity of $16,000 per year in consideration of the transfer to them of stock having a fair market value considerably in excess of the purchase price of the annuity. The difference between the amount paid to the annuitant prior to her death and the fair market value of the stock at the time of the transfer was a gift. Thus, the basis for computing gain realized in the subsequent sale of the stock by the children was the same as it would have been in the hands of the donor. *May Rogers et al.,* 31 B.T.A. 994 (1935).

Disposition By Corporation Of Its Own Stock

The disposition by a corporation of shares of its own stock (including treasury stock) for money or other property does not give rise to taxable gain or deductible loss to the corporation regardless of the nature of the transaction or the facts and circumstances involved. I.R.C. Section 1032(a).

This rule does not apply to the acquisition by a corporation of shares of its own stock except where the corporation acquires the shares in exchange for shares of its own stock (including treasury stock). Regulations Section 1.1032–1(b).

Stockholder Payment Of Corporate Deficiencies

Sometimes stockholders are obliged to pay taxes of a dissolved corporation in their capacity as transferees. Thus, a corporation was liquidated, and the shareholders reported their net proceeds as capital gain. Subsequently a judgment was rendered against the dissolved corporation, and the shareholders were required to pay this judgment as transferees of the corporate assets. The payments were held to be capital losses. The stockholders had to pay the judgment because of the liability imposed upon them as transferees of liquidation distribution assets. Their liability as transferees was not based on any ordinary business transactions of theirs apart from the liquidation proceedings. Even though each year ordinarily is a separate unit for tax accounting purposes, all of the liquidation transactions must be considered in order to classify the nature of the tax assessment. Thus, payments to dispose of the transferee liability were capital. *Arrowsmith et al. v. Commissioner,* 344 U.S. 6 (1952).

This rule applies to gain as well as loss. *Alvin B. Lowe et al.,* 44 T.C. 363 (1965).

Stockholder Receipts

A taxpayer sold the stock of a corporation to a buyer. The buyer made a partial payment of the purchase price and deposited the shares with the taxpayer as security. Three years later, the buyer defaulted. He transferred the stock back to the taxpayer, who released him from any further payments under the original purchase agreement. The amounts previously paid by the buyer were kept by the taxpayer. This was held to be capital gain, rather than ordinary income as claimed by the Internal Revenue Service. Inasmuch as the original transaction had been capital, the adjustments after it was closed also were capital. *United States v. Lease,* 346 F.2d 696 (2d Cir., 1965).

Chapter 6

Short Sales.
Puts. Calls

Short Sales

"A short sale is a contract for the sale of shares which the seller does not own or the certificates for which are not within his control so as to be available for delivery at the time when, under the rules of the Exchange, delivery must be made." *Provost v. United States,* 269 U.S. 443 (1926). "The term 'short sale' means any sale of a security which the seller does not own or any sale which is consummated by the delivery of a security borrowed by, or for the account of, the seller." Securities Exchange Act, Rule X–3B–3.

This may be elaborated upon in the words of one court in a tax case. "The short seller sells securities which he does not own. He is required by the rules of the Stock Exchange to make delivery of the stock sold to the purchaser on the next business day. Accordingly, he arranges to borrow an equal number of shares, usually from a broker, which shares are then delivered to the purchaser. The short seller deposits with the lender the full market price of the borrowed shares, and he maintains this deposit, equal to the value of such shares, until the borrowed shares are returned. He may or may not receive interest on this deposit, depending upon the agreement. The short seller completes the transaction by purchasing at a later date the stock which he borrowed and by delivering such purchased stock to the lender. During the period that the seller is 'short,' his loan contract requires him to give the lender all the benefits which the lender would have received if he had retained the stock and, accordingly, when dividends are declared on the stock the short seller must pay to the lender an amount equal to such dividends." *Commissioner v. Wiesler,* 161 F.2d 997 (6th Cir., 1947).

Gain or loss from the short sale of property is considered as gain or loss from the sale or exchange of a capital asset to the extent that the property (including a commodity future) used to close the short sale constitutes a capital asset in the hands of the taxpayer. I.R.C. Section 1233(a).

A short sale is not deemed to be consummated until delivery of the property to close the short sale. Generally, the period for which a taxpayer holds property delivered to close a short sale determines whether long-term or short-term capital gain or loss results. If the short sale is made through a broker, who borrows property to make a delivery, the short sale is not deemed to be consummated until the obligation of the seller created by the short sale is finally discharged by delivery of property to the broker to replace the property borrowed by the broker.

Section 1233 provides rules as to the tax consequences of a short sale of property if gain or loss from the short sale is considered as gain or loss from the sale or exchange of a capital asset and if, at the time of the short sale or on or before the date of the closing of the short sale, the taxpayer holds property substantially identical to that sold short. The term "property" is defined for this purpose to include only stocks and securities (including those dealt with on a "when-issued" basis) and commodity futures which are capital assets in the hands of the taxpayer. Special rules which will be described elsewhere apply to commodity futures and to arbitrages.

The first two rules are applicable whenever property substantially identical to that sold short has been held by the taxpayer on the date of the short sale for more than six months (determined without regard to Rule (2), below), or is acquired by him after the short sale and on or before the date of the closing thereof. These rules are:

Rule (1). Any gain upon the closing of such short sale will be considered as a gain upon the sale or exchange of a short-term capital asset (notwithstanding the period of time any property used to close that short sale has been held); and

Rule (2). The holding of such substantially identical property will be considered to begin (notwithstanding the general provisions of Section 1233) on the date of the closing of such short sale or on the date of a sale, gift, or other disposition of such property, whichever date occurs first. For the purpose of Rules (1) and (2), the acquisition of an option to sell property at a fixed price will be considered a short sale, and the exercise or failure to exercise the option will be considered as a closing of the short sale, except that any option to sell property at a fixed price acquired on or after August 17, 1954 (the day after enactment of the Internal Revenue Code of 1954) will not be considered a short sale and the exercise or failure to exercise that option will not be considered as the closing of a short sale, provided that the option and property identified as intended to be used in its exercise are acquired on the same date. This exception does not apply if the option is exercised, unless it is exercised by the sale of the property so identified. In the case of any option not exercised which falls within this exception, the cost of the option will be added to the basis of the property with which the option is identified. If the option itself does not specifically identify the property intended to be used in exercising the option, then the identification of the property will be made by appropriate entries in the taxpayer's records within fifteen days after the property is acquired.

Rule (3). Any loss upon the closing of such short sale will be considered as a loss upon the sale or exchange of a long-term capital asset, notwithstanding the period of time any property used to close such short sale has been held. For the purpose of this rule, the acquisition of an option to sell property at a fixed price is not considered a short sale, and the exercise or failure to exercise the option is not considered as a closing of a short sale. Regulations Section 1.1233–1(c)(2)–(4).

Rules (1) and (3), above, do not apply to the gain or loss attributable to so much of the property sold short as exceeds in quantity the substantially identical property referred to previously. Except as otherwise provided for in the arbitrage provisions, below, Rule (2) applies to the substantially identical property in the order of the dates of the acquisition of such property, but only to so much of this property as does not exceed the quantity sold short. If the property substantially identical to that sold short has been held by the taxpayer on the date of the short sale for not more than six months, or is acquired by him after the short sale and on or before the date of the closing thereof, and if property substantially identical to that sold short has been held by the taxpayer on the date of the short sale for more than six months, all three rules are applicable.

The regulations furnish these illustrations:

"*Example (1)*. A buys 100 shares of X stock at $10 per share on February 1, 1955, sells short 100 shares of X stock at $16 per share on July 1, 1955, and closes the short sale on August 2, 1955, by delivering the 100 shares of X stock purchased on February 1, 1955, to the lender of the stock used to effect the short sale. Since 100 shares of X stock had been held by A on the date of the short sale for not more than 6 months, the gain of $600 realized upon the closing of the short sale is, by application of rule (1) in subparagraph (2) of this paragraph, a short-term capital gain.

"*Example (2)*. A buys 100 shares of X stock at $10 per share on February 1, 1955, sells short 100 shares of X stock at $16 per share on July 1, 1955, closes the short sale on August 1, 1955, with 100 shares of X stock purchased on that date at $18 per share, and on August 2, 1955, sells at $18 per share the 100 shares of X stock purchased on February 1, 1955.

The $200 loss sustained upon the closing of the short sale is a short-term capital loss to which section 1233(d) has no application. By application of rule (2) in subparagraph (2) of this paragraph, however, the holding period of the 100 shares of X stock purchased on February 1, 1955, and sold on August 2, 1955 is considered to begin on August 1, 1955, the date of the closing of the short sale. The $800 gain realized upon the sale of such stock is, therefore, a short-term capital gain.

"*Example* (3). A buys 100 shares of X stock at $10 per share on February 1, 1955, sells short 100 shares of X stock at $16 per share on September 1, 1955, sells on October 1, 1955, at $18 per share the 100 shares of X stock purchased on February 1, 1955, and closes the short sale on October 1, 1955, with 100 shares of X stock purchased on that date at $18 per share. The $800 gain realized upon the sale of the 100 shares of X stock purchased on February 1, 1955, is a long-term capital gain to which section 1233(b) has no application. Since A had held 100 shares of X stock on the date of the short sale for more than 6 months, the $200 loss sustained upon the closing of the short sale is, by application of rule (3) in subparagraph (4) of this paragraph, a long-term capital loss. If, instead of purchasing 100 shares of X stock on October 1, 1955, A closed the short sale with the 100 shares of stock purchased on February 1, 1955, the $600 gain realized on the closing of the short sale would be a long-term capital gain to which section 1233(b) has no application.

"*Example* (4). A sells short 100 shares of X stock at $16 per share on February 1, 1955. He buys 250 shares of X stock on March 1, 1955, at $10 per share and holds the latter stock until September 2, 1955 (more than 6 months), at which time, 100 shares of the 250 shares of X stock are delivered to close the short sale made on February 1, 1955. Since substantially identical property was acquired by A after the short sale and before it was closed, the $600 gain realized on the closing of the short sale is, by application of rule (1) . . . a short-term capital gain. The holding period of the remaining 150 shares of X stock is not affected by section 1233 since this amount of the substantially identical property exceeds the quantity of the property sold short.

"*Example* (5). A buys 100 shares of X stock at $10 per share on February 1, 1955, buys an additional 100 shares of X stock at $20 per share on July 1, 1955, sells short 100 shares of X stock at $30 per share on September 1, 1955, and closes the short sale on February 1, 1956, by delivering the 100 shares of X stock purchased on February 1, 1955, to the lender of the stock used to effect the short sale. Since 100 shares of X stock had been held by A on the date of the short sale for not more than 6 months, the gain of $2,000 realized upon the closing of the short sale is, by application of rule (1) . . . a short-term capital gain and the holding period of the

100 shares of X stock purchased on July 1, 1955, is considered, by application of rule (2) . . . to begin on February 1, 1956, the date of the closing of the short sale. If, however, the 100 shares of X stock purchased on July 1, 1955, had been used by A to close the short sale, then, since 100 shares of X stock had been held by A on the date of the short sale for not more than 6 months, the gain of $1,000 realized upon the closing of the short sale would be, by application of rule (1) . . . a short-term capital gain, but the holding period of the 100 shares of X stock purchased on February 1, 1955, would not be affected by section 1233. If, on the other hand, A purchased an additional 100 shares of X stock at $40 per share on February 1, 1956, and used such shares to close the short sale at that time, then, since 100 shares of X stock had been held by A on the date of the short sale for more than 6 months, the loss of $1,000 sustained upon the closing of the short sale would be, by application of rule (3) . . . a long-term capital loss, and since 100 shares of X stock had been held by A on the date of the short sale for not more than 6 months, the holding period of the 100 shares of X stock purchased on July 1, 1955, would be considered, by application of rule (2) . . . to begin on February 1, 1956, but the holding period of the 100 shares of X stock purchased on February 1, 1955, would not be affected by section 1233.

"*Example* (6). A buys 100 shares of X preferred stock at $10 per share on February 1, 1955. On July 1, 1955, he enters into a contract to sell 100 shares of XY common stock at $16 per share when, as, and if issued pursuant to a particular proposed plan of reorganization. On August 2, 1955, he receives 100 shares of XY common stock in exchange for the 100 shares of X preferred stock purchased on February 1, 1955, and delivers such common shares in performance of his July 1, 1955, contract. Assume that the exchange of the X preferred stock for the XY common stock is a tax-free exchange pursuant to section 354(a)(1), and that on the basis of all of the facts and circumstances existing on July 1, 1955, the 'when issued' XY common stock is substantially identical to the X preferred stock. Since 100 shares of substantially identical property had been held by A for not more than 6 months on the date of entering into the July 1, 1955, contract of sale, the gain of $600 realized upon the closing of the contract of sale is, by application of rule (1) . . . a short-term capital gain." Regulations Section 1.1233–1(c)(6).

The term "substantially identical property", as applied to stocks or securities, has in general the same meaning as "substantially identical stock or securities" as used in Section 1091, relating to wash sales of stock or securities. (See Chapter 7.) Ordinarily, stocks or securities of one corporation are not considered substantially identical to stocks or securities of another corporation. In certain situations, they may be substantially identical: for example, in the case of a reorganization, the facts and circumstances may be such that the stocks and securities of a predecessor and of a successor corporation are substantially identical. Similarly, bonds or preferred stock of a corporation ordinarily are not considered substantially identical to the common stock of the same corporation. In certain situations, however, as, for example, where the preferred stock or bonds are convertible into common stock of the same corporation, the relative values, price changes, and other circumstances may be such as to make the bonds or preferred stock and the common stock substantially identical property. Likewise, depending on the facts and circumstances, the term may apply to the stocks and securities to be received in a corporate reorganization or recapitalization, traded in on a when-issued basis, as compared with the stocks or securities to be exchanged in such reorganization or recapitalization. Regulations Section 1.1233–1(d).

A call option contract and the shares of stock subject to call are not "substantially identical property." Revenue Ruling 58–384, 1958–2 CB 410.

In the case of futures transactions in any commodity on or subject to the rules of a board of trade or commodity exchange, a commodity future requiring delivery in one calendar month will not be considered as property substantially identical to another commodity future requiring delivery in a different calendar month. Similarly, futures in different commodities which are not generally through custom of the trade used as hedges for each other (such as corn and wheat, for example) are not considered substantially identical property. If commodity futures are likewise substantially identical property, the mere fact that they were procured through different brokers will not remove them from the scope of the term "substantially identical property." Commodity futures procured on different markets may come within this term depending upon the facts and circumstances in each case, with the historical similarity in the price movements in the two markets as the primary factor to be considered. Regulations Section 1.1233–1(d)(2).

Where a taxpayer enters into two commodity futures transactions on the same day, one requiring delivery by him in one market and the other requiring delivery to him of the same (or substantially identical) commodity in the same calendar month in a different market, and he subsequently closes both such transactions on the same day, Section 1233 will have no application to so much of the commodity involved in either transaction as does not exceed in quantity the commodity involved in the other. I.R.C. Section 1233(e)(3). Section 1233(f), relating to arbitrage operations in stocks or securities, has no application to arbitrage transactions in commodity futures.

In the case of a short sale of property by an individual, the term "taxpayer" means "taxpayer or his spouse." Thus, if the spouse of a taxpayer holds or acquires property substantially identical to that sold short by the taxpayer, and the other requirements of Section 1233 are met, then the rules are applicable to the same extent as if the taxpayer held or acquired the substantially identical property. "Spouse" does not include an individual who is legally separated from the taxpayer under a decree of divorce or of separate maintenance. Regulations Section 1.1233–1(d)(3).

In the case of a short sale of stock after December 31, 1957 by a dealer in securities, the holding period of substantially identical stock which he has held as an investment for not more than six months will be considered to begin on the date of the closing of the short sale, or on the date of a sale, gift, or other disposition of such property, whichever occurs first. Such is not the case, however, where the short sale is closed within twenty days of the date on which it was made. The acquisition of an option to sell property at a fixed price is considered to be a short sale, and the exercise or failure to exercise such option is considered a closing of such short sale. Regulations Section 1.1233–1(e).

Gain or loss on a short sale is realized only when the borrowed stock is delivered, "or at least not before the lender acquires an equitable interest in specific shares." *Richardson v. Commissioner,* 121 F.2d 1 (2d Cir., 1941). Even if under state law, delivery of stock certificates is necessary to complete a sale, a completed short sale without this formality may be enough to establish a short sale for Federal income tax purposes. *Dee Furey Mott,* 35 B.T.A. 195 (1936), *aff'd,* 103 F.2d 1009 (6th Cir., 1939).

Mere failure to deliver stock certificates is not enough to establish a short sale. *C. B. Feree,* 32 B.T.A. 725 (1935), *aff'd,* 84 F.2d 124 (3d Cir., 1936). Where stock belonging to the seller was inaccessible at the time of the sale, and hence was not turned over to the broker until the year after the sale, the broker had to borrow stock to carry out the selling order. Inasmuch as the seller had agreed with his broker to use his own stock, as soon as he could, to cover the transaction, no delivery was required to fix the gain or loss on the transaction. *Ruml v. Commissioner,* 83 F.2d 257 (2d Cir., 1936).

Arbitrage In Securities

"[A]rbitrage operations are transactions involving the purchase and sale of property entered into for the purpose of profiting from a current difference between the price of property purchased and the price of property sold. Assets required for arbitrage operations [for the purpose of Section

1233(f)] include only stocks and securities and rights to acquire stocks and securities. The property purchased may be either identical to the property sold or, if not so identical, such that its acquisition will entitle the taxpayer to acquire property which is so identical. Thus, the purchase of bonds or preferred stock convertible, at the holder's option, into common stock and the short sale of the common stock which may be acquired therefor, or the purchase of stock rights and the short sale of the stock to be acquired on the exercise of such rights, may qualify as arbitrage operations. A transaction will qualify as an arbitrage operation under section 1233(f) only if the taxpayer properly identifies the transaction as an arbitrage operation on his records as soon as he is able to do so. Such identification must ordinarily be entered in the taxpayer's records on the day of the transaction. Property acquired in a transaction properly identified as part of an arbitrage operation is the only property which will be deemed acquired for an arbitrage operation. The provisions of section 1233(f) and this paragraph shall continue to apply to property acquired in a transaction properly identified as an arbitrage operation although, because of subsequent events, *e.g.,* a change in the value of bonds so acquired or of stock into which such bonds may be converted, the taxpayer sells such property outright rather than using it to complete the arbitrage operation." Regulations Section 1.1233–1(f)(3).

In the case of a short sale entered into as part of an arbitrage operation in stocks and securities, Rule (2) as mentioned earlier in this chapter applies first to substantially identical property acquired for arbitrage operations and held by the taxpayer at the close of business on the day of the short sale. The holding period of substantially identical property not acquired for arbitrage operations is affected only to the extent that the amount of property sold short exceeds the amount of substantially identical property acquired for arbitrage operations and held by the taxpayer at the close of business on the day of the short sale. I.R.C. Section 1233(f).

If the substantially identical property acquired for arbitrage operations is disposed of without closing the short sale so that a net short position in assets acquired for arbitrage operations is created, a short sale in the amount of this net short position will be deemed to have been made on the day such position is created. Rule (2) will then apply to substantially identical property not acquired for arbitrage operations to the same extent as if the taxpayer, on the day this net short position is created, sold short an amount equal to the amount of the net short position in a transaction not entered into as a part of an arbitrage operation. Regulations Section 1.1233–1(f)(ii).

The following is an example of an arbitrage operation:

"Certain bonds traded on the New York Stock Exchange are convertible, at the option of the holder, into common stock of the issuing corporation. The market price of the bonds tends to fluctuate in direct relation to the market price of the stock. At times, however, there is a slight difference in the relative market prices of the bonds and stocks. When the price of the bonds is down, in relation to the price of the stock, members of the Exchange buy the bonds at the market price and as nearly simultaneously as possible sell the stock into which the bonds are convertible. The bonds purchased are then converted and the stock so received is used to close the sale. These transactions are known as arbitrage operations. *Held,* sales of stock in the manner described constitute short sales . . ." Revenue Ruling 154, 1953–2 CB 173.

Hedging Operations

The provisions of Section 1233 do not apply to *bona fide* hedging transactions in commodity futures entered into by flour millers, producers of cloth, operators of grain elevators, etc., for the purpose of their business. Gain or loss from a short sale of commodity futures which does not qualify as a hedging transaction is considered gain or loss from the sale or exchange of a capital asset in the hands of the taxpayer. I.R.C. Section 1233(g).

Hedging transactions are essentially to be regarded as insurance rather than dealing in capital assets, and gains and losses therefrom are ordinary gains and losses. G.C.M. 17322, XV–2 CB 151. "Furthermore, Congress has since specifically recognized the hedging exception here under consideration in the short sale rule of § 1233 (a) of the 1954 Code." *Corn Products Refining Company v. Commissioner,* 350 U.S. 46 (1955). This provides that capital treatment will be provided to gains and losses from short sales of property, other than a hedging transaction, to the extent that the property (including a commodity future) used to close the short sale constitutes a capital asset in the hands of a taxpayer.

In the *Corn Products* case, corn was an essential raw material in the taxpayer's business. The taxpayer had entered into a program of buying and selling corn futures to protect itself against a rise in the price of corn. These transactions in futures were an integral part of its business designed to protect its manufacturing operations. Thus, any gain or loss realized by the taxpayer from these transactions were ordinary and not capital in nature.

In an attempt to avoid possible losses from the reduction in the value of an international wool dealer's large inventory of "sterling area" and French wools, which could result from a rumored devaluation of the pound and the franc, the dealer dealt in sterling and franc currency futures. It was held that these futures transactions were in the nature of *bona fide* hedging operations conducted as part of the dealer's regular business and that the loss sustained by him in closing out the futures was an ordinary loss deductible in full against gross income. *Wool Distribution Co.,* 34 T.C. 323 (1960).

Losses in commodity futures contracts, however, were capital where trading in these futures was not conducted as an integral part of the business, being an independent speculative transaction. *Henry I. Seroussi,* T.C. Memo. 1963–233, filed August 29, 1963.

The Supreme Court has set forth three general classifications of dealing in commodity futures: speculation, legitimate capital transactions, and hedging. *United States v. New York Coffee & Sugar Exchange,* 263 U.S. 611 (1924).

Options

There is a fundamental distinction between a stock right and an option. The former is an equity inherent in stock ownership as a quality inseparable from the capital interest represented by the stock. *Miles v. Safe Deposit & Trust Co. of Baltimore,* 259 U.S. 247 (1922). An option to purchase stock is a right in no way based upon the ownership of stock. "[I]f Congress . . . had intended to link options with stock rights, it surely would have mentioned them specifically." *E. T. Weir,* 10 T.C. 996 (1948).

The principal forms of option are *puts* and *calls.* The terms thus were described in one case:

"A 'put' is an option to sell and a 'call' is an option to buy a specified number of shares of stock at a set price at any time within an agreed-upon period. These options are granted in consideration of a cash payment, the 'premium.' Standard-form contracts are used for puts and calls; each option is negotiable and is endorsed by a member firm of the New York Stock Exchange. Ordinarily, puts and calls are issued on blocks of 100 shares of a popular stock listed on a national exchange. The duration of the option ranges from thirty days to six months and ten days. The price at which the named stock can be put or called is ordinarily the market price when the option is written and is termed the 'striking price.' In order to exercise an option, it must be physically presented before expiration to the stock exchange firm that endorsed it. Options are customarily purchased by the public from put and call broker-dealers, but it is seldom they who create the option contracts they sell. Rather, that is the function of writers; the writer is in contact with the put and call broker. Either one or the other may suggest writing a particular option; then they negotiate the terms, the principal bargaining point being what premium the writer will receive. Premiums vary depending on numerous factors, including the risk to the writer the particular option involves and the demand from the public. The broker's gross profit is the difference between the premium he charges to his customer and what he must pay to the writer. The maximum profit an option writer can make from writing the option alone is the full premium he receives. This he keeps, of course, when the stock price either remains steady during the option life or fluctuates in his favor, *i.e.,* declines on a call or rises on a put. For then the optionee will find it unprofitable to exercise his rights." *Reinach v. Commissioner,* 373 F.2d 900 (2d Cir., 1967).

There are many variations on this theme. "For more sophisticated plungers, options come in varied forms with arcane names—'strips,' 'straps,' 'straddles' and 'spreads'—that conjure up visions of the Marquis de Sade. Actually, they are only combinations of puts and calls."*

In the case of a call on commodities, "[w]hen such a sale is made the right of possession passes to the buyer. The seller has the right to have the amount which he is to be paid fixed by the market price, plus or minus an agreed number of points, at a future date to be determined or 'called' by the seller. In such transactions the seller gains the advantage of rises in the market between the time of the contract and the date of the call. The seller has the right of market declines as well as the benefit of market rises and is required to keep the contract margined." *Patterson v. Hightower, Jr. et al.,* 245 F.2d 765 (5th Cir., 1957).

The amount (premium) received by the writer (issuer or optioner) of a put or call which is not exercised constitutes ordinary income, to be included in his gross income only for the taxable year in which the failure to exercise the option becomes final. Where a put is exercised, the amount received by the writer for granting it constitutes an offset against the option price, which he paid for the securities involved upon its exercise, in determining the (net) cost basis to him of the securities that he purchased pursuant thereto, for subsequent gain or loss purposes. Where a call is exercised, the amount received by the writer for granting it is includible by him, with the option price, which he received for the securities involved upon its exercise, in the (total) amount realized by him for the securities that he sold pursuant thereto, for the purpose of determining his gain or loss on their sale. For the latter purpose, if the amount received for granting a call is, under its terms, applicable, upon its exercise, on, to, or against the option price specified therein, such price thus adjusted (reduced) is considered the real option price. On the sale by the option holder (optionee) of the stock involved in a put, upon its exercise, the cost of the option to him should be offset against the option price, thereupon received or accrued, in computing

* *TIME Magazine,* October 6, 1967.

the (net) amount realized by him for the stock that he sold pursuant thereto, for the purpose of determining his gain or loss on its sale. Revenue Ruling 58–234, 1958–1 CB 279.

Gain or loss from the sale of an option to buy or to sell property which is (or if acquired would be) a capital asset in the hands of the taxpayer holding the option is considered as gain or loss from the sale or exchange of a capital asset. The period for which the taxpayer has held the option determines whether the capital gain or loss is long-term or short-term. I.R.C. Section 1234(a).

Section 1234 does not apply to gain or loss from the sale or exchange of an option to buy or to sell property, where, had the transaction been in the property covered rather than in the option, Section 1231 would have controlled taxability. Regulations Section 1.1234–1(a)(2).

Gain or loss from the sale or exchange of an option to buy or to sell property which is not (or if acquired would not be) a capital asset in the hands of the taxpayer holding the option is considered ordinary income or loss, unless Section 1231 controls taxability of the transaction.

If the holder of an option to buy or to sell property incurs a loss on failure to exercise the option, the option is deemed to have been sold or exchanged upon the date that it expired. Any such loss to the holder of the option is treated under the general rule of Section 1234(a). But any gain to the grantor of an option arising from the failure of the holder to exercise it is ordinary income. I.R.C. Section 1234(b).

Section 1234 does not apply to a loss on the failure to exercise an option to sell property at a fixed price which is acquired on the same day on which the property identified as intended to be used in exercising the option is acquired. The loss is not recognized, but the cost of the option is added to the basis of the property with which it is identified.

Any gain or loss realized by a dealer in options from the sale or exchange of property is deemed to be ordinary income or loss. A dealer in options to buy or to sell property is considered a dealer in the property subject to the option.

Section 1234 does not apply to gain resulting from the sale or exchange of an option—

(1) To the extent that the gain is in the nature of compensation.

(2) If the option is treated as Section 306 stock, which, in general, is a tax-free dividend on common stock paid in the form of preferred stock.

(3) To the extent that the gain is a distribution of earnings or profits taxable as a dividend.

(4) Acquired by the taxpayer before March 1, 1954, if in the hands of the taxpayer this option is a capital asset (whether or not the property to

which the option relates is, or would be if acquired by the taxpayer, a capital asset in his hands).

Losses to which Section 1234 applies are subject to the loss limitations of Section 165(c) (trade or business losses in the case of an individual) and Section 1211 (offset of capital losses only against capital gains in the case of a corporation and the same treatment plus $1,000 in the case of an individual). Section 1234 does not permit the deduction of any loss which is disallowed under any other provision of law. Nor does the section apply to an option to lease property, but it does apply to an option to buy or to sell a lease. If the section applies to an option to buy or to sell a lease, it is the character the lease itself (if acquired) would have in the hands of the taxpayer, and not the character of the property leased, which determines the treatment of gain or loss experienced by the taxpayer with respect to such an option.

The grantor of an option has ordinary income if the option expires unexercised. Revenue Ruling 58–234, 1958–1 CB 279. But this does not apply in the case of an option to acquire the taxpayer's own stock, for a corporation does not recognize gain when it sells its own stock. I.R.C. Section 1032.

Failure to exercise an option is covered by the rule of Section 1234 even if there was a sound business reason for this failure. *Southern Coast Corporation,* 17 T.C. 824 (1951).

There is no tax distinction between "non-exercise" and "failure" to exercise an option. *Milliken et al. v. Commissioner et al.,* 196 F.2d 135 (2d Cir., 1952).

Amounts received in partial payment for shares under an option which was forfeited by the buyer were ordinary income. *F. R. Ingram et al.,* T.C. Memo. 1961–277, filed September 29, 1961. The expiration of an option unexercised fixed the nature of the payment for the option as ordinary income. *Dill Company,* 33 T.C. 196 (1959), *aff'd,* 294 F.2d 291 (3d Cir., 1961).

If an option is allowed to lapse, the fee retained by the grantor of the option should be treated as ordinary income in the year the option lapses. Revenue Ruling 57–40, 1957–1 CB 266.

A *straddle,* although commonly referred to as one contract, embodying both a put and a call, is, in fact, two separate option contracts. Each, neither, or both may be sold or exercised, by the same or different persons. Thus, it is necessary to allocate the premium received for writing the straddle contract to the put option and to the call option. This allocation should be made on the basis of the relative market values, at the time of the issuance of the straddle, of the put and call options contained therein. "Accordingly, if the 'call' is exercised and the 'put' is not, the amount of the premium properly allocable to the 'put' would be considered ordinary income to the writer; conversely, if the 'put' were exercised and the 'call' were not the amount of premium properly allocable to the 'call' would be considered ordinary income to the writer. Naturally, if both options are exercised the amount of the premium allocated to the 'call' option would be added to the amount realized on the sale of the property 'called' from the writer, and the amount of the premium allocated to the 'put' option would reduce the cost basis of the property purchased by ('put' to) the writer. Also, if neither option is exercised the amount of premium received by the writer constitutes ordinary income." Revenue Ruling 65–31, 1965–1 CB 365.

"Straddles are one form of an option: namely, an offer both to purchase and to sell a specified amount of property at a stated price for a limited period of time. . . . A 'straddle' is a combination of a put and call, with respect to the same security, for the same quantity, at the same purchase or sale price and available for the same period of time.

"Straddles are likely to be written by persons with holdings of a security who believe that in the long run, the price of the stock will not vary greatly from its present price. Their inducement for writing the straddle is the receipt of a premium. Straddles generally are granted to brokers or dealers who, in turn, customarily sell the put and call components to different purchasers. The majority of puts and calls originate in straddles. While the use of puts and calls is not a new development in the securities markets, their significance in the securities markets is relatively limited; for example, the total number of shares covered by options sold in recent years on the New York Stock Exchange has rarely exceeded 1 percent of the total shares sold.

"Normally either (not both) the put or the call component of the straddle is exercised by the purchaser shortly before the end of the term for which the straddle is written. Frequently this is 6 months and 10 days after the straddle is issued. Which component of the straddle is exercised depends upon the market conditions at the time the straddle was written. If the market in that security has risen, the securities are likely to be 'called' from the writer; if the market has fallen, the stock is likely to be 'put' to the writer. While in the great majority of the cases, one component of the straddle is exercised and the other is allowed to lapse, occasionally (perhaps 10 to 15 percent of the time) neither option is exercised and in a few other cases (less than 1 percent of the cases) both components of the straddle are exercised.

"Although options are purchased for hedging and other similar purposes by some investors, their primary use probably is as a method of investing by individuals with small amounts of money." Senate Finance Committee Report on H.R. 13103, "The Foreign Investors Tax Act of 1966."

Gain derived from the lapse of an option written as part of a straddle is short-term capital gain. Thus, such gains are added to any other short-term capital gains, to be netted against any net short-term capital losses. Any remaining short-term capital gains are taxed as ordinary income. This treatment does not apply to a person who holds securities (including options to acquire or to sell securities) for sale to customers in the ordinary course of his trade or business. I.R.C. Section 1234(c).

If a person grants a multiple option (a put plus a call plus one or more additional puts or calls), he must identify in his records which two of the component options constitute the straddle, if it is not clear from the options themselves. If there is no identification by the writer, this provision relating to straddles does not apply. As a result, in such a case the gain on the lapsed option results in ordinary income.

A corporate security for purposes of the definition of a straddle is the same as defined in Section 1236(c) of the Code: that is, stocks, bonds, notes, etc. Accordingly, this treatment does not apply as to commodities futures.

Chapter 7

Disallowed Gains and Losses

Transactions Between Related Parties

Losses are not recognized for Federal income tax purposes in the case of transactions between certain related parties. Except in the case of distributions in corporate liquidations, no deduction is allowed for losses arising from direct or indirect sales or exchanges of property between persons who, on the date of the sale or exchange, are within any of these relationships:

(1) Member of a family. This will be defined below.

(2) An individual and a corporation more than 50% in value of the outstanding stock of which is owned, directly or indirectly, by or for that individual.

(3) Two corporations more than 50% in the value of the outstanding stock of which is owned, directly or indirectly, by or for the same individual, if either of these corporations in the taxable year preceding the date of the sale or exchange was (under the law applicable to that year) a personal holding company or a foreign personal holding company.

(4) A grantor and a fiduciary of any trust.

(5) A fiduciary of a trust and a fiduciary of another trust, if the same person is a grantor of both trusts.

(6) A fiduciary of a trust and a beneficiary of the same trust.

(7) A fiduciary of a trust and a beneficiary of another trust, if the same person is a grantor of both trusts.

(8) A fiduciary of a trust and a corporation more than 50% in value of the outstanding stock of which is owned, directly or indirectly, by or for the same trust or by or for a person who is a grantor of that trust.

(9) A person and a tax-exempt organization which is controlled directly

or indirectly by that person or (if the person is an individual) by members of his family. I.R.C. Section 267(a)(1), (b).

For the purpose of applying these rules, constructive ownership of stock is applied in this manner:

(1) Stock owned, directly or indirectly, by or for a corporation, partnership, estate, or trust will be considered as being owned proportionately by or for its shareholders, partners, or beneficiaries.

(2) An individual is considered as owning the stock owned, directly or indirectly, by or for his family.

(3) An individual owning (except by the application of (2), immediately above) any stock in a corporation is considered as owning the stock owned, directly or indirectly, by his partner.

(4) The family of an individual includes only his brothers and sisters (whether by the whole or half blood), spouse, ancestors, and lineal descendants.

(5) Stock constructively owned by a person by reason of the application of (1) will, for the purpose of applying (1), (2), or (3), be treated as actually owned by that person, but stock constructively owned by an individual by reason of the application of (2) or (3) will not be treated as owned by him for the purpose of again applying either of these provisions in order to make another the constructive owner of this stock. I.R.C. Section 267(c).

Inasmuch as Section 267 does not include members of a partnership and the partnership as related persons, transactions between partners and partnerships do not come within the scope of this section. These transactions are governed by Section 707, which provides that the partnership is to be considered as an entity separate from the partners. Any transaction described in Section 267 between a partnership and a person other than a partner is considered as occurring between the other person and the member of the partnership separately. Thus, if any other person and a partner are within any one of the relationships specified in Section 267, no deduction with respect to the transactions between the other person and the partnership will be allowed—

(1) To the related partner to the extent of his distributive share of the partnership deductions for losses resulting from the transactions.

(2) To the other person to the extent the related partner acquires an interest in any property sold or exchanged with the partnership by this other person at a loss. Regulations Section 1.267(b)–1(b).

"[T]he purpose of [the forerunner of Section 267] was to put an end to the right of taxpayers to choose, by intra-family transfers and other designated devices, their own time for realizing tax losses on investments which, for most practical purposes, are continued uninterrupted." *McWilliams et al. v. Commissioner,* 331 U.S. 694 (1947). "Section 267 was enacted to correct what Congress considered the abusive, frequently employed practice of creating losses for purposes of avoiding the income tax through transactions between certain specified persons. . . . To prevent this tax avoidance, Congress denied deduction of losses on all exchanges between these persons regardless of their subjective intent." *Dillard Paper Company,* 42 T.C. 588 (1964), *aff'd,* 341 F.2d 897 (4th Cir., 1965).

Section 267 applies where transactions are *directly or indirectly* between related parties. An individual managed his wife's investment account and his own. On various occasions, he ordered his broker to sell certain stock for one account and to buy the same number of shares of this stock for the other, at as nearly the same price as possible. He informed the broker that this was to establish tax losses. The transactions were negotiated through the New York Stock Exchange, and the identity of the other party to each trade never was known. The Internal Revenue Service disallowed the losses as being between related parties. The taxpayer claimed that neither spouse had sold to the other but, presumably, to a stranger. The court held that the phrase "directly or indirectly" covered the situation, and the losses were disallowed. *McWilliams et al. v. Commissioner,* 331 U.S. 694 (1947).

The *McWilliams* decision applies to over-the-counter sales as well as to listed stocks. *John B. Shethar et al.,* 28 T.C. 1222 (1957).

The operation of Section 267 does not depend upon the simultaneous execution of the transactions of purchase and sale. *Commissioner v. Kohn,* 158 F.2d 32 (4th Cir., 1946). Nor does it matter that one spouse sold securities *after* the other spouse had purchased similar ones. *John B. Shethar et al.,* 28 T.C. 1222 (1957).

The Internal Revenue Service cannot stretch Section 267 to cover other related persons, however close their ties may be. Thus, in one case the Service argued that "because of the close blood and personal relationship between the two families, the stock interests of the families should be combined for the purpose of deciding this issue." The court disagreed, saying that "the family of a shareholder includes 'only' the persons related as above described. We are not at liberty to bring in collateral relatives in determining the matter of stock ownership." *Graves Brothers Company,* 17 T.C. 1499 (1952).

Shares owned by the brother of the taxpayer's wife are not attributed to the taxpayer through a double family attribution. Revenue Ruling 67–262, I.R.B. 1967–34, 13. Where a sale or exchange between an estate and a corporation more than 50% in value of the stock of which is owned by the estate results in a loss, the transaction is not covered by Section 267 and hence the loss is not disallowed. *Ruth Hanna Estate v. Commissioner,* 319 F.2d 54 (6th Cir., 1963). Disallowance of loss on transfers between a grantor and a fiduciary of any trust is not confined to situations involving an *individual* grantor and the fiduciary of a *taxable* trust created by the grantor. *Dillard Paper Company v. Commissioner,* 341 F.2d 897 (4th Cir., 1965).

If a sale is made at a loss to joint buyers and one of these is a related party within the meaning of Section 267, the loss is to be apportioned between related and unrelated parties. The loss allocated to the unrelated party is disallowed. *Walter Simister, Jr.,* 4 T.C. 470 (1944).

Section 267 applies to sales in the ordinary course of the trade or business, as well as to capital transactions. *Melvin W. McGrew et al.,* T.C. Memo. 1965–256, filed September 22, 1965. The language of this section is so broad that it includes *bona fide* transactions without regard to hardships in particular cases. *Nathan Blum,* 5 T.C. 702 (1945). "The question of good faith is not controlling." *Federal Cement Tile Company v. Commissioner,* 338 F.2d 691 (7th Cir., 1964).

Involuntary sales are covered by the section. Thus, no loss was allowed to a mortgagor from an involuntary foreclosure sale of the mortgaged property to other members of his family. *Thomas Zacek et al.,* 8 T.C. 1056 (1947). But loss was allowed where property was sold by county officials in foreclosure proceedings, even though the purchaser was a corporation in which the taxpayer-seller owned more than 50% of the stock. Here, the taxpayer had no choice as to the time of sale; the county offiicals decided that. The price was set at a public auction, where the bidding was spirited. *McCarty et al. v. Cripe,* 201 F.2d 679 (7th Cir., 1953).

Where property is purchased from a relative and, as part of the consideration, it is provided that the property will revert to the seller if the buyer pre-deceases her, any loss on the transaction is not denied to the buyer's estate under Section 267. "The loss here was not a loss from a sale or exchange of property; it was a loss occasioned by death." *National Metropolitan Bank of Washington et al. v. United States,* 111 F. Supp. 422 (Ct. Cl., 1953).

If a taxpayer sells property on two different occasions to a related party, one transaction resulting in a gain and the other in a loss, the loss is not deductible and the gain must be reported in full. *United States Holding Co.,* 44 T.C. 323 (1965).

If a loss from a sale or exchange is not allowable to the transferor under Section 267(a) and the taxpayer sells or otherwise disposes of this property (or other property which takes its basis) at a gain, then this gain will be recognized only to the extent that it exceeds the disallowed loss. (This does not apply in the case of wash sales.) I.R.C. Section 267(d).

No loss is allowed on stock redemptions under Section 302(a), which involve related taxpayers within the purview of Section 267. Revenue Ruling 57–387, 1957–2 CB 225.

The statute applies only to the disallowance of *losses* between related taxpayers. "Section 267 specifically provides that no deduction shall be allowed in respect of losses from sales of property between specified persons. It does not provide that gains from such sales shall not be recognized." *Edwin H. Johnson Estate,* 42 T.C. 441 (1964).

Wash Sales

A taxpayer cannot deduct a loss from the sale or other disposition of stock or securities if, within a period beginning thirty days before the date of the sale or disposition and ending thirty days after this date (referred to as the "61-day period"), he has acquired by purchase or other non-tax-free transaction substantially identical stock or securities, or if he has entered into a contract or an option to acquire them. This rule does not apply in the case of:

(1) A taxpayer, not a corporation, if the sale or other disposition of stock or securities is made in connection with the taxpayer's trade or business, or

(2) A corporation, a dealer in stock or securities, if the sale or other disposition of stock or securities is made in the ordinary course of its business as a dealer. I.R.C. Section 1091(a).

Where more than one loss is sustained within the taxable year from the sale or other disposition of stock or securities, the wash sales provisions are applied to the losses in the order of disposition (starting with the earliest one) of the stock or securities sold at a loss. If the order of disposition where there have been several dispositions at a loss on the same day cannot be determined, the stock or securities will be deemed to have been disposed of in the order of their acquisition, starting with the earliest. I.R.C. Section 1091(b).

Deduction of a loss sustained on the sale of a portion of shares of stock purchased in one lot by a taxpayer less than thirty days before the sale will not be disallowed by the wash sales provisions merely because the taxpayer acquired in the original purchase more shares than he later sold. "For example, a taxpayer acquires 200 shares of the only outstanding stock of a corporation. Less than 30 days after its acquisition, he sells

100 of these shares at a loss. The loss.will not be disallowed unless during the period prescribed in section 1091(a) of the Code, he acquires, or enters into a contract or option to acquire, additional shares or securities which are substantially identical to those sold." Revenue Ruling 56–602, 1956–2 CB 527.

Where the amount of stock or securities acquired within the 61-day period is less than the amount sold or otherwise disposed of, the loss from the sale or other disposition which is not deductible will be that with which there is matching in accordance with this rule: the stock or securities acquired will be matched in accordance with the order of their acquisition (beginning with the earliest acquisition) with an equal number of the shares of stock or securities sold or otherwise disposed of.

Where the amount of stock or securities acquired within the 61-day period is not less than the amount sold or otherwise disposed of, then the particular shares of stock or securities the acquisition of which resulted in the loss non-deductibility will be those with which they are matched in accordance with this rule: the stock or securities sold or otherwise disposed of will be matched with an equal number of the shares or stock or securities acquired in accordance with the order of acquisition, beginning with the earliest. Regulations Section 1.1091–1(c), (d).

The acquisition of any share of stock or any security which results in the non-deductibility under the wash sales provisions will be disregarded in determining the deductibility of any other loss. Regulations Section 1.1091–1(e).

Where a taxpayer acquires stock through the exercise of subscription rights and within thirty days after the acquisition he sells an equal number of shares of the stock with respect to which the rights were issued, the wash sales provisions are applicable. I.T. 2890, XIV–1 CB 225. In the case of a contract for the sale of stock below cost and a purchase on the same day of an equal number of identical shares, where delivery of the stock covered by the sales contract will take place thirty-one or more days after the date of the contract, the loss sustained upon the sale of the stock is not an allowable deduction. Within the 61-day period prescribed in Section 1091(a), identical stock was purchased to replace the stock sold. Revenue Ruling 59–418, 1959–2 CB 184.

Substantially Identical. The wash sales provision is not concerned with the identity of shares sold, but provides only for the disallowance of loss deductions if substantially identical property is acquired within thirty days of the sale. *Richard Coulter,* 32 B.T.A. 617 (1935). "Generally, respective bonds are 'substantially identical' . . . if they are not substantially different in any material feature (unaffected by any related material feature, or as affected by such other feature or features), or because of differences in several material features considered together. On the other hand, they are not 'substantially identical,' within such meaning, if they are substantially different in any material feature (unaffected by any related material feature, or as affected by such other feature or features), or because of differences in several material features considered together (*i.e.,* even though each of such differences considered alone might not be regarded as substantial). In determining whether or not bonds purchased were substantially identical to bonds sold, the bonds purchased must, of course, be compared as they existed when purchased with the bonds sold as they existed when sold.

"The fact that bonds of one series have the same, or approximately the same, market value on a particular day, or days, as bonds of another series of the same obligor, equally secured, and bearing interest at the same rate, does not necessarily establish that the respective bonds are 'substantially identical,' for that market situation can occur even if such respective series of bonds have substantially different maturity dates (unaffected, or as affected, by earlier call provisions) but, where they so differ, their market prices often are substantially higher on the substantially longer term series (than on the substantially shorter term series) when the market for the bonds is strong (usually during periods of generally low interest rates) and the reverse frequently occurs when the market for the bonds is weak (usually during periods of generally high interest rates)." Revenue Ruling 58–211, 1958–1 CB 529.

"Ordinarily, stocks or securities of one corporation are not considered substantially identical to stocks or securities of another corporation. In certain situations they may be substantially identical: for example, in the case of a reorganization the facts and circumstances may be such that the stocks and securities of predecessor and successor corporations are substantially identical property. Similarly, bonds or preferred stock of a corporation are not ordinarily considered substantially identical to the common stock of the same corporation. However, in certain situations, as, for example, where the preferred stock or bonds are convertible into common stock of the same corporation, the relative values, price changes, and other circumstances may be such as to make such bonds or preferred stock and the common stock substantially identical property." Revenue Ruling 56–406, 1956–2 CB 523.

Bonds of a Federal Land Bank of one city are not "substantially identical" to bonds of a Federal Land Bank of another city. The Federal Land Banks are not alike liable on the individual bonds of each other because one bank's liability on the bonds of another is only contingent and not joint and several. *Hanlin et al. v. Commissioner,* 108 F.2d 429 (3d Cir., 1939). Bonds of different local housing authorities, issued under agreement with the Federal Public Housing Administration, are not "substantially identical" securities within the meaning of Section 1091. Revenue Ruling 59–44, 1959–1 CB 205.

Disposition. Loss on the sale of stock or securities is not allowed if there is a re-acquisition within the "61-day period" of the date of disposition. "The meaning of 'disposition' in Section [1091] has not been made more precise by regulations issued by the Commissioner." *Doyle et al. v. Commissioner,* 286 F.2d 654 (7th Cir., 1961). In that case, the putting up of securities as collateral for a short sale was deemed not to be a disposition. Here, there was no showing that the taxpayer was precluded from substituting other collateral for the protection of the broker had she chosen to do so or that she could not exercise any other control over these shares consistent with the purposes for which she originally hypothecated them.

Non-Applicability. The wash sales provisions do not apply to futures contracts in commodities. *Corn Products Refining Company v. Commissioner,* 215 F.2d 513 (2d Cir., 1954), *aff'd on other grounds,* 350 U.S. 46 (1955).

Losses on wash sales of securities were not allowed where the taxpayers could not establish that they were not dealers in securities. *Peyton G. Nevitt et al.,* 20 T.C. 318 (1953). Evidence that an individual had a brokerage account upon which he bought and sold securities in a series of transactions was insufficient to exclude a loss from the restrictions of the wash sales provisions. *Richard Coulter,* 32 B.T.A. 617 (1935).

A bank is not exempted from the wash sales provisions. *Merchants National Bank,* 9 T.C. 68 (1947).

Negative Proof. A taxpayer must prove not only that a purchase had not been made, but that no contract or option to re-acquire had been entered upon within thirty days of the sale. *A. W. Mellon,* 36 B.T.A. 977 (1937).

Basis. If the property consists of stock or securities the acquisition of which (or the contract or option to acquire which) resulted in the nondeductibility of the loss, then the basis will be the basis of the stock or securities disposed of, increased or decreased, as the case may be, by the difference, if any, between the price at which the property was acquired and the price at which the substantially identical stock or securities were sold or otherwise disposed of. I.R.C. Section 1091(d).

The regulations furnish these illustrations of the basis of stock or securities acquired in wash sales:

"*Example (1).* A purchased a share of common stock of the X Corporation for $100 in 1935, which he sold January 15, 1955, for $80. On February 1, 1955, he purchased a share of common stock of the same corporation for $90. No loss from the sale is recognized under section 1091. The basis of the new share is $110; that is, the basis of the old share ($100) increased by $10, the excess of the price at which the new share was acquired ($90) over the price at which the old share was sold ($80).

"Example (2). A purchased a share of common stock of the Y Corporation for $100 in 1935, which he sold January 15, 1955, for $80. On February 1, 1955, he purchased a share of common stock of the same corporation for $70. No loss from the sale is recognized under section 1091. The basis of the new share is $90: that is, the basis of the old share ($100) decreased by $10, the excess of the price at which the old share was sold ($80) over the price at which the new share was acquired ($70)." Regulations Section 1.1091–2.

Less Than Arm's Length Transactions

Disallowance of gain or loss may, in effect, be effected by the Internal Revenue Service under the arm's length provision of the Code, Section 482. That section is not supposed to *disallow* loss. "Under that section the Commissioner is given no authority to disallow a deduction truly sustained, but only to distribute, apportion or allocate it to prevent evasion." *Henry W. Breyer Co.,* B.T.A. Memo., Docket No. 90060, entered July 11, 1939. But if the re-allocation is to a taxpayer which cannot use it because there is no offsetting item, the re-allocation is effectively a disallowance. Such also is the case where a loss is re-allocated to a taxpayer the tax returns of which were closed by the statute of limitations.

Section 482 is "a relatively compact section of the Internal Revenue Code . . . containing words of delusive simplicity." *Eli Lilly and Company v. United States,* 372 F.2d 990 (Ct. Cl., 1967). This is what it says:

"In the case of two or more organizations, trades, or businesses (whether or not incorporated, whether or not organized in the United States, and whether or not affiliated) owned or controlled directly or indirectly by the same interests, the Secretary or his delegate may distribute, apportion, or allocate gross income, deductions, credits, or allowances between or among such organizations, trades, or businesses, if he determines that such distribution, apportionment, or allocation is necessary in order to prevent evasion of taxes or clearly to reflect the income of any of such organizations, trades, or businesses." I.R.C. Section 482.

"Two elements must coalesce for the Commissioner to use his section 482 power: "(1) The businesses must be under *common control.* (2) The reallocation must be necessary to *reflect the proper income* of the businesses or *prevent tax evasion." South Texas Rice Warehouse Co. v. Commissioner,* 366 F.2d 890 (5th Cir., 1966).

"Controlled" means more than 50%. A one-half interest does not constitute control for this purpose. *Q. I. Roberts et al.,* T.C. Memo., Docket Nos. 15773–5, entered January 19, 1949. Control for the purposes of this section "includes any kind of control, direct or indirect, whether legally enforceable, and however exercisable or exercised. It is the reality of control which is decisive, not its form or the mode of its exercise." *L. E. Shunk Latex Products, Inc.,* 18 T.C. 940 (1952).

Re-allocation in the case of parties under common control can only be made if the transaction is at less than arm's length. "An arm's length transaction generally means one between parties with adverse economic interests." *Turnbull, Inc.,* T.C. Memo. 1963–335, filed December 24, 1963.

If one party sells securities which have appreciated in value to a person under common control at cost, and the latter immediately re-sells them at a profit, the Internal Revenue Service may re-allocate the profit for tax purposes to the first seller. *Asiatic Petroleum Co. (Delaware) Limited v. Commissioner,* 79 F.2d 234 (2d Cir., 1935). This was a transaction at less than arm's length; for in dealing with an unrelated party, one would not sell at cost what could be sold at a gain.

Limitation On Capital Losses

In the case of a corporation, losses from sales or exchanges of capital assets are allowed as deductions only to the extent of such gains. In the case of other taxpayers, losses from sales or exchanges of capital assets are allowed as a deduction only to the extent of the gains from such transactions, plus the taxable income of the taxpayer or $1,000, whichever is smaller. I.R.C. Seciton 1211.

A corporation was not entitled to a capital loss deduction on a sale to a controlled corporation. "Where management's desire to retain the power to vote a bloc of shares is the sole 'business purpose' for a sale to a subsidiary there is no actual loss to the selling corporation." *Northern Pacific Railway Company v. United States,* 378 F.2d 686 (Ct. Cl., 1967).

For the treatment of unused capital loss carryovers, see Chapter 5.

Where a taxpayer incurred expenses in obtaining an alleged loan, and no true indebtedness actually was created, the expenses were not allowed as a deduction, despite the taxpayer's claim that this was the cost of a "right" to obtain a loan. Said the court: "The entire transaction, including the loan, was a sham. In my opinion, any 'right' to obtain a loan is infected with the same taint, regardless of the taxpayers' intentions. Accordingly, no capital loss deduction is allowable for the worthlessness of such 'right.' *Cf. Gregory v. Helvering*, 293 U.S. 465 (1935)." *Berenson et al. v. United States,* 257 F. Supp. 101 (D.C., S.D.N.Y., 1966).

Gain From Sale Of Certain Property Between Spouses Or Between An Individual And A Controlled Corporation

Capital treatment is not allowed on sales of depreciable property, including Section 1231 assets, between (1) husband and wife and (2) an individual and a corporation more than 80% of the stock of which is owned by him and his spouse and minor children and minor grandchildren. I.R.C. Section 1239. "Section 1239 prevents capital gain treatment of a 'sale or exchange' of depreciable property to a controlled corporation or spouse. Without this section a taxpayer who had property which has been depreciated to a low basis could sell that property to a controlled corporation or spouse and pay only capital gains rates on the gain. The transferee (who is virtually identical to the transferor in the proscribed area) could then redepreciate the property, using the sale price as a new basis. The depreciation, of course, would be deducted from ordinary income. Section 1239 renders such a scheme profitless by taxing the gain on the transfer at ordinary rather than capital rates." *United States v. Parker et al.,* 376 F.2d 402 (5th Cir., 1967).

Section 1239 applies where a taxpayer owns more than 80% in value of all of the outstanding stock in a corporation at the time of sale. This rule may apply even where the taxpayer owns exactly 80% of the stock, if there were restrictions upon the shares of the 20% owner which made them worth less per share than the stock of the majority owner. Thus, where there were restrictions upon the transfer of the minority shareholder's stock, his shares were in effect worth less than the purported 20%; and by the same token, the owner of the 80% interest had stock that was worth more than 80%. The same result might apply merely because the owner of the 20% interest did not have control whereas the owner of the 80% interest did. *United States v. Parker et al.,* 376 F.2d 402 (5th Cir., 1967).

The 80% rule did not apply in the case of a sale of depreciable property to a corporation where 80% of the stock could be arrived at only by including shares held by an irrevocable trust for the benefit of minor children. Beneficial ownership of stock is not included for this purpose. *Mitchell et al. v. Commissioner,* 300 F.2d 533 (4th Cir., 1962). Ownership does not mean "in effect," "tantamount to," or "in substance." Ownership rather than control is the criterion. *Trotz et al. v. Commissioner,* 361 F.2d 927 (10th Cir., 1966).

Other Disallowance Of Capital Gain

Capital gain will not be recognized but ordinary income where the buyer is in effect purchasing cash. Bethlehem Steel owned several corporations no longer used, where all of the assets had been converted into cash and the liabilities had been paid off. These subsidiaries could not be liquidated at a loss; for in the liquidation of a wholly-owned subsidiary under the Code conditions, no gain or *loss* is recognized. So the stocks were sold to an unrelated party: in one instance, for example, a corporation with net assets of $100,000 in the form of a bank account was sold for $93,000 in cash. After six months, the buyer liquidated the corporations, receiving the $100,000 cash for a $93,000 investment. The court held that she had, in effect, purchased cash at a discount, and that she had realized income on the dates she had purchased the stock, the income to be taxed to her as ordinary income on those dates. *Lowndes et al. v. United States,* 258 F. Supp. 193 (D.C., Md., 1966), *aff'd,* 384 F.2d 635 (5th Cir., 1967).

Loss On Worthless Securities

If any security which is a capital asset becomes worthless during the taxable year, the resulting loss is a capital one. I.R.C. Section 165(g)(1). But this rule does not apply in the case of securities of an affiliated corporation. Ordinary loss results if (1) the creditor corporation owns at least 95% of each class of the debtor's stock and (2) more than 90% of the aggregate of the debtor corporation's gross receipts for all taxable years has been from sources other than royalties, rents (except those derived from rental of properties to employees of the corporation in the ordinary course of its operating business), dividends, interest (except that received on any deferred purchase price of operating assets sold), annuities, and gains from sales or exchanges of stocks and securities. I.R.C. Section 165(g)(3).

In the case of banks, the 95% figure is 80%. I.R.C. Section 582(b).

Ordinary loss was not recognized where a corporation owning stock in a deficit corporation acquired enough of the latter's remaining shares to "qualify" for ordinary loss treatment. *Hunter Manufacturing Corporation,* 21 T.C. 424 (1953).

Reorganizations And Exchanges

No gain or loss is recognized in the case of a tax-free corporate reorganization. See Chapter 10.

Gain from the sale or exchange of stock of a collapsible corporation, or a distribution in liquidation of such a corporation in part or full payment in exchange for stock, is treated as ordinary income and not capital gain. I.R.C. Section 341(a). See Chapter 10. A similar situation exists in the case of partnerships. Any gain recognized upon the sale or exchange, directly or indirectly, of property which, in the hands of the transferee immediately after the transfer, is property other than a capital asset, will be treated as ordinary income if the transaction is between a partnership and a partner who owns, directly or indirectly, more than 80% of the capital interest or profits interest in the partnership. This rule also applies where such a transaction is between partnerships in which the same persons own, directly or indirectly, more than 80% of the capital interests or profits in each partnership. I.R.C. Section 707(b)(2).

There may be a tax-free exchange of stock without a formal corporate reorganization. No gain or loss is recognized if common stock in a corporation is exchanged solely for common stock in the same corporation, or if preferred stock in a corporation is exchanged solely for preferred stock in the same corporation. I.R.C. Section 1036(a). This rule is not limited to an exchange between two individual stockholders. It includes a transaction between a stockholder and the corporation. Regulations Section 1.1036–1(a).

Acquisition Of Stock To Get Assets

If stock is acquired, not for the purpose of making an investment, but merely as an incident in the achieving of some other objective, the transaction is not treated as a capital one for tax purposes. There are several variations on this theme.

To Get Inventory. At a time of wartime whiskey shortages, the taxpayer, a liquor wholesaler, needed inventories. American Distilling Company offered shareholders a stipulated quantity of whiskey at a cost of $30.20 per each share of stock held. In order to obtain the right to buy whiskey, the taxpayer acquired stock in American Distilling Company on the New York Stock Exchange, exercised the rights, and immediately sold the stock at a loss. It was held that the loss was not subject to capital loss limitations, for the purpose of the transaction was to get inventory. Thus, the loss was treated as part of the cost of the inventory. *Western Wine & Liquor Co.,* 18 T.C. 1090 (1952).

Two newspaper corporations, which were unrelated, were seriously affected by a newsprint shortage. At the suggestion of a paper consultant, each corporation purchased 50% of the stock of a paper manufacturing company, which then was utilized primarily to supply newsprint to the two purchasing corporations, the taxpayers. It was not until seven years later that the trade sources of newsprint were able to assure deliveries of the desired quantities. At that time, the stock of the paper manufacturing companies was sold at a loss. It was held that ordinary rather than capital loss has resulted. "[I]f securities are purchased by a taxpayer as an integral and necessary act in the conduct of his business, and continue to be so held until the time of their sale, any loss incurred as a result thereof may be fully deducted from gross income as a business expense or ordinary loss. If, on the other hand, an investment purpose be found to have motivated the purchase or holding of the securities, any loss realized upon their ultimate disposition must be treated in accord with the capital asset provisions of the Code." Here, the taxpayers were not investment-minded when they purchased the stock. Nor did their original business purpose change prior to the time they disposed of the stock. Thus, the stock was not a capital asset in their hands and ordinary loss resulted. *Booth Newspapers, Inc. et al v. United States,* 303 F.2d 916 (Ct. Cl., 1962).

The taxpayer, a manufacturer of electrical fittings, needed to obtain malleable iron castings. Its supplier needed its foundry for its own purposes. The taxpayer and three other parties organized a foundry corporation as a source of supply, the taxpayer owning 25% of the stock. Subsequent disposition of the stock of the foundry corporation resulted in a loss which was fully deductible. "Stock purchased as an investment is a capital asset; when sold, it creates capital gain or loss. But stock purchased in the ordinary course of business where the only purpose is to insure a vital source of inventory is not a capital asset, and the loss upon its sale is deductible from ordinary income." *Electrical Fittings Corporation,* 33 T.C. 1026 (1960).

A lumber dealer purchased debentures of a plywood manufacturer in order to insure a course of that material. The cost of the debentures was deductible in full as a business expense or loss upon worthlessness of the debentures when the obligor failed. *Tulane Hardware Lumber Co., Inc.,* 24 T.C. 1146 (1955).

The operator of a bowling alley had been experiencing difficulty in securing an adequate supply of duck pins of good quality. Shares were bought in the stock of a manufacturer, which then gave the taxpayer a 25% reduction in the price of these pins. The stock was not bought as an investment, and ultimate loss was not subject to capital loss limitations. *Arlington Bowling Corporation,* T.C. Memo. 1959–201, filed October 26, 1959.

The purchase of a minority interest (not control) in a corporation solely for the purpose of acquisition of inventory by the exercise of a right vested in the owner to purchase a specific amount of inventory was included in the cost of goods acquired, where the stock was sold forthwith when the inventory rights were acquired. *Charles A. Clark,* 18 T.C. 1090 (1952).

Although most of the litigated cases have involved situations where the taxpayer has purchased a minority capital interest in an already established source of supply (where the capital interest would be more likely to be marketable), the principle is not foreclosed to a corporation's acquiring a high percentage of the controlling interest in another corporation. *Old Dominion Plywood Corporation et al.,* T.C. Memo. 1966–135, filed June 20, 1966. In most cases of this type, the corporations purchased were promptly liquidated and the assets distributed. But the taxpayer still will prevail if there is a good business reason unconnected with investment for allowing the corporate form to continue. *John J. Grier Co. v. United States,* 328 F.2d 163 (7th Cir., 1963).

But the necessary lack of investment motivation is not demonstrated where the acquired stock is held after its retention no longer is necessary. Capital loss treatment was required where stock had been purchased in order to get whiskey rights in the case of a buyer which retained the stock for nine years after the rights had been exercised. The court considered that the long retention of the shares betokened a change of intention to that of *investment. Gulftex Drug Co., Inc.,* 29 T.C. 118 (1957), *aff'd,* 261 F.2d 238 (5th Cir., 1958). A manufacturer of paperboard acquired debentures of a supplier in order to assure a supply of raw materials: specifically, unbleached sulphite pulp. But the demand for such raw materials lessened, and ultimately the manufacturer used a different type of raw material. Sale of the debentures resulted in capital loss; for before the debentures were sold, the original business purpose had changed to an investment purpose motivation. *Missiquoi Corporation,* 37 T.C. 791 (1962). Where stock is acquired to be assured of a source of inventory, the period of holding these shares is not to be deemed unduly long where the problem of obtaining material persists for years. *Old Dominion Plywood Corporation et al.,* T.C. Memo. 1966–135, filed June 20, 1966.

Ordinarily, where stock is acquired in order to get a source of supply, the problem is how to treat the *loss;* for such customarily results, inasmuch as the shares are sold ex-rights or are purchased at too high a price in order to get the inventory. But when gain does result under such circumstances, it is deemed to be ordinary. *Mansfield Journal Company v. Commissioner,* 274 F.2d 284 (6th Cir., 1960).

To Keep A Good Line. The taxpayer, a department store, was requested by the manufacturer of a quality line of ladies' suits to purchase stock so that the manufacturer could expand. The manufacturer stated that unless this was done, the line would be turned over to a competitor of the taxpayer. Resultant loss on the manufacturer's stock was deductible as ordinary and necessary expense, in order to assure a source of supply. *Smith & Welton, Inc. v. United States,* 164 F. Supp. 605 (D.C., E.D. Va., 1958).

To Get An Outlet. A salesman who bought stock in the business of a customer who incorporated could deduct the ultimate worthlessness of this stock as a business expense. The purchase had been for the purpose of assuring the salesman the exclusive orders of the customer, "as the business purpose for which they were held continued until the very day they became worthless." *Hagan et al. v. United States,* 221 F. Supp. 248 (D.C., Ark., 1963).

To Attract Personnel. A manufacturing corporation was unable to attract and to hold competent sales management personnel. The corporation incorporated each of its sales offices, with the objective of selling the stock at book value to capable sales persons, who in time could own their own organizations. In two instances, the ventures were not successful, and the taxpayer corporation re-purchased the shares for ultimate sale to other individuals. Losses on such transactions were not capital. The taxpayer never intended to make a profit from the sale of this stock, either through appreciation or dividends. The stock was held solely for the purpose of selling it, as soon as possible, to qualified managers in order to further the sales of its manufactured products. *Weather-Seal, Inc.,* T.C. Memo. 1963–102, filed April 8, 1963.

To Pay For Services. Where shares of stock were acquired as payment for services, disposition of these shares was not treated as a capital loss. "It is not uncommon for engineering or contracting firms to take their pay in stock. . . . This stock was income when received; it remained income for two years; and thereafter it continued to be 'property held by the taxpayer primarily for sale in the course of his trade or business.' " *Gilbert et al. v. Commissioner,* 56 F.2d 361 (1st Cir., 1932).

To Secure A Lease. A corporation (the taxpayer) operated various restaurants, all adjacent to railroad stations. Declining railroad activity resulted in falling business, and the taxpayer sought a restaurant in a different type of location. A supper club was purchased. Then the taxpayer discovered that the club's lessor had the right to withhold approval to the assignment of the lease to the club's new owner. To protect itself, the taxpayer purchased the stock of the landlord corporation. Subsequent sale of this stock resulted in a loss, which was fully deductible. The stock had been purchased only to secure the lease, and its subsequent sale (to the supper club) achieved this business result. *John J. Grier Co. v. United States,* 328 F.2d 163 (7th Cir., 1963).

To Get Preferential Space. All applicants for concessions at a New York

World's Fair were required to invest in the fair's debentures, which were issued to finance the fair. The taxpayer obtained a concession until the fair closed. Shortly thereafter, the debentures were sold at a loss. It was held that the taxpayer had made an investment in the debentures and that they represented capital assets, loss on the sale of which was a capital loss. The taxpayer could not establish how much of the cost was the payment of a bonus for a desirable location. *Exposition Souvenir Corporation v. Commissioner,* 163 F.2d 283 (2d Cir., 1947).

To Get Rights. Stock of the Federal National Mortgage Association, purchased by a taxpayer (such as a bank or trust company or any other private source dealing in mortgages) in order to enable the taxpayer to sell mortgages to the Association, constituted a capital asset. Revenue Ruling 58–41, 1958–1 CB 86.

To Serve As Security Bond. A manufacturer entered into a contract with a foreign government, under which the manufacturer (the taxpayer) had to deposit United States Government bonds as security for the performance of the contract. When the contract was completed and the bonds were released, they were sold in a few days' time at a loss. This was not a capital loss but was an ordinary and necessary business expense. The cost of procuring security for the performance of the contract was not distinguishable from ordinary premium expense of a surety company, a usual part of a contractor's costs. The bonds were not treated as an investment on the taxpayer's books. *Commissioner v. Bagley & Sewell Co.,* 221 F.2d 944 (2d Cir., 1955).

To Terminate An Agency Contract. A corporation was permitted to deduct as ordinary and necessary business expense the cost of the stock of a company which was the purchaser's selling agency, where it appeared that the purchaser's reputation would have been injured had not this agency been eliminated from the economic scene *via* liquidation. The only way to achieve this result was to purchase the stock, which was not desired as an investment. *Helvering v. Community Bond and Mortgage Corporation,* 74 F.2d 727 (2d Cir., 1935).

To Aid Depressed Businesses. The purchase of stock in a non-profit corporation to aid business was held to be a business expense. Here, the shares were in a corporation that was to assist plans in a depressed area which needed assistance, and no dividends were to be declared. *Commissioner v. The Hub, Incorporated,* 68 F.2d 349 (4th Cir., 1934).

To Circumvent Ceiling Prices. Acquisition of worthless shares as part of a deal to pay over-ceiling prices at a time of price controls was treated as part of the cost of the merchandise. *William Young Co.,* T.C. Memo., Docket No. 30848, entered July 14, 1952.

Other Disallowances

Section 861 of the Code, dealing with foreign corporations, covers income from sources within the United States. "No deduction shall be allowed under this section for the amount of any item or part thereof allocable to a class or classes of exempt income." Regulations Section 1.861–8(d). This could cover bond or other interest.

Gain realized upon the sale of an endowment or annuity contract shortly before its maturity date is not given long-term capital gain treatment. *W. Stanley Barrett et al.*, 42 T.C. 993 (1964).

Other situations of non-recognition of gain or loss in the case of involuntary divestitures (*e.g.*, S.E.C.- or F.C.C.-ordered sales under Sections 1081 and 1071) are covered in Chapter 5. Consideration also is given there to orders enforcing the Anti-Trust Laws (Section 1111).

Chapter 8

Corporate Reorganizations

Stockholder Or Bondholder Interest

A tax-free corporate reorganization may be of tax benefit to the corporation, or to the security holders of all types, or to both. If it is not of tax benefit to them, certainly it is of tax significance to them. Typically, a corporate reorganization may not be effected unless and until there is tax clearance. Thus, in connection with the acquisition of *The Newark Evening News* by Time, Inc. in a stock transaction, the New York *Times* of February 15, 1968 stated: "The acquisition will be made through an exchange of stock . . . subject to a ruling by the Internal Revenue Service that the transaction will be tax-free."

It is not the purpose of this book to describe the ramifications of tax-free reorganizations to the corporation, except insofar as the stockholders or the bondholders may seek to evaluate how they will be affected by what affects the corporation.* But stockholders and bondholders may be affected directly as well as indirectly by a corporate reorganization. A substantial bulk of all of the litigated reorganization cases involves, not the corporation, but the security holders.

Nature Of The Tax-Free Reorganization

"Congress has determined that in certain types of transactions the economic changes are not definitive enough to be given tax consequences, and has clearly provided that gains and losses on such transactions shall not be recognized for income-tax liability but shall be taken into account later."

_____
* See Robert S. Holzman, *Tax-Free Reorganizations* (Lynbrook, New York: Farnsworth Publishing Company, Inc., 1967).

Commissioner v. Wheeler, 324 U.S. 524 (1945). "Congress . . . was trying to give to business enterprises leeway in readjusting their corporate arrangements to better [*sic*] suit their business purposes. If the rearrangement had that purpose, Congress was willing to concede them some possible tax advantages. If the rearrangement had no business purpose, let the taxes fall where they might." *Commissioner v. Wilson et al.,* 353 F.2d 184 (9th Cir., 1965).

It is not only the corporations involved in a tax-free reorganization which are the beneficiaries of this rule that there is no taxable gain upon the receipt of something which is in effect a continuum of what was surrendered. "We cannot conclude that mere change, for purposes of reorganization in the technical ownership of an enterprise . . . followed by issuance of new certificates constitutes gain separated from the original capital interest. Something more is necessary—something which gives the stockholder a thing really different from what he therefore had." *Weiss v. Stearn,* 265 U.S. 242 (1924).

In the case of corporate reorganizations, the question of whether a transaction begets capital or ordinary gain or loss comes up with great frequency, in many variations and ramifications. When something is exchanged for something else, or is changed in form itself, there frequently is some element of gain or loss. What is its character? Typical situations are:

Redemptions of stock. I.R.C. Section 302.

Redemption to pay death taxes. I.R.C. Section 303.

Preferred stock bail-outs. I.R.C. Section 306.

12-month liquidations. I.R.C. Section 337.

Collapsible corporations. I.R.C. Section 341.

Partial liquidations. I.R.C. Section 346.

Receipt of excess principal amount of bonds. I.R.C. Section 355.

Receipt of something in addition to what may be received tax-free. I.R.C. Section 356.

"Inherent in the concept of a 'reorganization' as used in the statute is that there must be a real continuity of interest in the owners of the old corporation and the owners of the new." *Southwell Combing Co.,* 30 T.C. 487 (1958). Usually, the shareholders (at least those who do not own enough stock to be heard at directors' meetings) have little to say about a corporate reorganization, but they are personally affected by it. "What was actually done by the corporation controls the tax consequences to the stockholder." *Sarah A. Young,* T.C. Memo., Docket No. 5557, entered October 30, 1945.

A tax-free reorganization may only be one of the following types, the letters referring to the subparagraph designations of Section 368(a)(1) of the Code:

"(A) a statutory merger or consolidation;

(B) the acquisition by one corporation, in exchange solely for all or a part of its voting stock (or in exchange solely for all or a part of the voting stock of a corporation which is in control of the acquiring corporation), of stock of another corporation if, immediately after the acquisition, the acquiring corporation has control of such other corporation (whether or not such acquiring corporation had control immediately before the acquisition);

(C) the acquisition by one corporation, in exchange solely for all or a part of its voting stock (or in exchange solely for all or a part of the voting stock of a corporation which is in control of the acquiring corporation), of substantially all of the properties of another corporation, but in determining whether the exchange is solely for stock the assumption by the acquiring corporation of a liability of the other, or the fact that property acquired is subject to a liability, shall be disregarded;

(D) a transfer by a corporation of all or a part of its assets to another corporation if immediately after the transfer the transferor, or one or more of its shareholders (including persons who were shareholders immediately before the transfer), or any combination thereof, is in control of the corporation to which the assets are transferred; but only if, in pursuance of the plan, stock or securities of the corporation to which the assets are transferred are distributed in a transaction which qualifies under section 354, 355, or 356 [these sections refer, respectively, to exchanges of stock and securities in certain reorganizations, distribution of stock and securities of a controlled corporation, and receipt of additional consideration];

(E) a recapitalization; or

(F) a mere change in identity, form, or place of organization, however effected."

"The Congress intended to encourage six types of reorganizations. They are defined in § 368 and designated by the letters 'A' through 'F.' The 'A' merger, the 'B' exchange of stock for stock, and the 'C' exchange of stock for substantially all of the properties of another are all amalgamating reorganizations. The 'D' reorganization is the divisive spin-off, while the 'E' and 'F' reorganizations, recapitalizations and reincorporations, are neither amalgamating nor divisive. All are sanctioned equally, however." *Commissioner v. Mary Archer W. Morris Trust,* 367 F.2d 794 (4th Cir., 1966).

If property (including stock or bonds) is disposed of, there is taxable gain or loss to the extent of the difference between the adjusted basis of the asset and what is received for it in cash or other property. But such is not the case in a tax-free reorganization. "Although the Code generally requires immediate recognition of gain or loss upon the sale or exchange of property, certain sections permit consummation of formal business readjustments without immediate taxation of the participating businesses or their shareholders." *J. O. Willett Estate et al. v. Commissioner,* 365 F.2d 760 (5th Cir., 1966).

A tax-free reorganization is tax-free only at the time of its execution. Gain or loss is computed when the transaction has taken on a more complete or definitive form. The asset received takes the basis of the asset surrendered in a completely tax-free reorganization; thus, when the former is disposed of, gain or loss will be determined in the light of the original basis. This is true despite the differences in value between what was relinquished and what was received therefor. "[S]ince it was the intention of Congress not to forgive, but only to defer taxes in the situation where a taxpayer has not received something new in an exchange, Congress also provided that when there has been a 'tax-free' exchange the taxpayer must retain as the tax basis of the property received, the basis of the property which was given in an exchange." *Barker v. United States,* 200 F.2d 223 (9th Cir., 1952).

If in a tax-free reorganization property is received in addition to what may be received tax-free, gain is recognized to the recipient, but not in excess of the amount of the money received plus the fair market value of any other property received. Loss to the recipient is not recognized. I.R.C. Section 356(a).

Dividends

A frequent consequence of a corporate reorganization is that a shareholder will receive something which is taxable as a dividend. Anything which a shareholder received from a corporation which has earnings and profits is presumed to be a dividend under Section 301(a), unless some statutory exception can be found. "To constitute a distribution taxable as a dividend, the benefit received by the shareholders need not be considered as a dividend either by the corporation or its shareholders, declared by the board of directors, nor other formalities of a dividend declaration need be observed, if on all the evidence there is a distribution of available earnings or profits under a claim of right or without expectation of repayment." *Clark v. Commissioner,* 266 F.2d 698 (9th Cir., 1959). "The motive, or expressed intent of the corporation is not determinative, and constructive dividends have been found contrary to the expressed intent of the corporation. The courts, as arbiters of the true nature of corporate payments, have consistently used as a standard the measure of receipt of economic benefit as the proper occasion of taxation." *Sachs v. Commissioner,* 277 F.2d 879 (8th Cir., 1961). Thus, a distribution of corporate property (including shares of another corporation) is treated as a dividend if the amount paid by a stockholder for the property is less than its fair market value. *Lacy et al. v. Commisisoner et al.,* 341 F.2d 54 (10th Cir., 1965). Expenses of a yacht maintained by a corporation for the benefit of a stockholder were deemed to be dividends to him. *Challenge Manufacturing Co.,* 37 T.C. 650 (1962). A dominant stockholder is taxable on a distribution of corporate earnings made at his request to a third party for some purpose that he wishes to serve, although he himself received no economic gain. *Binenstock v. Commissioner,* 321 F.2d 598 (3d Cir., 1963).

A corporation's distribution of earnings to shareholders is a taxable dividend, despite the fact that this may be a distribution of what the corporation received on a tax-free basis, such as municipal bond interest. I.T. 2222, III–2 CB 12.

If a shareholder receives a distribution which is in excess of his *pro rata* share of the corporation's earnings and profits, the excess portion will reduce the adjusted basis of his stock. I.R.C. Section 301(c)(2).

Redemption Of Stock. When a corporation makes a payment to a shareholder in exchange for ownership of his stock, the transaction may resemble, exactly or substantially, either a dividend or a sale. Has the shareholder received a distribution of corporate earnings by virtue of his being a stockholder? If so, he has received a dividend. Has he made a sale of a capital asset to the corporation in the same manner as he might have sold the stock to an outside party? If so, there is a capital transaction. He has the burden of proof as to which it is. The same distribution may be essentially equivalent to a taxable dividend to some stockholders but not to others. Revenue Ruling 56–521, 1956–2 CB 174. Thus it is not the redemption itself that is or is not taxable; it is the redemption of the shares of a particular shareholder.

Redemption of stock refers to any transfer of shares by a stockholder to the issuing corporation for a consideration, whether the corporation in fact redeems the shares or uses them in any other fashion. I.R.C. Section 317(b).

A redemption of a shareholder's stock will not be treated as a dividend if he can establish—

(1) That the redemption was not essentially equivalent to a dividend; or

(2) That there was a substantially disproportionate redemption of stock; or

(3) That the redemption was in complete redemption of all of the stock of the corporation which he owned; or

(4) That the redemption was of stock issued by a railroad corporation (as defined in Section 77(m) of the Bankruptcy Act, as amended), pursuant to a plan of reorganization under that act. I.R.C. Section 302(b).

As to (1), above, capital treatment is provided if the stockholder can prove that the cancellation or redemption of his shares was not "at such time and in such manner as to make it essentially equivalent to the distribution by the corporation of a taxable dividend." *Cote v. Keefe,* D.C., N.H., 1953, *aff'd,* 213 F.2d 651 (1st Cir., 1954). "Dividend equivalence is not an abstraction." *Penfield v. Davis,* 105 F. Supp. 292 (D.C., N.D. Ala., 1952), *aff'd,* 205 F.2d 798 (5th Cir., 1953). It deals with the net economic effect of a transaction. "It is just as if the statute read: 'If a corporation redeems its stock in whole or in part, so that the net effect of the transaction is the same as the payment of a taxable dividend, the amount so distributed shall be treated as a taxable dividend.' " *Commissioner v. Sullivan,* 210 F.2d 607 (5th Cir., 1954).

"The colors of the cloth of dividend equivalency are not completely fast. Indeed, the fabric 'bleeds,' madras-like, to such an extent that the decided cases have been described as a 'morass' . . . and the underlying statutory provisions referred to as 'exasperatingly complex.' " *Henry McK. Hasserot et al.,* 46 T.C. 864 (1966). The infinite variety of "essentially equivalent to a dividend" cases almost defies count.* A sound corporate business purpose may indicate that the redemption was not primarily for the benefit of stockholders and did not have the effect of a dividend. But "the existence of a sound business purpose will not, of itself, require that the transaction be classified as 'not essentially equivalent to a dividend.' " *Charles Swan et al.,* 42 T.C. 291 (1964), *aff'd,* 355 F.2d 795 (6th Cir., 1966). And "[w]hile the absence of any valid corporate purpose as motivating the redemption might constitute substantial evidence indicating that the redemption was essentially equivalent to a dividend, we do not believe that the presence of such corporate purpose establishes, *per se,* nonequivalence." *Neff et al. v. United States,* 305 F.2d 455 (Ct. Cl., 1962).

As to (2), above, capital treatment is provided for an amount received in redemption of stock if—

(a) Immediately after the redemption the shareholder owns less than 50% of the total combined voting power of all classes of stock.

(b) The ratio which the voting stock he owns immediately after the redemption bears to the total voting stock at that time is less than 80% of the ratio which his stock owned immediately before the redemption bears to the total voting stock at that time. The same percentage rule applies to his total common stockholdings, whether voting or non-voting.

(c) The redemption is not pursuant to a plan the purpose or effect of

---

* For an analysis of many hundred cases involving this question, see Paul D. Seghers, William J. Reinhart, and Selwyn Nimaroff, *Essentially Equivalent To A Dividend* (New York: The Ronald Press Company, 1960).

which is a series of redemptions resulting in a distribution which (in the aggregate) is substantially disproportionate with respect to him. Regulations Section 1.302–3(a).

For the purpose of (2), above [substantially disproportionate redemption of stock] and of (3), following [complete elimination of a shareholder], constructive ownership rules apply. An individual is deemed to own:

(a) Stock owned, directly or indirectly, by his spouse, children, grand-children, and parents.

(b) Stock owned, directly or indirectly, by or for a partnership or estate, to the extent of his *pro rata* interest as a partner or beneficiary.

(c) Stock owned, directly or indirectly, by or for a trust (other than an exempt employees' trust), to the extent that he is a beneficiary in this trust.

(d) Stock owned, directly or indirectly, by a corporation, to the extent of his proportionate stock ownership of this corporation, if he has a 50% or greater stock interest in this corporation.

(e) Stock covered by an option for its acquisition. I.R.C. Section 318(a).

As to (3), above, capital treatment is provided if the redemption is in complete redemption of all of the shares that a stockholder owns in the issuing corporation. The constructive ownership rules must be applied. Thus, an individual has not redeemed all of his shares if some stock is still held by relatives designated in the constructive ownership rules discussed under Section 318 in the preceding paragraph. But the constructive owner-ship rules will not be applied if:

(a) Immediately after the redemption the taxpayer has no interest in the corporation (such as officer, director, or employee), except an interest as a creditor;

(b) The taxpayer does not acquire any such interest (except stock he inherits) within ten years from the date of redemption; and

(c) The taxpayer, in accordance with the regulations, files an agree-ment to notify the Secretary of the Treasury or his delegates of any acquisition described in (b). I.R.C. Section 302(c)(2).

The redemption of preferred stock may be treated as a dividend as well as the more usual redemption of common. *Commissioner v. Berenbaum,* 369 F.2d 337 (10th Cir., 1966). But a dividend was not found where the redemption was not on a *pro rata* basis. The court pointed out in this case that the corporation had a good dividend-paying record. *Arthur F. Hinrich-sen Estate,* T.C. Memo. 1966–271, filed December 19, 1966.

Where the redemption of his shares by a corporation might have dividend implications, a shareholder could sell his stock to an outside party on a capital basis. *Stanley D. Beard,* 4 T.C. 756 (1945).

Redemption Of Stock To Pay Death Taxes. A redemption of stock to pay death taxes is treated as a capital transaction, without dividend implications, if the stock that is being redeemed has been included in the decedent's gross estate for Federal estate tax purposes to the extent of more than (1) 35% of the value of the gross estate or (2) 50% of the value of the taxable estate. For the purposes of these percentage requirements, stock of two or more corporations is treated as the stock of a single corporation if more than 75% in value of the outstanding stock of each corporation is included in the decedent's gross estate. I.R.C. Section 303.

This rule applies only to the extent that the stock is redeemed for the purpose of paying death taxes, a term which for this purpose includes the estate, inheritance, legacy, and succession taxes imposed by reason of the decedent's death, together with funeral and administrative expenses allowed as deductions on the estate tax return.

The rule applies to redemptions made after the death of the decedent and (1) before expiration of the 3-year period of limitations for the assessment of the estate tax, or within ninety days after the expiration of that period or (2) if a petition has been filed with the Tax Court, within sixty days after that court's decision becomes final.

The amount of stock which may be redeemed under Section 303 to pay death taxes at capital gains rates does not include a widow's award as made by a state court. *Majeros v. Coyle, Jr.,* 254 F. Supp. 214 (D.C., N.D. Ill., 1966).

Redemption Through Use of Related Corporation. Section 304 was enacted to prevent controlling stockholders from withdrawing earnings and profits from one of two controlled corporations at capital gains rates through the simple device of selling the stock of one corporation to the other corporation. There are separate rules for each of the following situations:

(1) Brother-sister corporations: that is, where the same persons own the shares of both corporations, which are not related except through stock ownership.

(2) Parent-subsidiary corporations, where the parent owns 50% or more of the stock of the subsidiary.

As to (1), if a corporation, B, in return for property, acquires stock of another corporation, S, from one or more persons and the person or persons from whom the S stock was acquired were in control of both such corporations before the acquisition, then the property will be treated as received in redemption of the stock of the acquiring corporation (B). The stock received (S) by the acquiring corporation (B) will be treated as a contribution to the capital of that corporation (B). The transferor's basis for his stock in the acquiring corporation (B) will be increased by the basis of the stock (S) surrendered by him. As to each person transferring stock, the amount received by him will be treated as a dividend, unless he can establish that this is a capital transaction under Section 302(a) or Section 303, discussed above. The constructive ownership rules mentioned under Section 302 apply for the purpose of establishing that there is control through stock ownership of 50% or more, except that Rule (d) as mentioned there will be applied without regard to its regular 50% limitation.

As to (2), if a subsidiary corporation, S, in return for property, acquires from a shareholder of the parent corporation, P, stock in that corporation (P), then this property will be considered as a distribution in redemption of P Corporation. Here, again, 50% or more stock is necessary to constitute control, although for most reorganization purposes a figure of 80% is necessary for the concept of control.

Persons controlling a corporation, P, which itself controls another corporation, S, are deemed to control the latter corporation, S, as well. *Radnitz, Jr. et al. v. United States,* 294 F.2d 577 (2d Cir., 1961).

A redemption may constitute a "distribution in redemption of the stock" within the meaning of Section 304 without being a dividend under Section 302. *Salvatori et al. v. United States,* D.C., S.D. Cal., 1966.

Distributions Of Stock And Stock Rights

"The right to subscribe to the new stock was but a right to participate, in preference to strangers and on equal terms with other existing stockholders, in the privilege of contributing new capital called for by the corporation— an equity that inheres in stock ownership under such circumstances as a quality represented by the old stock. . . . The stockholder's right to take part of the new shares therefore—assuming their intrinsic value to have exceeded the issuing price—was essentially analogous to a stock dividend." *Miles v. Safe Deposit and Trust Co. of Baltimore,* 259 U.S. 247 (1922).

Stock dividends are distributions paid in the stock of the corporation making the distribution. Such a dividend is not taxable, unless it is in lieu of money, which covers either of two situations:

(1) If the stock dividend is made in discharge of preferred stock dividends for the corporation for the taxable year of the distribution or of the immediately preceding year.

(2) If the dividend, at the election of any shareholder, is payable either in cash or in stock. I.R.C. Section 305.

The rule applies both to the distribution of stock and of rights. If the dividend is not taxable by virtue of Section 305, it is immaterial whether the distribution is of treasury stock.

If a taxpayer receives a tax-free stock dividend, the adjusted basis of the stock upon which the dividend is received becomes the basis both for the original stock and for the stock dividend. This total basis must be apportioned between the old and the new stock. I.R.C. Section 307(a).

Thus, if a taxpayer owned one share of stock which had cost $45 and he receives a stock dividend of two additional shares, each share would have a basis of $15.

If the receipt of rights is tax-free and, at the time these rights are distributed, their fair market value is less than 15% of the fair market value of the stock upon which they are issued (the old stock), the basis of the rights will be zero unless the taxpayer elects to have the following allocation apply. The adjusted basis of the old stock is allocated between the old stock and that part of the new stock or rights which is not includible in gross income, in proportion to the fair market values of each on the date of distribution. I.R.C. Section 307(b).

Assume that an individual held 100 shares of stock at a cost of $22 per share. The corporation gave him ten stock rights, allowing him to purchase ten additional shares of stock at $26 a share. At the time the rights were distributed, the stock had a market value of $30, ex-rights, and each right had a market value of $3. The taxpayer elected to allocate a portion of the basis of his stock to the rights. The basis of the rights, and of the old and the new stock, is computed as follows:

100 shares × $22 = $2,200, cost of old stock in respect of which rights were acquired.

100 shares × $30 = $3,000, market value of old stock.

10 rights at $3 = $30, market value of rights.

$\dfrac{3,000}{3,030}$ × $2,200 = $2,178.22, cost of old stock apportioned to such stock.

$\dfrac{30}{3,030}$ × $2,200 = $21.78, cost of old stock apportioned to the rights.

If the rights are sold, the basis for determining gain or loss is $2.178 per right. If the rights are exercised, the original basis of the new stock acquired is the subscription price paid ($26) plus the basis of the rights exercised ($2.178 each), or $28.178 per share. The remaining basis of the 100 shares of old stock for the purpose of determining gain or loss on a subsequent sale is $2,178.22, or $21.7822 per share.

The mere issue of rights to subscribe and their receipt by shareholders is not a dividend. *Palmer v. Commissioner,* 302 U.S. 63 (1937). But where this is coupled with the fact that, at the time of the distribution of rights, there is a spread between the fair market value of the stock and the purchase price as called for by the rights, an intention to declare a dividend is indicated. The amount of the dividend, determinable at the time the shareholder of the distributing corporation exercises his stock rights, is the lower of the spread on the date of issue or the spread on the date of exercise. *Commissioner v. Baan et al.,* 382 F.2d 485 (9th Cir., 1967), *aff'd,* 391 U.S. 83 (1968).

The date of distribution of stock dividends or rights is the date of distribution to the shareholder and not the record date. Regulations Section 1.307–1(a).

The election as to allocation of rights is in the form of a statement attached to the shareholder's Federal income tax return for the year in which the rights are received. This election is irrevocable with respect to the rights for which the election was made. Regulations Section 1.307–2.

Section 306 Stock

A very dangerous type of stock dividend is in the form of what is known as "Section 306 stock." Section 306 stock is any stock received as a tax-free stock dividend (except common stock issued with respect to other common stock), at a time when the issuing corporation had earnings and profits. The term may apply to stock received in a tax-free corporate reorganization or a corporate separation (spin-off, etc.), if the effect of that transaction was substantially the same as the receipt of a stock dividend. I.R.C. Section 306. Common stock may be treated as Section 306 stock if it has characteristics more typical of preferred stock than of common, such as a mandatory annual redemption provision. *Henry A. Rosenberg Estate,* 36 T.C. 716 (1961).

By definition, Section 306 stock is stock that is *received* as a tax-free stock dividend. But *disposition* generally is another matter. Here there are two major tax possibilities:

(1) If a shareholder sells his Section 306 stock or otherwise disposes of it other than by redemption, his gain will be treated as ordinary income to the extent that the fair market value of the stock sold (on the date the stock was distributed to him) would have been a dividend had he received cash rather than the stock: that is, if he had received his *pro rata* share of the corporation's earnings and profits in cash. Any excess of the proceeds of the stock over the amount treated as ordinary income plus the adjusted

basis of the stock is treated as capital gain. There is no loss recognized upon the disposition of Section 306 stock.

(2) If a shareholder redeems his Section 306 stock, the entire proceeds will be treated as a dividend. The amount of the earnings and profits of the corporation at the time the stock was issued is immaterial. I.R.C. Section 306(a)(1), (2).

If any change is made in the terms and conditions of the stock, a shareholder's ratable share of corporate earnings and profits will be the higher of the figure at the time the stock was issued or the time when the modification took place. I.R.C. Section 306(g).

Section 306 does not come into play in these situations:

(1) If a shareholder completely terminates his stock interest in a corporation other than by redemption or by a disposition to a person covered by the stock attribution rules.

(2) If there is a redemption of stock in complete or partial liquidation of the corporation.

(3) If the stock is disposed of in a tax-free corporate reorganization or in a tax-free exchange.

(4) If the Commissioner of Internal Revenue is satisfied that the disposition or redemption was not in pursuance of a plan having as one of its principal purposes the avoidance of Federal income tax. I.R.C. Section 306(b). For example, Section 306 stock might be given to a charitable organization with no understanding as to what that organization would do with the stock and with no understanding that the shares would be redeemed. Revenue Ruling 57–328, 1957–2 CB 227.

When Section 306 stock is issued as a tax-free stock dividend, there is an allocation of basis between this stock and the stock with respect to which it was issued. This allocated basis of the Section 306 stock is taken into account when that stock is sold but not when it is redeemed.

Imputed Earnings And Profits

The amount of a corporation's earnings and profits is of great concern to the shareholders, for a distribution can be treated as a taxable dividend only to the extent of the corporation's earnings and profits. "It is well settled that earnings and profits is a statutory concept which is not identical with either earnings (or earned surplus) as determined by corporate accounting practice, or taxable income as computed under the Internal Revenue Code." *Bloch et al. v. United States,* 261 F. Supp. 597 (D.C., S.D. Texas, 1966). For that reason, a dividend might be found even where the corporation's certified balance sheet showed no earnings or profits, or earnings and profits that were less than the amount of the distribution. "For some purposes, it may be entirely true that general financial statements do not always reflect all information pertinent to tax liability." *Dunning et al. v. United States,* 353 F.2d 940 (8th Cir., 1965).

This creates a very dangerous and frequently unsuspected tax trap. A shareholder may be taxed upon distributions which clearly appeared *not* to be dividends because of the absence of corporate earnings. The explanation is that under certain circumstances, a corporation will be deemed to have inherited for tax purposes the earnings and profits of a predecessor corporation.

If a corporation is a successor in a tax-free reorganization to another corporation which had earnings and profits at the time of the reorganization, the successor is deemed to have taken over the earnings and profits of the predecessor for tax purposes. Thus, even if the successor corporation had earnings and profits of its own that were insufficient to cover a distribution to shareholders, this distribution nonetheless will be treated as a taxable dividend if the predecessor's earnings and profits plus those of the successor would support a dividend. *Commissioner v. Sansome,* 60 F.2d 931 (2d Cir., 1932).

This refers to such tax-free reorganizations as a merger or consolidation, or the complete liquidation of a subsidiary into its parent corporation.

Even though a particular stockholder was not the owner of shares at the time of the reorganization, this treatment applies. *Commissioner v. Munter,* 331 U.S. 210 (1947).

If the predecessor corporation had a deficit in its earnings and profits account, earnings and profits of the successor corporation may be reduced by this deficit, provided that the successor had no earnings and profits of its own at the time of the reorganization which would indicate that the reorganization was for the purpose of this deficit carryover. *United States v. Snider,* 224 F.2d 165 (1st Cir., 1955).

Distributions In Liquidation

When a corporation is liquidated in whole or in part, amounts received by the shareholders are treated as if stock had been sold back to the corporation. That is, there is capital gain or loss. I.R.C. Section 331. If the corporation is deemed to be a collapsible one, however, ordinary income customarily results. This will be discussed later in the chapter.

"Complete and partial liquidations are treated, for the purpose of the statute, as sales with a consequent measure of gain or loss, even though the proceeds may to some extent be derived from earnings." *Zenz v. Quinlivan,* 213 F.2d 914 (6th Cir., 1954).

A parent corporation derives no taxable gain or loss upon the complete liquidation of a corporation in which there is an 80% or greater stock interest, if the reorganization is completed within three years. I.R.C. Section 332. But a minority stockholder in the liquidated corporation must determine gain or loss in the usual manner; it is only the parent corporation which has a tax-free liquidation in the case of the liquidated corporation. Regulations Section 1.332–5.

Qualified Electing Shareholders. Under certain circumstances, a corporation may be liquidated without gain to its shareholders, subject to certain limitations on such non-recognition with respect to earnings and profits of the corporation accumulated after February 28, 1913 and stock and securities acquired by the corporation after December 31, 1953. Here are the conditions:

(1) The corporation must be completely liquidated within one calendar month of the taxable year.

(2) The special tax treatment applies only to shareholders who affirmatively have elected to become *qualified electing shareholders.*

(3) The required minimum number of shares was the subject of such elections. I.R.C. Section 333.

Shareholders fall into one of two categories for this purpose: corporate and non-corporate. In the case of corporate stockholders, the owner of 50% or more of the shares is not eligible for Section 333 treatment and is called an *excluded corporation.* If elections have been filed by the owners of 80% or more of the remaining corporate-owned shares, all corporations so voting are treated as qualified electing shareholders.

In the case of non-corporate shareholders, if elections are filed by the owners of 80% or more of the stock which is not owned by corporations, the shareholders so voting are treated as qualified electing shareholders.

Thus, either or both of the corporate owners and the non-corporate owners may be treated as qualified electing shareholders, regardless of how the other category votes. But even if a category (such as non-corporate owners) is entitled to become qualified electing shareholders because 80% or more of such stock so elected, shareholders whose stock was not so elected are not entitled to this treatment.

The election is made by filing Form 964 within thirty days after the corporation adopts a plan of complete liquidation. This is an irrevocable election.

Only so much of the gain on each share of stock owned by a qualified electing shareholder at the time of the adoption of the plan of liquidation is recognized as does not exceed the greater of:

(1) The share's ratable proportion of the corporation's earnings and profits accumulated after February 28, 1913, computed as of the last day of the month of liquidation, without diminution by reason of distributions made during that month, and including in the computation all items of income and expense accrued up to the date on which the transfer of all the property under the liquidation is completed; or

(2) The share's ratable proportion of the sum of the amount of money received by the stockholder on shares of the same class and the fair market value of all the stock or securities so received which were acquired by the liquidating corporation after December 31, 1953.

In the case of a qualified electing shareholder other than a corporation, that part of the recognized gain on a share of stock owned at the time of the adoption of the plan of liquidation which is not in excess of his ratable share of the liquidating corporation's earnings and profits accumulated after February 28, 1913 is treated as a dividend. It retains its character as a dividend for all tax purposes. The remainder of the gain which is recognized is treated as capital gain (long-term or short-term, as the case may be). In the case of a qualified electing shareholder which is a corporation, the entire amount of the gain which is recognized is treated as capital. Regulations Section 1.333–4(b).

Basis Of Property Received In Liquidation

If property is received in a distribution in partial or complete liquidation of a corporation, and if gain or loss is recognized on the receipt of this property, the basis of the property in the hands of the stockholder is the fair market value of the property at the time of the distribution. This does not apply in the case of a qualified electing shareholder nor in the case of the complete liquidation of a subsidiary corporation. I.R.C. Section 334.

A corporation owning 80% or more of the stock of a liquidating subsidiary corporation has a choice of several basis treatments; but such an election has no effect upon the tax treatment of individual shareholders or of a corporation with a minority interest.

"Who Makes The Sale?"

When a corporation is liquidated, there is a persistent problem as to who should be taxed upon the sale of its assets: (1) the corporation when the sale is made and (as a duplicating tax) the shareholders when they receive distributions representing their shares of the profit on the sale; (2) the stockholders on the theory that the liquidating corporation was acting as their agent; or (3) the corporation on the theory that the shareholders who completed a sale of corporate assets may merely have been putting a formal touch to a transaction which previously the corporation had negotiated. The problem is compounded when the corporate officers and the shareholders are the same persons, so that it is not clear whether they are acting for the corporation or for the stockholders.

The problem may be resolved and double or duplicating tax may be avoided if the corporation is able to meet the requirements of Section 337. The corporation will have no gain or loss to report upon the sale of its assets if the corporation is completely liquidated within a period of twelve months after the adoption of the plan of liquidation, provided that all inventory items are sold to a single person in a single transaction. Only the shareholders are taxed.

This treatment does not extend to collapsible corporations.

Collapsible Corporations

A collapsible corporation is one that is used to convert ordinary income into capital gain by one of these two principal techniques:

(1) A corporation has unrealized gains from the enhancement in value of its assets; but before the corporation has realized (taxable) gain, the company is liquidated and the shareholders receive the difference between the cost of their stock and the appreciated value of the assets at capital gains rates: that is, redemption of stock upon the complete liquidation of the corporation.

(2) A corporation has assets which have appreciated in value; but before the assets are sold at ordinary income rates, the shareholders sell their stock, which, because of the unrealized appreciation, is worth more than it had cost.

An example of (1) is a corporation which, with the funds supplied by shareholders, buys film and properties, pays salaries, and makes a motion picture. The completed footage is worth more than the corporation had paid for raw materials and wages. Thus, the shareholders, upon the liquidation of the corporation, receive at capital gains rates property which includes a profit element that would have been taxed as ordinary income had the corporation not been liquidated or even created in the first instance. An example of (2) is a corporation that is used to manufacture or to buy whiskey. As the whiskey ages, it becomes more valuable. The shareholders sell their stock at capital gains rates. Had the whiskey been sold by the corporation or had the corporation never been utilized, there would have been ordinary income.

Section 341 of the Code was enacted to prevent this conversion of ordinary income into capital gain. It provides that if the conditions of the statute are met, the shareholders' gain that would have been capital under the regular tax law will be treated as ordinary income to the shareholders. If the corporation is deemed to be collapsible, it is the shareholders who feel the entire tax impact.

A collapsible corporation is one that was formed or used principally to manufacture or to buy certain designated types of property (known as Section 341 assets), or to hold stock in a corporation formed for such purpose, with a view to the shareholders selling the stock or liquidating the corporation before the corporation realized a substantial part of the taxable income to be derived from the property. Section 341 property embraces the following, if held for less than three years:

(1) Property held primarily for sale to customers in the ordinary course of the trade or business.

(2) Property used in the trade or business, as defined in Chapter 2 as Section 1231 assets, except machinery, etc., used to produce inventory.

(3) Unrealized receivables or fees.

"The purpose of this provision was to prevent taxpayers from forming or using a corporation for the purpose of converting gains and profits which generally would be taxable as ordinary income to gains and profits taxable at the lower capital gains rates." *Steves III et al. v. United States,* D.C., W.D. Texas, 1966. "The collapsible corporation provision as literally written applies regardless of whether the assets constructed by the corporation would have produced capital gain or ordinary income if constructed and sold by the shareholder. Although this occasionally produces unwarranted taxation of capital gains as ordinary income, for the courts to rewrite the very complex legislation embodied in . . . § 341 of the 1954 Code would produce even more confusion." *Braunstein et al. v. Commissioner,* 305 F.2d 949 (2d Cir., 1962), *aff'd,* 374 U.S. 65 (1963).

Section 341 condemns to ordinary income status not only the gain which might result from a sale or exchange, but also the gain resulting from a corporation's distributions to its shareholders. *Gelfand et al. v. United States,* 375 F.2d 807 (Ct. Cl., 1967). The characterization of collapsible corporation is not limited to corporations which were set up to be liquidated within a short time after incorporation. Any corporation may be availed of for the forbidden purpose and thus may be a collapsible corporation. *Glicksman v. Commissioner,* 256 F.2d 108 (2d Cir., 1958).

The key phrase in determining whether a collapsible corporation exists is "with a view to. . . ." Was it the intention that the corporation be collapsed before realization of income? "It is well settled that the requisite view exists if the intention to distribute funds is formed at any time prior to the completion of the construction [or production, etc.]." *Jesse Hartman,* 34 T.C. 1085 (1960), *aff'd,* 296 F.2d 726 (2d Cir., 1961). If the collapse of the corporation or the sale of its stock is attributable solely to circumstances which arose after the manufacture, production, purchase, etc., of the assets (other than circumstances which reasonably could be anticipated at the time of manufacture, production, purchase, etc.), the corporation will be deemed not to have been formed with a view to collapse, unless there is compelling evidence to the contrary. But if the collapse is attributable to circumstances present at the time of manufacture, production, purchase, etc., the corporation will be deemed to be collapsible unless the contrary can be established. Regulations Section 1.341–2(a)(3).

A taxpayer's purpose can change during the course of his holding of property, and in such cases it is the dominant purpose of his holding during the period prior to the sale which is critical. *Tibbals et al. v. United States,* 362 F.2d 266 (Ct. Cl., 1966).

There is a refutable presumption that a corporation is collapsible if at the time of its liquidation or the sale of its stock (1) the fair market value of its Section 341 assets constitutes 50% or more of the fair market value of its total assets and (2) the fair market value of the Section 341 assets is 120% of the adjusted basis of these assets. Cash and capital assets are not taken into account in arriving at fair market value of the total assets. I.R.C. Section 341(c).

There also is a presumption that a corporation is collapsible if:

(1) A shareholder sells his stock or receives a liquidating dividend or a distribution in excess of the basis of his stock;

(2) He receives gain attributable to Section 341 assets;

(3) The manufacturing, production, purchase, etc., of these assets was a substantial activity of the corporation; and

(4) The corporation had not by that time derived a substantial part of the taxable income to be derived from this property. Regulations Section 1.341–5(b).

Collapsible corporation treatment does not apply if any of these circumstances exists:

(1) The shareholder does not, at any time after the actual commencement of the manufacture, purchase, etc., of the assets or at any time thereafter own more than 5% of the corporation's stock.

(2) If not more than 70% of the gain recognized during a taxable year upon the stock in a collapsible corporation is attributable to Section 341 assets. If more than 70% of the gain is from this source, all is considered to be; if less, none.

(3) If any part of the shareholder's gain is realized more than three years after the actual completion of the manufacture, etc., of the Section 341 assets, collapsible corporation treatment does not apply to that part. I.R.C. Section 341(d).

The constructive ownership rules apply to (1).

There are four other areas where, in limited situations, collapsible corporation treatment is not applied:

(1) Sales or exchanges of stock (other than to the issuing corporation or to stipulated related persons).

(2) Certain distributions in complete liquidation taxed as capital gains under Section 331.

(3) Certain complete liquidations which are not taxed by virtue of Section 333.

(4) Certain sales or exchanges of property by a corporation under Section 337. I.R.C. Section 341(e).

Partial Liquidations

A distribution in partial liquidation of a corporation is treated as a return of capital rather than as a dividend. For this purpose, the distribution may not be essentially equivalent to a dividend and it must occur within the taxable year in which the plan of partial liquidation is adopted or in the following year. I.R.C. Section 346.

A distribution is deemed to be in partial liquidation if there is a termination of a corporation's business and these circumstances exist:

(1) The distribution is attributable to the termination of a trade or business which has been conducted actively for at least five years immediately before the distribution.

(2) Immediately after this distribution, the corporation was actively engaged in the conduct of a trade or business which was conducted actively throughout that 5-year period. I.R.C. Section 346(b).

Ordinarily, the partial liquidation results from a contraction of the business. The business continues to be carried on but in such a manner that the same amount of capital no longer is committed to the enterprise, and the partial liquidation represents a return of capital which once was needed but no longer is.

But there may be a valid liquidation without a contraction of the business, as where a corporation reduces its outstanding stock to improve its financial statement.

The transfer by a shareholder of his stock to the issuing corporation may fit the language both of Section 302(b)(3) [complete elimination of a shareholder] and Section 346 [partial liquidation]. Where such is the case, Section 346 will govern the tax treatment. Regulations Section 1.346–2.

Transfer To A Controlled Corporation

Ordinarily, if a taxpayer sells or exchanges property, he has taxable gain or loss. This rule, if applied to the exchange of property for stock in a newly-created corporation, might discourage the formation of corporations with valid business reasons for existence. Accordingly, the Code provides non-recognition of gain or loss if a taxpayer transfers property to a corporation solely for its stock, provided that, immediately after the transaction, he is in control of the corporation to which the property is transferred. If several transferors are involved, the transferors collectively must control the corporation. This rule "does not exempt from taxation entirely gain on property transferred in qualified transactions but merely postpones the recognition of that gain until the property is transferred in a taxable transaction." *Connolly Tool & Engineering Co.,* T.C. Memo. 1964–202, filed July 27, 1964.

"Control" for this purpose means at least 80% of the total combined voting power of all classes of stock entitled to vote and at least 80% of the total number of shares of all other classes of stock. I.R.C. Section 351(a).

It is not required that the transferors receive stock in proportion to the property they transfer. But if the stock received is disproportionate to the property transferred, the Internal Revenue Service may determine that the variance is attributable to an element of compensation, gift, or other taxable event; and the transaction may be taxed accordingly. Regulations Section 1.351–1(b)(1).

If the transferors receive anything other than stock or securities for the property transferred to the corporation, any gain is taxable, but not in excess of the boot received: that is, the property in addition to stock or securities. No loss is recognized in the case of receipt of boot. I.R.C. Section 351(b). Money is boot. *Burr Oaks Corporation v. Commissioner,* 365 F.2d 24 (7th Cir., 1966).

Stock rights are not stocks or securities. *Commissioner v. Baan et al.,* 382 F.2d 485 (9th Cir., 1967), *aff'd,* 391 U.S. 83 (1968).

The general rule of Section 351 does not apply (that is, gain or loss will be recognized) where property was transferred to an investment company after June 30, 1967. A transfer of property after that date will be considered to be a transfer to an investment company if:

(1) The transfer results, directly or indirectly, in diversification of the transferors' interests, and

(2) The transferee is (a) a regulated investment company, (b) a real estate investment trust, or (c) a corporation more than 80% of the value of the assets of which (excluding cash and non-convertible debt obligations from consideration) are held for investment and are readily marketable stocks or securities, or interests in regulated investment companies or real estate investment trusts. Regulations Section 1.351–1(c)(1).

Stocks and securities will be considered readily marketable if (and only if) they are part of a class of stock or securities which is traded on a securities exchange or traded or regularly quoted in the over-the-counter market. Regulations Section 1.351–1(c)(3).

In applying (c), above, stock and securities in subsidiary corporations will be disregarded and the parent corporation will be deemed to own its ratable share of its subsidiaries' assets. A corporation will be considered a subsidiary if the parent owns 50% or more of (1) the combined voting power of all classes of stock entitled to vote or (2) the total value of shares of all classes of stock outstanding. Regulations Section 1.351–1(c)(4).

"A transfer ordinarily results in the diversification of the transferors' interests if two or more persons transfer nonidentical assets to a corporation in the exchange. For this purpose, if any transaction involves two or more transfers of nonidentical assets which, taken in the aggregate, constitute an insignificant portion of the total value of assets transferred, such transferor shall be disregarded in determining whether diversification has occurred. If there is only one transferor (or two or more transferors of identical assets) to a newly organized company, the transfer will generally be treated as not resulting in diversification. If a transfer is part of a plan to achieve diversification without recognition of gain, such as a plan which contemplates a subsequent transfer, however delayed, of the corporate assets (or of the stock or securities received in the earlier exchange) to an investment company in a transaction purporting to qualify for nonrecognition treatment, the original transfer will be treated as resulting in diversification." Regulations Section 1.351–1(c)(5).

Exchanges Of Stock And Securities
In Certain Reorganizations

No gain or loss is recognized to a shareholder who surrenders his stock in exchange for other stock, or to a security holder who surrenders his securities for stock, provided the exchange is pursuant to a plan of reorganization. The stock and securities surrendered, as well as those received, must be those of a corporation which is a party to the reorganization. I.R.C. Section 354(a)(1).

If a greater *principal amount* of securities is received than the principal amount of the securities which are surrendered, the excess principal amount is taxable as boot. I.R.C. Section 354(a)(2). There is no comparable rule in the case of receipt of a larger amount of stock than is surrendered.

Exchanges of stock and securities are tax-free under Section 354 only if a transferor corporation transfers all or substantially all of its assets to a single corporation. Its remaining properties (if any) and the stock, securities, and other properties received in the exchange must be distributed by the corporate transferor to its shareholders or security holders in pursuance of the plan of reorganization. I.R.C. Section 354(b).

Distribution Of Stock And Securities
Of A Controlled Corporation

Ordinarily, a distribution to a shareholder from his corporation at a time when it has earnings and profits is treated as a taxable dividend. But an exception is made in the case of a corporate separation under Section 355. "[T]he general purpose of Congress in sanctioning, in proper cases, tax-free spin-offs was to permit the real owners of enterprises to rearrange their units and evidences of ownership to suit their own ideas of how best to carry on their businesses." *Commissioner v. Wilson et al.,* 353 F.2d 184 (9th Cir., 1965).

The objective of the divisive reorganization is to give stockholders of a corporation controlled by them the privileges of separating or "spinning off" from their corporation a part of its assets and liabilities, so that the separated part may be lodged in another corporation which is controlled by the same stockholders. Inasmuch as the real owners of the assets are the same persons who owned them before, the statute allows these shareholders to have their real ownership divided into smaller corporations than the original company, if there is any non-tax reason for this action. For example, where a corporation's efficiency was impaired by the existence of a department of a nature alien to the remainder of the operation, a corporate separation was justified. *Commissioner v. Mary Archer W. Morris Trust,* 367 F.2d 794 (4th Cir., 1966).

A *spin-off* occurs where a part of the assets of a corporation is transferred to a new corporation, the stock of which is distributed to the shareholders of the old corporation without the surrender by them of stock in the old corporation. A *split-off* involves the same kind of transaction except that the shareholders surrender part of their stock in the old corporation (the parent) in exchange for stock in the new company (the subsidiary). In a *split-up,* the parent corporation transfers substantially all of its assets to two or more corporations and then liquidates, its stockholders surrendering all of their stock in the parent corporation and receiving the stock of the new corporation. All three forms of divisive reorganization are to be tested under the provisions of Section 355. *Commissioner v. Baan et al.,* 382 F.2d 485 (9th Cir., 1967), *aff'd,* 391 U.S. 83 (1968).

Section 355(a) provides that (1) if a corporation distributes to its stockholders with respect to their stock, solely stock of a corporation which is controlled immediately before the distribution, (2) the transaction was not used principally as a device for distributing the earnings or profits of either corporation, (3) the specific requirements of Subsection (b) with reference to the active conduct of the business are satisfied, and (4) all of the stock of the controlled corporation held by the distributing corporation is distributed, then the shareholders will not have gain or loss recognized to them on receipt of the stock. The distribution of shares of the separated corporation need not be on a *pro rata* basis, nor need the arrangement call for the shareholder to surrender any of his stock in the original corporation.

This rule applies only if the distributing corporation and the controlled corporation are engaged immediately after the distribution in the active conduct of a trade or business. "Trade or business" means the active carrying on of a business as opposed to the passive receipt of income. But it is not necessary that the original corporation have been engaged in more than one trade or business in order to have a tax-free divisive reorganization. The trade or business must have been conducted actively throughout the 5-year period ending on the date of the distribution. I.R.C. Section 355(b).

The fundamental basis of non-recognition of gain or loss under Section 355 is that no tax should be imposed when the same people continue to own the same businesses with only formal changes in the business organization. Consistent with that concept, Section 355 provides that distributions made pursuant to that section must be made pursuant to a plan which contemplates distribution to the shareholders of the distributing corporation of a controlling portion of the stock or securities of the controlled corporation. *Commissioner v. Baan et al.,* 382 F.2d 485 (9th Cir., 1967) *aff'd,* 391 U.S. 83 (1968).

Securities received in a divisive reorganization which otherwise would be tax-free lose this exemption if the principal amount of the securities in the controlled corporation which are received exceeds the principal amount of the securities which are surrendered (if any) in connection with this distribution. I.R.C. Section 355(a)(3). Any additional property received (including excess principal amount of securities) is treated as boot. Regulations Section 1.355–2(a).

There must be a non-tax reason for the divisive reorganization, which usually is referred to as the sound business purpose. *Commissioner v. Wilson et al.,* 353 F.2d 184 (9th Cir., 1966). Ordinary dividend treatment is accorded to a divisive reorganization if the transaction is used principally as a device for distributing earnings to the shareholders of any corporation that is a party to the reorganization. *Commissioner v. Baan et al.,* 382 F.2d 485 (9th Cir., 1967), *aff'd,* 391 U.S. 83 (1968).

Assumption Of Liabilities

Ordinarily, if liabilities are assumed in connection with a corporate reorganization, they are not treated as boot: that is, the assumption is not regarded as "other property." But if the principal purpose of having the liabilities assumed is avoidance of Federal income tax, the assumption is treated as boot. I.R.C. Section 357.

Thus, if an individual transfers to a controlled corporation certain property in return for corporate stock and the assumption by the corporation of specified liabilities, this assumption is not boot if the principal purpose for the assumption is other than tax avoidance. In determining whether the principal purpose was tax avoidance, the motivation for the original incurring of the liabilities is irrelevant. "We read this language as excluding from identification as a purpose to avoid tax *on the exchange,* the original and unrelated motivation for borrowing the money which created the obligation." *Drybrough et al. v. Commissioner,* 376 F.2d 350 (6th Cir., 1967).

If, in a transfer to a controlled corporation, the sum of the amount of the liabilities assumed plus the amount of liabilities to which the property is subject exceeds the total of the adjusted basis of the property transferred, the excess will be treated as gain from the sale of an asset (capital or not, as the case may be). I.R.C. Section 357(c)(1). Thus, if the transferred property is subject to liabilities which exceed the transferor's basis in the property, the excess is recognized as gain. *Easson et al. v. Commissioner,* 294 F.2d 653 (9th Cir., 1961).

Insolvency Reorganizations

No gain or loss is recognized if, pursuant to a plan of reorganization, stock or securities in an insolvent corporation are exchanged solely for stock or securities in a corporation organized or availed of to effectuate the plan. This is limited to situations where stock in a corporation (other than a railroad corporation) is transferred in pursuance of an order of the court having jurisdiction of the corporation in a receivership, foreclosure, or similar proceeding, or in a proceeding under Chapter X of the Bankruptcy Act, to another corporation organized, or made use of, to effectuate a plan of reorganization approved by the court in such proceedings, in exchange solely for stock or securities in this other corporation. I.R.C. Section 371.

If the assets of the insolvent corporation are taken over by a bondholders' protective committee, which in turn transfers these assets to a new corporation formed for this purpose, Section 371 still applies. *Helvering v. Alabama Asphaltic Limestone Company,* 315 U.S. 179 (1942).

If the stockholder or security holder receives something other than stock or securities in the new corporation, this will be treated as boot. No loss is recognized on such a transaction.

Acquisitions To Evade Or To Avoid Tax

The Commissioner of Internal Revenue may disallow any deduction, credit, or other allowance if the principal purpose of the acquisition of a corporation was to secure such a benefit which otherwise would not be enjoyed. This rule applies in any case where any person or persons acquired, directly or indirectly, control of a corporation, or where any corporation acquires, directly or indirectly, property of another corporation (not controlled, directly or indirectly, immediately before this acquisition by the acquiring corporation or its stockholders), if the acquiring corporation's basis for the assets is the same as it was in the hands of the transferors. I.R.C. Section 269.

Ordinarily, Section 269 applies to acquisitions by corporations. But where individuals purchased the shares of a corporation with an accumulated deficit, transferred their own business to this corporation, and changed the old corporate name to one more appropriate to its new business, the individuals could not carry over the losses incurred by the corporation in its pre-acquisition type of business against profits of the business conducted after the individuals acquired the corporate stock. *Commissioner v. British Motor Car Distributors, Ltd.,* 278 F.2d 392 (9th Cir., 1960).

Where the shareholders of a profitable corporation acquire the stock of a deficit corporation, the acquisition itself produces no tax benefit to the shareholders. But if the profitable corporation is then merged into the deficit company, the Internal Revenue Service may ascertain whether the merger was an integral component of the entire scheme and whether the acquisition thus was a phase of an acquisition to avoid or to evade tax. *J. T. Slocomb Company v. Commissioner,* 334 F.2d 269 (2d Cir., 1964).

Recapitalizations

One of the six types of tax-free corporation reorganization is a recapitalization. I.R.C. Section 368(a)(1)(E). This includes such situations as:

(1) The funding by a corporation of a bond issue with its own preferred stock.

(2) The exchange by a corporation of its preferred stock on which there are dividend arrearages for other preferred stock of the corporation plus other of its shares with respect to the dividends in arrears. Regulations Section 1.368–2(e).

(3) The surrender to a corporation for cancellation of 25% of its preferred stock in exchange for no par value common stock.

(4) The issuance of a corporation of its preferred stock (previously authorized but unissued) for outstanding common stock.

(5) The exchange of a corporation's outstanding preferred stock, having certain priorities with reference to the amount and payment of dividends and the distribution of the corporate assets upon liquidation, for a new issue of the corporation's common stock having no such rights.

A recapitalization is not *per se* tax-free. There must be present the requirements laid down for reorganizations in general. A rcapitalization is not tax-free if it has the net economic effect of the distribution of a dividend. *Commissioner v. Edward T. Bedford Estate,* 325 U.S. 283 (1945).

The exchange of bonds and accrued interest thereon for stock of the corporation which issued the bonds is a recapitalization if the bonds have a long enough maturity not to be deemed the equivalent of cash. Revenue Ruling 59–98, 1959–1 CB 76. Here, the ruling was affirmative where the bonds had an average life of 6½ years when issued and were purchased for investment purposes by persons other than the stockholders.

Sound Business Purpose

"[I]n order to fit within a specified provision of the Internal Revenue Code a transaction must not only comply with the explicit requirements of the section, but it must also have a 'business purpose' that falls within the spirit of the section." *Moses L. Parshelsky Estate et al. v. Commissioner,* 303 F.2d 74 (2d Cir., 1962). This is especially true in the field of corporate reorganizations, where this doctrine had its genesis. *Gregory v. Helvering,* 293 U.S. 465 (1935).

Under this doctrine, the Commissioner may disregard the form and tax the transaction according to the substance. The converse has not been argued by taxpayers with conspicuous success. It is difficult for a taxpayer to say that the substance of a transaction should be the lodestar of taxation rather than form. This argument has been raised futilely on behalf of many corporations. The argument has been no more successful when raised on behalf of stockholders.

Thus, in one case, shareholders argued that there had been no business purpose in a plan of reorganization involving two corporations. The court, however, stated that it could not conceive of corporations remaining in existence for twelve and fifteen years, respectively, "without some valid business purpose." *Lewis B. Meyer Estate,* 15 T.C. 850 (1950). In another such situation, stockholders claimed that the transaction by which they got assets was not a reorganization inasmuch as "the transaction served no business purpose whatever, tax avoidance being the sole concern of the parties. . . ." But the court felt that there had been reasons for having formed and continued the company for several years; and "the purposes which prompt the organization of a holding company in the first instance are inherent in the reorganization of such company . . ." *Chester A. Souther et al.,* 39 B.T.A. 197 (1939).

Chapter 9

Dividends. Interest. Amortization

Dividends

Characteristics. A dividend is a distribution made by a corporation to its shareholders out of earnings and profits accumulated after February 28, 1913, or out of earnings and profits of the taxable year. I.R.C. Section 316(a). But, as was noted in Chapter 7, these earnings and profits may include those of a predecessor corporation where there has been a tax-free reorganization.

If a corporation makes a distribution at a time when it has accumulated earnings and profits, the shareholders have the burden of establishing that the distribution is not a fully taxable dividend. *Thorval J. Lockwood Estate,* T.C. Memo. 1964–205, filed August 3, 1964, *rev'd on another issue,* 350 F.2d 712 (8th Cir., 1965). In order to avoid tax upon corporate distributions, a stockholder must show that the corporation had no earnings and profits from which a dividend could be paid. *United States v. Kavanagh,* 308 F.2d 824 (8th Cir., 1962).

Essentially Equivalent To A Dividend. In order to tax a distribution as a dividend, the Internal Revenue Service need not even allege that it is one. "Needless to say, formal declaration of a dividend is not required." *Bradbury v. Commissioner,* 298 F.2d 111 (1st Cir., 1962). All that is required is that the transaction have the effect of one, deliberately or otherwise.

If corporate contributions to an employee benefit plan were made under circumstances where the chief stockholders were the principal beneficiaries, these payments may be regarded as dividends. Regulations Section 1.404(a)–1(b). Withdrawals from a corporation by a stockholder were treated as dividends where there was no evidence as to a maturity date for repayment. *Clarence L. Bibb,* T.C. Memo. 1965–296, filed November 8, 1965. Sale of stock to a controlled corporation may be treated for tax purposes as a dividend. *Ole Bardahl et al.,* T.C. Memo. 1965–116, filed April 29, 1965. Where a corporation paid bonuses to four officer-stockholders (who were not related) in direct proportion to their stockholdings, a dividend was found. *Northlich, Stolley, Inc. v. United States,* 368 F.2d 272 (Ct. Cl., 1966).

Where the grantor of a trust is the equitable owner of the trust corpus, dividends on stock owned by the trust are income to him, regardless of to whom paid. *Hyman v. Nunan,* 143 F.2d 425 (2d Cir., 1944).

A distribution is not so likely to be deemed a dividend if it can be established that the chief stockholder had no need or requirement for the cash distributed to him and he deposited it in his general bank account. See *Salvatori et al. v. United States,* D.C., S.D. Cal., 1966.

Unlike most income tax matters, the showing of a sound business purpose is not a redeeming factor, for "the existence of a business purpose will not, of itself, require that the transaction be classified as 'not essentially equivalent to a dividend.' " *Charles Swan et al.,* 42 T.C. 291 (1964), *aff'd,* 355 F.2d 795 (6th Cir., 1966).

"When an individual shareholder receives an economic benefit through a diversion of corporate earnings and profits, such a receipt may be taxable as a constructive dividend." *Sullivan et al. v. United States,* 363 F.2d 724 (8th Cir., 1966). "The motive, or expressed intent of the corporation is not determinative, and constructive dividends have been found contrary to the expressed intent of the corporation. The courts, as arbiters of the true nature of corporate payments, have consistently used as a standard the measure of economic benefit as the proper occasion for taxation." *Sachs v. Commissioner,* 277 F.2d 879 (8th Cir., 1960).

Taxable Status. Revenue Procedure 65–10, 1965–1 CB 738, provides instructions and guidelines relating to (1) the determination of the taxable status of corporate distributions to stockholders and (2) the data to be furnished to the Internal Revenue Service with the corporation's annual information return, Form 1096, in support of the corporate determination of the earnings and profits upon which the taxability of the distribution depends.

It is stated in this Revenue Procedure that "[i]n appropriate situations, the Service will process the returns of stockholders receiving corporate distributions claimed to be partly or wholly not taxable as dividends by relying upon good faith determinations made by the corporation, if such determinations are based upon a bona fide estimation of current year earnings and profits and a computation of accumulated earnings and profits reflecting latest information available at the date of determination. Under this procedure it will be possible in most cases to accept tentative determinations, particularly in the cases of companies whose stock is widely held, and those companies for which a reasonably current determination of accumulated earnings and profits has been made by the Service. However, in any case in which factors are present indicating that there may be gross inaccuracy in the corporation's determination, the Service will of necessity be required to consider the computations in detail before such determination can be accepted."

The basic authority is Section 6042(d) of the Code, which provides that if the Service so requests, a corporation must furnish data to determine the corporation's available earnings and profits, the names and addresses of the stockholders entitled to these earnings and profits, and the amount paid to each.

The taxable status of corporate distributions in the hands of the stockholder is determined by the source of the distribution. To determine this, it is necessary to make computations from March 1, 1913 (or the date of incorporation, if that is later) of the current earnings and profits of each year, the post-1913 earnings and profits, the March 1, 1913 earned surplus, and the appreciation at March 1, 1913 subsequently realized.

Historical year-by-year computations are necessary for a number of reasons. For example, earnings and profits, and deficits in earnings and profits carried over from the transferor corporations under Section 381, may not be combined with the accumulated earnings and profits existing at the time of the transfer but must be carried forward separately year-by-year inasmuch as deficits at any carryover date may be used only to offset earnings and profits accumulated after the date of transfer.

Where a corporation determines that its distributions are partly or wholly not taxable as dividends, the data supporting the corporate determinations are to be filed with the Earnings and Profits Section, Tax Rulings Division, Internal Revenue Service, Washington, D.C., 20224, on or before February 28, with the lower portion of Form 1096, the annual information return.

Illustrative forms and computations are included in this Revenue Procedure.

Time of Dividend. "[T]he date of payment, not the date of the declaration of the dividend, is the date of the distribution. . . ." *Mason v. Routzahn,* 275 U.S. 775 (1927).

Where dividend checks dated December 31 were mailed to shareholders on that date, they were income to cash basis shareholders in January, unless it could be shown that the shareholder could have received payment in December had he called for his check. *Avery v. Commissioner,* 292 U.S.

210 (1934). In the case of a widely-held stock, it is not likely that a shareholder could establish that the income was available to him in December. "Confusion would result if the stockholders of any large corporation descended in a body on the treasurer's office and demanded forthwith payment of their dividends." *Commissioner v. Fox,* 218 F.2d 347 (3d Cir., 1954).

If a dividend is paid in one year and then is cancelled or revoked in the subsequent year, the income of the first year is not modified. The stockholder received the dividend under a claim of right in the earlier year and hence is taxable at that time. *St. Regis Paper Co. v. Commissioner,* 157 F.2d 884 (2d Cir., 1946).

When stock is sold, and a dividend is both declared and paid after the sale, this dividend is not gross income to the seller. When stock is sold after the declaration of a dividend and after the date as of which the seller becomes entitled to it, the dividend ordinarily is income to the seller. When stock is sold between the time of declaration and the time of payment of the dividend, and the sale takes place at such time that the purchaser becomes entitled to the dividend, ordinarily it is income to him. The fact that the purchaser may have included the amount of the dividend in his purchase price in contemplation of receiving the dividend does not exempt him from tax. Nor can the purchaser deduct the added amount he advanced to the seller in anticipation of the dividend. That added amount is merely part of the purchase price of the stock. In certain cases, however, the purchaser may be considered to be the recipient of the dividend even though he has not received the legal title to the stock itself and does not himself receive the dividend. Thus, if the seller retains the legal title to the stock as trustee solely for the purpose of securing the payment of the purchase price, with the understanding that he is to apply the dividends received from time to time in reduction of the purchase price, the dividends are considered to be income to the purchaser. Regulations Section 1.61–9(c).

Dividends Received Exclusion—Individuals. Individuals may exclude from gross income the first $100 for dividends received during the taxable year. In the case of a joint return of husband and wife, each spouse is entitled to the exclusion in an amount not in excess of $100 with respect to the dividends he received. Where two or more persons hold stock as tenants by the entirety, the dividends received with respect to this stock will be considered as being received by each tenant to the extent that he is entitled under local law to a share of the dividends. Where dividends constitute community property under local law, each spouse will be considered as receiving one-half of the dividends. I.R.C. Section 116(a).

The dividend exclusion treatment does not extend to distributions from:

(1) China Trade Act corporations.

(2) Tax-exempt organizations.

(3) A corporation given the tax treatment afforded to those dealing with possessions of the United States (Section 931).

(4) A real estate investment trust which is taxed as such.

(5) Mutual savings banks, co-operative banks, and building and loan associations which are entitled to a deduction for dividends paid on deposits under Section 591.

(6) Regulated investment companies, to the extent provided in Section 854 (discussed in this book under "Regulated Investment Companies").

The availability of the dividend exclusion is limited in the case of non-resident aliens to dividends which are effectively connected with the conduct of a trade or business in the United States. The exclusion is also allowed in the case of an expatriate subject to tax under Section 877.

In the case of a simple trust (one which distributes its earnings currently), dividends distributed to beneficiaries retain their original character in the beneficiary's hands for the purpose of determining the availability to the beneficiaries of the dividend exclusion. Regulations Section 1.652(b)–1. In the case of a complex trust, distributions are treated as consisting of the same proportion of each class of items entering into the computation of distributable net income as the total of each class bears to the total distributable net income of the estate or trust unless the terms of the governing instruments specifically allocate different classes of income to different beneficiaries, or unless local law requires such an allocation. Regulations Section 1.662(b)–1.

In the case of partnerships, each partner takes into account, as part of the dividends received by him from domestic corporations, his distributive share of dividends received by the partnership, with respect to which the partner is entitled to an exclusion under Section 116. Regulations Section 1.702–1(a)(5).

Discussion of the treatment of dividends received by a common trust fund is considered in the commentary on such funds.

As to the time when dividends in general are deemed to have been received for the purpose of the exclusion, the regular rules as to actual and constructive receipt apply. But solely for purposes of determining the amount of the exclusion applicable to dividends received by a beneficiary from an estate or trust, the time of receipt of the dividends by the estate or trust is also considered the time of receipt by the beneficiary. Regulations Section 1.116–1(f), (g).

Dividends Received Deduction—Corporations. A corporation is allowed a deduction for dividends received from a domestic corporation which is subject to Federal income tax. With exceptions to be mentioned below, the dividends received deduction of a corporation is:

(1) 85%, in the case of dividends other than those described in (2) or (3), following.

(2) 100%, in the case of dividends received by a Small Business Investment Company operating under the Small Business Investment Act of 1958.

(3) 100%, in the case of qualifying dividends, as defined in the following paragraph.

The term "qualifying dividends" means dividends received by a corporation which, at the close of the day the dividends are received, is a member of the same affiliated group of corporations (as defined in Section 243 (b)(5)) as the corporation distributing the dividends, provided the necessary conditions are met.

The term "affiliated group" includes, for this purpose, those domestic corporations (including a corporation which is treated as a domestic corporation because it is a subsidiary of a domestic corporation that was chartered in a contiguous country solely to comply with rules as to ownership of property) where there is at least an 80% voting stock control by a common parent corporation. A corporation that is "includible" for this purpose may not be a tax-exempt organization, a foreign corporation, a corporation subject to special tax because it deals with possessions of the United States, a China Trade Act corporation, a regulated investment company, or a real estate investment trust. There are special rules for insurance companies.

An affiliated group which includes the distributing and recipient corporations must have made an election which is effective for the taxable years of its member corporations which include the day of receipt. The dividends involved must have been distributed out of earnings and profits of a taxable year which ends after December 31, 1963 and with respect to which two requirements are satisfied:

(1) On each day of the taxable year the distributing corporation and the recipient corporation must have been members of the affiliated group.

(2) An election under Section 1562 (relating to election of multiple surtax exemptions) must not be effective for that taxable year.

The election is made by the common parent corporation, with a consent form to be signed by each affiliate. The election may be terminated by filing notice with the Commissioner; the election is terminated if the affiliated group includes a member which was not a member in the preceding taxable year and which files a statement that it does not consent to the election.

In determining the dividends received deduction, any amount allowed as a deduction for dividends paid by mutual savings banks, co-operative banks, and domestic building and loan associations will not be considered as a dividend.

The dividends received deduction in the case of dividends received from a regulated investment company is subject to the limitations imposed by Section 854: that is, a capital gain dividend is not treated as a dividend, while other dividends by the corporation must have been set forth in notices to the shareholders within forty-five days after the close of its taxable year.

In the case of dividends received from a real estate investment trust, a dividends received deduction is not allowed for any year in which the real estate investment trust is taxed as such. I. R. C. Section 243(c).

If a domestic corporation accumulated earnings and profits during a period when it is subject to Federal income tax, and subsequently this company re-incorporates in a foreign country, any dividends paid out of earnings and profits after the re-incorporation are eligible for the dividends received deduction. Regulations Section 1.243–3(a).

Special treatment is provided for a corporation entitled to the dividends received deduction which is a party to an anti-trust court proceeding and which receives stock in an anti-trust distribution. In such a case, the amount of dividend income and the amount of the dividends received deduction both are determined by the fair market value of the stock distributed (without regard to the basis of this stock in the hands of the distributing corporation). The basis of the stock to the receiving corporation, however, is the fair market value of this stock diminished by that portion of the dividends received deduction attributable to the unrealized appreciation (if any) in the hands of the distributing corporation. I.R.C. Section 301(f).

The following corporations are not entitled to the dividends received deduction:

(1) Regulated investment companies.

(2) Real estate investment trusts.

(3) Tax option corporations.

(4) Non-resident foreign corporations.

Dividends Received On Certain Preferred Stock. A corporation is allowed a deduction for dividends received on certain preferred stock of stipulated public utility corporations which are subject to Federal income tax. The deduction is allowable only for such dividends where the distributing corporation was allowed the deduction for dividends paid provided in Section 247 (relating to dividends paid in certain preferred stock of public utilities).

To determine the amount of the deduction, it is necessary (1) to ascertain the amount of such dividends received and (2) to multiply this amount by a fraction, the numerator of which is 14% and the denominator of which is the sum of the normal and surtax rates for that year. There is then ascertained the amount which is 85% of the excess of (1) over (2). I.R.C. Section 244.

Dividends Received From Certain Foreign Corporations. A corporation is allowed a deduction for dividends received from a foreign corporation (other than a foreign personal holding company) which is subject to Federal income tax if, for an uninterrupted period of not less than 36 months ending with the close of the foreign corporation's taxable year in which the dividends are paid, this foreign corporation has been engaged in trade or business within the United States and if 50% or more of the gross income of the corporation from all sources for that period is effectively connected with the conduct of a trade or business within the United States. If the foreign corporation has been in existence for less than 36 months as of the close of the taxable year in which the dividends are paid, then the applicable uninterrupted period to be taken into consideration is the entire period the corporation has been in existence as of the close of the taxable year. An uninterrupted period which satisfies the twofold requirement with respect to business activity and gross income may start at a later date than the date on which the foreign corporation first commenced an uninterrupted period of engaging in trade or business within the United States, but the applicable uninterrupted period is in any event the longest uninterrupted period which satisfies this twofold requirement. I.R.C. Section 245.

The dividends received deduction from such foreign corporations is the sum of the following:

(1) 85% of the dividends received from earnings and profits of the taxable year. This amount may not exceed a figure which bears the same ratio to 85% of these dividends as the gross income from United States sources for the taxable year bears to gross income from all sources for that year.

(2) 85% of the dividends received from earnings and profits accumulated after February 28, 1913, which have accumulated after the beginning of the uninterrupted period referred to above. This amount may not exceed a figure which bears the same ratio to 85% of these dividends as the gross income from United States sources for the portion of the uninterrupted period bears to its entire gross income for the period. I.R.C. Section 245(a).

In the case of dividends of a foreign corporation that was engaged in trade or business within the United States for an uninterrupted period of not less than 36 months where 50% or more of the gross income from all sources for that period was actively connected with the conduct of a trade or business within the United States, an 85% dividends received deduction is allowed. The dividends received deduction is 100% where a domestic corporation receives the dividends from a wholly-owned foreign subsidiary which has a 100% effectively connected income. I.R.C. Section 245(b). In such a situation, a foreign corporation is subjected to United States tax on all of its income, just as is a domestic corporation.

Rules Applying To Deductions For Dividends Received. The sum of the deductions allowed by Section 243(a) (relating to dividends received by corporations), Section 244 (relating to dividends received on certain preferred stock), and Section 245 (relating to dividends received from certain foreign corporations) is limited to 85% of the taxable income of the corporation. But this limitation does not apply for any taxable year for which there is a net operating loss. I.R.C. Section 246(b).

The dividends received deduction is not allowed for the three sections mentioned in the preceding paragraph—

(1) If the dividend is in respect of any share of stock which is sold or otherwise disposed of where the taxpayer has held the share for fifteen or fewer days; or

(2) If and to the extent that the taxpayer is under an obligation to make corresponding payments with respect to substantially identical stock or securities. It is immaterial whether the obligation has arisen pursuant to a short sale or otherwise.

In the case of any stock having a preference in dividends, in lieu of the 15-day rule provided in (1), above, the holding period is 90 days if the taxpayer received dividends on the stock which are attributable to a period or periods aggregating in excess of 366 days. I.R.C. Section 246(c).

In computing the holding period for purposes of the above restriction provisions, the day of disposition but not the day of acquisition is taken into account. There is not taken into account any day which is more than fifteen days after the date on which the share of stock becomes ex-dividend. Thus, the holding period is terminated automatically at the end of the 15-day period without regard to how long the stock may be held after that date. In the case of stock having a preference in dividends, a 90-day period is substituted for the above-mentioned 15-day period. The tacking of the holding period of stock disposed of in a wash sale to the holding period of the stock acquired is not permitted for purposes of determining the holding period. I.R.C. Section 246(c)(3).

The holding periods will be appropriately reduced for any period that the taxpayer's stock holding is offset by a corresponding short position resulting from an option to sell, a contractual obligation to sell, or a short sale of substantially identical stock or securities. The holding periods of stock held for a period of fifteen days or less on the date the short position is created accordingly must be reduced to the extent of the short position. Where the amount of stock acquired within this period exceeds the amount as to which the taxpayer establishes a short position, the stock the holding period of which must be reduced because of the short position will be that most recently acquired within that period. If, on the date the short position is created, the amount of stock subject to the short position exceeds the amount, if any, of the stock held by the taxpayer for fifteen or fewer days, the excess shares of stock sold short will, to the extent thereof, postpone until the termination of the short position the commencement of the holding periods of subsequently acquired stock. Stock having a preference in dividends is also subject to these rules, except that the 90-day period applies in lieu of the 15-day period otherwise applicable. Regulations Section 1.246–3(d).

Dividends Paid On Certain Preferred Stock Of Public Utilities. A deduction is allowed for dividends paid during the taxable year by certain public utility corporations on specified preferred stock. This deduction is an amount equal to the product of a stipulated fraction times the lesser of—

(1) The amount of the dividends paid during the taxable year by a public utility on its preferred stock; or

(2) The taxable income for that year, computed without regard to the dividends paid on preferred stock of certain public utilities.

The fraction for any taxable year has as its numerator 14 and as its denominator the combined normal and surtax rates for that year.

Details of this deduction are contained in I.R.C. Section 247.

Interest

In general, all interest is allowed as a deduction, whether or not connected with the taxpayer's trade or business. But exceptions have been carved out in the case of (1) interest to purchase or to carry tax-exempt securities and (2) so-called interest where there is no *bona fide* indebtedness.

Production Of Exempt Interest. No deduction is allowed for expenses or interest relating to the receiving of tax-exempt interest. I.R.C. Section 265.

A loan not incurred to purchase tax-exempt securities but for the purpose of operating a taxpayer's business was not "incurred or continued to purchase or carry" tax-exempt securities, even though the securities were hypothecated as security for the loan. *R. B. George Machinery Co.,* 26 B.T.A. 594 (1932). When a loan not incurred originally to purchase tax-exempt securities is continued for that purpose, the interest ceases to be deductible. *Constance M. Bishop,* 41 T.C. 154 (1963).

"Interest" In The Absence Of Indebtedness. Sometimes a transaction is arranged whereby a taxpayer pays a sum to an entrepreneur, allegedly as interest to obtain funds for the acquisition of property which the taxpayer in fact never owns. Thus, where money is borrowed and Government bonds are purchased with the funds, the bonds being then collateralized, if in fact the transaction is entirely on paper, no interest deduction is allowed. "[T]he question for determination is whether what was done, apart from the tax motive, was the thing which the statute intended." *Knetsch v. United States,* 364 U.S. 361 (1960).

In such a transaction, the taxpayer never owns anything and never owes anything (for the "purchased" securities are collateral in full for the loan). This type of arrangement has been characterized as a "financial round robin. . . ." *Broome v. United States,* 170 F. Supp. 613 (Ct. Cl., 1959). "There must be an actual 'indebtedness' on which the 'interest' is paid. Here there was none; all that took place were transactions which lack substance and which must be ignored for tax purposes." *Benenson et al. v. United States,* 257 F. Supp. 101 (D.C., S.D.N.Y., 1966). No matter how genuine the intentions of the taxpayers may have been as to the transactions, their intentions do not control. *Jockmus v. United States,* 335 F.2d 23 (2d Cir., 1964).

Although such deals customarily are concerned with Government bonds, the finding is the same in the rare situations when other securities are the subject. *Cahn et al. v. Commissioner,* 358 F.2d 492 (9th Cir., 1966).

Tax-Exempt Interest. Interest upon obligations of a state, territory, or any political subdivision thereof, or the District of Columbia is not included in gross income. I.R.C. Section 103(a). "Obligations issued by or on behalf of a State, Territory, or possession of the United States, or a duly organized political subdivision acting by constituted authorities empowered to issue such obligations, are the obligations of a State, Territory, or possession of the United States, or a political subdivision thereof. Certificates issued by a political subdivision for public improvements (such as sewers, sidewalks, streets, etc.) which are evidences of special assessments against specific property, which assessments become a lien against such property and which the political subdivision is required to enforce, are, for purposes of this section, obligations of the political subdivision even though the obligations are to be satisfied out of special funds and not out of general funds or taxes. The term 'political subdivision,' for purposes of this section, denotes any division of the State, Territory, or possession of the United States which is a municipal corporation, or to which has been delegated the right to exercise part of the sovereign power of the State, Territory, or possession of the United States. As thus defined, a political subdivision of a State, Territory, or possession of the United States may or may not, for purposes of this section, include special assessment districts so created, such as road, water, sewer, gas, light, reclamation drainage, irrigation, levee, school, harbor, port improvement, and similar districts and divisions of a State, Territory, or possession of the United States." Regulations Section 1.103–1.

The so-called "industrial development bonds" are bonds issued by a municipality or other political subdivision. But the debtor, in reality, is the private corporation which will use the facility constructed with the proceeds of the bond issue. In the case of such bonds sold on or before March 15, 1968, interest was deemed to be exempt on the theory that they were municipal or other exempt bonds. But in the case of bonds issued after that date, the securities are not considered to be obligations of a state, territory, or possession of the United States, or any political subdivision thereof, or the District of Columbia within the meaning of Section 103(a)(1). T.I.R. 972, March 6, 1968. Exceptions are made if (1) the bond issue is of $1,000,000 or less and substantially all the proceeds are for land or depreciable property, or (2) the proceeds are used for residential property for family units, sports facilities, specified public utilities facilities, air or water pollution facilities, and facilities for industrial parks. Under P.L. 90–634 (enacted October 25, 1968), a municipality may elect a $5,000,000 limit.

Tax-exempt bonds are tax-exempt only as to interest. Any gain upon sale is taxable. *Wilcutts v. Bunn,* 282 U.S. 216 (1931).

Income consisting of dividends on stock of Federal land banks, Federal land bank associations, Federal home loan banks, and Federal Reserve banks is not, in the case of shares issued before March 28, 1942, includible in gross income. Income consisting of dividends on share accounts of Federal savings and loan associations is includible in gross income but, in the case of shares issued before March 28, 1942, is not subject to the normal tax on income. Dividends from shares and stock of these Federal agencies or instrumentalities issued on and after March 28, 1942 are includible in gross income.

The tax exemption provisions of the preceding paragraph do not apply in the case of stock or shares issued on or after March 28, 1942. Regulations Section 1.103–2(a), (b).

Regardless of the exemption from income tax of dividends paid on the stock of Federal Reserve banks, dividends paid by member banks are treated the same as dividends of ordinary corporations.

Dividends on the stock of the central bank for co-operatives, the production credit corporations, and banks for co-operatives, organized under the provisions of the Farm Credit Act of 1933, constitute income to the recipients, subject to both the normal and the surtax. Regulations Section 1.103–2(a).

Interest upon notes secured by mortgages executed to Federal land banks, joint-stock land banks, or Federal intermediate credit banks is not subject to Federal income tax. Regulations Section 1.103–3.

Interest upon obligations of the United States issued on or before September 1, 1917 is exempt from tax. In the case of obligations issued after September 1, 1917 and in the case of obligations of a corporation organized under Act of Congress, if the corporation is an instrumentality of the United States, the interest is exempt from tax only if and to the extent provided in the acts authorizing the issue, as amended and supplemented. Interest on Treasury bonds issued before March 1, 1941 is exempt from Federal income taxes except surtaxes imposed upon the income or profits of individuals, associations or corporations. But interest on an aggregate of not exceeding $5,000 principal amount of these bonds is also exempt from surtaxes. Interest in excess of the interest on an aggregate of not exceeding $5,000 principal amount of such bonds is subject to surtax and must be included in gross income.

Interest upon obligations issued on or after March 1, 1941 by the United States, or any agency or instrumentality thereof, are not exempt from Federal income tax except in the case of such obligations which the Federal Maritime Board and Maritime Administration (formerly United States Maritime Commission) or the Federal Housing Administration has, before March 1, 1941, contracted to issue at a future date. The interest on such obligations so contracted to be issued bears such tax-exemption privileges as were at the time of the contract provided in the law authorizing the issuance. In the case of obligations issued as the result of a funding obligation, as, for example, where a corporation exchanges bonds for previously issued bonds, the refunding obligations are deemed, for the purposes of this section, to have been issued at the time of the exchange rather than at the time the original bonds were issued. Regulations Section 1.103–4(b).

When the income of a trust is taxable to beneficiaries (as in the case of a trust the income of which is to be distributed to the beneficiaries currently), each beneficiary is entitled to exemption as if he owned directly a proportionate part of the Treasury bonds held in trust. When, on the other hand, the income is taxable to the trustee (as in the case of a trust the income of which is accumulated for the benefit of unborn or unascertained persons), the trust, as the owner of the bonds held in trust, is entitled to the exemption on account of this ownership. Regulations Section 1.103–5(a). Inasmuch as the income of a partnership is taxable to the individual partners, each partner is entitled to the exemption as if he owned directly a proportionate part of the bonds held by the partnership. Regulations Section 1.103–5(b).

Partially Tax-Exempt Interest. Section 35 provides a credit for partially tax-exempt interest received by individuals. This is an anachronism, for all bonds subject to this treatment have been retired.

Amortization Of Bond Premium

If a taxpayer pays a premium in acquiring bonds, the premium may or must, under varying circumstances, be amortized. That is, there would be deducted a *pro rata* portion of the premium each year over the life of the bond. This is covered by Section 171 of the Code.

The term "bond," as used in this section, means any bond, debenture, note, or certificate or other evidence of indebtedness, issued by any corporation and bearing interest (including any similar obligation issued by a government or political subdivision thereof). The term does not, however, include any such obligation which constitutes stock in trade of the taxpayer or any such obligation of a kind which would properly be included in the inventory of the taxpayer if on hand at the close of the taxable year, or any such obligation held by the taxpayer primarily for sale to customers in the ordinary course of his trade or business. This definition of a bond applies regardless of whether the bond has coupons or is in registered form. This section has no application to bonds held by dealers in securities other than bonds held by such dealers for investment purposes pursuant to Section 1236, relating to dealers in securities. Regulations Section 1.171–4.

Bond premium is amortizable by the owner of a bond in either of two categories:

(1) Amortization of bond premium is mandatory in the case of:
   (a) Fully tax-exempt bonds (the interest on which is excludible from gross income), whether the owner is a corporation, individual, or other taxpayer.
   (b) Partially tax-exempt bonds owned by a corporation.

(2) Amortization of bond premium is optional (at the election of the taxpayer) in the case of:
   (a) Fully taxable bonds, whether the owner is a corporation, individual, or other taxpayer.
   (b) Partially tax-exempt bonds owned by taxpayers other than corporations. I.R.C. Section 171(a).

In the case of a fully tax-exempt bond, the amortizable bond premium for the taxable year is simply an adjustment to the basis or adjusted basis of the bond. If the premium is $1, the basis or adjusted basis of the bond is reduced by $1. No deduction is allowable on account of this amortizable bond premium.

In the case of a fully taxable bond to which Section 171 applies, the amortizable bond premium is applied both as an adjustment to the basis or adjusted basis of the bond and as a deduction in computing taxable income.

In the case of a partially tax-exempt bond, the amortizable bond premium for the taxable year is used for the following purposes:

(1) As an adjustment to the basis or adjusted basis of the bond.

(2) As a deduction in computing taxable income.

(3) In the case of individuals, estates, or trusts, as a reduction of the amount which otherwise would be taken into account in computing the credit for partially tax-exempt interest under Section 35.

(4) In the case of corporations, as a reduction of the amount allowed as a deduction for partially tax-exempt interest under Section 242.

The regulations provide this example:

"In the case of an individual who has elected to amortize the premium on a partially tax-exempt bond, if the interest on such bond with an adjusted basis of $1,024 is $30 for the taxable year and the amortizable bond premium thereon is $4 for the taxable year, then the $30 is included in gross income, the $4 is allowable as a reduction, the adjusted basis of $1,024 is reduced by $4 to $1,020, and a credit amounting to $0.78 (3 percent of $30 minus $4) is allowed against the tax for such taxable year. In the case of a corporation, which is required to amortize the premium on such bond, no credit is allowed against the tax, but the deduction under section 242 on account of the interest is $26 ($30 minus $4)." Regulations Section 1.171–1(b)(4).

Where no specific deduction is permitted under Section 171(a) for amortization of bond premium as such (because the tax is computed by use of the optional tax tables, or because the taxpayer elects to use the standard deduction), it will be presumed, if the taxpayer has elected to amortize bond premium in accordance with Section 171, that the deduction for amortization of bond premium has been allowed for the purpose of determining the adjusted basis of the bond.

Bonds Owned By Decedents. Where a decedent who used the cash method owned fully taxable bonds to which Section 171 applies, the interest accruing thereon during the period ending with his death is deemed to be income in respect of a decedent (Section 691) and is included upon its receipt in the gross income of the estate or legatee, whichever acquires the right to receive the interest. The amount of amortizable bond premium properly allowable for that period is a deduction for the period to the decedent and is not allowable as a deduction to the estate or legatee.

Where a decedent who used the cash method owned partially tax-exempt bonds to which Section 171 applies, the interest accruing thereon during the period ending with his death is, by reason of Section 691, included upon its receipt in the gross income of the estate or legatee, whichever acquires the right to receive the interest. The amount of the amortizable bond premium properly allowable for that period is a deduction for the period to the decedent, as in the case of a fully taxable bond. The amount of the amortizable bond premium will not be applied to reduce the credit or deduction of the estate or legatee for the interest for that period.

Where a decedent using the accrual method owned fully taxable bonds and partially tax-exempt bonds to which Section 171 applies, in the case of fully taxable bonds, both the interest accruing thereon during the period ending with his death and the deduction on account of the amortizable bond premium for that period are taken into account in computing the taxable income of the decedent. In the case of partially tax-exempt bonds, the rule as to the accrued interest and the amortization deduction is the same as in the preceding sentence, and the amount which would otherwise be taken into account in computing the decedent's credit against tax for this interest must be reduced by the amount of the amortizable bond premium for the period ending with the decedent's death. Regulations Section 1.171–1(c).

Determination Of Bond Premium. In general, bond premium on any bond to which Section 171 applies is the excess of the amount of the basis of the bond over the amount payable at maturity or, in the case of a callable bond, the earlier call date.

In the case of wholly taxable bonds which are issued after January 22, 1951 and are acquired after January 22, 1954 but before January 1, 1958, the earlier call date may be used in computing the amortizable bond premium only if this earlier call date is a date more than three years after the date of original issue. If a bond described in the preceding sentence is subject to a call date which falls within three years of the date of original issue, the amortizable bond premium will be computed by reference to the amount payable on maturity. If a wholly taxable bond is acquired after December 31, 1957, the amortizable bond premium will be computed by reference to the amount payable on maturity, or if it results in a smaller amortizable bond premium attributable to the period of earlier call date, the computation will be made by reference to the amount payable on the earlier call date.

In the case of a wholly taxable bond which has a call date, the amount of bond premium attributable to the taxable year in which the bond is called will include an amount equal to the excess of the amount of the adjusted basis of the bond as of the beginning of the taxable year over the amount received on redemption of the bond or (if greater than the amount received on redemption) the amount payable on maturity.

If the date as of which the basis of the bond was established precedes the first taxable year to which Section 171 applies to the bond, proper adjustments must be made to reflect unamortized bond premium on this bond for the period including the holding period before the date as of which Section 171 first becomes applicable to the bond in the hands of the taxpayer. Such adjustment is required whether or not an election was made under Section 171 or its forerunner and applies to all bonds to which the election is applicable.

Amortizable bond premium on any bond to which Section 171 applies is that part of the bond premium on the bond which is attributable to the taxable year.

Callable Bonds. In the case of a callable bond, the earlier call date will be considered as the maturity date, with two exceptions:

(1) If the earliest call date is more than three years from the date of original issue, provided further that the bonds are fully taxable, were issued after January 22, 1951, and were acquired after January 22, 1954 but before January 1, 1958.

(2) If the purchase and immediate transfer of callable bonds (such as in the form of gifts or contributions) "occurs in such a manner as to make the entire transaction not bona fide. . . ." Regulations Section 1.171–2(a)(3).

The amount due on the earlier call date will be considered as the amount payable on maturity unless it is determined under a different method of amortization regularly employed by the taxpayer that another amount should be the amount payable on maturity. Thus, in the case where a bond premium is to be amortized to the earlier call date, the bond premium must be spread over the period from the date as of which the basis for loss of the bond is established down to the earlier call date, rather than to the maturity date. The earlier call date may be the earliest call date specified in the bond as a day certain, the earliest interest payment date if the bond is callable at that date, the earliest date at which the bond is callable at par, or any other call date, prior to maturity, specified in the bond as may be selected by the taxpayer.

Where a deduction for amortizable bond premium may be determined with respect to alternative call dates, the amount of amortizable bond premium calculated with reference to a particular call date must be calculated thereafter with reference to the same call date. If, however, the bond has not in fact been called upon the call date originally selected, the bond premium then unamortized must be amortized to a succeeding call date or to maturity. "Thus, assume a $100 bond is acquired at time of issue for $125. The bond is callable in five years at $115 and in 10 years at $110. The taxpayer may amortize $10 of premium during the first five years and, if the bond is not then called, an additional $5 of premium during the next five years. If the bond is not called at the end of ten years, the remaining $10 of premiums must be amortized to maturity." Regulations Section 1.171–2(b)(2).

Convertible Bonds. The fact that a bond is convertible into stock does not, in itself, prevent the application of the bond premium amortization rule. A convertible bond is within the scope of Section 171 if the option to convert on a date certain specified in the bond rests with the holder. For the purpose of determining the amount of amortizable bond premium on a convertible bond for the taxable year, however, the amount of bond premium may not include any amount attributable to the conversion feature of the bond. For this purpose, the term "convertible bond" includes a bond issued with detachable stock purchase warrants.

The value of the conversion features of a particular bond is to be ascertained as of the time of acquisition by reference to the assumed price at which this bond would be purchased on the open market if without conversion features, and by subtracting this assumed price from the cost of the bond. The assumed price of the bond without conversion features will be ascertained by comparison to the yields on which bonds of similar character, not having conversion features, are sold on the open market and adjusting the bond in question to this yield. The adjustment may be made by the use of standard bond tables. In selecting quotations for comparative purposes, obviously, bonds of the same classification and grade must be used.

If a convertible bond acquired on or before June 15, 1950 is held during the taxable year, the amortizable bond premium is to be computed as if the provisions for the determination of the bond premium without the inclusion of any amount attributable to the conversion features of the bond were applicable for each year for which the bond was held prior to that taxable year.

Capitalized Expenses. In the case of a bond to which Section 171 otherwise applies, on which the bond premium is attributable only to capitalized expenses (such as buying commissions), if a taxpayer regularly employs a reasonable method of amortization (whether or not capitalized expenses are included in it), he is permitted but is not required to amortize capitalized expenses in accordance with this method. The same option exists where there is bond premium exclusive of capitalized expenses.

Years Where There Is No Interest. In a taxable year in which interest is not received or accruable, if the taxpayer—

(1) Regularly employs a reasonable method of amortization under which the bond premium for the taxable year is amortized, or

(2) Is required by the regulations to use the amortization method prescribed by Regulations Section 1.171–2(f), below, or

(3) Regularly employs a reasonable method of amortization under which the bond premium for the taxable year is not amortized,

the taxpayer is permitted, but not required, to amortize bond premium for the year in accordance with this method.

Methods Of Amortization. Determination of the bond premium and amortizable bond premium on any bond to which Section 171 applies will be made in accordance with:

(1) The method of amortization regularly employed by the taxpayer, if this method is reasonable; or

(2) In all other cases, the method of amortization to be described in the second succeeding paragraph.

A taxpayer who regularly employs a method of amortization may be one, for example, who is subject to the jurisdiction of a Federal or state regulatory agency and who, for the purposes of this agency, amortizes the bond premium on his bonds in accordance with a method prescribed or approved by this agency. But it is not necessary that the taxpayer be subject to the jurisdiction of such an agency or that the method be prescribed or approved by an agency. It is sufficient if he regularly employs a method of amortization and this method is reasonable.

The bond premium to be amortized is to be determined as follows. The amortizable bond premium attributable to the taxable year will be an amount which bears the same ratio to the bond premium as the number of months in the taxable year during which the bond was held by the taxpayer bears to the number of months from the beginning of the taxable year (or, if the bond was acquired in the taxable year, from the date of acquisition) to the date of maturity or earlier call date. A fractional part of a month is to be disregarded unless it amounts to more than half a month, in which case it will be considered as a month. Bond premium is to be ascertained by determining the excess of the amount of the basis of the bond (adjusted to date for amortizable bond premium) over the amount payable at maturity or, in the case of a callable bond, the earlier call date, unless one of the exceptions previously mentioned applies. Regulations Section 1.171–2(f).

Election As To Taxable And Partially Taxable Bonds. In the case of a corporation, the election of Section 171 may be made only with respect to fully taxable bonds. In the case of a taxpayer other than a corporation, the election may be made with respect to these classes:

(1) Fully taxable bonds only.

(2) Partially tax-exempt bonds only.

(3) Both fully taxable and partially tax-exempt bonds.

The election is made by the taxpayer by claiming a deduction for the bond premium in his return for the first taxable year to which he desires the election to be applicable. No other method of making the election will be recognized. If the election is made, the taxpayer should attach to his return a statement showing the computation of the deduction. The election will apply to all the bonds in respect of which it was made owned by the taxpayer at the beginning of the first taxable year to which the election applies and also to all the bonds of that class (or classes) thereafter acquired by him. The election is binding for all subsequent taxable years, unless the Commissioner authorizes a revocation of the election subject to whatever conditions are imposed.

If a trust owning partially tax-exempt bonds elects to amortize the bond premium thereon, the credits of the trust and the credits and deductions of the beneficiaries on account of the interest must be reduced by the portion of the amortizable deduction attributable to their shares of the interest. A similar rule is applicable in the case of partially tax-exempt bonds owned by estates, common trust funds, partnerships, and foreign personal holding companies. Regulations Section 1.171–3.

Other Considerations. Where wholly taxable bonds were sold by a taxpayer at a profit and immediately thereafter the same kind of bonds was purchased at a premium, the taxpayer may elect, with respect to the bonds so purchased, to make an adjustment to the bases of the bonds for the amortizable bond premium. The amount of the amortization attributable to the taxable year constitutes an allowable deduction from gross income. Revenue Ruling 55–353, 1955–1 CB 381.

Premiums paid by a corporation on the purchase of its callable convertible notes in excess of the amounts for which it was legally bound to pay upon calling the notes constituted ordinary and necessary expenses. *Roberts & Porter, Inc. v. Commissioner,* 307 F.2d 745 (7th Cir., 1962). The Internal Revenue Service has announced that it will not follow this decision. Revenue Ruling 67–409, I.R.B. 1967–47, 8.

Bond redemption premium was disallowed to the extent that it was unreasonable. *United States v. Haskel Engineering & Supply Company,* 380 F.2d 786 (9th Cir., 1967).

Chapter 10

Business and Non-Business Bad Debts. Worthless Securities

Bad Debts

Section 166 of the Code provides for an ordinary loss for bad debts when they are "created or acquired in connection with a trade or business of the taxpayer" and a short-term capital loss for all other bad debts. In general, loans made by corporations and by partnerships which are engaged in business are presumed to be business bad debts. *Robert Cluett,* 3d, 8 T.C. 1178 (1947). Thus, ordinary loss results from worthlessness thereof.

A non-business bad debt is one other than—

(1) A debt created or acquired in connection with a taxpayer's trade or business, or

(2) A debt the loss from the worthlessness of which is incurred in the taxpayer's trade or business. I.R.C. Section 166(d).

A debt must be enforceable to be written off for Federal income tax purposes if it becomes worthless. Regulations Section 1.166–1(a). Where a state law declared that any obligation with annual interest in excess of 6% was void, the holder of a note with 20% semi-annual interest could not write off the debt for tax purposes when this debt became bad. *William K. Harriman et al.,* T.C. Memo. 1967–190, filed October 4, 1967.

"[I]t suffices for deduction that the creation of the debt should have been significantly motivated by the taxpayer's trade or business, even though there was a non-qualifying motivation as well." *Weddle et al. v. Commissioner,* 325 F.2d 849 (2d Cir., 1963).

In distinguishing between a bad debt and a capital advance by a stockholder, one court declared: "This question is one of fact. And in deciding whether or not a debtor-creditor relation resulted from advances, the parties' true intent is relevant. Bookkeeping, form, and the parties' expressions of intent or character, the expectation of repayment, the relation of advances to stockholdings, and the adequacy of the corporate capital previously invested are among the circumstances properly to be considered, for the parties' formal designations of the advances are not conclusive, but must yield to 'facts which even indirectly may give rise to inferences contradicting' them." *Martin M. Dittmar,* 23 T.C. 789 (1955). Thus, in ascertaining whether advances were, in fact, contributions to capital, one pertinent circumstance is that the stock of the alleged "debtor" was wholly owned by the creditors. *Arlington Park Jockey Club v. Sauber,* 262 F.2d 902 (7th Cir., 1959).

For a discussion of the distinctions between debt and capital for tax purposes, see Chapter 3.

Stockholder Advances As Bad Debts. If a stockholder is to obtain a bad debt deduction for an advance to his corporation which becomes bad, "[h]e must not only prove that his participating in various enterprises was greater than that of an investor seeking profits from the operation of the businesses, but also that his purpose in organizing or rehabilitating companies was to develop them into going concerns for sale in the ordinary course of business." *Syer, Jr. et al. v. United States,* 380 F.2d 1009 (4th Cir., 1967). Investing in a business is not a trade or business, and the return from such investing arises from the corporation's business rather than a stockholder's, even though what the shareholder receives is substantially the product of his services to the corporation. Furnishing management or other services to a corporate employer does not constitute the operation of a trade or business by a stockholder-investor so as to permit a business bad debt deduction in the absence of substantial additional evidence of the incidental and proximate relationship of his loans to his trade or business. "The business of promoting corporations is one where the return is other than an investor's return, such as fees, commissions, or profits from the sales of corporations to customers in the regular course of the promoter's business. Even if a taxpayer demonstrates such an independent business activity, bad debt losses arising from his own business must be carefully distinguished from those of an investor participating in the conduct of corporate affairs." *Louis Schwartz et al.,* T.C. Memo. 1964–247, filed September 22, 1964.

As was stated in the landmark case of this series: "Devoting one's time and energies to the affairs of a corporation is not of itself, and without more, a trade or business of the person so engaged." In order to sustain a finding that the taxpayer is engaged in the trade or business of promoting or financing corporations, he must show that his reward or compensation from these corporations is different from that flowing to an investor and that he had an intention of "developing the corporations as going businesses for sale to customers in the ordinary course." *Whipple v. Commissioner,* 373 U.S. 193 (1963). "Without this additional evidence, the furnishing of organizational, promotional and managerial services to corporations is not a trade or business within the meaning of the statute." *United States v. Clark et al.,* 358 F.2d 892 (1st Cir., 1966).

For a promoter to be entitled to a business bad debt deduction, he must show that compensation which he receives as promoter is "received directly for his own services rather than indirectly through the corporate enterprise." *I. Hal Millsap, Jr. et al.,* 46 T.C. 751 (1966). Even if a taxpayer can show that he was in the business of promoting corporations, he still must establish that he was in the business of promoting the particular corporation which resulted in a loss to him. *United States v. Clark et al.,* 358 F.2d 892 (1st Cir., 1966).

A taxpayer was in the trucking business. He had a 25% stock interest in a boat manufacturing company, the bulk of the shipments of which were handled by the taxpayer's trucking service. When the manufacturing company failed, the loans which he had made to it were uncollectible and were treated as a business bad debt. The loans by the taxpayer to the manufacturing corporation were proximately related to his freight business. *Decker et al. v. United States,* 244 F. Supp. 31 (D.C., N.D. Iowa., 1965). A business bad debt was allowed in the case of a wealthy individual who invested in stocks but who also lent money to various corporations. Specifically, he guaranteed loans in return for a percentage fee. "However, a taxpayer may have more than one business or trade for income tax purposes." *Carpenter v. Erickson,* 255 F. Supp. 613 (D.C., Ore., 1966).

An individual was a developer of shopping centers. In each instance, he selected a site, took an option, secured prospective tenants, negotiated a loan commitment, prepared building plans, and approached potential investors; he carried on all of these activities as an individual. After all of these matters had been taken care of, a shopping center corporation was formed with the investors as stockholders. Then the individual assigned the options and leases to the corporation. He supervised construction. If the venture was successful, he would receive a certain amount of stock, usually from 40% to 50%, but he was not reimbursed for his expenses. Loss on the stock of one such corporation resulted in a business bad debt to him. His business was not serving his own corporations but was promoting projects with a view to a present reward flowing directly from his personal efforts. He was in the business of promoting shopping centers, and his loss was incurred in that business. *Ralph Biernbaum et al.,* T.C. Memo. 1963–210, filed August 6, 1963.

On the other hand, where a stockholder advanced funds to a corporation with the expectation that corporate utilization of the money could enhance the value of his stock, the unpaid loans were not business bad debts. His activities with respect to the affairs of the corporation were those of an investor. His activities did not constitute the carrying on of a trade or business. *Charles Oster,* T.C. Memo. 1964–335, filed December 30, 1964. An individual owned all of the stock of a corporation which sold supermarket check-out counters. He was president and treasurer. He advanced funds to the corporation when it was unable to borrow from banks. Losses on the loans were capital. The advances did not constitute valid debts but were in the nature of capital contributions. And the stockholder was not in the business of lending money to or promoting business enterprises or organizations. *George T. Smith et al.,* T.C. Memo. 1964–278, filed October 22, 1964. An individual who advanced funds to corporations which he had formed is not entitled to a business bad debt deduction unless he can establish that he had organized the corporations with a view to quick and profitable sale after each business had become established, rather than to long-range investment gains. *United States v. Byck,* 325 F.2d 551 (5th Cir., 1963).

An individual was in the real estate and building business in his individual capacity. He made advances to two corporations in which he was a major stockholder. These corporations had been formed upon a representation from the Federal Housing Administration that moneys would be lent to finance a housing complex only if the borrower were a corporation. His advances to the subsequently-insolvent corporation could not be treated as business bad debts. Even though he had to use corporations if he wanted the F.H.A. loans, the fact remained that he voluntarily had set up the corporations. The success or failure of the corporate venture could only remotely affect his individual building business and there was no evidence that it did. "The mere fact that [the taxpayer] happens to be in a business similar to that of a corporation, without more, does not provide the causal connection necessary to qualify advances made by [him] to the corporation as a business debt of [the taxpayer]." *William E. Dunn et al.,* T.C. Memo. 1963–301, filed November 1, 1963.

A taxpayer was a stock and security broker and operated through a corporation, of which he was president and a 25% stockholder. The corporation underwrote an issue of stock of a corporation known as Devco, Inc., and shares were sold to about eighty persons, including the taxpayer. When Devco became financially involved, the taxpayer advanced funds to it. Upon ultimate failure, the taxpayer claimed a business bad debt, on the ground that the loan had not been made in an attempt to salvage his investment in Devco but rather to preserve his reputation and good will with those to whom he and his corporation had sold Devco stock and to retain the confidence of his customers. Thus, he claimed, the loss was related to his business as a stockbroker and should be considered a business bad debt. The court disagreed. The taxpayer was not in the brokerage business as an individual. He was in the business of being president of a corporation, but he was not in the brokerage business merely because that happened to be the business of his corporation. This was a capital loss to him. *Johnson et al. v. McLeod,* 241 F. Supp. 178 (D.C., E.D.S.C., 1965).

Stockholder-Employee Loans To Corporation. If a stockholder-employee makes loans to a corporation in order to protect his job, the resulting debt is a business bad debt. This is especially so where he was virtually unemployable because of age or personality factors. *Isidor Jaffe et al.,* T.C. Memo. 1967–215, filed October 30, 1967.

The vice-president of a corporation, who was a minority shareholder, was informed by the president that he (the vice-president and present taxpayer) would be expected to make loans to the company and to an affiliate until their cash conditions improved. On eleven occasions, he did so. Some of the advances were re-paid. On a subsequent occasion, he was informed that he would be discharged if he did not make an additional loan to the company. He refused and was discharged. The advances were deductible as business bad debts, for the loans were made in connection with the taxpayer's trade or business of rendering services for pay. *Trent et al. v. Commissioner,* 291 F.2d 669 (2d Cir., 1961).

Where the chief stockholder of a corporation advanced funds to it, a resultant loss was not deductible as a business bad debt. As the largest stockholder, he could not say that he was obliged to make the loan in order to keep his job. He was in the business of being an employee. His loans to the company were not proximately related to any business activity he carried on and they were not deductible as business bad debts. *Leonard Lundgren et al.,* T.C. Memo. 1965–314, filed December 7, 1965.

The majority stockholder of a corporation made loans to it, but the company nonetheless failed. He claimed a business bad debt on the ground that the advances had been made in order to save his job and hence were proximately related to his trade or business as an employee. It was held that his financial investment in the company was substantial as compared to the salary received. There was no proof that the loans had not been made as an investment, and only indirectly to protect his job through saving the investment. *Kelly v. Patterson,* 331 F.2d 753 (5th Cir., 1964).

Where the majority stockholder of a corporation also was the president, amounts she lost as guarantor of corporate indebtedness were not treated as business bad debts. It was not certain whether she made the guarantee to protect her investment or her job. As majority stockholder, she did not have to fear being fired by a superior; but she would have lost her job if the company had ceased operations because of inability to obtain credit. Inasmuch as she could not prove which motivation was dominant, the Commissioner's finding that she had acted as an investor prevailed. *Weddle et al. v. Commissioner,* 325 F.2d 849 (2d Cir., 1963).

Guarantees

Where a stockholder personally guarantees debts of his corporation, any loss he must make good is fully deductible as a business bad debt if the loss was proximately related to a business that the stockholder conducted. *Putnam v. Commissioner,* 352 U.S. 82 (1957). Such was the case where a stockholder "was by no means a mere 'passive investor' in these enterprises but he personally was a most important factor in each." *Jack M. Gamble et al.,* T.C. Memo. 1960–238, filed November 8, 1960. In the case of a stockholder-guarantor: "In order to prevail here he must show (1) that he was individually in the *business* of seeking out, promoting, organizing, financing and managing business ventures as claimed; (2) that his activities with regard to [the insolvent corporations] were a part of that business; and (3) that his said guarantees and the losses resulting therefrom were proximately related to said individual business." *United States v. Clark et al.,* 358 F.2d 892 (1st Cir., 1966).

A wealthy individual was permitted to take a bad debt deduction for a guarantee of loans of a corporation in which he had no other interest. In the past seven years, he had financed at least seven corporations in return for a fee for guaranteeing the loans. "He was known in his community for financing local business he thought would succeed." Although he may have been an investor, he also was in the business of financing businesses by lending money. *Carpenter v. Erickson,* 253 F. Supp. 613 (D.C., Ore., 1966).

Guarantees by a major stockholder of the corporation's indebtedness did not, upon honoring the indebtedness, result in a business bad debt where this stockholder's motivation in making the guarantees was her desire to see her grandson-in-law (who had been given an executive position) make a success of the venture. The chief stockholder's guarantees were regarded as contributions to capital. *United States v. Henderson, Jr.,* 375 F.2d 36 (5th Cir., 1967).

An individual owned 10% of the stock of a corporation. Believing that such action would enhance the value of his stock, he joined others in guaranteeing paper of the corporation's subsidiaries. Later he sold the stock at cost. Without being called upon to honor his guarantee (there was no danger of insolvency of the companies), he paid a sum to be discharged from the guarantee. This was deductible as an ordinary loss on a transaction entered upon for profit. *J. J. Shea et al.,* 36 T.C. 577 (1961).

A taxpayer owned a very substantial minority interest in a corporation of which he was board chairman and general manager. As general manager, his responsibilities were primarily financial. He could not take a business bad debt for corporate obligations he had to make good upon insolvency. "There is no proof that the guaranteeing of corporate loans was a required duty of [the taxpayer] as chairman of the board or that [the corporation] took corporate action requesting him to do so." *Eugene H. Rietzke et al.,* 40 T.C. 443 (1963).

Where the dominant stockholder of a corporation sustained a loss on guarantees which she had made because she felt it was her responsibility to do so as "practically owner of the business," there was no business bad debt. The guarantee had been made in her capacity as investor. *Weddle et al. v. Commissioner,* 325 F.2d 849 (2d Cir., 1963).

Worthless Securities

An individual may deduct a worthless securities loss only if it was incurred in a trade or business or in a transaction entered into for profit. I.R.C. Section 165(c).

If a security which is a capital asset in a taxpayer's hands becomes worthless, the resultant loss will be treated as a loss from the sale or exchange of a capital asset on the last day of the taxable year. I.R.C. Section 165(g)(1).

An amount paid by an individual pursuant to an indemnity agreement to hold the guarantor of a corporate note harmless in return for which the individual received stock of the corporation whose loan was guaranteed was a loss from worthlessness of securities. This was a transaction entered into for profit. *Albert J. Harvey, Jr. et al.,* 35 T.C. 108 (1960).

Where a corporation's assets were nationalized by the Czechoslovakian Government, this had the effect of rendering the shares of the stockholders worthless. This resulted in capital loss to such a shareholder. *Erwin De Reitzes-Marienwert,* 21 T.C. 846 (1954). But the problem of proof in the case of foreign securities often is difficult to establish. Thus, no deduction for Polish bonds was allowed where the taxpayer could not establish cost basis and the year of worthlessness. *Kupiszewski et al. v. Commissioner,* 366 F.2d 778 (5th Cir., 1966).

Assessment On Double Liability Stock

An assessment paid on worthless, double liability bank stock by a shareholder on the cash method constitutes a part of the original stock investment and any loss sustained on the disposition thereof will constitute a capital loss. Where a stockholder effects recoveries on his investment, these will be capital gain to the extent that the assessment had produced a capital loss that had been utilized for tax purposes. Revenue Ruling 55–619, 1956–2 CB 52.

Where an individual owned stock in a holding company of national bank stocks and compromised his double liability upon insolvencies by contributing to a settlement fund, this payment could be added to the cost of the stock; and this total was to be reduced by any amount as to which he had prior tax benefits. *Tuttle v. United States,* 101 F. Supp. 532 (Ct. Cl., 1951).

The payment of an assessment upon bank stock is an additional capital cost of the stock. *Porter Property Trustees, Ltd.,* 42 B.T.A. 681 (1940).

Chapter 11

Valuations

The valuation of capital assets is significant in such tax areas as the computation of Federal estate and gift taxes, ascertainment of the amount of compensation where payment is in the form of capital assets, the amount of a charitable contributions deduction, the determination of gain or loss upon the disposition of assets, stock option computations, and the allocation of consideration in the case of a bulk purchase and sale. "There is no distinction, for most purposes . . . in the meaning of fair market as used in an estate tax return and one involving income tax." *Champion v. Commissioner,* 303 F.2d 887 (5th Cir., 1962).

Fair Market Value

"Value" has many meanings. "The term 'value,' as used in the cited statutory provision, means 'fair market value.'" *Leonard B. McKitterick Estate,* 42 B.T.A. 130 (1940).

"What is the 'market' value is not always the 'fair' value, and vice versa. In many situations there is no market for the property in question." *Ames v. O'Malley,* 91 F. Supp. 463 (D.C., Nev., 1950), *aff'd,* 197 F.2d 256 (8th Cir., 1952). But the Treasury regulations take a different view. "Only in rare and extraordinary cases does property have no fair market value." Regulations Section 1.453–6(2). Yet such situations do exist. In one case, it was held that stock had no fair market value where it was subject to numerous restrictions. *Robert Lehman,* 17 T.C. 652 (1951).

"The term 'fair market value' comes from the realm of business and economics, and from the viewpoint of the court is a fact,—an existing condition, which must be ascertained, but not created or altered by any rule of law. Primarily, it means the price at which a specified quantity of a given economic good is actually sold. It is an accomplished fact. More frequently, however, it means general or future power in exchange. But when we speak of fair market value as of a given past date, the term means the price that probably would have resulted had the good been exchanged between a willing, informed, and normal buyer and a similar seller." *Jenkins et al. v. Smith,* 21 F. Supp. 251 (D.C., Conn., 1937).

More succinctly: "The definition may be stated as the price which would probably be agreed upon by a seller willing, but under no compulsion, to sell, and a buyer willing, but under no compulsion, to buy, when both have reasonable knowledge of the facts." *John J. Newberry et al.,* 39 B.T.A. 1123 (1939). A record of offering or "ask" price is not a proper method of evaluation, for this is not necessarily what a willing buyer would pay. *Meridan Corporation v. United States,* 253 F. Supp. 636 (D.C., S.D.N.Y., 1966). As Judge Learned Hand declared: "Perhaps there need not be a 'market' to establish a 'market value,' but there must be some assurance that the value is what a 'market' would establish; and a 'market' itself presupposes enough competition between buyers and sellers to prevent the exigencies of an individual from being exploited. It may well imply that the goods have several possible buyers, so that a necessitous seller shall not be confined to one; and that there are several possible sellers of the same goods or their substantial equivalent, so that a hard-pressed buyer shall not have to accept the first offer." *Helvering v. Walbridge,* 70 F.2d 683 (2d Cir., 1934).

Actual realized prices usually are believed to be the best indication of fair market value; but there are some important exceptions to this belief. "[I]n the absence of exceptional circumstances which deprive them or reduce their evidentiary worth, prices at which stock is actually traded on an open public market on the basic date have been held generally to be the most dependable evidence of their value on that date." *Zanuck et al. v. Commissioner,* 149 F.2d 714 (9th Cir., 1948). But this concept is not an absolute one. "Stock market quotations have been held to be the best evidence of value of a traded stock in a number of cases. . . . While we are quick to recognize the persuasive importance of stock exchange prices in a stock valuation case . . . nonetheless, we are convinced that we must carefully consider all of the evidence in the record which indicates the true fair market value . . ." *Moore-McCormack Lines, Inc.,* 44 T.C. 745 (1965).

"It is unquestioned that in proving the fact of market value, accredited price current lists and market reports, including those published in trade journals or newspapers which are accepted as trustworthy, are admissible in evidence." *Virginia v. West Virginia,* 238 U.S. 202 (1915).

Fair market value depends on the market and not on intrinsic worth. *Millie Langley Wright Estate,* 43 B.T.A. 551 (1941). Book value is not synonymous with fair market value, for good will, patents, etc., may not be on the books at more than nominal figures. *Joseph Soss,* B.T.A. Memo., Docket No. 97021, entered October 25, 1940. Book value does not necessarily represent actual value even where books are correctly kept: for example, cost carried forward may not be the same as present value. *Virginia v. West Virginia,* 238 U.S. 202 (1915). Book value cannot be used to value shares where equipment was carried at its depression cost less depreciation reserve. *Peavey Paper Mills (Inc.),* T.C. Memo. 1960–237, filed November 4, 1960. "[I]t is an oversimplification to look only to the nominal stated capital of [a corporation] in determining the value of the [stockholders'] equity investment." *Murphy Logging Co. et al. v. United States,* 378 F.2d 222 (9th Cir., 1967).

Valuation Factors

Where securities have no ready or an exceedingly limited market, fair market value may be ascertained upon considerations bearing upon its intrinsic worth. *Doric Apartment Company v. Commissioner,* 94 F.2d 895 (6th Cir., 1938). Thus, the circulation structure of a newspaper or magazine is a most important element in the valuation of its stock. *Meredith Publishing Company v. Commissioner,* 64 F.2d 890 (8th Cir., 1933).

Earnings. Valuation need not always be on the basis of earnings. A corporation may have been run for long-range appreciation rather than current earnings and dividends. *William Hamm, Jr.,* T.C. Memo. 1961–347, filed December 28, 1961, *aff'd,* 325 F.2d 934 (8th Cir., 1963). "Prior earnings records usually are the most reliable guide as to future expectancy, but resort to arbitrary five-or-ten year averages without regard to current trends or future prospects will not produce a realistic valuation. If, for instance, a record of progressively increasing or decreasing net income is found, then greater weight may be accorded the most recent years' profits in estimating earning power." Revenue Ruling 54–77, 1954–1 CB 187.

Underlying Assets. Where a stock is to be valued by reference to the underlying assets, obsolescence and the need for physical improvements are limiting factors. *South Carolina National Bank et al. v. McLeod,* 256 F. Supp. 913 (D.C., S.C., 1966).

The liquidating value of a corporation sometimes furnishes a basis of valuation. "If a corporation is about to go into liquidation, the entire answer may be found in liquidating values. . . ." *J. Luther Snyder Estate v. United States,* 285 F.2d 857 (4th Cir., 1961). Liquidating value might be used to value stock in the case of a shareholder large enough to compel liquidation of the corporation. *Bartram v. Graham,* 157 F. Supp. 757 (D.C., Conn., 1957). But liquidating value is not binding in the case of a minority stockholder who cannot compel the liquidation of the corporation. *Colonial Trust Co. v. Kraemer,* 63 F. Supp. 866 (D.C., Conn., 1945). Where the stock is insufficient to vote for liquidation of a corporation, valuation of shares in accordance with the value of the underlying assets may be subject to a discount. *Obermer v. United States,* 238 F. Supp. 29 (D.C., Hawaii, 1964).

In a manufacturing company as opposed to an investment company, liquidating value may have little relevancy, for the corporation may be one that is scarcely likely to be liquidated, being worth more alive than dead. *Inga Bardahl et al.,* T.C. Memo. 1965–158, filed June 15, 1965.

Comparisons. "In the case of stock and securities of a corporation the value of which, by reason of their not being listed on an exchange and by reason of the absence of sales thereof, cannot be determined with reference to bid and asked prices or with reference to sales prices, the value thereof shall be determined by taking into consideration, in addition to all other factors, the value of stock or securities of corporations engaged in the same or in a similar line of business which are listed on an exchange." I.R.C. Section 2031(b).

But it is not possible to compare all corporations with comparable ones the stock of which is listed on an exchange. Some stock must be characterized as unique. *Obermer v. United States,* 238 F. Supp. 29 (D.C., Hawaii, 1964). Comparisons must be approached with great caution. "While the comparative appraisal is a valid approach where no other information as to stock transactions is available its validity is diminished when only one comparative is used since no two companies are exactly alike, and in the instant case there is no showing that [the selected comparison company] matched [the corporation to be valued] in its growth pattern." *Jungbluth v. United States,* 253 F. Supp. 338 (D.C., E.D. Wis., 1966), *aff'd,* 371 F.2d 416 (7th Cir., 1966). Discount may be in order when comparing unlisted shares with those of listed corporations, to represent the cost of publicly underwriting the shares. A 12.17% discount factor was used in *Central Trust Company v. United States,* 305 F.2d 393 (Ct. Cl., 1962).

Appraisers' Valuations. An independent appraiser's valuation of property may be an offering price and is not necessarily the price that a willing buyer would pay. This would not be a proper method of evaluation for tax purposes. *Meridan Corporation v. United States,* 253 F. Supp. 636 (D.C., S.D.N.Y., 1966). The valuation set by an expert cannot be used in the case of a gift of property which the donee immediately re-sells for a lower figure. *Philip Kaplan et al.,* 43 T.C. 663 (1965). Thus, the donor is penalized upon his tax return if the donee sells the property for too low a figure.

Where an appraiser is employed, his valuations may be suspect. He may have been instructed by his client to concentrate upon certain factors. "Parenthetically we find the appraiser's testimony quite amusing as he relates how he was coaxed by the oldest brother to keep the value up and by the younger one to keep it down." *Murphy Logging Co. et al. v. United States,* 378 F.2d 222 (9th Cir., 1967).

Dividends. The dividend factor is a material element in the valuation of a minority stockholders' interest. *The South Carolina National Bank et al. v. McLeod,* 256 F. Supp. 913 (D.C., S.C., 1966).

Stock Split. Stock is subject to a higher valuation where there is evidence that the shares are about to be split, thus increasing marketability. *Jungbluth v. United States,* 253 F. Supp. 338 (D.C., E.D. Wis., 1966), *aff'd,* 371 F.2d 416 (7th Cir., 1966).

Capital Gain Lock-In. Stock would tend to have a lower value if the corporate assets were primarily securities and there was a "built-in" capital gains tax. *Obermer v. United States,* 238 F. Supp. 29 (D.C., Hawaii, 1964).

How The Owner Valued The Shares. A *bona fide* offer, made by a willing and able potential purchaser, which is rejected by the taxpayer, is some evidence of what he as owner considered the lower limits of such value to be. *Edward W. Payne,* 12 B.T.A. 781 (1928). But that does not conclusively establish the fair market value of the property. *Hiram S. Brown Estate,* T.C. Memo. 1956–240, filed October 31, 1956.

Valuations used by a decedent on gift tax returns a year or two before his death are significant, especially if book value and/or earnings of the corporation rose in the meantime. *Houghton et al. v. United States,* D.C., E.D. Wis., 1965.

If shareholders use their pre-emptive rights to acquire additionally issued stock, the figure at which the rights were issued indicates an actual transaction at fair market value. *Jungbluth v. United States,* 253 F. Supp. 338 (D.C., E.D. Wis., 1966), *aff'd,* 371 F.2d 416 (7th Cir., 1966).

Use Of A Formula. "Because valuations cannot be made on the basis of a prescribed formula, there is no means whereby the various applicable factors in a particular case can be assigned mathematical weights in deriving the fair market value. For this reason, no useful purpose is served by taking an average of several factors (for example, book value, capitalized earnings and capitalized dividends) and basing the valuation on the result. Such a process excludes active consideration of other pertinent factors, and the end result cannot be supported by a realistic application of the significant facts in the case except by mere chance." Revenue Ruling 59–60, 1959–1 CB 237.

Formulae are evidence probative of intrinsic value which is more appropriate to an unlisted stock valuation than to a listed stock for which there is an active market demand. *Leonard B. McKitterick Estate,* 42 B.T.A. 130 (1940).

How significant are averages to a typical investor? "A prudent investor, searching for a basis for a reasonable estimate of the future, does not depend upon averages alone. He searches for significant trends, and his use of data that measures past performance must be governed by all of those considerations which enter into managerial projections of sales and earnings." *J. Luther Snyder Estate v. United States,* 285 F.2d 857 (4th Cir., 1961).

It is one thing to make use of yardsticks or formulae. Even after such factors have been agreed upon, there is still the question of "the weight to be given to the several factors. . . ." *King v. United States,* D.C., N.D. Cal., 1965.

Stock Of Closely-Held Corporations

There are few problems more difficult in taxation that the valuation of shares in a closely-held corporation where there has been no arm's length market for stock. "[A] 'close corporation' means, in the vernacular, a corporation in which the stock is held in few hands, or in few families, and wherein it is not at all, or only rarely dealt in by buying or selling." *Brooks v. Willcuts,* 78 F.2d 270 (8th Cir., 1935).

The most comprehensive rules for the valuation of stocks of closely-held corporations were set forth in Revenue Ruling 59–60, 1959–1 CB 237, which states in part as follows:

"Closely held corporations are those corporations the shares of which are owned by a relatively limited number of stockholders. Often the entire stock issue is held by one family. The result of this situation is that little, if any, trading in the shares takes place. There is, therefore, no established market for the stock and such sales as occur at irregular intervals seldom reflect all of the elements of a representative transaction as defined by the term 'fair market value.' . . .

"The fair market value of specific shares of stock will vary as general economic conditions change from 'normal' to 'boom' or 'depression,' that is, according to the degree of optimism or pessimism with which the investing public regards the future at the required date of appraisal. Uncertainty as to the stability or continuity of the future income from a property decreases its value by increasing the risk of loss of earnings and value in the future. The value of shares of stock of a company with very uncertain future prospects is highly speculative. . . .

"Valuation of securities is, in essence, a prophecy as to the future and must be based on facts available at the required date of appraisal. . . .

"It is advisable to emphasize that in the valuations of the stock of closely held corporations or the stock of corporations where market quotations are either lacking or too scarce to be recognized, all available financial data, as well as all relevant factors affecting the fair market value, should be considered. The following factors, although not all-inclusive are fundamental and require careful analysis in each case:

(a) The nature of the business and the history of the enterprise from its inception.

(b) The economic outlook in general and the condition and outlook of the specific industry in particular.

(c) The book value of the stock and the financial condition of the business.

(d) The earning capacity of the company.

(e) The dividend-paying capacity.

(f) Whether or not the enterprise has goodwill or other intangible value.

(g) Sales of the stock and the size of the block of stock to be valued.

(h) The market price of stocks of corporations engaged in the same or a similar line of business having their stocks actively traded in a free and open market, either on an exchange or over-the-counter. . . .

"The valuation of closely held corporate stock entails the consideration of all relevant factors as stated. . . . Depending upon the circumstances in each case, certain factors may carry more weight than others because of the nature of the company's business."

Because of its importance, the full text of this Revenue Ruling is reproduced in Appendix 2 of this book.

Revenue Ruling 59–60, above, sets forth the proper approach to use in the valuation of closely-held corporate stocks for estate and gift tax purposes. But the general approach, methods, and factors outlined therein are equally applicable to valuations of corporate stocks for income and other tax purposes. Revenue Ruling 65–192, 1965–2 CB 259.

In the case of stock in a closely-held corporation, one factor is fear of loss of the chief customer. Where the arrangement was beneficial to the chief customer and that party in any event would be in no position to terminate the contract for several years, the possibility would not be regarded as a value depressant. *Houghton et al. v. United States,* D.C., E.D. Wis., 1965.

In setting the valuation of stock in a closely-held corporation, the court in one case considered the fact that the company's activities were not diversified. This served to lessen the valuation. *Dorothy Cookson Estate,* T.C. Memo. 1965–319, filed December 14, 1965.

The valuation of shares of a decedent held in a corporation could not be written down to reflect the corporation's loss of its guiding spirit and chief executive. Despite the respect accorded him in the industry and his management talents, the evidence revealed that an extremely able and experienced management team was capable of assuming his duties. The death of the decedent would not have led a willing buyer to believe that the general outlook of the corporation was unfavorable. *Houghton et al. v. United States,* D.C., E.D. Wis., 1965. But where a corporation is in fact a 1-man company, the death of that person can serve to lessen the value of the stock. *James D. McDermott Estate,* T.C. Memo., Docket No. 31207, entered April 30, 1953.

The amount of dividends paid may be a primary factor in the valuation of corporate stock where a corporation is closely held and the shareholder does not own enough stock to have an effective voice in management. *Augustus E. Staley,* 41 B.T.A. 752 (1940).

A limiting factor upon stock of a corporation exists where, because of appreciation in value of the investments held, there is a so-called "built-in" capital gains tax. *Obermer v. United States,* 238 F. Supp. 29 (D.C., Hawaii, 1964).

A discount was allowed in the valuation of shares where stockholder litigation was underway and any potential buyer would be disinclined to buy into a family squabble. *Champlin Refining Co. v. Commissioner,* 123 F.2d 202 (10th Cir., 1941).

Stock of a closely-held corporation was adversely affected by the fact that it was widely known that the corporation was to be subjected to substantial additional Federal tax liability. *Samuel Want,* 29 T.C. 1223 (1958), *rev'd in part on other grounds,* 280 F.2d 777 (2d Cir., 1960).

The value of closely-held stock would tend to be depressed by the existence of a heavy debenture retirement commitment. *Obermer v. United States,* 238 F. Supp. 29 (D.C., Hawaii, 1964).

The price at which directors' qualifying shares are sold to a new director in a closely-held corporation may not be determinative of true value. *South Carolina National Bank et al. v. McLeod,* 256 F. Supp. 913 (D.C., S.C., 1966).

"Closely held corporate stock cannot be valued reasonably by the application of any inflexible formula. . . . Financial data is [sic] important only to the extent it furnishes a basis for an informed judgment of the future performance of the particular company, for investors buy stock of this kind out of reasoned hope in the future, not out of pride in the past." *J. Luther Snyder Estate v. United States,* 285 F.2d 857 (4th Cir., 1961).

Discount For Minority Interest. Unlisted stock, representing a minority interest in a family-controlled or close corporation, has limited marketability. *Betty Hansen et al.,* T.C. Memo., Docket Nos. 29419–21, entered

July 28, 1952. Unless offered a discount, who would be apt to buy a less than controlling interest in a closely-held corporation when it would appear that his plans and policies would lack the votes to be effected and the existing shareholders probably would "gang up" against him?

"In a closely held corporation, where the transfer is of a minority interest, stocks may be inclined to have a fair market value less than book value since a minority stockholder is in no position to bring about dissolution to obtain the book value." *Inga Bardahl et al.,* T.C. Memo. 1965–158, filed June 15, 1965. "[M]inority stock interests in a 'closed' corporation might be worth less than the proportionate share of assets to which they attach." *Irene de Guebriant Estate,* 14 T.C. 611 (1950), *rev'd on another issue,* 186 F.2d 307 (2d Cir., 1951). In the case of a minority interest in one family-owned company, the court felt that a buyer could be found in the family. But a discount of 20% nonetheless was allowed. *Bartram et al. v. Graham,* 157 F. Supp. 757 (D.C., Conn., 1957).

A decedent owned one-eighth of the common stock in a family holding company, the principal assets of which were unlisted stock in a closely-held corporation and an interest in a joint venture, neither of which was engaged in active business operations. It was held that such interests have a fair market value less than the proportionate share of the underlying assets. The taxpayer reported $48.80 per share; the Internal Revenue Service, $82; the court, $70. *Jesse Ring Garrett Estate,* T.C. Memo., Docket No. 35955, entered October 7, 1953.

A minority interest in a closely-held corporation was not entitled to a discount where it was purchased, not by an outsider, but by the owner of the largest block of shares. *Rufus F. Turner et al.,* T.C. Memo. 1964–161, filed June 10, 1964.

After-Events

The valuation of a capital asset is to be determined from the facts known at the time of the taxable event, such as a gift. *Elsie McK. Morgan et al.,* 42 T.C. 1080 (1964). "Valuation . . . must be based on facts available at the required date of appraisal." Revenue Ruling 59–60, 1959–1 CB 237. As was stated in the leading case in this series, "The valuation of stock must be made as of the relevant dates without regard to events occurring subsequent to the crucial dates." *Bader v. United States,* 172 F. Supp. 833 (D.C., S.D. Ill., 1959).

But "Evidence of a sale taking place after a valuation date has probative force bearing on the value as of the earlier critical date—where there has been no material change of conditions or circumstances in the interim." *Mabel Lloyd Ridgely Estate v. United States, . . .* F.2d . . . (Ct. Cl., 1967).

Actual Sales Prices May Not Be Controlling

"The prices at which shares of stock are actually traded on an open market on the pertinent date have been held generally to be the best evidence of the fair market value on that date, in the absence of exceptional circumstances." *Catherine McCulloch Spencer Estate,* 5 T.C. 904 (1945). But on occasion, the courts have recognized the existence of these "exceptional circumstances."

Reasonable Knowledge. "[T]he price at which shares are sold is ordinarily the best test of their value. It is quite true that, even in wide markets where there are many buyers and sellers, these often do not know the more important facts about the company; and their consensus of opinion is not necessarily a proper measure of value, if by that is meant a truly informed judgment; nevertheless, sales are usually the most reliable evidence, and in any case they should weigh heavily." *Rogers et al. v. Helvering,* 107 F.2d 394 (2d Cir., 1939).

In the case of actual sales on the New York Stock Exchange, a court should consider these quotations and at the same time give some weight to all of the facts and circumstances which surrounded that market on the date in question. *Strong v. Rogers,* D.C., N.J., 1933, *aff'd,* 72 F.2d 455 (3d Cir., 1934). In this case, expert witnesses testified that stock quotations in July, 1929, were unreasonably high. The court noted: "It appears that at the time the market was greatly affected by the presence of thousands of unskilled and unreasoning buyers who entered the market in ignorance of the true facts underlying values and purely for the purpose of speculation." Such always is the case to some degree; but ordinarily "their presence is not in sufficient numbers to produce such wild and unreasonable prices. . . ." Of the two stocks in question, one sold on the Stock Exchange at 89¾ and the other at 106 on the critical date. The court accepted values of 55 and 65, respectively.

Shares of a closely-held corporation were valued by the executor of a decedent's estate at $3 per share, upon the basis of actual over-the-counter sales of the stock. The Internal Revenue Service used $10, claiming that these shares did not represent a free and open market, for the sellers were unaware of the corporation's improved financial position. The court found that only a few stockholders who directed the business knew of the improved financial condition, and these were not the persons who sold their shares. The sellers did not have adequate knowledge of the material factors affecting the value of their stock; they were not sufficiently experienced in business and corporate accounting to determine from the reports the increased earnings and the real intrinsic value of the stock. In setting a valuation of $6.50, the court observed: "These sales were apparently between uninformed sellers and uninformed buyers." *Schnorbach v. Kavanagh*, 102 F. Supp. 828 (D.C., W.D. Mich., 1951). That negates the element in the definition of "fair market value" that buyer and seller "both have reasonable knowledge of the facts." *John J. Newberry et al.*, 39 B.T.A. 1123 (1939).

A taxpayer vainly argued that the Internal Revenue Service erred in valuing a stock gift at the New York Stock Exchange mean of the day. The taxpayer's position was that valuation of a gift on October 5, 1939 should have reflected the adverse effect on values of the outbreak of World War II, which would seriously impair earnings of a motion picture company. This circumstance, argued the taxpayer, was something "which the public knew but did not know how to weigh." But specific proof of the effect of this intelligence could not be established. *Zanuck et al. v. Commissioner*, 149 F.2d 714 (9th Cir., 1945).

Shares of S.M.A. Corporation had a mean value on the Cleveland Stock Exchange of $10.50 on the date of a decedent's death. But at that time, a much larger corporation, American Home Products, was actively considering a merger with S.M.A. The public was not aware of this contemplated merger and the stock exchange quotations reflected this fact. Evidence showed that the majority stockholders of both corporations were ready and able to have the merger effected on the terms which were adopted subsequent to the decedent's death: that is, the giving of American's shares worth $14.04 for each share of S.M.A. The court set a value on the S.M.A. stock of $14 per share on the date of the decedent's death. *W. E. Telling Estate*, T.C. Memo., Docket No. 106694, entered June 28, 1944.

Of little probative value were sales to unsophisticated investors who were willing to spend relatively small sums to speculate on a cheap unlisted stock without regard to the underlying financial structure. *J. K. Downer et al.*, 48 T.C. 86 (1967).

Actual sales prices on the New York Stock Exchange were not to be disregarded upon the ground that there was concealment and misrepresentations of which both buyers and sellers were unaware. The fact was, the shares could have been traded in on the critical date at that figure. *Millie Langley Wright Estate*, 43 B.T.A. 551 (1941).

Less Than Arm's Length Sale. Actual sales are not a determination of value if made at less than arm's length. *Cora R. Fitts Estate v. Commissioner*, 237 F.2d 729 (8th Cir., 1956).

Where The Consideration Covers More Than Sale Of Stock. Even in a transaction between unrelated parties, the actual price of stock is not determinative of value if the purchases and sales were actuated by other considerations than the sale of the stock. Value was not set by sales prices of stock where the buyers secured something of substantial value in addition to the stock, such as the presidency of a corporation or employment as its counsel. *Betty Hansen et al.,* T.C. Memo., Docket Nos. 29419–21, entered July 28, 1952. In one case, the price paid by minority stockholders for enough stock to get control of a corporation was not deemed to be the fair market value of the stock. Here there was no willing buyer. It was a payment to assure continued employment of the purchasers in the only business in which they had any expert knowledge. *Frank Pidgeon et al.,* B.T.A. Memo., Docket Nos. 45689–91, entered January 19, 1933.

Because of the possibility that their stock holdings might be in violation of the Clayton Anti-Trust Act, certain shareholders wished to withdraw from a corporation. They sold their entire interests for an amount equivalent to their cash investments in the company. "That sale," said the court, "was made under circumstances somewhat comparable to a forced sale. It was not a typical representation or open market sale and is not a criterion of value." *Magee Furnace Co.,* 11 B.T.A. 1216 (1928).

Amounts paid to a minority stockholder by a corporation do not set a value for the stock, where the minority stockholder had no other available market. S.M. 2522, III–2 CB 23. Actual sales of stock might be unrepresentative of fair market value, when shares are re-purchased by a corporation from a dissenting stockholder, perhaps to get rid of him at any price. See *Jungbluth v. United States,* 253 F. Supp. 338 (D.C., E.D. Wis., 1966), *aff'd,* 371 F.2d 416 (7th Cir., 1966). He may have been paid too much, part of the payment being for nuisance value. Where a principal stockholder of a corporation purchased the shares of a dissident stockholder and immediately re-sold the shares at a lower figure to key employees, deduction was denied. The purchase of stock by him did not establish its value under these circumstances, for he might have set some value on the managerial services the company was obtaining. Without establishment of how much of the consideration was for the stock itself, there was no basis for a loss deduction. *Leo Sack et al.,* 33 T.C. 805 (1960).

The prices obtained upon a sacrifice sale do not necessarily represent the true value of a listed stock. *Laird et al. v. Commissioner,* 85 F.2d 598 (3d Cir., 1935). Sales made under peculiar and unusual circumstances, such as sales of small lots, forced sales, and sales in a restricted market, "may neither signify a fair market price or value . . ." *Heiner v. Crosby,* 24 F.2d 191 (3d Cir., 1928). Prices obtained at public auction sales "are not always the best criterion of value, and are certainly not conclusive, particularly where there is evidence that the property would sell for more under different circumstances." *Daniel S. McGuire et al.,* 44 T.C. 801 (1965).

A realized price is not determinative of value if it can be established that this was the result of a quick sale. *Bell's Booteries, Inc. v. United States,* 91 F. Supp. 155 (D.C., M.D. Tenn., 1948).

Actual sales prices of shares were not determinative of value when banks had been interested only in obtaining enough for these collateralized shares to cover their loans upon them. *Walter v. Duffy,* 287 F. 41 (3d Cir., 1923). "A single transaction between a husband and wife made under the emotion, tension and practical necessities involved in a divorce proceeding does not comply with this rule." *Commissioner v. Marshman et al.,* 279 F.2d 27 (6th Cir., 1960).

Although the best evidence of value usually is the sales record of stock in an open market, the prices at which such sales were made is not determinative of the fair market value where market sales were supported or stimulated so as not to be truly representative. *Champion v. Commissioner,* 303 F.2d 887 (5th Cir., 1962).

An acceptable valuation was not set by actual sales of a security on a stock exchange where the transaction was the very first sale of a stock of a new company which was relatively unknown to the investing public. *American Steel Foundries v. United States,* 299 F.2d 300 (Ct. Cl., 1961).

The Blockage Theory

"It is common knowledge that sales of small lots of stock on an exchange afford no reliable criterion of value per share for large lots which if disposed of rapidly are likely to flood the market and thus depress the price. Every skillful broker who wishes to dispose of a block of stock larger than the market is likely to absorb without sacrifice in price will liquidate slowly by sales of small units. If he disposes of the stock too slowly, he runs the risk that a recession in current prices may occur and that the prices of sales may suffer on that account. If he sells too quickly, he is likely to suffer from forcing an amount of stock on the market which exceeds the normal demand so that purchasers will only buy at less than going rates. . . . If the block is large enough and the market thin, size will certainly count under ordinary circumstances. To be sure some unusual factor like a struggle for corporate control might cause a large block to sell at a higher rate than a small lot would had no struggle begun, but the size of the block is surely a matter for consideration in finding value." *Groff v. Munford,* 150 F.2d 825 (2d Cir., 1945).

Courts recognize "the obvious economic fact that a market in which sales of small lots can be accomplished at a specific price may lack the body and breadth necessary to support sales of large blocks of securities at the same unit price." *Richardson v. Commissioner,* 151 F.2d 102 (2d Cir., 1945). This is the blockage theory. " 'Blockage' is a term used to characterize the depressing effect on the market price of a stock traded on a stock exchange caused by sale of a larger block substantially in excess of the normal level of trading. The necessity to liquidate such a block is likely to depress prices because it creates an available supply far in excess of normal demand." *Seas Shipping Company, Inc.,* T.C. Memo. 1965–240, filed August 31, 1965, *aff'd,* 371 F.2d 528 (2d Cir., 1967).

" 'Blockage' is not a law of economics, a principle of law, nor a rule of evidence. If the value of a given number of shares is influenced by the size of the block, this is a matter of evidence and not of doctrinaire assumption." *Safe Deposit & Trust Company of Baltimore,* 35 B.T.A. 259 (1939), *aff'd,* 95 F.2d 806 (4th Cir., 1938).

Infrequent transactions fall short of furnishing a satisfactory indication of the value of a large block of stock. *Virginia v. West Virginia,* 238 U.S. 202 (1915). But a taxpayer cannot establish how the theory of blockage applies to his particular lot of shares without the testimony of brokers who are familiar with the market in that particular stock and with distribution methods. The court is not required to accept the opinions of the taxpayer's experts as to value, especially if there is contradictory testimony. *Gamble v. Commissioner,* 101 F.2d 565 (6th Cir., 1939).

Here is a typical example of the blockage principle. A decedent owned 14,700 of the 180,000 shares of South Bend Lathe Works, which was listed on the Chicago Stock Exchange. The executor used a valuation of $25.92 per share. The Internal Revenue Service used $45.50, the mean between the highest and lowest prices on the days immediately before and after the date of death. The court accepted the blockage principle yet felt that contemporary sales should be the starting point, but that allowance should be made for the expenses of utilization of secondary distribution that would maintain existing prices. A $5 reduction was allowed, which included the spread allowed secondary dealers of about $3.50 per share and handling expenses of $1.50 which the executor might have to expend. *St. Joseph Bank and Trust Company v. United States,* D.C., N.D. Ind., 1953.

"A 'secondary distribution' is a process by which a large block of stock is placed on the market through an underwriting syndicate and distributors, immediately after the close of the market, to be sold at the closing price of the day. This method of the sale of stock by blocks is practically equivalent to a sale by wholesale. Adequate compensation must be paid by the seller to those engaged in this operation. The approval of the stock exchange is required before such a distribution is offered. Protective measures covering the seller, the brokers, and the buying public are carefully imposed and meticulously observed. The net price realized by the vendor varies from $1 to $2 below the price to the public." *Sewell L. Avery,* 3 T.C. 963 (1944).

Another method of implementing the blockage theory is the *special offering.* "The special offering is a method of stimulating demand for a stock and greater volume of sales, with a safeguard against price 'rigging' and fluctuations of the market place, so that although demand is stimulated and sales are increased, market price is stabilized and the market is unmolested. The difference between the selling of stock on an exchange under ordinary circumstances and the selling of stock on an exchange through a special offering is that in the former instance the buyers come into the market voluntarily (they put orders with the broker), whereas in the latter instance they come into the market as the result of solicitation by salesmen (the salesman goes out to get the order). Under ordinary circumstances, the average public does not know what or how much stock is being offered unless he is solicited by salesmen. When there is not a ready market for stock, buyers have to be solicited. Many who are willing to buy small lots of stock are brought into the market by paying salesmen a higher sales commission. The original seller of the stock makes a concession from the market price, so that the dealer purchasing the stock from him will be able to pay salesmen to solicit orders from customers. The net price realized by the original seller is usually about $1 per share under the market price for a stock selling in the middle thirties. Under the 'Special Offering' method of selling stock, protective measures covering the buying public, the brokers, and the sellers are imposed by the stock exchange and are meticulously observed." *Thomas A. Standish,* 8 T.C. 1204 (1947).

Where Blockage Was Allowed. Gifts were made aggregating 12,800 shares of Melville Shoe Corporation common stock. The taxpayer used a valuation of $27.50. The Internal Revenue Service used $29.50, the mean of the stock market sales on the day nearest the date of gift. Noted the court: "If the record shows that by reason of a 'thin market' or other circumstances a block of the size in question could not have been sold through normal channels by sales on the market without seriously depressing the price, this fact becomes important." Witnesses testified that the market was thin, aggregating 1,600 shares in a week. There was testimony that the normal and most satisfactory way to market this stock would be through a wholesale house, the charges thereto approximating $2 per share. The taxpayer's valuation was sustained. *J. Franklin McElwain et al.,* T.C. Memo., Docket Nos. 11033 and 110442, entered December 28, 1942.

Gifts of 16,000 shares of Armstrong Cork Co. were made, at a time when 1,411,000 shares were outstanding. The donor used a valuation of

$36.295 per share; the Internal Revenue Service used $37.25, the mean between the highest and lowest quoted selling prices on the day of the gift. In the judgment of the court, the shares were not closely held. The court found that the shares could not be absorbed without breaking the market. Value was set at $36.295 per share, 95½ ¢ below the mean. Considered were the price at which the block could be sold over a reasonable period of time, the fact that the market was thin, and the fact that on the day of the gift there was a special offering of 4,000 shares of the stock on the New York Stock Exchange. *Thomas A. Standish,* 8 T.C. 1204 (1947).

A decedent owned 2,700 shares of Weyerhaeuser Timber Company stock, which was not listed on an exchange but which was traded over-the-counter. On the critical date, the bid and ask prices were 61 and 63. These quotations were for 100-share lots. The court felt that such a block would have depressed the market and could not have been sold by a skillful broker within a reasonable time at the current bid price. If handled by a broker, the stock would be considered a wholesale transaction and would have involved expense. The court accepted the estate's valuation of $59.50. *Jessie Ring Garrett Estate,* T.C. Memo., Docket No. 35955, entered October 7, 1953.

Where Blockage Was Not Allowed. "Whether a large block of stock is to be valued at the same unit value as a small lot actually sold on the market is not a question to be answered dogmatically, but one which must be considered in each case upon evidence specifically applicable to the problem in hand." *Archibald M. Chisholm Estate,* 37 B.T.A. 167 (1938).

In one case, the taxpayers claimed that, had they dumped on the market large blocks of a listed stock, they could not have obtained prices even approximating the Commissioner's figure of mean average on the critical date, for which reason, it was alleged, the stock should be valued at the prices which the taxpayers' experts testified probably could be obtained on a forced sale. The court upheld the Government, stating that the value of stock could be proved by evidence of book values, intrinsic values, good will, and the prospects of the company involved. Inasmuch as the taxpayers had not availed themselves of such procedures, the Commissioner's presumption as to the value would not be upset. *Laird et al. v. Commissioner,* 85 F.2d 598 (3d Cir., 1935).

The mean price of General Motors stock on the date for which shares were to be valued was $52.75, on a volume of 7,900 shares. The taxpayer's witnesses testified that the 100,000 shares to be valued could not have been sold at that price, and they estimated values ranging from $50 to $47. The court upheld the Commissioner, stating that "[i]t does not appear that the block of 100,000 shares could not have been sold at its quoted prices within a reasonable time by skilled brokers following prudent liquidation practices." In fact, in the next two months, more than 375,000 shares were sold at average prices between $53 and $54. *Mott v. Commissioner,* 139 F.2d 317 (6th Cir., 1943).

"In a reasonably ready market shares of stock might be worth the price quoted on a particular date even though no purchaser would have been available for a large block if in the near future all the shares could have been 'peddled out' according to the practice of prudent executors at the price realizable on the critical date for a small number of shares. The stock may well have been worth the market price realizable for the smaller number of shares because the owner could realize that amount by an efficient liquidation with a loss of only a negligible sum for a few days' interest." *Bull et al. v. Smith,* 119 F.2d 490 (2d Cir., 1941). That places a burden upon the owner of shares to show that a skillful broker could not have "peddled out" the stock without depressing the market.

The blockage rule was not applied where there was no need or intention to dump any stock. *Seas Shipping Company, Inc.,* T.C. Memo. 1965–240, filed August 31, 1965, *aff'd,* 371 F.2d 528 (2d Cir., 1967).

Under certain circumstances, the existence of a large block of stock will not serve to reduce the valuation. "When a block of stock as large as 13 percent is purchased the net asset value (or book value) of the stock becomes an important consideration." *Moore McCormack Lines, Inc.,* 44 T.C. 745 (1965).

Lack Of A Consistent Pattern. The blockage discount may vary as between dates. National Tea Company had 631,400 shares outstanding on March 12, 1946 and 651,150 on March 6, 1947. It was held that a transaction involving 6,250 shares on the earlier date did not involve blockage as these shares could have been absorbed by the market; but as to the same number of shares on the later date, blockage was justified because the record showed that the market had gotten considerably thinner. A discount of 87½¢ per share was allowed for the later date. *Harley V. McNamara,* 19 T.C. 1001 (1953), *rev'd on other grounds,* 210 F.2d 505 (7th Cir., 1954).

The discount may vary because of different secondary distribution factors for two stocks on the same day. Gifts were made of an aggregate of 26,000 shares of Montgomery Ward & Co. and 8,000 shares of United States Gypsum Co. stock. The donor reported the stock at $36 and $62.50, respectively, figures that were 1½ and 2 points, respectively, below the mean quotations for the day of the gift. The Commissioner sought to use the mean averages on the New York Stock Exchange for the day: $37.50 and $64.50, respectively. The court used $36.50 and $64.50. This took into account the charges that would have been made by secondary distributors, market absorption being somewhat different for the two stocks. *Sewell L. Avery,* 3 T.C. 963 (1944).

Negative Blockage. The existence of a large block of shares may increase the per share value of each of these shares under appropriate circumstances.

A decedent owned 62,982 shares of Seatrain Lines, Inc., of a total of 1,412,891 shares outstanding. The estate valued these at $3; the Internal Revenue Service used $7.375, the mean between bid and asked of this over-the-counter stock. The court used a figure of $5.50. Noting that more than two-thirds of the outstanding shares were owned directly or beneficially by investors of three principal groups or classes, the court stated that "the substantial number of shares held by the decedent's estate may for such reason have had greater value as a single block, because of their potential for affording 'leverage' to a potential buyer or buyers in acquiring a controlling stock interest." *Marjorie Gilbert Brush Estate,* T.C. Memo. 1963–186, filed July 8, 1963.

An individual made three gifts, each of 24,500 shares of Soss Manufacturing Company stock, or a total of 73,500 shares. Outstanding were 195,000 shares. For gift tax purposes, the value was shown at $3.0085 a share, obtained by dividing the adjusted capital of the company by the number of shares outstanding. The Commissioner used $7.25, the mean of the bid and ask quotations on the New York Curb Market on the date of the gift. The court used $5.75, saying: "Stock representing absolute control of a profitable and going business might well command a better price than a number of shares not representing control or representing probable control." *Joseph Soss,* B.T.A. Memo., Docket No. 97021, entered October 25, 1940.

Sale of a large block of shares does not necessarily mean a break in the market price. "The opposite condition might possibly have prevailed, for the influence of the ownership of a large number of shares upon corporate control might give them a value in excess of prevailing market quotations; in which event the application of the administrative rule (the use of a lower value) would be unfair to the government." *Helvering v. Safe Deposit & Trust Company of Baltimore,* 95 F.2d 806 (4th Cir., 1938).

Restrictions On Sale Of Stock

Stock is worth less than its aliquot part of the total share value where it is subject to a restriction, such as upon transfer. *United States v. Parker et al.,* 376 F.2d 402 (5th Cir., 1967). Thus, where some of the shares of a corporation were not qualified for sale to the public, they were valued at 20% less than qualified shares. *Matthew I. Heinold Estate v. Commissioner,* 363 F.2d 329 (7th Cir., 1966).

Where stock is subject to restrictions that make sale impossible, the stock has no market value. *Helvering v. Tex-Penn Oil Company et al.,* 300 U.S. 481 (1937). But a restriction on the public sale of stock does not prevent private sale, even though the restriction may have the effect of depressing the fair market value of this stock as compared to the fair market value of unrestricted shares. *Edward C. Victorson et al.,* T.C. Memo. 1962–231, filed October 1, 1962, *aff'd,* 326 F.2d 264 (2d Cir., 1964).

Certain certificates of a stock traded on the American Stock Exchange bore this notation: "The shares represented by this certificate have not been registered under the Securities Act of 1933. The shares have been acquired for investment and may not be sold or transferred in the absence of an effective registration statement for the shares under the Securities Act of 1933 or an opinion of counsel to the company that registration is not required under said Act." The taxpayer claimed that the shares had no value as they could not be sold. But the court held that the restrictive statement did not rob the shares of ascertainable value, inasmuch as they could have been sold privately. *Specialty Paper & Board Co.,* T.C. Memo. 1965–208, filed July 28, 1965. The Commissioner used as the value the actual sales price of that day, $5.125, but he lowered this to $4.50 upon the evidence of his own witness. The court accepted this.

Evidence of the price of unrestricted shares in active trading on the New York Curb Market at the time restricted shares were received by the taxpayer was more probative of the fair market value of the restricted shares than evidence of book value or past earnings. *T. W. Henritze et al.,* 28 B.T.A. 1173 (1933).

The holder of *investment letter stock* cannot sell it on the open market for a stipulated period (say, one or two years) without violating the Securities Act of 1933 unless there is a *bona fide* change in circumstances. The holder thus would be obliged to retain the stock or to sell it privately to some one who would hold it. This should entitle the stock to a discount in valuation; but a 20% factor assigned by the Tax Court in one case was reversed on the ground that there was no evidence supporting this particular figure. *LeVant et al. v. Commissioner,* 376 F.2d 434 (7th Cir., 1967). In another case, the court considered that shares which were subject to an investment letter should not be valued at the selling price of free stock of $11 but, in terms of that factor and the size of the block, at $7. *William H. Husted,* 47 T.C. 664 (1967).

It has long been recognized that a restriction on the sale of investment letter stock reduces the value of this stock below the fair market value of the stock without the restriction. *Edith G. Goldwasser,* 47 B.T.A. 445 (1942), *aff'd,* 142 F.2d 556 (2d Cir., 1944). There, the stock being valued was received by the taxpayer under an arrangement whereby she was to make no public offering of the shares but was to hold them as an investment. The court nonetheless determined the stock had value and in the course of its opinion said that while this provision did not constitute a restrictive covenant preventing her from disposing of the stock if she had seen fit to do so, "we think it did have the effect of depressing the market for her particular shares."

Where stock was bound by a restriction that it could not be sold for six months, the court found that "there was no market value until the restriction should be removed." Regard being had to the speculative quality of this stock, it did not have a market value capable of being ascertained with reasonable certainty six months hence, when it would be saleable. *Schuh Trading Co. et al. v. Commissioner,* 95 F.2d 408 (7th Cir., 1938).

An over-the-counter broker entered into an underwriting agreement with a corporation for the public issue of the latter's stock. If the entire issue were sold, the broker could buy 50,000 additional shares at a low figure, which shares would not be registered nor exempted from registration and which could not be sold for a stipulated period, which still had six months to run. The broker argued that because of the speculative nature of the stock, a private sale was not possible and a public one was not permitted. The court held, on the basis of testimony of the Commissioner's expert witness, that a private placement was possible. A value of 50¢ per share was assigned, the price of the unrestricted stock ranging from 75¢ to 93¾¢ in that month. *Victorson et al. v. Commissioner et al.,* 326 F.2d 264 (2d Cir., 1964).

It does not follow that shares which cannot be presently sold are without value, if the corporation is one that is likely to be in existence when the restriction is lifted. "The *restricted* shares which the taxpayer had received subject to an agreement not to sell them for a year were not worthless. They had a value, as opposed to an ascertainable market value, in the sense that undoubtedly someone could be found to pay something for a contract for their delivery at the end of the year. Whether anyone could be found to promise a price at which a sensible owner would contract to make such a delivery is entirely problematical. Clearly enough no reasonable person would undertake to pay as much for the restricted shares deliverable in a year as for the unrestricted shares deliverable at once." Here, no fair market value was found. *State Street Trust Company v. United States,* 37 F. Supp. 846 (D.C., Mass., 1941), *aff'd,* 124 F.2d 948 (1st Cir., 1942). In this case, unrestricted shares were found to have had a value of about $44 per share, while the restricted shares were given a value of zero. Where a sale of stock was completely barred for one year by a restriction and the enterprise was a new one of a speculative nature, no ascertainable value for the shares was found. *Helvering v. Tex-Penn Oil Company et al.,* 300 U.S. 481 (1937).

The value of stock may be limited for estate tax purposes by an enforceable agreement which fixes the price to be paid therefor, and where the seller if he desires to sell during his lifetime can receive only the price fixed by the contract and at his death, his estate can receive only the price theretofore agreed on. *Albert L. Salt Estate,* 17 T.C. 92 (1951). On the other hand, where the agreement made by the decedent and the prospective purchaser of his property fixed the price to be received therefor by his estate at the time of his death, but carried no restriction on the decedent's right to dispose of his property at the best price he could get during his lifetime, the property owned by the decedent at the time of his death would be included as a part of his estate at its then fair market value. *George Marshall Trammel Estate,* 18 T.C. 662 (1952).

If shareholders have the right to purchase stock at the figure an outsider offers, an outsider would hesitate to go to the expense entailed in investigating the facts essential to his making an offer. This would tend to restrict the marketability of the shares. *Eugene H. Kelly Estate,* T.C. Memo. 1955–129, filed May 20, 1955.

Where stock is received subject to a contract right of the seller to re-purchase, the fair market value of the stock when received does not exceed the re-purchase price regardless of how much greater its intrinsic value may be. *Helvering v. Salvage,* 297 U.S. 106 (1936). Likewise, if there is an option in another to purchase stock at the date it is received by the taxpayer, the value does not exceed the option price. *Phil Kalech,* 23 T.C. 672 (1955). Fair market value "is not to be determined in a vacuum" but must "be determined with respect to the particular property in question . . . subject to any conditions or restrictions on marketability." *Daniel H. Deutsch et al.,* T.C. Memo. 1967–142, filed June 28, 1967.

Subchapter S of the Internal Revenue Code will restrict the marketability of shares. This deals with the so-called "tax option corporations," where an election is made not to be taxed as a corporation. There are limitations upon the classes of persons who may hold such stock, and potential purchasers might be unwilling to accept the tax attributes. I.R.C. Section 1371(a); Section 1373.

The Burden Of Proof

Sometimes it is a *stockholder* who argues that the value of his stock should be higher than was claimed by the Internal Revenue Service. A sale by a corporation to a shareholder at a low price might be deemed to be a dividend. *Trianon Hotel Co.,* 30 T.C. 156 (1958). The taxpayer has the burden of proving that an actual sale did not represent a true value. *Jungbluth v. United States,* 253 F. Supp. 338 (D.C., E.D. Wis., 1966), *aff'd,* 371 F.2d 416 (7th Cir., 1966).

The taxpayer has the burden of proving that notes are worth less than face value. *Whitlow et al. v. Commissioner,* 82 F.2d 569 (8th Cir., 1936). On the other hand, losses are not allowed where the taxpayer had made the assumption that the basis of securities was their par value. *Hunt v. Commissioner,* 82 F.2d 668 (5th Cir., 1936).

Chapter 12

Estate Planning

The Pattern

Estate planning is one area where the stockholders legitimately may utilize a corporation to effect their own financial chores, such as redemption of shares under appropriate circumstances, or valuation of their own stock.

Estate planning may furnish a sound business purpose that justifies an arrangement for Federal income tax purposes. *V. H. Monette and Company, Incorporated et al.,* 45 T.C. 115 (1965), *aff'd,* 374 F.2d 116 (4th Cir., 1967). Estate planning considerations were found to be valid business purposes supporting the allowance to newly formed corporations of the right to the benefits of the $25,000 surtax exemptions. *Cronstroms Mfg. Co. et al.,* 36 T.C. 500 (1960).

Plans should be made so that, if a major stockholder's shares must be sold upon his death by his estate, the corporation would not have its continued existence jeopardized by inexperienced persons who might acquire the stock. See *Salvatori et al. v. United States,* D.C., S.D. Cal., 1966.

A recapitalization may be effected to reduce one's ultimate gross estate. Thus, a recapitalization which is tax-free under Section 368(a)(1)(E) may be used to change 1-class common stock into preferred and common stock, or non-voting and voting stock. Thereafter, the non-voting shares may be given away under a regular gift program, or shares may be given to charitable organizations, without diluting one's voting interest in a corporation.

The Federal estate tax is not a property tax but is, rather, a tax upon the privilege of transmitting property at the time of one's death. "The estate tax is an excise tax to tax a particular event, or a transaction, or to apply to a particular property, at a specific time. In that respect it differs from the income tax which taxes the net and continuing result of a flow of transactions." *Barritt v. Tomlinson,* 129 F. Supp. 642 (D.C., S.D. Fla., 1955).

Gross Estate

"The gross estate of the decedent is the starting point for the computation of the estate tax." *Waldrop v. United States,* 137 F. Supp. 753 (Ct. Cl., 1956). Gross estate includes all of the decedent's property or interests in property, whether the property is real or personal, tangible or intangible. I.R.C. Section 2031(a). The question of situs of intangibles of non-resident aliens will be discussed in Chapter 16.

Gross estate may include property which the decedent in fact no longer owned at the time of his death. Thus, there may be included in gross estate, shares subject to a buy-sell agreement in a family-owned corporation, if this agreement had been made at a time when the health of one of the parties was failing. This might be regarded as an arrangement that was testamentary in character, a device for the avoidance of Federal estate taxes. *Slocum v. United States,* 256 F. Supp. 753 (D.C., S.D.N.Y., 1966).

An oral agreement to give away property does not take it out of gross estate where oral agreements are not valid contracts under state law. *Grossman v. Campbell, Jr.,* D.C., N.D. Texas, 1964, *aff'd on this issue,* 368 F.2d 206 (5th Cir., 1966).

Even if bonds are tax-exempt, they are nonetheless includible in gross estate, the tax exemption extending only to taxability of income. *Greiner v. Lewellyn,* 258 U.S. 384 (1922).

If property is registered in two names as co-owners, it will be includible in the gross estate of the person who furnished the property or who supplied the funds for its purchase. Mimeograph 5202, 1941–2 CB 241, substantially restated in Revenue Ruling 68–269, I.R.B. 1968–22, 19.

The name appearing on registered bonds is significant in ascertaining the Federal estate tax consequences. Illustrative are the following situations:

"If 'John Jones' purchases with his separate funds savings bonds and has them registered in his name as owner, and the bonds are so held at the time of his death, the redemption value of the bonds constitutes a part of his gross estate for Federal estate tax purposes.

"If 'John Jones' purchases with his separate funds savings bonds and has them registered in his name as owner, payable on death to an individual as beneficiary, for example, 'John Jones, payable on death to Miss Mary Jones,' no gift results from the transaction. In such case 'John Jones' alone, as the registered owner, may during his lifetime redeem the bonds and retain the proceeds. For Federal estate tax purposes, however, upon the death of 'John Jones' while the bonds are so held, their entire redemption value at the time of death would form a part of his gross estate.

"If 'John Jones' purchases with his separate funds savings bonds and has them gratuitously registered in the name of 'Mary Jones' as owner, the transaction results in a gift from 'John Jones' to 'Mary Jones' during the year in which the bonds are purchased and registered, and the cost of the bonds must be considered in determining the donor's gift tax liability for such year. If 'Mary Jones' dies while the bonds are registered, the redemption value of the bonds at the time of her death would be includible in her gross estate for Federal estate tax purposes.

"If 'John Jones' purchases with his separate funds savings bonds and gratuitously has them registered in the name of 'Miss Mary Jones, payable on death to Miss Helen Jones,' he has made a gift in the amount of the purchase price and such amount must be considered in determining his gift tax liability, if any, for the calendar year in which the gift was made. 'John Jones' having made, during his lifetime, a gift of his investment in the bonds (and provided the transfer was not made in contemplation of death), his estate will not be subject to any Federal estate tax liability in respect of the bonds.

"If 'John Jones' purchases with his separate funds savings bonds and gratuitously has them registered in the name of 'Miss Mary Jones or Miss Helen Jones,' he has made a gift, for Federal gift tax purposes, to each of them of one-half of the amount of the purchase price of the bonds, and (provided the gifts were not made in contemplation of death) his estate will not be subject to any Federal estate tax liability in respect of the bonds.

"If 'John Jones' purchases with his separate funds savings bonds and has them registered in his name and that of another individual in the alternative as coowners, for example, 'John Jones or Mrs. Ella S. Jones,' there is no gift for Federal gift tax purposes, unless and until he during his lifetime gratuitously permits 'Mrs. Ella S. Jones' to redeem them and retain the proceeds as her separate property, in which event a gift of the then redemption value of the bonds would be made. Of course, such bonds if not previously redeemed would, on the death of 'John Jones' be includible in his gross estate for estate tax purposes at their full redemption value.

"If savings bonds are purchased with the separate funds of two individuals and registered in their names as coowners, for example, 'John Jones or Ella S. Jones,' the amount includible in the gross estate, for Federal estate tax purposes, of the first coowner to die (if the bonds were not previously redeemed) is the full redemption value of the bonds less such part thereof as is proportionate to the amount of the purchase price furnished by the survivor and not acquired from the decedent for less than an adequate and full consideration in money or money's worth." Mimeograph 5202, 1941–2 CB 241, substantially restated in Revenue Ruling 68–269, I.R.B. 1968–22, 19.

Property is includible in a decedent's gross estate only to the extent that he had an interest in this property. I.R.C. Section 2033. "Factors bearing on the question of the extent of a taxpayer's interest in such an account include the nature of the tenancy created under State law. . . ." Revenue Ruling 55–187, 1955–1 CB 197. The entire value of property owned by the decedent and his wife as tenants by the entirety was included in the decedent's gross estate where the wife had contributed nothing to the tenancy other than property given to her by the decedent. *William MacP. Hornor Estate v. Commissioner,* 130 F.2d 649 (3d Cir., 1942).

In the eight community property states, each spouse is deemed to own one-half of the property acquired by either since the establishment of the community interest. These states are Arizona, California, Idaho, Louisiana, Nevada, New Mexico, Texas, and Washington.

There is includible in gross estate any transfers made by the decedent for insufficient consideration, the amount thus to be included being the excess of the fair market value over the consideration received. I.R.C. Section 2043. "The type of consideration comprehended by 'adequate and full consideration' is not the same as common law contractual consideration. . . . Not only consideration, but 'adequate and full' consideration must be received. The statute excepts only those bona fide sales where the consideration received was of a comparable value which would be includable in the transferor's gross estate." *Lillian B. Gregory Estate,* 39 T.C. 1012 (1963). "[T]here must be the kind of consideration which in an arm's length business transaction provides the transferor of property with the full value thereof, in exchange; and that if the consideration is not paid in money, property, or services, but is represented by some benefit, then the benefit must be of the *equivalent money value* in order to constitute the required 'adequate and full consideration.' " *John M. Goetschius Estate,* 17 T.C. 495 (1951).

Retained Interests. Gross estate includes not only property which the decedent owned at the time of his death but transfers where he retained the right (either alone or in conjunction with another party) to designate the person who was to possess or to enjoy the property or the income from it. *Commissioner v. Ellis Branson Ridgway Estate,* 291 F.2d 257 (3d Cir., 1961). Thus, where the decedent reserved the power to change the ultimate beneficiaries or to vary the amounts distributable to each, he had a power to alter, to amend, or to revoke, and the corpus was includible in his gross estate. The transfer was incomplete at the time of his death. *Bank of New York & Trust Co.,* 20 B.T.A. 677 (1930).

Where trusts were subject to alteration only as to remainder interests, only the value of the remainder interests was includible in gross estate. *Fanny M. Dravo et al.,* 40 B.T.A. 309 (1939), *aff'd,* 119 F.2d 97 (3d Cir., 1941).

Gross estate includes any property which the decedent had transferred (except for adequate consideration), by trust or otherwise, if possession or enjoyment of the property could be obtained only by surviving the decedent and the decedent had retained a reversionary interest in the property which (immediately before his death) exceeded 5% of the value of the property. I.R.C. Section 2037(a). For example, under a trust agreement, the settlor was to have a reverter only if the income of an irrevocable trust was not needed for beneficiaries: his wife, his daughter, and descendants of the daughter. Here the court believed that "the possibility of enjoyment by the decedent's estate of this contingent reversion was so remote at the date of death that the reversion had no ascertainable value." *Walter J. Hill Estate v. Commissioner,* 193 F.2d 724 (2d Cir., 1952).

Gross estate includes the value of any interest in property transferred by the decedent (in trust or otherwise), if the enjoyment of the interest was subject at the date of his death to any change through the exercise of a power by him to alter, to amend, to revoke, or to terminate, or if he relinquished such a power in contemplation of death. I.R.C. Section 2038.

There are three exceptions to this rule:

(1) Where there was full consideration for the transfer.

(2) Where the decedent's power could be exercised only with the consent of all parties having an interest in the property.

(3) Where the power was held solely by a person other than the decedent. If the decedent could have replaced the person holding the power and take his place, the decedent would be considered to hold this power. Regulations Section 20.2038–1(a).

There is no power to alter if an ascertainable standard for invasion of corpus by the trustee existed and corpus in fact had not been invaded. *Jennings et al. v. Smith,* 161 F.2d 74 (2d Cir., 1947).

A decedent had transferred securities to an irrevocable trust for the equal benefit of her daughter and three grandchildren. The decedent named herself as co-trustee with a bank, but she was to have the right to possess sole judgment in the management and investment of the trust corpus for life or until she renounced that authority. The bank was to be merely custodian of the securities if she managed the corpus. It was held that her retention of powers was not broad enough to throw the corpus into her gross estate. *Aline Peters Peters,* T.C. Memo. 1964–167, filed June 18, 1964.

Where an individual and his wife set up trusts for the benefit of their minor children, with themselves as trustees, and the grantors as trustees were empowered to pay the principal and/or the income in whole or in part to the children at any time before they reached age 21, the trust corpus was includible in the grantors' gross estates. The grantors had retained the right to terminate the trusts by these powers. *Russell Harrison Varian Estate,* 47 T.C. 34 (1967).

Use Of Trusts

Among the uses of trusts where capital assets are concerned are these:

(1) To insulate the grantor or the beneficiaries from claims of creditors.

(2) To have the assets under the active management of competent and experienced persons.

(3) To divest oneself of control of a business.

(4) To provide that property may go to the beneficiaries upon the death of the grantor without administration delays and expenses and without publicity.

If the grantor has properties of different types, he may set up several trusts, so that each one has as its trustee an expert in that field: securities, real estate, and the like.

A trust may not be recognized for tax purposes where the grantor reserves significant powers: for example, in the conveyance of property by him to the trustee, where this property could not be disposed of by the trustee without the grantor's written permission. *Irvine K. Furman et al.,* 45 T.C. 360 (1966), *aff'd,* 381 F.2d 22 (5th Cir., 1967).

Where an individual set up a trust for the benefit of herself and stipulated relatives, with a bank and an individual as co-trustees, the trustees were given the right in their sole discretion to pay the settlor any income they deemed appropriate. They paid all of the income to her. Upon her death, the corpus was includible in her estate. The court pointed out that any one could find trustees who, if given absolute discretion, would exercise it in accordance with the grantor's wishes. *Maria M. Coxe Skinner Estate v. Commissioner,* 316 F.2d 517 (3d Cir., 1963).

"One of the pivotal factors is the *actual independence* of the trustee." *Alden B. Oakes et al.,* 44 T.C. 524 (1965). Where the grantor of an irrevocable trust was one of the three trustees that could, in their sole discretion, pay trust income to the beneficiary or accumulate the income, he reserved the power to accumulate or to distribute income. Thus, where he held the power until the moment of his death, there was included in his gross estate all of the trust principal, including those portions representing accumulated income. *United States v. O'Malley et al.,* 383 U.S. 627 (1966).

"The taxable gross estate . . . must include those property interests the ultimate possession or enjoyment of which is held in suspense until the moment of the grantor's death or thereafter." *Fidelity-Philadelphia Trust Company et al. v. Rothensies,* 324 U.S. 108 (1945). Property of a trust is includible in gross estate not only when the grantor himself had a right to its income but also where he had the right to designate those who could possess and enjoy it. *United States v. O'Malley et al.,* 383 U.S. 627 (1966).

Short-Term Trusts. A short-term trust generally is regarded as one where the grantor has a reversionary interest in either the corpus or the income, which will (or may reasonably be expected to) take effect in possession or enjoyment within ten years. I.R.C. Section 673(a). He is subject to Federal income tax upon such trust income. But the grantor will not be taxed upon trust income if the corpus or income will come to him only if the income beneficiary dies within ten years, regardless of the life expectancy of the beneficiary. I.R.C. Section 673(c).

Where the grantor of a trust has a reversionary interest in the corpus which will revert to his estate at his death, the income therefrom will not be taxed to him under Section 673(a) if his life expectancy, according to appropriate United States life and actuarial tables, is more than ten years at the time of the transfer. But the grantor will be taxable on the income from that portion of the trust attributable to securities or other property added to the principal of the trust after the date of its creation and within ten years prior to its termination date, measured by the life expectancy of the grantor on the date that such additions are made. Revenue Ruling 56–601, 1956–2 CB 458.

Where the grantor has a life expectancy based on appropriate United States life and actuarial tables of less than ten years, and he establishes a trust with the corpus reverting to his estate at his death, the income therefrom is taxable to the grantor inasmuch as the specific event provided in the trust instrument (that is, the life expectancy of the grantor) is the practical equivalent of the expiration of a period of less than ten years. Revenue Ruling 55–34, 1955–1 CB 226.

The grantor is treated as the owner of any portion of a trust in respect of which the beneficial enjoyment of the corpus or income therefrom is subject to a power of disposition by him, or a non-adverse party, or both, without the approval or consent of the adverse party. I.R.C. Section 674.

The grantor also is treated as the owner of any portion of a trust if, without the approval or consent of any adverse party, trust income may be distributed to the grantor, or held or accumulated for future distribution to him. I.R.C. Section 677(a).

There is what might be styled as a "very short-term trust." If a trust is set up with a term of two years or more, the grantor will not be taxed upon its income, provided that this income is irrevocably payable to a church, a convention or association of churches, a religious order, a hospital, or an educational organization with a regular faculty and curriculum. The income for the trust's stated duration must be payable to a single named beneficiary. I.R.C. Section 673(b).

Trusts For Benefits Of Minors. Minors are legally competent to receive stock. *Edward H. Keller,* 41 B.T.A. 1020 (1940). But ordinarily a trust is set up for the benefit of the minor, so that a competent party may act in a fiduciary capacity for the minor. Trusts for minor children may be disregarded for tax purposes as shams: that is, the income may be taxed to the grantor. *Emil Morton et al.,* 46 T.C. 723 (1966).

An individual created a trust for the benefit of his children by the transfer of certain property. The trust was to exist for a period of fifteen years. His brother created an identical trust for the benefit of *his* children. The two brothers and their father were trustees of both trusts and were empowered to invest and reinvest the trusts' earnings. The grantors could not reach any part of the corpus or income, but after the expiration date, the grantors had the option to call for the return of their original property. Income of the trust was taxable to the grantors, the trustees being deemed non-adverse parties. *Humphrey et al. v. United States,* 245 F. Supp. 49 (D.C., Kansas, 1965).

Trust corpus is taxable to the settlor where he can have the income used to meet his own obligations. *Commissioner v. Arthur S. Dwight Estate,* 205 F.2d 298 (2d Cir., 1953).

Where the decedent made valid transfers under a custodianship arrangement as provided in the Gift To Minors Act, these funds could not be used to discharge his own obligations and hence he could not be said to have retained a life estate. *Jack F. Chrysler Estate v. Commissioner,* 361 F.2d 508 (2d Cir., 1966).

Power Of Appointment

A power of appointment often is used to drop into someone else's hands the making of difficult decisions, such as which of a person's children is to get specific properties. But sometimes a person believes that the designation of which relative is to get property or income depends upon circumstances which are not yet known or may not be known at the time of his death. Then he would like to leave the making of the decision until some later time when a named person, as his deputy, will make the decision.

There is included in gross estate the value of a general power of appointment created after October 21, 1942 if the decedent still had this power at the time of his death, or if he relinquished it in contemplation of death. The value of a special or limited power of appointment is not included in gross estate. I.R.C. Section 2041.

A general power of appointment is one which an individual may exercise in favor of himself, his estate, his creditors, or the creditors of his estate. Where a person has a power of appointment which he may not exercise in that manner, it is a special or limited power of appointment.

A general power of appointment is not included in a decedent's estate if his power to use it for himself, his estate, or creditors was limited by an ascertainable standard relating to his health, education, support, or maintenance.

In one case, the sole life beneficiary and trustee held the power, as trustee, to appoint principal to herself "at any time necessary or advisable in order to provide for the reasonable needs and proper expenses or the benefit or comfort" of the beneficiary. It was held that neither the fact that the power was held as trustee, nor the state's implied standard of good faith for the exercise of a power of appointment, created an ascertainable standard that would characterize the power of appointment as other than a general power. *Strite v. McGinnes,* 330 F.2d 234 (3d Cir., 1964).

The exercise or complete release of a general power of appointment created after October 21, 1942 (and under certain circumstances the exercise of a special power of appointment created after that date by the creator of another power of appointment) is a taxable gift. I.R.C. Section 2514.

Transactions In Contemplation Of Death

There is included in gross estate the value of all property in which the decedent had an interest which he had transferred at any time (other than for full consideration), by trust or otherwise, in contemplation of death. If within a 3-year period ending with his death, the decedent (other than for full consideration) transferred an interest in property or released a general power of appointment, it will be deemed to have been in contemplation of death, unless the contrary can be proven. I.R.C. Section 2035.

The age of a decedent at the time of a gift or other transfer is not necessarily decisive in ascertaining whether there had been a transaction in contemplation of death. In one case, gifts by a nonagenarian were deemed not to have been in contemplation of death. He had been complaining violently about the size of his income tax and had been very responsive to a suggestion that he could reduce the income tax by giving away some of his income-producing property. A statement as to such motivation had been overheard at the breakfast table by the maid. *Kniskern, Jr. et al. v. United States,* 232 F. Supp. 7 (D.C., S.D. Fla., 1964).

"The law is clear that . . . the good health of a deceased taxpayer, standing alone, is not controlling. He need not be in fear of imminent death nor expect death in the near future." *Speights v. United States,* 214 F. Supp. 24 (D.C., N.J., 1962). When one decedent was 55, his physician told him that he had angina pectoris and hypersensitive heart disease. There was no substantial change in the decedent's activities after he learned of his condition and he continued to work from ten to twelve hours a day. Two years later, he made certain gifts. Two years thereafter, he died of another ailment, of the existence of which he had not known. The gifts were held not to have been in contemplation of death, for knowledge of his heart condition had not changed his way of life. The modest size of his estate suggested to the court that he had not been concerned with his estate tax burden. *Benjamin Beurman Estate,* T.C. Memo. 1965–114, filed April 27, 1965.

A gift was held not to have been in contemplation of death where a mother explained to her daughters in letters why she was setting up trusts for them: "The principal alloted to each of you is assumed to be sufficient to provide a monthly income equal to that which I have given you many years out of my own resources.

"In this way, you will see, the burden of responsibility on my shoulders will be considerably eased." *The Colorado National Bank of Denver v. Nicholas,* 127 F. Supp. 498 (D.C., Colo., 1954).

A gift of stock to one's son to kindle his interest in a family corporation is associated with life rather than death and hence was not a gift in contemplation of death. *D. I. Cooper Estate,* 7 T.C. 1236 (1945). Gifts within three years of death were not included in gross estate where they were part of a continuing gift policy for her children. *Jessie E. Bond Estate,* T.C. Memo. 1966–21, filed January 26, 1966.

United States Government savings bonds are included in a decedent's gross estate if, in contemplation of death, the purchaser had had the bonds registered in names other than his own. Mimeograph 5202, 1941–2 CB

241, substantially restated in Revenue Ruling 68–269, I.R.B. 1968–22, 19. But registration of such bonds in the names of a decedent's minor children was held not to have been in contemplation of death where there was testimony that the taxpayer had wanted to provide for the education and welfare of his children and to put the bonds beyond the reach of his wife, whose financial demands upon him he had considered to be excessive. *Browarsky et al. v. Granger,* 148 F. Supp. 665 (D.C., W.D. Pa., 1956).

Unlike most tax matters, a tax avoidance motive is not fatal here—unless the avoided tax is one associated with death, such as the estate tax. Thus, where a gift was motivated by desire to avoid an increased burden of income tax (such as transfer of income-producing securities), this was a motive associated with life. *First National Bank of Kansas City v. Nee,* 67 F. Supp. 815 (D.C., W.D. Mo., 1946). Avoidance of gift tax by numerous small gifts is a purpose associated with life rather than with death. *Fletcher Awerey Estate,* 5 T.C. 222 (1945).

In the case of a restrictive agreement upon the disposition of shares of any officer-stockholder of a corporation who should die, the question may arise as to whether the transaction is in contemplation of death. "Absent a transfer by a decedent in his lifetime, section [2035, transactions in contemplation of death] has no application and decedent's interest in the partnership at the time of his death is to be included in the estate. . . ." *Lionel Weil Estate,* 22 T.C. 1267 (1954).

Marital Deduction

In arriving at taxable estate, gross estate of a married person is reduced by the marital deduction. This is an amount equal to the value of any interest in property which passes or has passed from the decedent to his surviving spouse, but only to the extent that this interest is included in determining the value of the gross estate. A terminable interest is not available for use in the marital deduction: that is, an interest passing to the surviving spouse which is not absolute. If the interest which passes to the surviving spouse will terminate upon that spouse's death or upon the occurrence or non-occurrence of any contingency, there is a terminable interest. I.R.C. Section 2056(a).

A property interest devolving upon any person through survivorship-ownership is considered as having passed from the decedent to such survivor. *Robertson v. United States,* 199 F. Supp. 78 (D.C., N.D. Ala., 1968).

In order to obtain the marital deduction with respect to any property, the executor must establish the following:

(1) The decedent was survived by his spouse.

(2) The property interest for which the deduction is sought passed from the decedent to his spouse.

(3) The property interest is not a terminable one.

(4) The value of the property interest was a specified amount.

(5) The value of the decedent's adjusted gross estate was a specified amount. Regulations Section 20.2056(a)–1. The significance of (5) is that the marital deduction may not exceed 50% of adjusted gross estate.

Charitable Contributions

An estate is entitled to a deduction of charitable bequests in arriving at taxable estate. "Only charitable bequests capable of being stated in terms of money are deductible; conditional bequests are not." *Hammerstein, Jr. v. Kelly,* 349 F.2d 928 (8th Cir., 1965). A gift of non-voting stock of a closely-held corporation to a foundation had ascertainable value, for it was not subject to legal conditions, powers, or restrictions that would make it doubtful if the foundation ever would receive or keep the donated property. Overlapping control did not make the value unascertainable. *Richard P. Makoff et al.,* T.C. Memo. 1967–13, filed January 30, 1967.

Contributions are deductible to a trust for the benefit of the grantor's needy relatives. *Schoellkopf v. United States,* 124 F.2d 482 (2d Cir., 1942). "[T]here may be a public charity even where the creator has given a preference to relatives." *Agnes C. Robinson Estate,* 1 T.C. 19 (1942).

Charitable Remainders

A charitable remainder involves the creation of a trust with a designated person (or persons) as lifetime income beneficiary, with a charitable organization being named as remainderman. Upon the death of the life tenant, the corpus goes to the charity. A charitable deduction is available to the grantor in the amount of the property transferred to the trust less the value of the life tenant's interest. Frequently this arrangement is coupled with a power of invasion of corpus being available to the trustee. Despite the existence of this power, a charitable deduction is available if there is an ascertainable external standard for invasion, as a result of which it appears that the possibility that the charity will not receive the corpus is negligible.

"In general, an ascertainable standard has been found when the language of the will allows invasion only to the extent necessary to sustain the beneficiary's customary mode of living. . . . We have found no case which goes beyond this in finding a reasonable standard." *Charles H. James Estate,* 40 T.C. 494 (1963). "The likelihood of an invasion of principal and the possible extent thereof depends upon the facts of the particular case. One of the main factors to be considered is whether the trust instrument fixes a definite standard, or whether the extent of the invasion is calculable in accordance with some ascertainable standard. Other factors are the life expectancy of the life beneficiary, the cost per annum of the beneficiary's present standard of living, the income of the trust after reinvestment of the sale proceeds, and the expected income of the beneficiary from sources other than the trust." Revenue Ruling 66–367, 1966–2 CB 241.

The will or other creating instrument must provide a sufficiently definite standard limiting the extent of possible invasion for the benefit of non-charitable interests, so that the value of the charitable remainder is "presently ascertainable" at the time of the testator's death. *Mercantile-Safe Deposit and Trust Company v. United States,* 252 F. Supp. 191 (D.C., Md., 1966). There was no permissible deduction where invasion of principal was authorized "for reasonable support, care and comfort, or for expenses of accident, illness or other misfortune, whether included in the foregoing classification or not. . . ." The standard of invasion of corpus was, at the date of death of the trustor, not capable of being interpreted in a monetary sense, for "misfortune" was not defined. *Title Insurance and Trust Company v. United States,* 249 F. Supp. 386 (D.C., S.D. Cal., 1965).

Valuation Date Of Estate

Ordinarily, a decedent's estate is valued as of the date of death. At the election of the executor, an alternate valuation date of one year after the date of death may be used. This includes property in which the decedent had an interest, dower or curtesy interests, transactions in contemplation of death, transfers with retained life estate, transfers taking effect at death, revocable transfers, annuities, joint interests, powers of appointment, proceeds of life insurance, transfers for insufficient consideration, and prior interests. Such property interests are referred to as "included property." These interests remain "included property" for the purpose of valuing the gross estate under the alternate valuation method even though they change in form during the alternate valuation period by being actually received, or disposed of, in whole or in part, by the estate. On the other hand, property earned or accrued (whether received or not) after the date of the decedent's death and during the alternate valuation period with respect to any property interest existing at the date of the decedent's death, which does not represent a form of "included property" itself or the receipt of "included property" is excluded in valuing the gross estate under the alternate valuation method. Such property is referred to as "excluded property."

Interest-bearing obligations, such as bonds or notes, may comprise two elements of "included property" at the date of the decedent's death, namely, (1) the principal amount of the obligation itself and (2) interest accrued to the date of death. Each of these elements is to be valued separately as of the applicable valuation date. Interest accrued after the date of death and before the subsequent valuation date constitutes "excluded property." But any part payment of principal made between the date of death and the subsequent valuation date, or any advance payment of interest for a period after the subsequent valuation date made during the alternate valuation period which has the effect of reducing the value of the principal obligation as of the subsequent valuation date, will be included in the gross estate and valued as of the date of the payment.

Shares of stock in a corporation and dividends declared to stockholders of record on or before the date of the decedent's death and not collected at the date of death constitute "included property" of the estate. On the other hand, ordinary dividends out of earnings and profits (whether in cash, shares of the corporation, or other property) declared to shareholders of record after the date of the decedent's death are "excluded property" and are not to be valued under the alternate valuation method. Regulations Section 20.2032–1.

Where a decedent owned shares of stock of a corporation which, a few months after his death, authorized a tax-free stock dividend, this dividend was included in the value of the gross estate in a case where the alternate valuation method was used. *John Schlosser Estate v. Commissioner,* 277 F.2d 268 (3d Cir., 1960).

In order to eliminate changes in value attributable only to a mere lapse in time, Section 2032(a)(3) provides that any interest or estate "affected by a mere lapse of time" is included in a decedent's gross estate under the alternate valuation method at its value as of the date of the decedent's death, but with adjustment for any difference in its value as of the subsequent valuation date not due to mere lapse of time. Properties, interests, or estates which are "affected by mere lapse of time" include patents, estates for the life of persons other than the decedent, remainders, reversions, and the like. That phrase has no reference to obligations for the payment of money, whether or not interest-bearing, the value of which changes with the passing of time.

Character Of Income

In the absence of specific provisions in the governing instrument for the allocation of different classes of income, or unless local law requires an allocation, the amount deductible for distributions to beneficiaries of estates or complex trusts is treated as consisting of the same proportion of each class of items entering into the computation of distributable net income as the total of each class bears to the total distributable net income. Regulations Section 1.661(b)–1.

But a settlor could provide that all tax-exempt income be paid to a specified beneficiary or that capital gains be allocated to a particular beneficiary unless local law declared to the contrary.

Pecuniary Bequests

No gain or loss is recognized by a trust or estate by reason of the distribution of property in kind unless the distribution is in satisfaction of a right to receive a distribution in a specified dollar amount. When property other than money is distributed by an estate to any beneficiary (including a trust) in satisfaction of a cash bequest, the estate realizes gain or loss measured by the difference between the amount of the bequest satisfied and the basis to the estate of the property so distributed. *Kenan, Jr. et al. v. Commissioner,* 114 F.2d 217 (2d Cir., 1940).

In that case, a will provided that the trustees were to pay a named beneficiary $5,000,000, but that they could, in their sole discretion, substitute marketable securities of a value equal to that amount. The trustees paid the bequest in cash and securities which had appreciated in value since acquisition. The trustees derived capital gain to the extent of the appreciation of the securities.

A final distribution by the executor of an estate of appreciated-value property, in order to satisfy a pecuniary legacy, will result in a gain to the estate, even though this distribution is of an insufficient amount completely to satisfy the bequest. Revenue Ruling 66–207, 1966–2 CB 43.

If there is a bequest of a certain amount to a beneficiary who agrees to accept securities of that value, the transaction is a sale or other disposition of the securities insofar as the estate is concerned. *Suisman v. Eaton,* 83 F.2d 1019 (2d Cir., 1936).

Payment Of Estate Tax

The Federal estate tax return is due fifteen months after the date of death of decedent, at which time payment of the tax is due. I.R.C. Section

6075(a). An extension of up to ten years is available upon a showing of undue hardship in making the payment. Regulations Section 1.6161–1(b).

Where the value of an interest in a closely-held business, which is included in the gross estate of a citizen or resident of the United States, exceeds either (1) 35% of the value of his gross estate or (2) 50% of the taxable estate, the executor may elect to pay all or part of the estate tax in installments. This election applies to deficiencies as well as tax, unless the deficiency is due to negligence, intentional disregard of the rules and regulations, or fraud. Inasmuch as the election must be made on or before the due date of the return, this treatment does not extend to a deficiency in a case where (for whatever reason) no election was made to pay in installments the tax shown on the return. The amount of estate tax which the executor may elect to pay in installments is limited to an amount, A, which bears the same ratio to B (the gross Federal estate tax, reduced by the authorized credits) as C (the value of the interest in a closely-held business which is included in the gross estate) bears to D (the value of the gross estate). I.R.C. Section 6166(b).

The term "interest in a closely-held business" means, among other things, stock in a corporation carrying on a trade or business if 20% or more in value of the voting stock of the corporation is included in determining the decedent's gross estate or if the corporation had ten or fewer shareholders. Regulations Section 20.6166–2(a). Interests in two or more closely-held businesses are treated as an interest in a single closely-held business if more than 50% of the total value of each such business is included in determining the value of the decedent's gross estate. For purposes of this 50% requirement, an interest in a closely-held business which represents the surviving spouse's interest in community property is considered as having been included in determining the value of the decedent's gross estate.

That portion of the Federal estate tax represented by reversionary or remainder interests may be postponed up to six months upon the posting of a bond. I.R.C. Section 6163(a).

Payment In United States Treasury Bonds. The Secretary of the Treasury or the Commissioner of Internal Revenue must receive at par, with an adjustment for accrued interest, Treasury bills, notes, and certificates of indebtedness issued by the United States in payment of Federal estate taxes to the extent and under the conditions provided in the regulations. I.R.C. Section 6312(a).

The following are the Treasury bonds which may be redeemed at par and accrued interest for this purpose, regardless of the price below par at which the bonds had been purchased:

The list below sets forth the series of Treasury bonds, whether in registered or coupon form, that may be redeemed at par plus accrued interest for the purpose of applying the proceeds to the payment of Federal estate taxes.

TREASURY BONDS

Series	Dated	Due
2½ % 1962–67	May 5, 1942	June 15, 1962–67
2½ % 1963–68	Dec. 1, 1942	Dec. 15, 1963–68
2½ % 1964–69	Apr. 15, 1943	June 15, 1964–69
2½ % 1964–69	Sept. 15, 1943	Dec. 15, 1964–69
2½ % 1965–70	Feb. 1, 1944	Mar. 15, 1965–70
2½ % 1966–71	Dec. 1, 1944	Mar. 15, 1966–71
2½ % 1967–72	June 1, 1945	June 15, 1967–72
2½ % 1967–72	Nov. 15, 1945	Dec. 15, 1967–72
2¾ % (Investment Series B) 1975–80	Apr. 1, 1951	Apr. 1, 1975–80
3¼ % 1978–83	May 1, 1953	June 15, 1978–83
3% 1995	Feb. 15, 1955	Feb. 15, 1995
4% 1969	Oct. 1, 1957	Oct. 1, 1969
3⅞ % 1974	Dec. 2, 1957	Nov. 15, 1974
3½ % 1990	Feb. 14, 1958	Feb. 15, 1990
3¼ % 1985	June 3, 1958	May 15, 1985
4% 1980	Jan. 23, 1959	Feb. 15, 1980
4¼ % 1975–85	Apr. 5, 1960	May 15, 1975–85
3½ % 1980	Oct. 3, 1960	Nov. 15, 1980
3½ % 1998	Oct. 3, 1960	Nov. 15, 1998
4¼ % 1987–92	Aug. 15, 1962	Aug. 15, 1987–92
4% 1988–93	Jan. 17, 1963	Feb. 15, 1988–93
4⅛ % 1989–94	Apr. 18, 1963	May 15, 1989–94
4¼ % 1974	May 15, 1964	May 15, 1974
4⅛ % 1973	July 22, 1964	Nov. 15, 1973
4⅛ % 1974	Jan. 15, 1965	Feb. 15, 1974

The series of bonds listed above bearing interest of more than 4 per cent per annum are redeemable for this purpose by the terms of their issue and by virtue of the provisions of Title 31 U. S. Code, Sec. 765, which provides, generally, that any United States bonds bearing interest of more than 4 per cent per annum may be received at par in payment of Federal estate taxes. All of the other series of bonds listed above are redeemable for this purpose solely by the terms of their issue and not by virtue of the provisions of Title 31 U. S. Code, Sec. 765.

To be redeemable at par, the bonds must have been owned by the decedent at the time of his death and thus constitute a part of his estate. The redemption on this basis may not exceed the amount of estate tax due.

Bonds submitted for redemption must be accompanied by Form PD 1782 and Form GB 596.

For further details, see Appendix to Operating Circular No. 17 as issued by the Federal Reserve Bank of New York.

Income In Respect Of A Decedent

"Income in respect of a decedent" means amounts to which a decedent was entitled but which were not properly includible in computing his taxable income for the taxable year ending with the date of his death or for a previous taxable year under the accounting method he used. This includes:

(1) Accrued income if he reported his income on the cash basis.

(2) Income accrued solely by reason of his death if he reported on the accrual basis.

(3) Income to which he had a contingent claim at the time of his death. I.R.C. Section 691.

Also included are items of gross income in respect of a prior decedent, if (1) the right to receive these amounts was acquired by the decedent by reason of the death of the prior decedent or by bequest or inheritance from the prior decedent and if (2) the amount of gross income in respect of the prior decedent was not properly includible in computing the decedent's taxable income for the taxable year ending with the date of his death or for a previous taxable year. Regulations Section 1.691(a)–1(c).

"[I]ncome in respect of a decedent includes payments attributable to the decedent's activities—such as personal services, sales, deferred-compensation contracts, or investment income accruing before death—even though he may not have had the right to payment before his death. On the other hand, it does not include payments in the nature of return after the date of death on property passing to the estate—such as rents under a lease, royalties on a patent assignment, or interest on a coupon bond." *Levin v. United States,* 373 F.2d 434 (1st Cir., 1967).

A decedent owned shares of a corporation, which owned preferred stock in another company. There were arrearages on the preferred stock held by the corporation. The executors dissolved the corporation the shares of which the decedent had held, and in time the beneficiaries received the arrearages on the preferred stock which the dissolved corporation had held. This was not income in respect of a decedent. Even if the arrearages constituted a right to income, the right to the income was the dissolved corporation's and not the decedent's. *Boyle et al. v. United States,* 355 F.2d 233 (3d Cir., 1965).

The right to receive an amount of income in respect of a decedent is treated in the hands of the estate or the person entitled to receive the amount by bequest or inheritance from the decedent or by reason of his death as if it had been acquired in the transaction by which the decedent acquired this right, or a prior decedent had done so. It has the same character it would have had if the decedent (or a prior decedent) had lived and received the amount: that is, capital gain, exempt income, etc. I.R.C. Section 691(a)(3).

Deductions Of Persons Receiving Income In Respect Of A Decedent. A person who must include in gross income an amount of income in respect of a decedent may deduct for that year that portion of the estate tax imposed upon the decedent's estate which is attributable to the inclusion in that estate of the right to receive this amount. If a person must include in gross income an amount of income in respect of a prior decedent, he may deduct that portion of the estate tax imposed upon the prior decedent's estate which is attributable to the inclusion in the prior decedent's estate of the value of the right to receive that amount. Regulations Section 1.691(c)–1.

Federal Gift Tax

Similar in operation to the Federal estate tax is the Federal gift tax. There is a tax upon the *privilege* of making gifts.

In the computation of this tax, there is a specific lifetime exemption of $30,000. I.R.C. Section 2521. In addition, there is an annual exclusion of $3,000 per donee. I.R.C. Section 2503(b). This exclusion does not cover gifts of future interests in property, which includes such items as reversions and remainders. But certain types of gifts to minors are not treated as gifts of future interests. I.R.C. Section 2503(c).

Under Section 2503(c), no transfer for the benefit of a donee who has not attained age 21 on the date of the gift will be considered a gift of a future interest if all three of the following conditions are satisfied by the terms of the transfer:

(1) Both the property itself and its income may be expended by or for the benefit of the donee before he attains age 21.

(2) Any portion of the property and its income not disposed of under (1) will pass to the donee when he attains age 21.

(3) Any portion of the property and its income not disposed of under (1) will be payable either to the estate of the donee or as he may appoint under a general power of appointment if he dies before attaining age 21.

A transfer will not fail to qualify merely because:

(1) There is left to the discretion of a trustee the determination of the amounts (if any) of the income or property to be expended for the benefit of the minor and the purpose for which the expenditure is to be made, provided that there are no substantial restrictions under the terms of the trust instrument on the exercise of this discretion.

(2) The donee, upon reaching age 21, has the right to extend the term of the trust.

(3) The governing instrument contains a disposition of the property or income not expended during the donee's minority to persons other than the donee's estate in the event of the default of appointment by the donee. Regulations Section 25.2503–4(b).

A $3,000 exclusion was permitted where income earned during minority was accumulated, the principal of the trust to go to the beneficiary when he was 30, provided accumulations until age 21 was reached would go to the minor's estate, if he died before attaining age 30. *Arlean I. Herr,* 35 T.C. 732 (1961), *aff'd,* 303 F.2d 780 (3d Cir., 1962). Here the agreement provided: "All unexpended sums of accumulated income and principal shall be paid to the minor at his or her majority or to his or her estate if the minor dies before majority."

An individual (the decedent) had securities registered in his own name as custodian for his children. The securities so registered were kept in a separate safe deposit box for each child, held in the name of the decedent and his wife as joint tenants. No other securities were kept in the box. Income tax returns were filed for each child, tax being paid from the child's account. The decedent filed gift tax returns reflecting the gifts. The securities were not included in his gross estate. They were not purchased with his funds, nor were they securities he previously had transferred to himself as custodian for the children. He had relinquished all beneficial interest in the sources from which the securities could have been purchased. He could not have used funds from any of these sources to discharge his own obligations to support his minor children, and hence he had not retained a life estate under Section 2036. He had retained no power to alter or to terminate the children's enjoyment of the property transferred to them, so as to require the inclusion of the property in his gross estate under Section 2038. "The circumstances of the transfers—the careful keeping of ledgers, the reporting of each transfer as a gift, the absence of any use of the funds for the father's benefit—makes clear that the property was to be the children's, to be preserved until their majority." *Jack F. Chrysler Estate v. Commissioner*, 361 F.2d 508 (2d Cir., 1966).

An alleged transfer of stock to a minor will not be recognized if the language on the certificate does not comply with the wording required by state law, such as a Gift To Minors Act. *Henry D. Duarte et al.*, 44 T.C. 193 (1965). There may be tax to the grantor of a trust set up for the benefit of minor children, if the arrangement appears to have been a sham. *Emil Morton et al.*, 46 T.C. 723 (1966).

The Federal gift tax rates are 75% of the Federal estate tax rates, bracket for bracket. But if gifts are made over a period of time and are spaced properly, the rate will be considerably less than 75% of the potential estate tax liability, by reason of the lifetime exemption, annual exclusions, a gift-splitting procedure for married spouses, and a marital exemption. In determining the amount of taxable gifts in the case of a donor who was a citizen or resident of the United States at the time the gift was made, there is deducted an amount equal to one-half of the value of any property interest transferred by gift to a donee who at the time of the gift was the donor's spouse. This rule does not apply to a terminable interest or to any property interest that is not included in the total amount of gifts made during the calendar year. I.R.C. Section 2523. A gift made by one spouse to a person other than his spouse may be considered as made 50% by him and 50% by his spouse, but only if at the time of the gift each spouse was a citizen or resident of the United States. Both spouses must consent to this treatment by way of an election on the Federal gift tax form. I.R.C. Section 2513.

Non-Resident Aliens. Bonds issued by United States persons, unlike other debt obligations, are considered to be situated where the instrument is located for purposes of the Federal gift tax applicable to non-resident aliens. (For a discussion of non-resident aliens, see Chapter 15.) Debt obligations of a United States person or of the United States, a state or political subdivision thereof, or the District of Columbia which are owned by persons who within the past ten years became expatriates to avoid Federal taxes are deemed to be situated in the United States. I.R.C. Section 2511(b).

Gifts of intangible property by non-resident aliens are not subject to the Federal gift tax. But this rule does not apply to gifts by donors who within the ten years immediately before the gift became expatriates of the United States with a principal purpose of avoiding United States income, estate, or gift taxes. If the Secretary of the Treasury or his delegates establishes that it is reasonable to believe that the individual's loss of United States citizenship will result in a substantial reduction in the gift tax payable by the donor, the burden of proving that tax avoidance was not one of the principal purposes rests with the donor. This does not refer to losses of citizenship under Sections 301(b), 350, or 355 of the Immigration and Nationality Act. I.R.C. Section 2501.

Basis. If a gift is made in property, its value at the date of the gift is considered to be the amount of the gift. Regulations Section 25.2512–1. This differs from the income tax treatment, where the donor's basis carries over to the donee. I.R.C. Section 1015(a). The basis of property acquired by inheritance or devise is the fair market value at the date of death or one year thereafter, as used by the executor on the estate tax return. I.R.C. Section 1014. If property is included in the donor's gross estate as a transaction in contemplation of death, basis to the donee is as though a gift had been made.

The basis of property acquired by gift may be increased by the amount of any Federal gift tax paid upon the transfer, but the total value may not exceed fair market value at the time of the gift. I.R.C. Section 1015(d)(1)(A).

Estate planning thus should take into account what the basis of the property of the client will be in the hands of his beneficiary.

Completed Gifts. No gift of stock is recognized for tax purposes where the donor merely makes a verbal assignment. Transfer of stock by a form of assignment or on the transfer agent's books is necessary. There must be constructive or symbolic delivery, "a delivery as perfect as the nature of the property and surroundings of the parties reasonably permitted." *Lunsford Richardson,* 39 B.T.A. 927 (1939), *aff'd,* 126 F.2d 562 (2d Cir., 1942).

In the case of a gift of stock, the gift customarily is not regarded as complete until the names on the certificates are changed. *Ralph Owen Howard Estate,* 9 T.C. 1192 (1947).

The tax applies to *indirect gifts.* In a family corporation, the father owned 1,509 shares of stock, while each of his three sons owned one of the remaining shares. The father transferred 1,508 of his shares to the corporation without consideration, and the corporation held these as treasury stock. This was held to be a gift by him to each son of one-fourth of his stock, inasmuch as he retained only a one-fourth interest. Basis to each son was the original cost of his one share plus the basis in the father's hands of the stock transferred to each son. This was not regarded as a capital contribution to the corporation. *Julie B. Hitchon Estate,* 45 T.C. 96 (1965).

An individual endorsed his stock certificate in a closely-held corporation to his wife. He gave the certificate to her in an envelope marked: "Property of [the husband]." He then placed the envelope in a vault to which he and his wife each had access. After his death, it was held that he had not not made a gift to his wife during his lifetime: the stock thus was included in his gross estate. When he had given her the certificate, he merely told her to safeguard it with her life; he never indicated that it was a gift, and he never had given up control of the stock. *Gorski et al. v. United States,* D.C., N.D. Ill., 1964.

Where Series E bonds were registered in the names of two persons as alternative co-owners, and the purchaser had the bonds re-issued in the name of the other party as a gift, the redemption value of the bonds at the time of re-issue was the value to be used for gift tax purposes. Revenue Ruling 55–278, 1955–1 CB 471.

Chapter 13

Tax-Sheltered Investments

Section 1231 Assets

Section 1231 assets represent a generous extension of capital gains rates to non-investment items. See Chapter 2. As was stated in that chapter, the general rule is that long-term capital gain treatment is afforded to Section 1231 assets held for more than six months which are disposed of at a gain. Losses are fully deductible.

The tax shelter stems from the fact that capital gain treatment is possible in the case of non-capital assets. In certain instances, it might appear that a taxpayer actually is engaged in business, but his profits are not taxed as ordinary income.

Section 1231 assets include these items which are favored as a form of investment:

(1) Property used in the trade or business of a character which is subject to depreciation, and also real estate, held for more than six months, which is not inventory and which is not held primarily for sale to customers in the ordinary course of the trade or business. I.R.C. Section 1231(b)(1).

(2) Timber, coal, or domestic iron ore. I.R.C. Section 1231(b)(2).

(3) Livestock, regardless of age, held by the taxpayer for draft, breeding, or dairy purposes, and held by him for twelve months or more from the date of acquisition. The term does not include poultry. I.R.C. Section 1231(b)(3).

(4) Unharvested crops on land used in the trade or business and held for more than six months, if the crop and the land are sold or exchanged (or compulsorily or involuntarily converted) at the same time and to the same person. I.R.C. Section 1231(b)(4).

Realty

Real property purchased by a taxpayer specifically for use in its business, which is thereafter found to be unsuitable for its use and is sold more than six months after purchase at a loss, constitutes "property used in the trade or business" within the meaning of Section 1231(b)(1). Revenue Ruling 58–133, 1958–1 CB 277.

Stock in a co-operative apartment building may be characterized as a capital asset. *Junius B. Peake et al.,* T.C. Memo., Docket No. 27636, entered June 15, 1951.

In the case of a taxpayer who was not a dealer in leases, a leasehold with 30 years to run constituted real property and was a Section 1231 asset in the hands of a realty corporation. Revenue Ruling 60–4, 1960–1 CB 303.

When a taxpayer permits another party to extract minerals from the taxpayer's land at a fixed price per unit extracted, the question arises as to whether this is a sale or a lease. "If the taxpayer has retained no economic interest in the minerals the arrangement is to be considered a sale of a capital asset and thus entitled to capital gains treatment." *Peeler et al. v. United States,* 238 F. Supp. 640 (D.C., M.D. Ga., 1964). Here, the court found that the taxpayer had retained no economic interest in the minerals. There was no time limit for extraction. Thus, capital gains treatment was allowed.

Timber, Coal, Domestic Iron Ore

Timber. Section 631(a) provides that an election may be made by certain taxpayers to treat the difference between the actual cost or other basis of specified timber cut during the taxable year and its fair market value as standing timber on the first day of such year as a sale or exchange of a capital asset under Section 1231. Thereafter, any subsequent gain or loss will be determined in the manner to be described below. Regulations Section 1.631–1(a). The election may be made only if the taxpayer has owned, or has a contract right to cut, this timber for a period of more than six months before the beginning of that year.

If the election is made, gain or loss is recognized to the taxpayer in an amount equal to the difference between the fair market value of the timber and the adjusted basis for depletion of the timber in his hands. Fair market value for this purpose will be the fair market value as of the first day of the taxable year in which the timber is cut; henceforth this will be considered as the cost of the cut timber to the taxpayer for all purposes for which this cost is a necessary factor. The adjusted basis for depletion of the cut timber is based upon the number of units of timber cut during the taxable year which are considered to be sold or exchanged and upon the depletion unit of the timber in the timber account or accounts pertaining to the timber cut. The computation will be in the regular manner provided for depletion in Section 611, to be discussed later in this chapter. Regulations Section 1.631–1(d).

If a taxpayer makes this election, it will apply with respect to all timber which he owns or which he has a contract to cut. This election is binding for that year and for all subsequent years, unless the Commissioner, on a showing of undue hardship, permits him to revoke the election; but such a revocation will bar any further elections unless the Commissioner permits otherwise. I.R.C. Section 631(a).

In the case of the disposal of timber held for more than six months by the owner under any form of contract by virtue of which he retains an economic interest in the timber, the difference between the amount realized from the disposal of the timber and the adjusted depletion basis thereof will be considered as though it were a gain or loss on the sale of the timber. The date of disposal of the timber will be deemed to be the date it is cut; but if payment is made to the owner under the contract before the timber is cut, he may elect to treat the date of the payment as the date of disposal of the timber. The term "owner" for this purpose means any person who owns an interest in the timber, including a sublessor and a holder of a contract to cut timber. I.R.C. Section 631(b).

In case the products of the timber are sold after cutting, either in the form of logs or lumber or manufactured products, the income from these actual sales will be considered ordinary income. When the election under Section 631(a) is in effect, the cost of standing timber cut during the taxable year is determined as if the taxpayer had purchased this timber on the first day of the taxable year. Thus, in determining the cost of the products so sold, the cost of the timber will be the fair market value on the first day of the taxable year in which the standing timber was cut, in lieu of the actual cost or other basis of the timber. Regulations Section 1.631–1(e).

The taxpayer who would claim the benefit of the statute must be the one who has not only the right to cut but also the right to sell on his own account. *Carlen et al. v. Commissioner*, 220 F.2d 338 (9th Cir., 1955). "In order to have a 'contract right to cut timber' within the meaning of section 631(a) and this section, a taxpayer must have a right to sell the timber cut under the contract on his own account or to use such cut timber in his trade or business." Regulations Section 1.631–1(b)(1). The litigated cases under Section 631 turn on whether the taxpayer held a mere personal service logging contract or whether he held a right to sell the timber on his own account. See *Dean Lansing et al.,* T.C. Memo. 1964–82, filed March 30, 1964.

To be entitled to the benefits of Section 631 as the holder of a "contract right to cut," a taxpayer must have acquired under this contract a proprietary interest in the timber which he cuts. Whether he has such an interest depends upon the substance of the grant to him as determined in the light of all of the pertinent facts. Where a taxpayer is granted a contractual right to cut and to remove all of a described part of the merchantable timber on a particular tract of land, he has a proprietary interest in the timber cut by him if at the time of the cutting he has an unrestricted right to sell the logs or to use them in his trade or business. If the circumstances are such that the grantor in fact takes for his own use or for sale on his own account substantially all of the logs cut (whether or not in the exercise of a right in the form of an option to purchase), the taxpayer-grantee will not be deemed to have an unrestricted right to sell the logs or to use them in his trade or business. Revenue Ruling 58–295, 1958–1 CB 249.

The requirements of the statute are met if the timber either has been owned or held by the taxpayer under a cutting contract for more than six months before the beginning of the taxable year. It is immaterial that a change is made from one form of right to another, provided there is no interruption or cessation of the taxpayer's right to cut the timber involved for sale or for use in his trade or business. Revenue Ruling 61–57, 1961–1 CB 243.

The term "disposal" as used in Section 631 is not synonymous with "sale," and "something other than a sale was sufficient" to qualify under the statute. Even without a sale, the statute is satisfied. *Springfield Plywood Corporation,* 15 T.C. 697 (1950).

Although Section 631 is limited to timber actually cut or felled, for practical timber operations it generally is impossible to obtain a reasonably accurate measurement of quantity at the time the timber is cut or felled. Therefore, for the purpose of this section, timber is considered cut at the time when, in the ordinary course of business, the quantity of timber felled is first definitely determined, rather than at the time of felling. "Taxpayers are required to hold to a consistent scaling practice and may not shift the scaling point to obtain a tax advantage." Revenue Ruling 58–135, 1958–1 CB 519.

Coal–Iron Ore. Rather similar to the treatment of timber is the disposal of coal or domestic iron ore with a retained economic interest. The difference between the amount realized from disposal of the coal or iron ore in any taxable year and the adjusted depletion basis thereof plus the deductions disallowed for the taxable year under Section 272 (expenditures attributable to administering the contracts and to the preservation of the economic interest retained under the contract) will be gain or loss upon the sale of the coal or iron ore. I.R.C. Section 631(c).

No allowance for percentage depletion is allowed with respect to amounts which are considered to be realized from the sale of coal or iron ore under Section 631(c). Regulations Section 1.631–3(b).

Livestock

Section 1231 applies to the sale, exchange, or involuntary conversion of livestock, regardless of age, held by the taxpayer for draft, breeding, or dairy purposes, and held by him for twelve months or more from the date of acquisition. "Livestock" includes cattle, hogs, horses, mules, donkeys, sheep, goats, fur-bearing animals, and other mammals. It does not include poultry, geese, chickens, turkeys, pigeons, other birds, fish, frogs, reptiles, etc. Regulations Section 1.1231–2(a).

"Whether or not livestock is held by the taxpayer for draft, breeding, or dairy purposes depends upon all of the facts and circumstances in each case. The purpose for which the animal is held is ordinarily shown by the taxpayer's actual use of the animal. However a draft, breeding, or dairy purpose may be present if an animal is disposed of within a reasonable time after its intended use for such purpose is prevented or made undesirable by reason of accident, disease, drought, unfitness of the animal for such purpose, or a similar factual circumstance. Under certain circumstances, an animal held for ultimate sale to customers in the ordinary course of the taxpayer's trade or business may be considered as held for draft, breeding, or dairy purposes merely because it is suitable for such purposes or merely because it is held by the taxpayer for sale to other persons for use by them for such purposes. Furthermore, an animal held by the taxpayer for other purposes is not considered as held for draft, breeding, or dairy purposes merely because of a negligible use of the animal for such purposes or merely because the use of the animal for such purposes as an ordinary or necessary incident to the other purposes for which the animal is held." Regulations Section 1.1231–2(b).

It was held that cattle were not held for breeding purposes but for sale in the ordinary course of the trade or business, where advertisements of the cattle stated that "All are sensibly priced. . . ." *John Clark et al.,* 27 T.C. 1006 (1957).

In the case of bulls rented for breeding purposes, renting the bulls "in order to realize profit, while growing and fattening them for market does not establish that the primary purpose in holding them was for rental for breeding purposes." Thus, where the bulls were purchased with the intention of selling them after they had been raised and fattened, the animals were held primarily for sale in the course of business and were not Section 1231 assets. *Albert T. Erickson et al.,* 23 T.C. 458 (1954).

Unharvested Crops

Section 1231 does not apply to a sale, exchange, or involuntary conversion of an unharvested crop, if the taxpayer retains any right or option to re-acquire the land the crop is on, directly or indirectly (other than a right customarily incident to a mortgage or other security transaction). The length of time for which the crop, as distinguished from the land, is held is immaterial. A leasehold or estate for years is not "land" for purposes of Section 1231. Regulations Section 1.1231–1(f).

Natural Resources

Natural resource properties have several features which are attractive to investors: depletion, intangible drilling and development costs, and exploration expenditures.

Depletion. "Oil and gas reserves, like other minerals in place, are recognized as wasting assets. The production of oil and gas, like the mining of ore, is treated as an income-producing operation, not as a conversion of capital investment as upon a sale, and is said to resemble a manufacturing business carried on by the use of the soil. . . . The depletion effected by production is likened to the depreciation of machinery or the using up of raw materials in manufacturing." *Anderson et al. v. Helvering,* 310 U.S. 404 (1940).

In the case of mines, oil and gas wells, other natural deposits, and timber, there is allowed as a deduction a reasonable amount for depletion and for depreciation of improvements, according to the peculiar conditions in each case. For this purpose, the term "mines" includes deposits of waste or residue, the extraction of ores or minerals from which is treated as mining under the percentage depletion rules of Section 613 (c). Where it is ascertained as a result of operations or of development work that the recoverable units are greater or less than the prior estimate, then this prior estimate (but not the basis for depletion) is to be revised and the allowance for depletion for subsequent taxable years will be based on the revised estimate. I.R.C. Section 611(a).

Provision is made for the equitable apportionment of depletion among the several owners of economic interests in a mineral deposit or standing timber, for example, between the lessor and the lessee. I.R.C. Section 611(b).

The basis upon which *cost depletion* is to be allowed in respect of any mineral property is the basis provided for in Section 612, to be discussed below.

After the amount of the basis applicable to the mineral property has been determined for the taxable year, the cost depletion for that year will be computed by dividing that amount by the number of units of mineral remaining as of the taxable year and by multiplying the depletion unit so determined by the number of units of mineral sold within the taxable year. "In the selection of a unit of mineral for depletion, preference shall be given to the principal or customary unit or units paid for in the products sold, such as tons of ore, barrels of oil, or thousands of cubic feet of natural gas." Regulations Section 1.611–2(a).

The depletion unit of timber in a given year is the quotient obtained by dividing (1) the adjusted basis of the timber on hand at the beginning of the year plus the cost of the number of units of timber acquired during the year plus proper additions to capital by (2) the total number of units on hand at the beginning of the year plus the number of units acquired during the year plus (or minus) the number of units which must be added (or deducted) by way of correcting the estimate of the number of units remaining available in the account. The number of units cut during any taxable year multiplied by the depletion unit applicable to that year will be the amount of depletion allowable for the taxable year. Regulations Section 1.611–3(b).

In the case of cost depletion, the deduction is allowed upon the adjusted basis of the property for determining gain upon the sale or other disposition of the property. I.R.C. Section 612.

The basis for cost depletion of mineral or timber property does not include:

(1) Amounts recoverable through depreciation deductions, deferred expenses, and deductions other than depletion.

(2) The residual value of land and improvements at the end of operations.

In the case of any mineral property, the basis for cost depletion does not include amounts representing the cost or value of land for purposes other than mineral production. In the case of certain mineral properties, the basis does not include exploration or development expenditures which are treated under Sections 615(b) or 616(b) as deferred expenses to be taken into account as deductions on a ratable basis as the units of minerals benefited thereby are produced and sold. But there is included in the basis for cost depletion of oil and gas property the amounts of capitalized drilling and development costs which are recoverable through depletion deductions. In the case of timber property, the basis for cost depletion does not include amounts representing the cost or value of land.

Where a taxpayer elects to treat the cutting of timber as a sale or exchange of the timber, the basis for cost depletion is the fair market value of the timber as of the first day of the taxable year in which such timber is cut and this value will be considered for the taxable year and for all subsequent taxable years as the cost of the timber for all purposes for which the cost is a necessary factor. Regulations Section 1.612–1(b).

For the purpose of computing the depletion allowance in the case of mines, wells, and other natural deposits, the term "property" means each separate interest owned by the taxpayer in each mineral deposit in each separate tract or parcel of land. I.R.C. Section 614(a). The term denotes an economic interest in a mineral deposit. It includes working or operating interests, royalties, overriding royalties, production payments, and net profits interests. Regulations Section 1.614–1(a)(2).

In the case of a taxpayer computing depletion with respect to minerals by means of *percentage depletion,* the allowance is the applicable percentage of the gross income from the property, excluding from gross income an amount equal to any rents or royalties paid or incurred by the taxpayer in respect of the property. This allowance may not exceed 50% of the taxpayer's taxable income from the property (computed without allowance for depletion). For purposes of the preceding sentence, the allowable deductions taken into account with respect to expenses of mining in computing the taxable income from the property will be decreased by an amount equal to so much of any gain which (1) is treated as gain from the sale or exchange of property which is neither a capital asset nor a Section 1231 asset and (2) is properly allocable to the property. In no case will the depletion allowance be less than it would be if computed without reference to this section. I.R.C. Section 613(a).

The rates of percentage depletion are:

(1) 27½%—oil and gas wells.

(2) 23%—

    (a) sulphur and uranium; and

    (b) if from deposits in the United States—anorthosite, clay, laterite, and nephelite syenite (to the extent that alumina and aluminum compounds are extracted therefrom), asbestos, bauxite, celestite, chromite, corundum, fluorspar, graphite, ilmenite, kyanite, mica, olivine, quartz crystals (radio grade), rutile, block steatite talc, and zircon, and ores of the following metals: antimony, beryllium, bismuth, cadmium, cobalt, columbium, lead, lithium, manganese, mercury, nickel, platinum and platinum group metals, tantalum, thorium, tin, titanium, tungsten, vanadium, and zinc.

(3) 15%—

    (a) metal mines (if Paragraph (2)(b) does not apply, rock asphalt, and vermiculite; and

    (b) if neither Paragraph (2)(b), (5), or (6)(b) applies, ball clay, bentonite, china clay, sagger clay, and clay used or sold for use for purposes dependent on its refractory properties.

(4) 10%—asbestos (if Paragraph (2)(b) does not apply), brucite, coal, lignite, perlite, sodium chloride, and wollastonite.

(5) 7½%—clay and shale used or sold for use in the manufacture of sewer pipe or brick, and clay, shale, and slate used or sold for use as sintered or burned lightweight aggregates.

(6) 5%—

    (a) gravel, peat, pumice, sand, scoria, shale (except shale described in Paragraph (5)), and stone (except stone described in Paragraph (7));

    (b) clay used, or sold for use, in the manufacture of drainage and roofing tile, flower pots, and kindred products; and

    (c) if from brine wells—brimine, calcium chloride, and magnesium chloride.

(7) 15%—all other minerals (including, but not limited to, aplite, barite, borax, calcium carbonates, diatomaceous earth, dolomite, feldspar, fullers earth, garnet, gilsonite, garnite, limestone, magnesite, magnesium carbonates, marble, mollusk shells (including clam shells and oyster shells), phosphate rock, potash, quartzite, slate, soapstone, stone (used or sold for use by the mine owner or operator as dimension stone or ornamental stone), thenardite, tripoli, trona, and (if Paragraph (2)(b) does not apply) bauxite, flake graphite, fluorspar, lepidolite, mica, spodumene, and talc, including pyrophyllite), except that, unless sold on bid in direct competition with a *bona fide* bid to sell a mineral listed in Paragraph (3), the percentage will be 5% for any such other mineral (other than slate to which Paragraph (5) applies) when used, or sold for use, by the mine owner or operator as rip rap, ballast, road material, rubble, concrete aggregates, or for similar purposes. For purposes of this paragraph, the term "all other purposes" does not include—

    (a) soil, sod, dirt, turf, water, or mosses; or

    (b) minerals from sea water, the air, or similar inexhaustible sources.

Intangible Drilling And Development Costs. Intangible drilling and development costs incurred by an operator (one who holds a working or operating interest in any tract or parcel of land either as a fee owner or under a lease or any other form of contract granting working or operating rights) in the development of oil and gas properties may at his option be chargeable to capital or to expense. This option applies to all expenditures made by an operator for wages, fuel, repairs, hauling, supplies, etc., incident to and necessary for the drilling of wells and the preparation of wells for the production of oil or gas. These expenses are termed "intangible drilling and development costs." They include the cost to operators of any drilling or development work (excluding amounts payable only out of production or gross or net proceeds from production, if these amounts are depletable income to the recipient, and amounts properly allocable to cost of depreciable property) done for them by contractors under any form of contract, including turnkey contracts. This option applies to such items as amounts paid for labor, fuel, repairs, hauling, and supplies, which are used—

(1) In the drilling, shotting, and cleaning of wells,

(2) In such clearing of ground, draining, road making, surveying, and geological works as are necessary in preparation for the drilling of wells, and

(3) In the construction of such derricks, tanks, pipelines, and other physical structures as are necessary for the drilling of wells and the preparation of wells for the production of oil or gas.

In general, this option applies only to expenditures for those drilling and development items which in themselves do not have a salvage value.

Optional items, if capitalized, may thus be recovered:

(1) *Items returnable through depletion.* If the taxpayer charges such expenditures as fall within the option to capital account, the amounts so capitalized and not deducted as a loss are returnable through depletion insofar as they are not represented by physical property.

(2) *Items returnable through depreciation.* If the taxpayer charges such expenditures as fall within the option to capital account, the amounts so capitalized and not deducted as a loss are returnable through depreciation insofar as they are represented by physical property.

If the operator has elected to capitalize intangible drilling and development costs, then an additional option is accorded with respect to intangible drilling and development costs incurred in drilling a non-productive well. Such costs may be deducted as an ordinary loss provided a proper election is made in the return for the first taxable year in which a non-productive well is completed. This is a binding election for all future years. Regulations Section 1.612–4.

Exploration Expenditures. In the case of expenditures paid or incurred during the taxable year for the purpose of ascertaining the existence, location, extent, or quality of any deposit of ore or other material, and paid or incurred before the beginning of the development stage of the mine or deposit, there will be allowed as a deduction in computing taxable income so much of these expenditures as does not exceed $100,000. This rule applies only to the amount of those expenditures which otherwise would not be allowable as a deduction for the taxable year. This treatment does not apply to expenditures for the acquisition or improvement of property subject to the depreciation allowance; but allowance for depreciation will be considered, for purposes of this section, as expenditures paid or incurred. "In no case shall this section apply with respect to amounts paid or incurred for the purpose of ascertaining the existence, location, extent, or quality of any deposit of oil or gas." I.R.C. Section 615(a).

A taxpayer may elect to treat as deferred expenses any portion of the amount deductible for the taxable year under the preceding paragraph, whereupon this amount will be deductible on a ratable basis as the units of produced ores or minerals discovered or explored by reason of these expenditures are sold. The election is binding for that year. I.R.C. Section 615(b).

Section 615 does not apply to any amount paid or incurred to the extent that it would, when added to the amounts which would have been deducted under Subsection (a) and the amounts which have been treated as deferred expenses under Subsection (b), exceed $400,000.

Section 617 (to be discussed in the next paragraph) waives these $100,000 and $400,000 limitations under certain circumstances. Section 615 and Section 617 elections are mutually exclusive. I.R.C. Section 615(f).

Additional Exploration Expenditures In The Case Of Domestic Mining. In addition to Section 615 (Exploration Expenditures), Section 617 provides for the deduction of mining exploration expenditures in the taxable year in which they are paid or incurred without regard to the $100,000 and $400,000 limitations of Section 615. This provision is applicable only to mineral expenditures in the United States. Taxpayers may elect to deduct their mining exploration expenditures either under Section 617 without dollar limitations, or they may deduct such expenditures subject to these limitations. If taxpayers elect Section 617, any of these deductions is subject to the recapture rules to be mentioned below.

A taxpayer may initially elect to come under Section 615 and then subsequently (for example, if he desires to incur exploration expenditures in excess of either of these limitations) may elect to apply Section 617. In the event he elects to apply Section 617, the recapture provisions apply not only with respect to the amounts deducted in excess of the limitations, but also any amounts deducted under Section 615 for expenditures incurred after the enactment of Section 617.

A taxpayer may make an election to deduct exploration expenditures under Section 617 without limitations at any time during the period for making a claim for refund for the year involved. An election applies to all exploration expenditures covered by Section 617 for the year in question and all subsequent years. Assessment of a deficiency attributable to an election or revocation may be made within two years after the election or revocation is made.

Section 617 provides for the recapture of exploration expenditure deductions when a mine reaches the producing stage. When this occurs, the taxpayer may either (1) elect to include in income for that year the deductions chargeable to the mine or (2) to forego depletion from the property which includes or comprises the mine until the deductions foregone equal the amounts previously deducted.

The election to include the prior deductions in income must be made for all mines reaching the producing stage in a year with respect to which the taxpayer has deducted exploration expenditures under Section 617. Under this alternative the bases of the properties are increased by the amount recaptured and this may subsequently be recoverable through the depletion allowance. This, in effect, places the taxpayer essentially in the position he would have been in, had he initially capitalized the expenditures rather than deducting them currently.

Under the election to forego depletion deductions from a property until this equals the exploration expenditures, the amount of the depletion allowance disallowed is limited to the amount of the "adjusted exploration expenditures" with respect to a mine. This term is defined in general as the excess of the exploration expenditures previously allowed as deductions over the reduction in the depletion allowance which occurred because the taxpayer deducted exploration expenditures. This is further reduced for any amounts previously recaptured. A special recapture rule provides for a similar reduction in the depletion allowance where a taxpayer receives a bonus or royalty payment.

Section 617 also provides for the recapture of exploration expenditures (to the extent not already recaptured, in line with the above commentary) on the sale or other disposition of a mining property. In the case of a sale, exchange, or involuntary conversion, the adjusted exploration expenditures are recaptured only to the extent of the gain on the sale. In the case of other forms of disposition, the adjusted exploration expenditures are recaptured only to the extent the fair market value of the property exceeds its cost or other basis. The amount recaptured on sale or other disposition is treated as ordinary income. Dispositions for this purpose include disposals of iron ore which receive capital gain treatment under Section 631(c).

If only a portion of a mining property (other than an undivided interest) is disposed of, the entire adjusted exploration expenditures are attributed to the portion disposed of, to the extent of the gain (or the excess of the fair market value over the basis of the property). But if an undivided interest in a mining property is disposed of, a proportionate part of the adjusted exploration expenditures is attributed to this interest but only to the extent of the gain on the disposition (or the excess of fair market value over the basis).

Despite these rules, the recapture rules do not apply to the extent the taxpayer establishes to the satisfaction of the Secretary of the Treasury that the expenditures do not relate to the portion disposed of (or to any mine in the property which already has reached the producing stage).

There are certain exceptions to the recapture rules. In the case of gifts, inasmuch as the recapture rules do not apply at the time of the gift, the adjusted exploration expenditures go over to the donee. As a result, the recapture provisions apply and may result in ordinary income to the donee if he sells the property or takes a depletion deduction. In addition, where a mineral property is given to a charitable organization, the amount of the charitable deduction is reduced by the amount which would have been treated as ordinary income (under the recapture rules) had the property been sold at its fair market value.

A second exception applies in the case of transfers at death. In this case, the adjusted exploration expenditures do not go over to the heir and as a result this recapture is not applied upon the sale of the property by the heir.

A third series of exceptions to the recapture provisions relate to dispositions in transactions which generally are tax-free but where the basis of the property in the hands of the transferor is carried over to the transferee. (But in these transactions, where any gain is recognized because the exchange is accompanied by boot—that is, money or the equivalent—then to the extent of this gain, ordinary income may be realized.) To the extent gain is not recognized, the adjusted exploration expenditures go over to the transferee and may result in ordinary income. The tax-free transactions involved are those occurring on the complete liquidation of a subsidiary (Section 332) where the subsidiary's basis goes over to the parent; a transfer of mining property to a corporation controlled by the transferor (Section 351); a transfer by a corporation which is a party to a reorganization of property in pursuance of a plan of reorganization solely for stock or securities in another corporation also a party to the reorganization (Section 361); and transfers occurring in reorganizations pursuant to certain receiverships and bankruptcy proceedings (Sections 371 and 374).

Recapture is to occur on the contribution of property to a tax-exempt organization (other than a tax-exempt farm co-operative) in exchange for stock or securities in the exempt organization.

The recapture rules do not apply to property contributed to a partnership in exchange for an interest in the partnership nor to certain distributions by a partnership in partial or complete liquidation of an interest. In the case of a distribution of a mineral property by a partnership to a partner, the recapture rules are applied at the time of the distribution in those cases (and to the extent) gain is recognized. Where gain is recognized on such a distribution (as the result of the treatment of mineral property as an unrealized receivable to the extent of the adjusted exploration expenditures), the amount of the exploration expenditure which is to be recaptured subsequently is reduced by the amount of the gain attributable to the expenditures which was recognized on the distribution. This applies whether the mining property with respect to which gain is realized is distributed or whether the distributee partner realizes gain with respect to mineral property remaining in the partnership. Where the property goes over to the partner without recognition of gain, the recapture rules in the case of mineral properties distributed do not apply at that time. But provision is made for their application at any subsequent time when the partner (or a former partner) disposes of the mineral property or when a depletion deduction would be allowable.

Development Expenditures. Deduction is allowed for all expenditures paid or incurred during the taxable year for the development of a mine or other natural deposit (other than an oil or gas well) if paid or incurred after the existence of ores or minerals in commercially marketable quantities has been disclosed. This rule does not apply, however, to expenditures for the acquisition or improvement of property which is subject to the depreciation allowance; but allowance for depreciation may be considered, for purposes of this rule, as expenditures. I.R.C. Section 616(a).

A taxpayer may elect to have the above expenditures treated as deferred expenditures, to be deductible on a ratable basis as the units of produced ores or minerals benefitted by these expenditures are sold. In the case of such expenditures paid or incurred during the development stage of the mine or deposit, the election will apply only with respect to the excess of such expenditures during the taxable year over the net receipts during that year from the ores or minerals produced from the mine or deposit. If this election is made, it must be for the total amount of the expenditure, or the total amount of the excess, with respect to the mine or deposit. The election is binding for that taxable year. I.R.C. Section 616(b).

Payments To Encourage Exploration, Development, And Mining For Defense Purposes. A taxpayer may exclude from gross income amounts which are paid to him—

(1) By the United States or by any agency or instrumentality of the United States;

(2) As a grant, bounty, bonus, premium, incentive, subsidy, loan, or advance;

(3) For the encouragement of exploration for, or development of, a critical and strategic mineral or metal;

(4) Pursuant to or in connection with an undertaking by the taxpayer to explore for, or to develop or to produce, such mineral or metal and to expend or to use any amounts so received for the purpose and in accordance with the terms and conditions upon which these amounts are paid, which undertaking has been approved by the United States or by an agency or instrumentality thereof; and

(5) For which the taxpayer has accounted, or is required to account, to an appropriate agency of the United States Government for the expenditure or use thereof for the purpose and in accordance with the terms and conditions upon which these amounts are paid. Regulations Section 1.621–1(a).

The term "critical and strategic minerals or metals" means "minerals and metals which are considered by those departments, agencies, and instrumentalities of the United States charged with the encouragement of exploration for, and development and mining of, critical and strategic minerals and metals for defense purposes. See, for example, 30 CFR 301.3 (Regulations for Obtaining Federal Assistance in Financing Explorations for Mineral Reserves, excluding Organic Fields, in the United States, its Territories and Possessions." Regulations Section 1.621–1(d).

ABC Contracts. The classic ABC transaction has been popularized by the oil and gas industry. A production payment (a stipulated percentage of annual gross production paid in kind, or cash, and secured only by such production, until a pre-determined amount has been paid the vendor by the vendee) is retained by the assignor, A (the seller) from his sale of the lease or fee to the buyer, B (the operator) which may be sold separately, or at the same time, to C (a third party) for capital gain. The third party realizes ordinary depletable income upon receipt of amounts with respect to the production payment, while the assignor realizes capital gain upon his sale of the entire production payment. *Olin Bryant et al.,* 46 T.C. 848 (1966).

In resisting the issuance of a favorable Revenue Ruling involving an ABC acquisition of depletable mineral interests other than oil and gas,

Senator Gore (D., Tenn.) referred to the "notorious ABC scheme" which is "a sophisticated tax gimmick." 112 *Congressional Record* 12080–12083 (June 8, 1966), 18146–18147 (August 11, 1966), 18685 (August 16, 1965). "The ABC transaction is a tax dodge, pure and simple. Taxation is the principal reason for setting it up." *Congressional Record* 12081 (June 8, 1966).

Patents

Section 1235 provides, basically, that a transfer of all substantial rights to a patent, or an undivided interest in all such rights to a patent, by a holder (as defined) to a person (other than a related person, as defined) constitutes a sale or exchange of a long-term capital asset irrespective of whether the payments made in consideration bear a general resemblance to the payment of royalties. *Elmo Meiners et al.,* 42 T.C. 653 (1964).

The yardstick for determining whether a transfer of patent rights constitutes an "assignment" so as to entitle the transferee to capital gains treatment, as opposed to a mere "license," is whether the transferor has parted with "all substantial rights" under the patents. *C. A. Norgren Co. v. United States,* 268 F. Supp. 816 (D.C., Colo., 1967). The best method of ascertaining what has or has not been transferred is to examine what rights have been *retained* by the grantor. *Allied Chemical Corporation v. United States,* 370 F.2d 697 (2d Cir., 1967). The fact that a transferor contemporaneously assigned patent rights to *two* companies, one receiving the right to sell and the other the right to manufacture and to use, would make no difference. The transferor still has parted with all substantial rights to the patent. *Armco Steel Corporation v. United States,* 253 F. Supp. 749 (D.C., S.D. Ohio, 1966). All substantial rights were not transferred where the agreement covered a shorter period than the life of the properties, and even that period could have been accelerated by an unremedied default of the licensee.

To be an assignment rather than a mere license, the agreement must provide for all three of the rights of the inventor, that is, to make, to use, and to vend. *Kimble Glass Co.,* 9 T.C. 183 (1947). It is not necessary that these rights be spelled out in the agreement if they may be inferred from all of the circumstances. *Arthur C. Ruge,* 26 T.C. 138 (1956).

Payments made by the transferee of patent rights pursuant to a transfer satisfying the requirements of Section 1235 are payments of the purchase price for the patent rights and are not the payment of royalties. Regulations Section 1.1235–1(d).

Sale Or Exchange. In determining whether a sale or exchange of a patent or invention has occurred, the court must look not only to the documents themselves but to the "total factual complex surrounding the transaction," to determine the real intent of the parties. *Switzer v. Commissioner,* 226 F.2d 329 (6th Cir., 1955). The transaction will be treated as a sale only if the holder of the patents intended to surrender all of his interest in the patents or inventions and such surrender did in fact occur. *Rose Marie Reid,* 26 T.C. 622 (1956). Anything less than such a transfer is a mere license and the proceeds constitute ordinary income. *Gregg v. Commissioner,* 203 F.2d 954 (3d Cir., 1953).

A transfer (other than by gift, inheritance, or devise) of all substantial rights to a patent, by a holder to a person other than a related person constitutes the sale or exchange of a long-term capital asset, whether or not the payments therefor are—

(1) Payable periodically over a period co-terminous with the transferee's use of the patent, or

(2) Contingent on the productivity, use, or disposition of the property transferred. I.R.C. Section 1235(a).

If a transfer is not one as described in the preceding paragraph, Section 1235 is to be disregarded in determining whether the transfer is the sale or exchange of a capital asset. Thus, a transfer by a person other than a holder or a transfer by a holder to a related person is not governed by this section.

Provisions for the re-vesting of title in the assignor of a patent interest are not inconsistent with a sale or exchange of all substantial rights. *Waterman v. Mackenzie,* 138 U.S. 252 (1891). But an agreement providing for termination at will of the so-called assignor constitutes a mere license. *Lynne Gregg et al.,* 18 T.C. 291 (1952), *aff'd,* 203 F.2d 954 (3d Cir., 1953).

A taxpayer, in granting a license under a patent, retained the right to manufacture the patented items in the United States. The retention of this right, without establishing the fact that it had no value, was sufficient to defeat the taxpayer's claim that he had transferred all of his substantial rights under the patent. *Kirby II v. United States,* 297 F.2d 466 (5th Cir., 1961). Royalties under a licensing agreement whereby a taxpayer transferred the exclusive right to sell in the United States certain patented foods made in Japan were ordinary income. The taxpayer had retained the option to cancel the license agreement upon giving six months' notice. He thus had not transferred all of his substantial rights under the patent to the licensee. *Franz Martini et al.,* 38 T.C. 168 (1962).

Meaning Of "Patent." For this purpose, "patent" means a patent granted under the provisions of the United States Code, or any foreign patent granting rights generally similar to those under a United States patent. The patent or patent application for the invention need not be in existence if the requirements of Section 1235 are otherwise met.

The term "all substantial rights to a patent" means all rights (whether or not held by the grantor) which are of value at the time the rights to the patent (or an undivided interest therein) are transferred. This term does not include a grant of rights to a patent—

(1) Which is limited geographically within the country of issuance;

(2) Which is limited in duration by the terms of the agreement to a period less than the remaining life of the patent;

(3) Which grants rights to the grantee, in fields of use within trades or industries, which are less than all the rights covered by the patent, which exist and have value at the time of the grant; or

(4) Which grants to the grantee less than all the claims or inventions covered by the patent that exist and have value at the time of the grant.

"The circumstances of the whole transaction, rather than the particular terminology used in the instrument, shall be considered in determining whether or not all substantial rights to a patent are transferred in a transaction." Regulations Section 1.1235–2(b)(1).

Rights which are not considered substantial for purposes of Section 1235 may be retained by the holder. Examples are:

(1) The retention by the transferor of legal title for the purpose of securing performance or payment by the transferee in a transaction involving transfer of an exclusive license to manufacture, to use, and to sell for the life of the patent.

(2) The retention by the transferor of rights in the property which are not inconsistent with the passage of ownership, such as the retention of a security interest (*i.e.,* a vendor's lien), or a reservation in the nature of a condition subsequent (*i.e.,* a provision for forfeiture on account of nonperformance).

Examples of rights which may or may not be substantial, depending upon the circumstances of the whole transaction in which rights to a patent are transferred, are:

(1) The retention by the transferor of an absolute right to prohibit sublicensing or sub-assignment by the transferee.

(2) The failure to convey to the transferee the right to use or to sell the patent property.

The retention of a right to terminate the transfer at will is the retention of a substantial right for the purposes of Section 1235. Regulations Section 1.1235–2(b)(2).

A person owns an "undivided interest" in all substantial rights to a patent when he owns the same fractional share of each and every substantial right to the patent. It does not include, for example, a right to the income from a patent, or a license limited geographically, or a license which covers some but not all of the valuable claims or uses covered by the patent. A transfer limited in duration by the terms of the instrument to a period less than the remaining life of the patent is not a transfer of an undivided interest in all substantial rights to a patent. Regulations Section 1.1235–2(c).

A transfer of a fraction of a whole patent which includes a share of each of the substantial rights under the patent equal to that fraction constitutes a transfer of an undivided interest in all substantial rights to a patent within the meaning of Section 1235(a). Revenue Ruling 59–175, 1959–1 CB 213. It is not necessary that the payment be a lump sum in order to constitute capital gain. It may be cast in the form of a percentage of sales or profits, or an amount per unit manufactured or sold, or any combination of these items. *Carl C. Dreymann,* 11 T.C. 153 (1948).

It is not significant that the patents had not been issued or even applied for when the transfer was made. *Milton B. Laurent, Sr.,* 34 T.C. 385 (1960). Where a taxpayer paid all the expenses incidental to the design and building of the prototype of a machine when it still was under development, the interest which he acquired in the machine, in exchange for the payment, was perforce acquired prior to the actual reduction to practice of the machine. "[G]enerally, actual, as opposed to constructive, reduction cannot occur prior to the successful testing of a *completed* device." *Elmo Meiners et al.,* 42 T.C. 653 (1964).

The applicability of Section 1235 to transfers of undivided interests in patents, or to successive transfers of these rights, will be determined separately with respect to each transfer. "For example, X, who is a holder, and Y, who is not a holder, transfer their respective two-thirds and one-third undivided interests in a patent to Z. Assume the transfer by X qualifies under section 1235 and that X in a later transfer acquires all the rights with respect to Y's interest, including the rights to payments from Z. One-third of all the payments thereafter received by X from Z are not attributable to a transfer to which section 1235 applies." Regulations Section 1.1235–1(c)(3).

Meaning of "Holder." The term "holder" means an individual—

(1) Whose efforts created the patent property and who would qualify as the "original and first" inventor, or joint inventor, within the meaning of Title 35 of the United States Code, or

(2) Who has acquired his interest in the patent property in exchange for a consideration paid to the inventor in money or money's worth prior to the actual reduction of the invention to practice, provided that he was neither

the employer of the inventor nor related to him. The requirement that this individual is neither the employer of the inventor nor related to him must be satisfied at the time when the substantive rights as to the interest to be acquired are determined, and at the time when the consideration to be paid is definitely fixed. Thus, if prior to the actual reduction to practice of an invention an individual who is neither the employer of the inventor nor related to him agrees to pay the inventor a sum of money definitely fixed as to amount in return for an undivided one-half interest in rights to a patent and at a later date, when this individual has become the employer of the inventor, he pays the definitely fixed sum of money pursuant to the earlier agreement, this individual will not be denied the status of a holder because of the employment relationship.

Although a partnership cannot be a holder, each member of a partnership who is an individual may qualify as a holder as to his share of a patent owned by the partnership.

An individual may qualify as a holder whether or not he is in the business of making inventions or in the business of buying and selling patents. Regulations Section 1.1235–2(d).

Related Person. The term "related person" means one whose relationship to another person at the time of the transfer is described in Section 267(b) (which was discussed in Chapter 6), except that the term does not include a brother or sister.

If, prior to September 3, 1958, a holder transferred all his substantial rights to a corporation in which he owned more than 50% in value of the outstanding stock, he is considered as having transferred these rights to a related person for the purpose of Section 1235. On the other hand, if a holder, prior to that date, transferred all of his substantial rights to a corporation in which he owned 50% or less in value of the outstanding stock and his brother owned the remaining stock, he is not considered as having transferred these rights to a related person, inasmuch as the brother relationship is disregarded for this purpose.

If, subsequent to September 2, 1958, a holder transfers all his substantial rights to a patent to a corporation in which he owns 25% or more in value of the outstanding stock, he is considered as transferring these rights to a related person. On the other hand, if a holder subsequent to that date transfers all his substantial rights to a patent to a corporation in which he owns less than 25% in value of the outstanding stock, he is not considered as transferring these rights to a related person, inasmuch as the brother relationship is disregarded for this purpose.

If a relationship described in Section 267(b) exists independently of family status, the brother-sister exception does not apply. Thus, if a holder transfers all his substantial rights to a patent to the fiduciary of a trust of which the holder is the grantor, the holder and the fiduciary are related persons for this purpose. The transfer, therefore, would not qualify under Section 1235(a). Such is the situation whether or not the fiduciary is the brother or sister of the holder, inasmuch as the disqualifying relationship exists by reason of the grantor-fiduciary status and not by reason of family status. Regulations Section 1.1235–2(f).

Payments To An Employee. Payments received by an employee as compensation for services rendered *as an employee* under an employment contract requiring him to transfer to the employer the rights to any invention by the employee are not attributable to a transfer to which Section 1235 applies. Whether payments received by an employee from his employer (under an employment contract or otherwise) are attributable to the transfer by the employee of all substantial rights to a patent (or an undivided interest therein) or are compensation for services rendered to the employer by the employee is a question of fact. "In determining which is the case, consideration shall be given not only to all the facts and circumstances of the employment relationship but also to whether the amount of such payments depends upon the production, sale, or use by, or the value to, the employer of the patent rights transferred by the employee. If it is determined that payments are attributable to the transfer of patent rights, and all other requirements under section 1235 are met, such payments shall be treated as proceeds derived from the sale of a patent." Regulations Section 1.1235–1(c)(2).

If a person is employed by another to "invent" a specified product or products, the fruits of the employee's labor (the invention) belong to his employer. *United States v. Dubilier Condenser Corporation,* 289 U.S. 178 (1933). The payment to the employee is for his labor, and not the product, the invention. *Arthur N. Blum,* 11 T.C. 101 (1948), *aff'd,* 183 F.2d 281 (3d Cir., 1950). An employee, in consideration of his employment by a corporation, assigned to the corporation all inventions relating to that business which he might make during the employment. Subsequently the corporation announced to its employees a program for paying employee-inventors a certain percentage of any income received by the corporation as the result of its sale or licensing of employee inventions to third parties. Amounts thus received by the employee qualified as capital gains. *Thomas McClain et al.,* 40 T.C. 841 (1963). Capital treatment was proper where an individual was hired by a corporation as a design supervisor at a salary, with the added agreement that certain patentable inventions would be transferred to the corporation in consideration of specified payments (which had no connection with his salary payments) contingent upon the corporation's selling or licensing the invention. *T. Gardner et al.,* T.C. Memo, 1963–211, filed August 7, 1963.

A taxpayer had assigned his full right, title, and interest in an invention, subsequently patented, to his employer in consideration of a percentage of the sales price of the item when marketed. The invention had been perfected on his own time, but work on a pilot model thereof had been done on the employer's premises with its material and with the help of two other employees. Payments he received under the assignment were treated as long-term capital gain. Such shop rights as his employer had in the invention did not dilute the taxpayer's substantial rights in his patent. *Hans Jordan et al.,* 27 T.C. 265 (1956).

Chapter 14

Special Situation Companies

In the case of certain types of corporations, the Federal income tax may be paid entirely by the shareholders, as in the case of a regulated investment company, so that there is not the customary pattern of duplicate taxation. In the case of other types of corporations, such as a life insurance company, the income tax may be paid by the corporation but under beneficially preferential statutes, so that the stockholder (although his tax is not directly affected) is the beneficiary of special treatment in that his company has more of its after-tax earnings available for him.

In certain instances, there are elections or options as to taxability.

Banks

For Federal income tax purposes, "the term 'bank' means a bank or trust company incorporated and doing business under the laws of the United States (including laws relating to the District of Columbia), of any State, or of any Territory, a substantial part of the business of which consists of receiving deposits and making loans and discounts, or of exercising fiduciary powers similar to those permitted to national banks under the authority of the Comptroller of the Currency, and which is subject by law to supervision and examination by State, Territorial, or Federal authority having supervision over banking institutions. Such term also means a domestic building and loan association." I.R.C. Section 581.

A bank, as thus defined, is subject to the regular corporation income taxes.

Mutual savings banks, building and loan associations, and co-operative banks not having capital stock represented by shares are subject to tax as in the case of other corporations. But there are certain exceptions and special rules governing the computation in the case of such institutions. There are special rules for:

(1) Additions to reserves for bad debts. I.R.C. Section 593.

(2) Dividends paid by banking corporations. Deductions for amounts paid to or credited to the accounts of depositors or holders of withdrawal accounts as dividends. I.R.C. Section 591.

(3) Deductions for repayment of certain loans. I.R.C. Section 592.

(4) Net operating loss deduction. Any taxable year for which a mutual savings bank, building and loan association, or a co-operative bank not having capital stock represented by shares was exempt from tax will be disregarded. Regulations Section 1.581–2.

Bad Debt And Loss Deduction With Respect To Securities Held By Banks. A bank, as defined above, is allowed a bad debt deduction in the customary manner with respect to a debt which has become worthless in whole or in part and which is evidenced by a security (a bond, debenture, note, certificate, or other evidence of indebtedness to pay a fixed or determinable sum of money) issued by any corporation (including governments and their political subdivisions), with interest coupons or in registered form.

For purposes of the deduction for losses involving worthless securities, if the taxpayer is a bank and owns directly at least 80% of each class of stock of another bank, stock in this other bank will not be treated as a capital asset.

If the losses of the taxable year from sales or exchanges of bonds, debentures, notes, or certificates, or other evidences of indebtedness, issued by any corporation (including one issued by a government or political subdivision thereof) exceed the gains of the taxable year from sales or exchanges, no such sale or exchange will be considered a sale or exchange of a capital asset. I.R.C. Section 582.

Dividends Paid Deductions. In computing the taxable income of any national banking association, or of any bank or trust company organized under the laws of any state, territory, possession of the United States, or the Canal Zone, or of any other banking corporation engaged in the business of industrial banking and under the supervision of a state banking department or of the Comptroller of the Currency, or of any incorporated 'domestic insurance company, there is allowed as a deduction from gross income any dividend (not including a distribution in liquidation) paid, within the taxable year, to the United States or one of its instrumentalities that is exempt from Federal income taxes on the preferred stock of the corporation owned by the United States or of the instrumentality. The amount thus allowable as a deduction will reduce the deduction for dividends paid otherwise computed under Section 561 (dividends paid deduction). I.R.C. Section 583.

"In the case of mutual savings banks, cooperative banks, domestic building and loan associations, and other savings institutions chartered and supervised as savings and loan or similar associations under Federal or State law, there shall be allowed as deductions in computing taxable income amounts paid to, or credited to the accounts of, depositors or holders of accounts as dividends or interest on their deposits or withdrawable accounts, if such amounts paid or credited are withdrawable on demand subject only to customary notice of intention to withdraw." I.R.C. Section 591.

Deduction For Repayment Of Certain Loans. "In the case of a mutual savings bank not having capital stock represented by shares, a domestic building and loan association, or a cooperative bank without capital stock organized and operated for mutual purposes and without profit, there shall be allowed as deductions in computing taxable income amounts paid by the taxpayer during the taxable year in repayment of loans made before September 1, 1951, by (1) the United States or any agency or instrumentality thereof which is wholly owned by the United States, or (2) any mutual fund established under the authority of the laws of any State." I.R.C. Section 592.

A mutual savings bank not having capital stock represented by shares, a domestic building and loan association, or a co-operative bank without capital stock organized and operated for mutual purposes and without profit may, as an alternative to the customary deduction from gross income for specific debts which become worthless in whole or in part, deduct amounts credited to a reserve for bad debts in the manner and under the circumstances prescribed in Section 593 and, *in extenso,* Regulations Section 1.593–1 and 1.593–2. The gist of these lengthy and elaborate regulations is that there may be deducted as an addition to reserves for bad debts an amount which is the total of (1) a reasonable addition to a reserve for non-qualifying loans (as defined) and (2) an amount determined to be a reasonable addition to a reserve for qualifying real property loans.

Foreclosure On Property Securing Loans. In the case of a creditor which is a mutual savings bank not having capital stock represented by shares, domestic building and loan association, or co-operative bank without capital stock organized and operated for mutual purposes and without profit, no gain or loss will be recognized, and no debt will be considered as becoming worthless or partially worthless, as the result of a transaction by which this creditor bids in at foreclosure, or reduces to ownership or possession by agreement or process of law, any property which was security for the payment of any indebtedness. This treatment is mandatory if, for the taxable year in which the property is bid in at foreclosure, or reduced to ownership or possession by agreement or by process of law, the creditor is one of the types described in the preceding sentence, even though the creditor subsequently ceases to be such an organization. I.R.C. Section 595(a).

Alternative Tax For Mutual Savings Banks Conducting Life Insurance Business. Section 594 applies to the case of a mutual savings bank not having capital stock represented by shares which conducts a life insurance business, if:

(1) The conduct of the life insurance business is authorized under state law.

(2) The life insurance business is carried on in a separate department of the bank.

(3) The books of account of the life insurance business are maintained separately from other departments of the bank.

(4) The life insurance department of the bank would, if it were treated as a separate corporation, qualify as a life insurance company under Section 801.

If these conditions obtain, Section 594 provides that the tax upon the bank is the total of the following:

(1) A partial tax under the regular Federal income tax laws upon the taxable income of the bank determined without regard to any items of income or deduction properly allocable to the life insurance department.

(2) A partial tax on the income (as defined in Section 803, dealing with life insurance companies) of the life insurance department determined without regard to any items of income or deduction not properly allocable to such department, at the rates and in the manner provided in Subchapter L with respect to life insurance companies.

Special Deduction For Bank Affiliates. In the case of a holding company affiliate (as defined in Section 2 of the Banking Act of 1933), there is allowed as a deduction for purposes of computing the accumulated earnings tax and the personal holding company tax, the amount of the earnings and profits which the Board of Governors of the Federal Reserve System certifies to the Secretary of the Treasury has been devoted by this affiliate during the taxable year to the acquisition of readily marketable assets other than bank stock in compliance with Section 5144 of the Revised Statutes. The amount of this deduction for the taxable year may not exceed the taxable income for that year without regard to the special deductions for corporations in general. Nor may the aggregate of the deductions allowable under this section for all taxable years exceed the amount which must be devoted under Section 5144 to the acquisition of readily marketable assets other than bank stock. I.R.C. Section 601.

Common Trust Funds. A common trust fund maintained by a bank is not subject to Federal income tax; it is not considered to be a corporation. Participants of the common trust fund are taxed on their proportionate shares of income from the fund. In general, the term "participants" refers to any trust or estate, the moneys of which have been contributed to the common trust fund.

Two conditions must be satisfied by a fund maintained by a bank (as defined in Section 581, above) before the fund may be designated as a common trust fund. These conditions are that the fund must be maintained by the bank—

(1) Exclusively for the collective investment and re-investment of moneys contributed to it by the bank, whether acting alone or in conjunction with one or more co-fiduciaries, but solely in its capacity as:

    (a) A trustee of a trust created by will, deed, agreement, declaration of trust, or court order.

    (b) An executor of the will of, or as an administrator of the estate of, a deceased person.

    (c) A guardian (by whatever name known under local law) of the estate of an infant, or an incompetent individual, or of an absent individual.

(2) In conformity with the rules and regulations, prevailing from time to time, of the Comptroller of the Currency. I.R.C. Section 584(a), (b).

Each participant in a common trust fund must include in computing its taxable income for its taxable year within which or with which the taxable year of the fund ends, whether or not distributed and whether or not distributable:

(1) Its proportionate share of the gains and losses from sales or exchanges of capital assets held for not more than six months as part of its gains and losses from sales or exchanges of short-term capital assets.

(2) Equivalent treatment for long-term capital assets.

(3) Its proportionate share of the ordinary income or the ordinary net loss of the common trust fund.

Each participant's proportionate share in the amount of dividends (subject to any dividend exclusion of Section 116) received by the fund will be deemed to have been received by the participant as such dividends.

Each participant's proportionate share in the amount of partially tax exempt interest received by the fund will be deemed to have been received by the participant as such interest. If the fund elects to amortize the premium on these obligations, for purposes of the preceding sentence the proportionate share of each participant of this interest received by the fund will be his proportionate share of the interest (determined without regard to this sentence) reduced by so much of the bond premium amortization deduction as is attributable to that share.

Any tax withheld at the source from the fund's income will be deemed to have been withheld proportionately from the participants to whom the income is allocated.

The proportionate share of each participant in short-term and long-term capital gains and losses, ordinary taxable income or ordinary net loss, dividends received, partially exempt interest, and tax withheld at the source will be determined under the method of accounting adopted by the bank in accordance with the written plan under which the fund is established and administered, provided this method clearly reflects the income of each participant. The items of income and deductions are, therefore, to be allocated to the periods between valuation dates within the taxable year established by the plan in which they are realized or sustained, and the category of tax classification is to be computed for each such period. The proportionate shares of the participants in these items are then to be determined.

The taxable income of the common trust fund is computed in the same manner and on the same basis as in the case of an individual, except that—

(1) No charitable deduction is allowed.

(2) The gains and losses from sales or exchanges of capital assets of the common trust fund must be segregated. The fund is not allowed the benefit of the capital loss carryover.

(3) The ordinary taxable income (the excess of the gross income over deductions) or the ordinary net loss (the excess of the deductions over the gross income) will be computed after excluding all items of gain or loss from sales or exchanges of capital assets.

(4) The standard deduction is not allowed. I.R.C. Section 584(d).

The fund realizes no gain or loss by the admission or withdrawal of a participant, and the basis of the assets and the period for which they are deemed to have been held by the fund are unaffected. If a participant withdraws the whole or any part of its participating interest from the fund, this withdrawal will be treated as a sale or exchange by the participant of the participating interest which is so withdrawn. A participant is not deemed to have withdrawn any part of its participating interest in the fund so as to have completed a closed transaction by reason of the segregation and administration of an investment of the fund for the benefit of all of the then participants in the fund. This segregated investment will be considered as held by, or on behalf of, the fund for the benefit ratably of all participants at the time of segregation, and any income or loss arising from its administration and liquidation will constitute income or loss to the fund apportionable among the participants for whose benefit the investment was segregated.

The participant's gain or loss upon withdrawal of its participating interest (or portion of it) is measured by the difference between the amount received upon the withdrawal and the adjusted basis of the interest withdrawn plus the additions prescribed in the following paragraph and minus the reductions prescribed in the second following paragraph. The amount received by the participant will be the sum of any money plus the fair market value of other property received upon the withdrawal. The basis of the interest withdrawn will be the sum of any money plus the fair market value of any other property contributed by the participant to the fund to acquire the interest withdrawn. This basis will not be reduced on account of the segregation of any investment in the fund. For the purpose of making these adjustments to basis, the ward, rather than the guardian, will be deemed to be the participant; and the grantor, rather than the trust, will be deemed to be the participant, to the extent that the income of the trust is taxable to the grantor.

In computing the gain or loss upon the withdrawal of a participating interest, there will be added to the basis of the interest withdrawn an amount equal to the aggregate of the following items (to the extent that they were properly allocated to the participant for a taxable year of the fund and were not distributed to the participant prior to withdrawal):

(1) Wholly exempt income of the fund for any taxable year.

(2) Net income of the fund for the taxable years beginning after December 31, 1935 and prior to January 1, 1938.

(3) Net short-term capital gain of the fund for each taxable year beginning after December 31, 1937.

(4) The excess of the gains over the losses recognized to the fund upon sales or exchanges of capital assets held (a) for more than eighteen months for taxable years beginning after December 31, 1937 and before January 1, 1942 and (b) for more than six months for taxable years beginning after December 31, 1941.

(5) Ordinary net or taxable income of the fund for each taxable year beginning after December 31, 1937.

As mentioned above, in computing the gain or loss upon the withdrawal of a participating interest, the basis of the interest withdrawn will be reduced by such portions of the following items as were allocable to the participant with respect to the interest wihdrawn:

(1) The amount of the excess of the allowable deductions of the fund over its gross income for the taxable years beginning after December 31, 1935 and before January 1, 1938.

(2) The amount of the net short-term capital loss, net long-term capital loss, and ordinary net income of the fund for each taxable year beginning after December 31, 1937. Regulations Section 1.584–4.

The net operating loss deduction is not allowed to a common trust fund.

Each participant in a fund, however, will be allowed the benefits of such deduction. In the computation of the deduction, a participant in a fund will take into account its *pro rata* share of items of income, gain, loss, deduction, or credit of the fund. The character of any such item will be determined as if .the participant had realized this item directly from the source from which realized by the fund, or incurred the item in the same manner as incurred by the fund. Regulations Section 1.584–6.

Life Insurance Companies

Special rules apply to the taxation of life insurance companies. The term "life insurance company" means an insurance company which is engaged in the business of issuing life insurance and annuity contracts (either separately or combined with health and accident insurance) or non-cancellable contracts of health and accident insurance, if—

(1) Its life insurance reserves, plus

(2) Unearned premiums, and unpaid losses on non-cancellable life, health, or accident policies not included in life insurance reserves, comprise more than 50% of its total reserves. I. R. C. Section 801(a).

The tax imposed on life insurance companies consists of a normal tax and surtax computed as though the life insurance company taxable income (as defined in Section 802(b)) were the taxable income referred to in the regular income tax provisions.

The term "life insurance company taxable income" is the sum of:

(1) The *taxable investment income* (as defined in Section 804) or, if smaller, the *gain from operations* (as defined in Section 809). This is referred to as the Phase 1 tax.

(2) If the gain from operations (underwriting) exceeds the taxable investment income, an amount equal to 50% of that excess. This is referred to as the Phase 2 tax.

(3) The amount subtracted from the policyholders' surplus account for the taxable year, as determined under Section 815. This is referred to as the Phase 3 tax.

(1), (2), and (3) will be examined below.

If, for any taxable year, there is a loss from operations, the amount taken into account under (1) and (2) will be zero. But even in such a case, there may still be an amount includible in life insurance company taxable income (and hence subject to tax) by reason of (3). Regulations Section 1.802–4(a).

Phase 1 Tax. In order to determine taxable investment income, a life insurance company must first determine its gross investment income. The next step is to determine its investment yield. The third step is to determine the policyholders' share of each item of its investment yield, as this share is excluded from taxable investment income. Thus, only the life insurance company's share of the items comprising investment yield (less certain reductions) is taken into account in computing taxable investment income.

The percentage used in determining the life insurance company's share of each item of investment yield (including tax-exempt interest and dividends received) will be the percentage obtained by subtracting that part of the investment yield belonging to the policyholders under the policy and other contract liability requirements.

"Taxable investment income," then, is an amount (not less than zero) equal to the amount (if any) by which the net long-term capital gain exceeds the net short-term capital loss, plus the sum of the life insurance company's share of each item of investment yield (including tax-exempt interest and dividends received), reduced by the life insurance company's share of exempt interest, dividends received, and the small business deduction. Regulations Section 1.804–2.

"Gain for operations" is the excess of the sum of:

(1) The life insurance company's share of each item of investment yield;
(2) Premiums, decreases in certain reserves, and other amounts not included in investment yield which are includible in gross income; and
(3) The amount (if any) by which the net long-term capital gain exceeds the net short-term capital loss

over the following deductions: death benefits, increases in certain reserves, dividends to policyholders, operations loss deductions, certain non-participating contracts, certain accident and health insurance and group life insurance, assumption by another person of liabilities under insurance, tax-exempt interest, dividends, and specified other items. I.R.C. Section 809(b).

The "operations loss deduction" refers to an 8-year carry-forward of net operation losses of life insurance companies, if the corporation is a new one in the year of the loss. I.R.C. Section 812.

Phase 3 Tax. Any distributions to shareholders of life insurance companies are treated as made—

(1) first out of the shareholders' surplus account, to the extent thereof,
(2) then out of the policyholders' surplus account, to the extent thereof, and
(3) finally out of other accounts. I.R.C. Section 815(a).

Each stock life insurance company is required by Section 815(b) to maintain a shareholders' surplus account. Amounts in this account may be distributed to shareholders without the imposition of the so-called Phase 3 tax (the tax imposed by reason of distributions considered as made out of the policyholders' surplus account). The amount added to the shareholders' surplus account for any taxable year includes items for life insurance company taxable income and the excess of long-term capital gain over short-term capital loss.

Investment income attributable to a life insurance company's reserves for contracts sold under qualified pension and profit-sharing plans of private industry is not taxable at the company level, nor is income from reserves attributable to retirement annuity contracts purchased by tax-exempt educational, charitable, and religious organizations. Retirement annuities of public school systems are similarly treated. Committee Report on Public Law 88–571.

Capital Gains. Life insurance companies also are subject to capital gains tax.

In applying the rules as to capital gains treatment, life insurance companies have a special provision for the application of Section 1231—that is, property used in the trade or business and involuntary conversions. (See Chapter 2.) "Property used in the trade or business" means only property used in carrying on an insurance business. I.R.C. Section 817(a)(1).

For taxable years beginning after December 31, 1961, if the net long-term capital gain of any life insurance company exceeds its net short-term capital loss, there is an alternative tax, provided it is less than the regular tax. The alternative tax is the sum of (1) a partial tax on the life insurance company taxable income determined by reducing the taxable investment income, and the gain from operations, by the amount of the excess of its net long-term capital gain over its net short-term capital loss, and (2) an amount equal to 25% of that excess. I.R.C. Section 802(a)(2).

Mutual Insurance Companies

Special rules apply to the taxation of mutual insurance companies. See I.R.C. Section 821.

Foreign Life Insurance Companies Carrying On A Life Insurance Business In The United States

With respect to their life insurance business, foreign life insurance companies are taxed in substantially the same manner as domestic life insurance companies. But a special rule is provided where the surplus of a foreign life insurance company held in the United States is less than a specified minimum figure. This figure is expressed as the same percent of the foreign life insurance company's liabilities on United States business as the average surplus of domestic corporations is of their total liabilities. The Secretary of the Treasury determines this ratio each year. If the foreign insurance company's surplus held in the United States is less than this proportion of the taxpayer's total insurance liabilities on United States business, then the policy and other contract liability requirements for computing gain from operations are reduced by this deficiency multiplied by the rate of earnings on investments.

The remainder of the United States source income of this type of corporation is taxed in the same manner as income of other foreign corporations which is not effectively connected with a United States trade or business: that is, a flat 30% rate, unless a special treaty establishes a lower figure. I.R.C. Section 819.

Regulated Investment Companies

Regulated investment companies which meet various requirements with respect to asset diversification, capital structure, and operations and which distribute at least 90% of their ordinary income are treated as conduits of income and are taxed only on their undistributed income. Thus, the ordinary duplicating tax on corporation and on shareholders is substantially or entirely eliminated. Dividends paid by these companies are taxed in the usual manner to shareholders except that dividends arising from capital gains realized by the company are identified and receive capital gains treatment in the hands of the recipient. This method permits investors to pool their funds through the use of a corporation in order to obtain skilled, diversified investment in corporate securities without having to pay an additional layer of corporate tax.

A regulated investment company is any domestic corporation (other than a personal holding company as defined in Section 542) which is—

(1) Registered at all times during the taxable year, under the Investment Company Act of 1940, as amended, either as a management company or a unit investment trust, or

(2) A common trust fund or similar fund excluded by Section 3(c)(3) of that act from the definition of "investment company" and not included in the definition of "common trust fund" by Section 584(a), discussed earlier in this chapter.

But a corporation will not be considered a regulated investment company for any taxable year unless—

(1) It files with its return for the taxable year an election to be a regulated investment company or previously had made such an election;

(2) At least 90% of its gross income is derived from dividends, interest, and gains from the sale or other disposition of stock or securities;

(3) Less than 30% of its gross income is derived from the sale or other disposition of stock or securities held for less than three months; and

(4) At the close of each quarter of the taxable year,

    (a) at least 50% of the value of its total assets is represented by—

        (i) Cash and cash items, including receivables;

        (ii) Government securities;

        (iii) Securities of other regulated investment companies; or

        (iv) Securities (other than those described in (ii) and (iii) of any one or more issuers which meet these limitations: (A) The entire amount of the issuer's securities owned by the taxpayer corporation is not more than 5% of the value of the taxpayer's total assets and (B) The entire amount of the issuer's securities owned by the taxpayer does not represent more than 10% of the issuer's outstanding voting securities.

    (b) not more than 25% of the value of the taxpayer's total assets are invested in securities (other than Government securities or securities of other regulated investment companies) of one company or two or more companies under the taxpayer's control and engaged in similar trades or businesses.

Exceptions are made to the general investment diversification rules in the case of investment companies principally engaged in financing so-called development companies. Development companies are defined as companies principally engaged in the development or exploitation of inventions, technological improvements, new processes, or products not previously generally available. A company which is certified by the Securities and Exchange Commission as investing in a development company may, contrary to the general rule for regulated investment companies, hold more than 10% of the voting securities of a development company; but the waiver of the 10% voting restriction is, in general, limited to a period of ten years with respect to any one development company. The limitation that not more than 5% of the value of the company's assets may be invested in any one company is here construed to mean 5% of the value of the investment company's assets at the time the investment was made; it may subsequently increase its investments in the development company, even though the value of the initial investment rises, so long as the total cost to the investment company of these investments does not exceed 5% of the value of its total assets at the time of the second investment. I.R.C. Section 851.

Taxation Of Regulated Investment Companies. Regular corporate taxes are imposed upon investment company taxable income, which is taxable with these adjustments:

(1) The excess, if any, of the net long-term capital gain over the net short-term capital loss is excluded.

(2) The net operating loss deduction is not allowed.

(3) These special deductions are not allowed: for partially tax-exempt interest, for dividends received, for certain dividends paid.

(4) The deduction for dividends paid is allowed but is computed without regard to capital gains dividends.

(5) Taxable income for a period of less than twelve months is not annualized, even though the short taxable year results from a change of accounting period.

As to capital gains, there is a tax of 25% on the excess, if any, of the net long-term capital gain of a regulated investment company over the sum of its net short-term capital loss and its deduction for dividends paid determined with reference to capital gain dividends only.

A regulated investment company, which is taxable as such, may designate an amount of undistributed capital gains to each shareholder of the company. The earnings and profits of the company will be reduced each taxable year by the amount of undistributed capital gains so designated and its capital account will be increased by 75% of that amount.

Taxation Of Shareholders Of Regulated Investment Companies. Shareholders receiving dividends from regulated investment companies treat such receipts in the customary dividend manner. Capital gain dividends, however, are treated as gains from the sale of long-term capital assets in the taxable year of the shareholder in which the dividend was received. Undistributed capital gains of the regulated investment company also must be reported by a shareholder as long-term capital gain. The term "undistributed capital gains" means the amount designated as undistributed capital gains but may not exceed the shareholder's proportionate part of the amount subject to tax as capital gains. This amount must be included in gross income for the shareholder's taxable year in which falls the last day of the regulated investment company's taxable year in respect of which the undistributed capital gains were designated. Any shareholder who must include undistributed capital gains in his income will be deemed to have paid a tax equal to 25% of such amount for his taxable year for which this amount is so included. He is then entitled to a credit or refund of the tax so deemed paid. He increases the adjusted basis of the shares with respect to which the amount is so includible by 75% of that amount.

For purposes of determining whether the purchaser or seller of a share of regulated investment company stock is the shareholder at the close of the company's taxable year who must include an amount of undistributed capital gains in gross income, the amount of the undistributed capital gains will be treated in the same manner as a cash dividend payable to shareholders of record at the close of the company's taxable year. "Thus, if a cash dividend paid to shareholders of record as of the close of the regulated investment company's taxable year would be considered income to the purchaser, then the purchaser is also considered to be the shareholder of such company at the close of its taxable year for purposes of including an amount of undistributed capital gains in gross income. If, in such a case, notice on Form 2439 is . . . mailed by the regulated investment company to the seller, then the seller shall be considered the nominee of the purchaser and, as such, shall be subject to [these provisions]." Regulations Section 1.852–4(b)(2)(iv).

If the shareholder required to include an amount of undistributed capital gains in gross income is a partnership, each partner will include in his own income his distributive share of partnership capital gains and losses reflecting such gain, and the tax with respect to the undistributed capital gains is similarly treated.

A capital gain dividend is any dividend which is designated by a regulated investment company as a capital gain dividend in a written notice mailed to its shareholders not later than 45 days after the close of its taxable year. If the aggregate amount so designated with respect to the taxable year (including capital gain dividends paid after the close of the taxable year pursuant to an election under Section 855) is greater than the excess of the net long-term capital gain over the net short-term capital loss of the taxable year, the portion of each distribution which will be a capital gain dividend will be only that proportion of the amount so designated which this excess bears to the aggregate amount so designated.

If any person holds stock of a regulated investment company for less than 31 days and is required to include in his income as long-term capital gain any capital gain dividend or any undistributed capital gains, he will, to the extent of this amount, treat any loss on the sale or exchange of this stock as long-term capital loss. I.R.C. Section 852(b)(4).

Investment Trust of Tax-Exempt Securities. If a corporation owns tax-exempt bonds, the interest income, when distributed by the corporation, will be fully taxed to the shareholders, even if this distribution is entirely of tax-exempt interest; for all corporate distributions of earnings are treated as ordinary income to the shareholders. *James v. Commissioner,* 49 F.2d 707 (2d Cir., 1931). But unlike the conduit rule that exists in the case of distributions by corporations, income distributed by a trust retains the same character in the hands of the beneficiary that it had in the hands of the trust. I.R.C. Secion 652(b). For example, tax-exempt bonds were placed in a trust, and certificates were issued by the creator of the trust and approved by the trustee, certifying that the beneficiaries were to participate in the income from the bonds. The beneficiaries did not have to include these amounts in gross income. I.T. 2067, III–2 CB 78.

Where the purchaser of certificates issued by a trustee did not have an interest in the securities assigned to the trustee, nor could the certificate holder demand payment from the trustee before maturity, the income was taxable to him. *Bess Schoellkopf et al.,* 32 B.T.A. 88 (1935). But where the certificates provided that the purchaser acquired his ratable portion of all rights and interests in the bonds which the creator of the trust had owned, the income was tax-exempt. *Carson Estate Company,* 31 B.T.A. 607 (1934), *aff'd,* 80 F.2d 1007 (9th Cir., 1936).

"An 'investment' trust of the type commonly known as a management trust is an association, and a trust of the type commonly known as a fixed investment trust is an association if there is power under the trust agreement to vary the investment of the certificate holders. . . . However, if there is no power under the trust agreement to vary the investment of the certificate holders, such fixed investment trust shall be classified as a trust." Regulations Section 301.7701–4(c).

It is a cardinal principle of Federal income taxation that "[t]he grantor shall be treated as the owner of any portion of any trust, whether or not he is treated as such owner under any other provision of this part, where at any time the power to revest in the grantor title to such portion is exercisable by the grantor or a non-adverse party, or both." I.R.C. Section 676(a). But such is not the case where a certificate holder is given the right under his indenture to tender his certificate to the trustee for liquidation.

Records To Be Kept. Every regulated investment company must retain permanent records showing the information relative to the actual owners of its stock contained in the written statements for these shareholders. Various other informational requirements are imposed upon the company. Regulations Section 1.852–6.

A regulated investment company must submit to each shareholder a statement on Form 2439, stating the amount designated by the company for inclusion by the shareholder in computing his long-term capital gains and the tax paid with respect thereto by the company, which tax is deemed to have been paid by the shareholder. This form must be mailed to the shareholder not later than 45 days following the close of the company's taxable year. Copy A of this form must accompany the undistributed capital gains tax return of the company (Form 2438). The shareholder must attach Copy B of Form 2439 to his own income tax return.

The tax paid by the regulated investment company with respect to the undistributed capital gains required to be included by a shareholder in his computation of long-term capital gains for any taxable year is deemed paid by the shareholder and this payment constitutes an advance payment of income tax. Claim for refund or credit of the tax deemed to have been paid by a shareholder is to be made on the shareholder's tax return for the taxable year in which the undistributed capital gains is includible in gross income. A refund claim may be filed on Form 843.

Unit Investment Trust. In the case of a unit investment trust—

(1) which is registered under the Investment Company Act of 1940 and issues periodic payment plan certificates (as defined in that act), and

(2) substantially all of the assets of which consist of securities issued by a management company (as defined in that act),

the rule of Section 562(c) as to preferential dividends will not apply to a distribution by this trust to a holder of an interest in the trust in redemption of part or all of the interest, with respect to the net capital gain of the trust attributable to the redemption. I.R.C. Section 852(d). Section 562(c) provides that the amount of any distribution will not be considered as a dividend unless this distribution is *pro rata,* with no preference to any share of stock as compared to other shares of the same class, and with no preference to one class of stock as compared to another class except to the extent that the former is entitled to such preference.

Foreign Tax Credit Allowed To Shareholders. A regulated investment company which meets the requirements may make an election with respect to the income, war profits, and excess profits taxes (as described in Section 901(b)(1)) which it pays to foreign countries or possessions of the United States during the taxable year, including such taxes as are deemed paid by it under a foreign tax treaty with the United States. If an election is made, the shareholders of the regulated investment company will apply their proportionate shares of such foreign taxes paid (or deemed to have been paid) as either a credit (Section 901) or as a deduction (Section 164(a)). The election is not applicable with respect to taxes deemed to have been paid under Section 902 (relating to the credit allowable to corporate stockholders for taxes paid by the foreign corporation). I.R.C. Section 853.

To qualify for this election, a regulated investment company—

(1) must have more than 50% of the value of its total assets, at the close of the taxable year for which the election is made, invested in stocks and securities of foreign corporations, and

(2) must also, for that year, comply with the detailed requirements set forth.

A regulated investment company making a valid election is, for that year, denied both the deduction for foreign taxes and the credit for foreign taxes which it has paid to any foreign country or possession of the United States. But the regulated investment company may add the amount of foreign taxes paid to its dividends paid deduction for that taxable year.

A shareholder of an investment company which has made this election is, in effect, placed in the same position as a person directly owning stock in foreign corporations, in that he must include in his gross income (in addition to taxable dividends actually received) his proportionate share of such foreign taxes paid and must treat this amount as foreign taxes paid by him for the purpose of the foreign tax deduction and credit. For such purposes he must treat as gross income from a foreign country or possession of the United States (1) his proportionate share of the taxes paid by the regulated investment company to the foreign country or possession and (2) the portion of any dividend paid by the investment company which represents income derived from such sources. Regulations Section 1.853–2.

If a regulated investment company makes this election, the company must furnish its shareholders with a written notice mailed not later than 45 days after the close of its taxable year. The notice must designate the shareholder's portion of foreign taxes paid to each country or possession and the portion of the dividend which represents income derived from sources within each one. The shareholder may not report a larger amount than the company's notice stated; if the statement shows an excessive amount, he is limited to the correct figure.

To make the election, the company must file information returns on Forms 1099 and 1096, showing income derived and taxes paid with respect to each foreign country and possession; the date and contents of the forms sent to shareholders; the proportionate share of the taxes attributable to each share of stock. The company must file as part of its return Form 1118 (statement to support claim for credit by a domestic corporation for taxes paid or accrued to a foreign country or United States possession). The election is irrevocable.

Limitations As To Dividends Received. Limitations are provided as to dividends received from a regulated investment company for purposes of the dividends received credit and deduction.

A capital gain dividend is not considered to be a dividend for the above purposes. Other dividends are limited as to the amount that may be treated as a dividend for those purposes, where the investment company receives substantial amounts of income (such as interest, etc.) from sources other than dividends from domestic corporations which qualify. I.R.C. Section 854.

Where the "aggregate dividends received" (to be defined) during the taxable year by a regulated investment company eligible to be taxed as such are less than 75% of its gross income for that year, only that portion of the dividend paid by the regulated investment company which bears the same ratio to the amount of such dividends paid as the aggregate dividends received by the company, during the taxable year, bears to its gross income for that year (computed without regard to gains from the sale or other disposition of stock or securities) may be treated as a dividend for the purposes of the dividends received credit or deduction. Regulations Section 1.854–1.

The term "gross income" includes gains from the sale or other disposition of stock or securities undiminished by losses from such sales or other dispositions. The term does not include interest upon state, county, or municipal obligations. Revenue Ruling 63–118, 1963–1 CB 121.

For the purpose of computing the dividends limitation, the term "gross income" does not include gain from the sale or other disposition of stock or securities. Capital gains arising from the disposition of *other* capital assets are not excluded from gross income for this purpose.

The term "aggregate dividends received" includes only dividends received from domestic corporations (other than dividends not eligible for exclusion from gross income).

Dividends Paid After Close Of Taxable Year. In determining whether the deduction for dividends paid during the taxable year (without regard to capital gain dividends) by a regulated investment company equals or exceeds 90% of its investment company taxable income, and in computing its investment company taxable income, and in determining the amount of capital gain dividends paid during the taxable year, any dividend declared by the company before or after the close of the taxable year (but before the filing date of the tax year, including extensions) will, to the extent that the company so elects in its return, be treated as having been paid during that year. This rule is applicable only if the entire amount of the dividend actually is distributed to the shareholders in the 12-month period following the close of the taxable year and not later than the date of the first regular dividend payment made after the declaration. I.R.C. Section 855.

The election is made in the return filed by the company for the taxable year. The election is made by the company's treating the dividend to which the election applies as a dividend paid during the taxable year in computing its taxable income, or if the dividend to which the election applies is to be designated as a capital gain dividend, in computing the amount of capital gain dividends paid during that taxable year. The election may be made only to the extent that the earnings and profits of the taxable year (without reduction for any amount which is not allowable as a deduction in computing its taxable income for that year) exceed the total amount of distributions out of these earnings and profits actually made during the taxable year. The dividend, with respect to which the company has made an election, will be considered as paid out of the earnings and profits of the taxable year for which the election is made. The election is irrevocable.

The dividend with respect to which the election is made will be includible in the gross income of the shareholders for the taxable year in which the dividend is received by them.

Any dividends with respect to which the election was made must be reported not later than 45 days after the close of the taxable year in which the distribution is made.

Distribution Of Securities. No gain is recognized to a regulated investment company upon the distribution of a dividend consisting of certain of its portfolio securities, which had appreciated in value, where the dividend is declared and paid in such securities. Each shareholder must include in his gross income as a dividend the amount of property distributed by the company. The treatment by the shareholders of such dividends as capital gain distributions is limited to the excess of net long-term capital gain over net short-term capital loss of the investment company during the taxable year. Revenue Ruling 47–421, 1957–2 CB 367.

Allocation Of Capital Gain Distributions. With respect to allocation of capital gain distributions of regulated investment companies, the general rule is that such distributions are allocable to capital. Section 6(c) of the Revised Uniform Principal and Income Act (1962) has adopted this rule, and some of the states have enacted legislation to this effect.

If the trustee of a trust has the authority to invest in regulated investment companies and to treat capital gain distributions as income (whether by the express provisions of the governing instrument or by virtue of local law), he has the power to divert corpus from the remainder beneficiaries for the benefit of the income beneficiaries. If there are non-charitable income beneficiaries, a charitable remainder interest in corpus which is subject to such a power of investment (and diversion) cannot be severed from the non-charitable income interest in the absence of an acceptable formula for ascertaining the value of the remainder interest. But no generally acceptable formula for this purpose is known. Thus, a charitable deduction is not allowable under Section 170 (income tax), Section 2055 (estate tax), or Section 2522 (gift tax) with respect to a charity's remainder interest in the corpus of a trust where the trustee may invest in stock of regulated investment companies and treat capital gain distributions as income. Deduction will be allowed where the governing trust instrument clearly provides for the allocation of capital gain distributions to principal. Revenue Ruling 67–33, I.R.B. 1967–5, 9.

Change Of Status. A corporation which qualified as a regulated investment company but which, in a particular year, failed to meet all the requirements because less than 90% of its investment company taxable income was distributed as dividends, will be taxed as an ordinary corporation in that year. But it will again be taxed as a regulated investment company in any subsequent year in which all of the tests (including the 90% distribution rule) are met. Revenue Ruling 58–466, 1958–2 CB 379.

A corporation which otherwise meets the requirements of the Code at the close of any quarter will not lose its status as a regulated investment company because of a discrepancy during a subsequent quarter between the value of its various investments and these requirements unless the discrepancy exists immediately after the acquisition of any security and is wholly or partly the result of such acquisition. Further, where the acquisition of any security results in a discrepancy between the value of the corporation's total assets and these requirements at the close of any quarter, the corporation will not lose its status as a regulated investment company if the discrepancy is eliminated within thirty days after the close of the quarter. I.R.C. Section 851(d).

The term "acquisition" for this purpose includes the receipt of securities as a result of either a reorganization or an anti-trust order. Revenue Ruling 63–170, 1963–2 CB 286.

Capital Loss Carryover. A regulated investment company is entitled to capital loss carryovers. Revenue Ruling 60–217, 1960–1 CB 301.

Real Estate Investment Trusts

Real estate investment trusts which meet the requirements to be mentioned are treated as mere conduits and are taxed only on their undistributed income. The term "real estate investment trust" means an unincorporated trust or unincorporated association which (1) meets the qualifying conditions to be mentioned in the following paragraph and (2) satisfies certain gross income and asset diversification requirements that will be outlined below. I.R.C. Section 856(a).

To qualify as a real estate investment trust, an unincorporated organization must be one—

(1) which is managed by one or more trustees,

(2) the beneficial ownership of which is evidenced by transferable shares or by transferable certificates of beneficial interest.

(3) which would be taxable as a domestic corporation except for the provisions of Section 856 (dealing with real estate investment trusts),

(4) which does not hold any property primarily for sale to customers in the ordinary course of its trade or business,

(5) the beneficial ownership of which is held by 100 or more persons, and

(6) which would not be a personal holding company (as defined in Section 542) if all of its adjusted gross income constituted personal holding company income.

The conditions described in (1) through (4), above, must be met during the entire taxable year and the condition described in (5) must exist during at least 335 days of a taxable year of twelve months (or a proportionate part of a shorter taxable year).

For this purpose, "trustee" means a person who holds legal title to the property of the real estate investment trust and has such rights and powers as will meet the requirement of centralization of management. "An organization has centralized management if any person (or any group of persons which does not include all the members) has continuing exclusive authority to make the management decisions necessary to the conduct of the business for which the organization was formed." Regulations Section 301.7701–2(c). The existence of a mere fiduciary relationship does not, in itself, make one a trustee for this purpose.

The requisite 100 or more persons is determined without reference to constructive ownership or rules of attribution.

Limitations. A trust, even though it satisfies all the other requirements, will not be considered to be a real estate investment trust for tax purposes unless it elects to be one, or has made such an election for a previous taxable year which began after December 31, 1960. The election is made by the trust by computing taxable income as a real estate investment trust in its Federal return for the first taxable year for which it desires the election to apply, even though it may have qualified in earlier years. No other election method is permitted. The election is irrevocable.

A trust will not be considered a real estate investment trust for a taxable year unless for that year:

(1) At least 90% of its gross income is derived from:
    (a) Dividends;
    (b) Interest;
    (c) Rents from real property;
    (d) Gain from the sale or other disposition of stock, securities, real property, and interests in mortgages on real property; and
    (e) Abatements and refunds of taxes on real property;

(2) At least 75% of its gross income is derived from:
   (a) Rents from real property;
   (b) Interest on obligations secured by mortgages on real property;
   (c) Gain from the sale or other disposition of real property and interests in mortgages on real property;
   (d) Dividends or other distributions on, and gain from the sale or other distribution of, transferable shares in another qualified real estate investment trust which is so qualified for its taxable year to which the dividends or other distributions relate or during which the gain was realized; and
   (e) Abatements and refunds on taxes on real property; and
(3) Less than 30% of its gross income is derived from the sale or other disposition of:
   (a) Stock or securities held for less than six months; and
   (b) Real property, not compulsorily or involuntarily converted (within the meaning of an involuntary conversion as defined in Section 1033), held for less than four years.

All three of these gross income requirements must be met for the taxable year. Thus, at least 75% of gross income must be derived from the sources described in (2), above, and another 15% must be from sources described in (1) or (2), or from a combination of these sources. A maximum of 10% of gross income is not restricted as to source. Regulations Section 1.856–2(c)(1).

The 90% requirement in (1) permits the inclusion of dividends generally, while the 75% requirement in (2) includes dividends only to the extent that they represent dividends or other distributions on transferable shares in other qualified real estate investment trusts.

Diversification Of Investment Requirements. At the close of each quarter of the taxable year, at least 75% of the total assets of the trust must be represented by one or more of the following:

(1) Real estate assets;
(2) Government securities; and
(3) Cash and cash items (including receivables. But the receivables are only those which arise in the ordinary course of the trust's operation and do not include receivables purchased from another person).

The character of the remaining 25% (or less) of the value of the total assets is not restricted.

The ownership of securities under the above 25% limitation is further limited in respect of any one issuer to an amount not greater in value than 5% of the value of the trust's total assets and to not more than 10% of the outstanding voting securities of that issuer.

In order to determine the application of the percentage rules to total assets of the trust, a re-valuation of the assets of the trust is to be made at the end of any quarter in which there has been an acquisition of any property.

The term "value," as used in these mathematical limitations, means, with respect to securities for which market quotations readily are available, the market value; and with respect to other securities and assets, the fair value as determined in good faith by the trustees. "In the case of securities of other qualified real estate investment trusts, fair value shall not exceed market value or asset value, whichever is higher." Regulations Section 1.856–3(a).

The term "rents from real property" means, generally, the gross amounts received for the use of, or the right to use, real property of the trust. But certain amounts received for the use of the trust's real property are not considered as rent for this purpose:

(1) Where the amount of rent depends on the income or profits of any person.

(2) Where rent is received from a person (such as a corporation) in which the trust owns 10% or more of the total combined voting power of all classes of stock entitled to vote or 10% or more of the total number of shares of all classes of outstanding stock. If the person is not a corporation, rent is not included where the trust owns a 10% or greater interest in its assets or net profits.

(3) Where the trust furnishes services or manages property through an independent contractor.

For the purposes of (2) and (3), the stock attribution rules of Section 318(a) apply, except that in Section 318(a)(2)(C) (attribution through ownership of stock in a corporation), the figure to be used is 10% rather than 50%.

The term "rents from real property" as used in Section 856 does not apply to revenue derived from a property interest which is specifically excluded from qualification as a "real estate asset." Revenue Ruling 64–75, 1964–1 (Part 1) CB 228.

"Government securities" for this purpose include the securities of the (1) Federal Housing Administration, (2) Federal National Mortgage Association, (3) Federal Home Loan Bank, (4) Federal Land Bank, (5) Federal Intermediate Credit Banks, (6) Banks for Cooperatives, and (7) Public Housing Administration. Revenue Ruling 64–85, 1964–1 (Part 1) CB 230.

Qualified pension and profit-sharing trusts are persons for the purposes of the 100-person requirement of Section 856(a)(5). Revenue Ruling 65–3, 1965–1 CB 267.

Taxation Of Real Estate Investment Trusts And Their Beneficiaries.

The trust is not taxed on ordinary, taxable income which it distributes to its beneficiaries if 90% or more is distributed; if all is distributed, none is taxed to the trust. A real estate investment trust will not be taxed as such unless—

(1) The deduction for dividends paid for that year amounts to at least 90% of its real estate investment trust taxable income for that year, computed without regard to capital gain dividends, and

(2) The trust keeps the records which must be maintained by a real estate investment trust.

If the trust does not meet these requirements, it will, even though it may otherwise be classified as a real estate investment trust, be taxed in that year as an ordinary corporation. Then none of the other tax provisions relating to real estate investment trusts will apply. I.R.C. Section 857(a). "[I]f more than 10 percent of a real estate investment trust's ordinary taxable income were not distributed to shareholders during the taxable year, the trust would be taxed as a corporation and not as a real estate investment trust." Revenue Ruling 64–292, 1964–2 CB 182.

Method Of Taxation Of Real Estate Investment Trusts. Regular normal and surtax is imposed at standard income tax rates on the "real estate investment trust taxable income" for each taxable year. In computing the normal tax, the real estate investment trust taxable income and the dividends paid deduction (computed without regard to capital gain dividends) are both reduced by the deduction for partially tax-exempt interest provided by Section 242, as is the case with any corporation.

There also is imposed a tax of 25% for each taxable year on the excess (if any) of the net long-term capital gain of a qualified real estate investment trust over the sum of its net short-term capital loss and its deduction for dividends paid, determined with reference to capital gain dividends only.

To convert taxable income of the trust to "real estate investment trust taxable income," the following adjustments must be made:

(1) The excess, if any, of the net long-term capital gain over the net short-term capital loss is excluded.

(2) The special deductions allowed to corporations (except the deduction for organizational expenditures) is not allowed. Not allowed are the deduction for partially tax-exempt interest, the deduction for dividends received, and the deduction for certain dividends paid.

(3) The deduction for dividends paid is allowed, but without regard to capital gain dividends.

(4) The taxable income is not annualized, even if a short taxable year results from a change of accounting period.

(5) The net operating loss deduction is not allowed. I.R.C. Section 857(b)(2).

Method Of Taxation Of Shareholders. In the case of ordinary income, a shareholder receiving dividends from a real estate investment trust will include these dividends in gross income for the taxable year in which they are received. In the case of capital gain dividends, shareholders of the trust will treat these as gains from the sale or exchange of long-term capital assets that were realized in the taxable year of the shareholder in which the dividend was received.

If any person held a share of a real estate investment trust for less than 31 days but is required to include in gross income as long-term capital gain the amount of a capital gain dividend, he may, to the extent of this amount, treat any loss on the sale or exchange of this share as a loss from the sale or exchange of a long-term capital asset. I.R.C. Section 857(b).

Any dividend received from a real estate investment trust which is qualified as such for the taxable year to which the dividend relates is not eligible for the dividends received credit or deduction.

A capital gain dividend is any dividend which is designated by a real estate investment trust as such in a written notice mailed to its shareholders not later than thirty days after the close of its taxable year. If the aggregate amount so designated with respect to the taxable year (including capital gain dividends paid after the close of the taxable year pursuant to a valid election) is greater than the excess of the net long-term capital gain over the net short-term capital loss of the taxable year, the portion of each distribution which will be a capital gain dividend will be only that proportion of the amount so designated which this excess bears to the aggregate of the amount so designated. "For example, a real estate investment trust making its return on the calendar year basis advised its shareholders by written notice mailed December 30, 1961, that of a distribution of $500,-000 made December 15, 1961, $200,000 constituted a capital gain dividend, amounting to $2 per share. It was later discovered that an error had been made in determining the excess of the net long-term capital gain over the net short-term capital loss of the taxable year and that such excess was $100,000 instead of $200,000. In such case, each shareholder would have received a capital gain dividend of $1 per share instead of $2 per share." Regulations Section 1.857–4(e).

Earnings And Profits Of Real Estate Investment Trust. In the determination of the earnings and profits of a real estate investment trust (whether it qualifies for taxation as such or not), such earnings and profits for any taxable year (but not the accumulated earnings and profits) will not be reduced by any amount which is not allowable as a deduction in computing its taxable income for the taxable year.

Records To Be Kept. A real estate investment trust is required to keep such records as will disclose the actual ownership of its stock, and the person who must include in gross income the dividends received on his stock. The trust must demand written statements from shareholders of record disclosing the actual owners of stock. To ascertain whether the trust is a personal holding company, the trust records must show the maximum number of shares considered to be owned (actually or constructively) by each of the actual owners of stock at any time during the last half of the taxable year.

The written statements required of shareholders must be demanded—

(1) in the case of a trust having 2,000 or more shareholders of record on any dividend record date, from each record holder of 5% or more of its stock; or

(2) in the case of a trust having fewer than 2,000 and more than 200 shareholders on any dividend record date, from each record holder of 1% or more of its stock; or

(3) In the case of a trust having 200 or fewer shareholders on any dividend record date, from each record holder of one-half of 1% or more of its stock.

The demands for statements are to be made by the trust within 30 days after the close of the trust's taxable year. A list of persons who refuse to comply must be maintained by the trust.

Information Required Of Shareholders. Any person who refuses to supply the trust with a written statement must supply this information on his own tax return which ends with, or includes, the last day of the trust's taxable year. If the shareholder of record is not the actual owner of the stock, he must indicate who is.

Dividends Paid By Trust After Close Of Taxable Year. In—

(1) determining whether the deduction for dividends paid during the taxable year (without regard to capital gain dividends) by a trust equals or exceeds 90% of its real estate trust taxable income (computed without regard to capital gain dividends),

(2) computing its real estate trust taxable income, and

(3) determining the amount of capital gain dividends paid during the taxable year,

any dividend declared by the trust either before or after the close of the taxable year but in any event before the filing date (including extensions) of the return will, to the extent the trust so elects in its return, be treated as having been paid during this taxable year. This rule is applicable only if the entire amount of the dividend actually is distributed to the shareholders in the 12-month period following the close of this taxable year and not later than the date of the first regular dividend payment made after this declaration. I.R.C. Section 858.

The election must be made in the return filed by the trust for the taxable year. The election is made by the trust by treating the dividend to which this election applies as a dividend paid during the trust's taxable year in computing its real estate investment trust taxable income, or if the dividend to which the election applies is to be designated by the trust as a capital gain dividend, in computing the amount of capital gain dividend paid during the taxable year. The election may be made only to the extent that the earnings and profits of the taxable year exceed the total amount of distributions out of earnings and profits actually made during the taxable year (not including distributions with respect to which an election has been made for a prior year). The dividend with respect to which the trust has made a valid election will be considered as paid out of the earnings and profits of the taxable year for which the election is made, and not out of the earnings and profits of the taxable year in which the distribution actually is made.

After the expiration of the time for filing the return for the taxable year for which an election is made, the election is irrevocable.

The dividend, with respect to which a valid election has been made, will be includible in the gross income of the shareholders of the trust for the taxable year in which the dividend is received by them.

Notice To Shareholders. In the case of dividends with respect to which a real estate investment trust has made an election, any notice to shareholders with respect to the amounts must be made not later than thirty days after the close of the taxable year in which the distribution is made. If the notice relates to an election with respect to any capital gain dividend, such dividends will be aggregated by the trust with the designated capital gain dividends actually paid during the taxable year to which the election applies (not including dividends with respect to which an election has been made for a prior year) for the purpose of determining whether the aggregate of the designated capital gain dividends with respect to the trust's taxable year is greater than the excess of the net long-term capital gain over the trust's net short-term capital loss.

Farmers' Co-operatives

Co-operative associations engaged in the marketing of farm products for farmers, fruit growers, livestock growers, dairymen, etc., and turning back to the producers the proceeds of the sales of their products, less the necessary operating expenses, on the basis of either the quantity or the value of the products furnished by them, are exempt from Federal income tax. I.R.C. Section 521(a). Thus, co-operative dairy companies which are engaged in collecting milk and disposing of it or its product and distributing the proceeds, less necessary operating expenses, among the producers upon the basis of either the quantity or the value of milk or of butterfat in the milk furnished by the producers, are exempt from tax. The association is not exempt if the proceeds of the business are distributed in any way other than on a proportionate basis. That is, non-member patrons must be treated the same as members insofar as the distribution of patronage dividends is concerned.

Co-operative organizations engaged in occupations dissimilar to those of farmers, fruit growers, and the like are not exempt. Regulations Section 1.521–1(d).

Exemption from income tax is not denied to a farmers' co-operative association by reason of its having capital stock, if the dividend rate of the stock is fixed at not to exceed the legal rate of interest in the state of incorporation or 8% per annum, whichever is greater, on the value of the consideration for which the stock was issued and if substantially all of the stock (other than non-voting preferred stock, the owners of which are not entitled or permitted to participate in the profits of the association, upon dissolution or otherwise, beyond the fixed dividends) is owned by producers who market their products or purchase their supplies and equipment through the association. I.R.C. Section 521(b).

Registered Holding Companies

As was noted in Chapter 5, no gain is recognized to a transferor corporation which is a registered holding company, if this corporation, in obedience to an order of the Securities and Exchange Commission, transfers property in exchange for property. Any gain, to the extent that it cannot be applied in reduction of basis under Section 1082(a)(2), must be recognized. I.R.C. Section 1081.

According to Section 1082(a)(2), any gain not recognized on a transfer by reason of Section 1081 will reduce the basis of certain property in the hands of the transferor immediately after the transfer, or acquired within twenty-four months, in the following order: depreciable property, amortizable property, depletable property, securities in stipulated categories.

Form 982A is to be used by a corporation excluding from gross income under Section 1081 any amounts of income attributable to the transfer of property.

If the taxpayer desires to have basis adjusted other than under the general rule, the desired method must be offered and explained on a rider attached to the tax return.

Tax-Sheltered Companies

This subject is treated in Chapter 13.

Anti-Trust Stock

An anti-trust distribution is a distribution made in pursuance of a court order enforcing the anti-trust laws. Where stock is received in an anti-trust distribution by an individual shareholder (or any shareholder who is not entitled to the corporate dividends received deduction), the distribution is treated as a return of capital, and its full fair market value reduces the basis of the stock with respect to which it is made. If, however, the fair market value of the stock distributed exceeds the basis of the stock with respect to which the distribution is made, then gain is recognized to the extent of the excess and is taxable as any other gain would be taxed. I.R.C. Section 1111. This is the same as the income tax treatment of distributions made by corporations which have no earnings and profits.

This section applies only if the order, pursuant to which the distribution is made, requires the divestiture of stock to be completed within three years or less from the date the order becomes final.

To date, the section has been limited to distributions in the Du Pont anti-trust case, where General Motors Corporation stock was distributed.

Losses On Small Business Investment Company Stock

Any taxpayer who sustains a loss as a result of the worthlessness, or from the sale or exchange, of the stock of a small business investment company (whether or not this stock was originally issued to him) will treat this loss as a loss from the sale or exchange of property which is not a capital asset (that is, it is an ordinary loss), if at the time of the loss—

(1) The company which issued the stock is licensed to operate as a small business investment company pursuant to regulations promulgated by the Small Business Administration (13 C.F.R. Part 107) and

(2) This loss would, but for the provisions of Section 1242, be a loss from the sale or exchange of a capital asset. I.R.C. Section 1242.

For purposes of the net operating loss deduction, any amount of loss treated by reason of this section as a loss from the sale or exchange of a non-capital asset will be treated as attributable to the trade or business of the taxpayer. Accordingly, the limitation on the allowance of non-business deductions in computing a net operating loss does not apply to any loss with respect to the stock of a small business investment company.

Loss Of Small Business Investment Company

A small business investment company which sustains a loss as a result of the worthlessness, or the sale or exchange, of the securities of a small business concern (as defined in Section 103(5) of the Small Business Investment Act of 1958 and in 13 C.F.R. 107.103–1) will treat this loss as a loss from the sale or exchange of property which is not a capital asset if—

(1) The securities are either the convertible debentures, or the stock issued pursuant to the conversion privilege thereof, acquired in accordance with the provisions of Section 304 of the Small Business Investment Act and the regulations thereunder,

(2) This loss would, but for the provisions of Section 1243, be a loss from the sale or exchange of a capital asset, and

(3) At the time of the loss, the company is licensed to operate as a small business investment company pursuant to regulations promulgated by the Small Business Administration. I.R.C. Section 1243.

Loss On Small Business Stock Treated As Ordinary Loss

Subject to certain conditions and limitations, Section 1244 provides that a loss on the sale or exchange (including a transaction treated as a sale or exchange, such as worthlessness) of "Section 1244 stock" which would otherwise be treated as a loss from the sale or exchange of a capital asset will be treated as ordinary loss. Such a loss is allowed as a deduction from gross income in arriving at adjusted gross income. These requirements relate to the stock itself and the corporation issuing the stock.

The allowance of an ordinary loss deduction for a loss on Section 1244 stock is permitted only to the following two classes of taxpayers:

(1) An individual sustaining the loss to whom such stock was issued by a small business corporation, or

(2) An individual who is a partner in a partnership at the time the partnership acquired this stock in an issuance from a small business corporation and whose distributive share of partnership items reflects the loss sustained by the partnership.

In order to claim a deduction under Section 1244, the individual, or the partnership sustaining the loss, must have continuously held the stock from the date of issuance. A corporation, trust, or estate is not entitled to ordinary loss treatment under Section 1244 regardless of how the stock was acquired. An individual who acquires stock from a shareholder by purchase, gift, devise, or in any other manner is not entitled to an ordinary loss under Section 1244 with respect to this stock. Stock acquired through an investment banking firm, or other person, participating in the sale of an issue may qualify for ordinary loss treatment only if the stock is not first issued to that firm or person. Thus, for example, if the firm acts as a selling agent for the issuing corporation, the stock may qualify. On the other hand, stock purchased by an investment firm and subsequently re-sold does not qualify as Section 1244 stock in the hands of the person acquiring this stock from the firm. Regulations Section 1.1244(a)–1.

The aggregate amount which may be treated as ordinary loss may not exceed $25,000 or, in the case of a husband and wife filing a joint return, $50,000. I.R.C. Section 1244(b).

Section 1244 stock must be common stock (either voting or non-voting) in a domestic corporation. This does not include securities of a corporation convertible into common stock nor common stock convertible into other securities of the corporation. Regulations Section 1.1244(c)–1(b).

A corporation is regarded as a "small business corporation" if at the time of the adoption of the plan—

(1) The sum of—
    (a) The aggregate amount which may be offered under the plan, plus
    (b) The aggregate amount of money and other property received by the corporation after June 30, 1958, for stock, as a contribution to capital, and as paid-in surplus,

does not exceed $500,000; and

(2) The sum of—
    (a) The aggregate amount which may be offered under the plan, plus
    (b) The equity capital of the corporation (determined on the date of the adoption of the plan),

does not exceed $1,000,000.

For purposes of (2), the equity capital of a corporation is the sum of its money and other property (in an amount equal to the adjusted basis of this property for determining gain), less the amount of its indebtedness (other than indebtedness to shareholders). I.R.C. Section 1244(c)(2).

The offering of stock under Section 1244 must be acted upon within a time set in the plan, not to exceed two years. In one case, the plan stated that the offer would terminate when the stock had been purchased "or on the . . . day of . . . , 196 . . . , whichever occurs earlier." Inasmuch as, through oversight, no time was set, the $25,000 ordinary loss was not allowed. *James A. Warner,* 48 T.C. 49 (1967).

Stock received in a corporate reorganization does not qualify as Section 1244 stock: that is, it may not be treated as Small Business Corporation stock because it was not issued to the taxpayer in exchange for a transfer by him of money or other property.

Western Hemisphere Trade Corporation

A corporation is entitled to a special deduction against its Federal income tax if the requirements of a Western Hemisphere Trade Corporation are met. The deduction is a fraction, the numerator of which is 14 and the denominator is the combined normal and surtax rate for that year.

The requirements are:

The corporation must be a domestic corporation all of the business of which (other than incidental purchases) is done in any country or countries in North, Central, or South America, or in the West Indies, and which satisfies the following conditions:

(1) If 95% or more of the gross income of the corporation for the 3-year period immediately preceding the close of the taxable year (or the period of its existence if it was less than three years) was derived from sources without the United States; and

(2) If 90% or more of its gross income for such period was derived from the active conduct of a trade or business. I.R.C. Section 921.

Income From Sources Within Possessions Of The United States

A domestic corporation is taxable only on its United States source income (plus amounts received in the United States)—

(1) If 80% or more of its gross income for the 3-year period immediately preceding the close of the taxable year (or the period of its existence if it was less than three years) was derived from sources within a possession of the United States; and

(2) If 50% or more of its gross income for such period was derived from the active conduct of a trade or business within a possession of the United States. I.R.C. Section 931.

This includes the Panama Canal Zone, Guam, American Samoa, Wake and Midway Islands, and Puerto Rico. Regulations Section 1.931–1(a).

Tax Option Corporations

The earnings of certain small business corporations may be taxed to the shareholders of the corporation rather than to the corporate entity in a manner somewhat similar to the way partnership earnings are taxed to the partners rather than to the partnership. Where the election is made under Section 1371, the shareholders include in their own income for Federal income tax purposes the current taxable income of the corporation, both the dividends which have been distributed and the portion of the earnings which still are retained by the corporation.

A "small business corporation" for this purpose (as opposed to the small business corporation of Section 1244, mentioned earlier in this chapter) means a domestic corporation which is not a member of an affiliated group (as defined in Section 1504) and which does not—

(1) have more than 10 shareholders;

(2) have as shareholders a person (other than an estate) who is not an individual;

(3) have a non-resident alien as a shareholder; and

(4) have more than one class of stock. I.R.C. Section 1371(a).

Conditions of election, termination of an election, and other technical requirements are spelled out in Sections 1371 through 1378 and the corresponding regulations.

The "pass-through" election of Section 1371 could be used as a device for the avoidance of corporate capital gains tax. A corporation could arrange to have a large amount of capital gains realized in one year, elect the "pass-through" treatment for that year, distribute these realized capital gains, and then cause the "pass-through" status to be terminated. This would avoid capital gains tax at the corporate level and substitute capital gains tax for an ordinary (dividend) income tax at the shareholder level. Normally, this could be done where a corporation sold its assets and completely liquidated within a 12-month period under the provisions of Section 337 (gain or loss on sales or exchanges in connection with certain liquidations). By using the "pass-through" treatment, the shareholders could obtain the same result without liquidating the business.

In 1966, Section 1378 was enacted to impose a tax upon capital gains of a corporation which has elected the "pass-through" treatment under certain limited conditions. This tax is imposed only when the electing corporation has an excess of net long-term capital gain over net short-term capital loss which exceeds its other income and also exceeds $25,000. In addition, where the corporation would have a loss for the year but for the excess of capital gain referred to in the preceding sentence, the tax will apply only if the taxable income (taking into account this capital gain) is more than $25,000.

Inasmuch as this provision was intended to apply only in those situations where the "pass-through" treatment was elected to avoid taxes on capital gains, the tax is not applied in the case of corporations which have been under a "pass-through" election for at least the three immediately prior years. Alternatively, the tax does not apply in the case of new corporations which have been in existence for less than the three prior years but have made the "pass-through" election for the entire period of their existence.

Where these elections exist, a tax is imposed upon the electing corporation equal to 25% of the excess of the net long-term capital gain over net short-term capital loss, but only to the extent that this exceeds $25,000. But the tax may not exceed the tax which would have been imposed if the corporation had not elected the "pass-through".

The tax thus imposed on an electing corporation reduces the undistributed taxable income of the corporation and therefore reduces the amount of income taxable to the shareholders by a like amount. As a result, the shareholders will not be required to pay a tax upon an amount which the corporation in fact paid out as its own tax. The income taxable to the shareholders, however, retains its character as capital gain.

The special 25% tax will apply in those cases where the property in question was acquired in a tax-free transaction (such as the various types of corporate reorganization) and the corporation from which the property was acquired had not used the "pass-through" election during any of the 3-year period up to the time of the acquisition. Where that corporation had itself acquired the property in a tax-free transaction, then this test applies to the corporation from which that company had acquired the property.

Where election has been made that corporate earnings will be taxed at the shareholder level, and the corporation sells a capital asset or a Section 1231 asset and distributes the proceeds within 2½ months after the close of the taxable year, the corporation may elect to treat the distribution as having been made on the last day of the year of sale. I.R.C. Section 1375(e).

Deficit Companies

A corporation with a net operating loss carryover is a useful corporation, for under certain circumstances the company may be acquired, with the deficit being used as an offset against future earnings. Or a profitable enterprise may be added to the deficit company's activities so that the losses will not be wasted. But the Internal Revenue Service has various weapons to combat this situation. See Chapter 7.

Chapter 15

Foreign Aspects

Non-Resident Alien Individuals

United States trade or business income of non-resident alien individuals is subject to the regular individual Federal income tax rates. Other income is subject to the regular rates only if it is effectively connected with a United States trade or business. United States-source fixed or determinable income of non-resident aliens which is not so connected is subjected to a flat 30% rate (or a lower rate if provided by a tax treaty). Fixed or determinable income includes interest, dividends, rents, salaries, annuities, and certain income accorded capital gain treatment, such as lump-sum distributions from exempt employees' trusts; amounts paid to beneficiaries under qualified annuity plans; timber, coal, and iron ore royalties; amounts received on transfers of patent rights; and amounts received on the retirement or exchange of bonds and other evidences of indebtedness issued after September 28, 1965, which are treated as gains from the sale of property which is not a capital asset.

In the case of a non-resident alien's net United States source capital gains (other than those specifically included in the preceding paragraph as taxable at the 30% rate) which are not effectively connected with the conduct of a trade or business within the United States, no United States tax is imposed unless the non-resident alien has been present in the United States for at least 183 days during the taxable year. If he has been present for a period or periods aggregating 183 days or more during the taxable year, a tax of 30% is imposed on the amount by which his gains, derived from the sale or exchange at any time during that year exceed his losses, allocable to sources within the United States, from the sale or exchange at any time during that year of capital assets. For this purpose, gains and losses are taken into account only if, and to the extent that, they would be recognized and taken into account if they were effectively connected with the conduct of a trade or business within the United States, except that the gains and losses are determined without regard to Section 1202 (relating to the deduction for capital gains) and the losses are determined without the benefit of the capital loss carryover provided in Section 1212. I.R.C. Section 871(a)(2).

Income of a non-resident alien individual that is effectively connected with the conduct of a trade or business in the United States is taxable at the regular graduated rates applicable to individuals.

Foreign Beneficiaries Of
Estates And Trusts

If a trust, whether a foreign or domestic one, is engaged in a trade or business in the United States, its beneficiaries are deemed also to be engaged in that trade or business. I.R.C. Section 875.

Foreign Income Of Foreign Corporations
Not Connected With United States
Business

A United States shareholder of a foreign corporation will be interested in its United States tax status. Foreign corporations not engaged in a trade or business in the United States are taxed at the regular Federal income tax rates in the case of income which is effectively connected with a United States trade or business. In the case of foreign corporations with United States source fixed or determinable income which is not effectively connected with a United States trade or business, a flat 30% rate is applied. I.R.C. Section 882.

Investment income which is not related to a trade or business carried on in the United States is taxed at the flat 30% rate (or lower treaty rate) rather than at the regular corporate rates.

All United States source investment income (fixed or determinable) of foreign corporations which is not effectively connected with a trade or business in the United States is taxed at 30%. But all investment income effectively connected with a United States trade or business is taxed in the same manner as other income of that trade or business, and in the same manner as similar income of a domestic corporation.

Trade Or Business In the United States

The trading in stocks, securities, or commodities in the United States, for one's own account, whether by a non-resident alien physically present in the United States, through an employee located in that country, or through a resident broker, commission agent, or other agent—whether or not that agent has discretionary authority—does not constitute a trade or business in the United States. This treatment, however, does not apply to dealers in stocks, securities, or commodities or to a foreign investment corporation if it has its principal office in the United States. I.R.C. Section 864(b)(2).

Even though that subsection does not free some dealers in stocks, securities, or commodities, and investment companies, from the possibility that they may be considered as engaged in a trade or business in the United States, this does not mean that all such dealers or investment companies are so engaged. In such a situation, the question of whether a dealer or investment company is conducting a trade or business in the United States remains a question of fact.

"Effectively Connected." Investment income realized by a non-resident alien individual engaged in business within the United States by reason of his performing personal services in the United States will not be treated as income effectively connected with the conduct of a trade or business within the United States, unless there is a direct economic relationship between his holding of the assets from which such income results and his business of performing the personal services. Where there is such a relationship, as, for example, where an individual purchases stock in a domestic corporation to assure the opportunity of performing personal services in the United States for that corporation, income derived from these assets may be effectively connected with his conduct of such business within the United States. I.R.C. Section 864(c).

Controlled Foreign Corporations

Sections 951 through 964 of the Internal Revenue Code provide that certain types of income of controlled foreign corporations are subject to United States income tax even though such amounts are not currently distributed to the United States shareholders of these corporations. The amounts so taxed to certain United States shareholders are what will be described below as Subpart F income, previously excluded Subpart F income withdrawn from investments in less developed countries, and increases in earnings invested in United States property.

Controlled Foreign Corporation Defined. The term "controlled foreign corporation" means any foreign corporation of which more than 50% (or more than 25% in case Section 957(b), dealing with income from insurance of United States risks, applies) of the total combined voting power of all classes of stock entitled to vote is owned (actually or constructively) by United States shareholders on any date of the foreign corporation's taxable year. I.R.C. Section 957(a). A United States shareholder is a United States person (individual, partnership, corporation, trust, or estate) who owns, actually or constructively, 10% or more of the total combined voting power of all classes of stock entitled to vote of this foreign corporation. I.R.C. Section 951(b). A foreign corporation is one which was organized other than in the United States or of any state or territory. I.R.C. Section 7701(4), (5).

Less Developed Country. The term "less developed country" means any foreign country (other than an area within the Sino-Soviet bloc) or any possession of the United States with respect to which, in the first day of the taxable year, there is in effect an executive order by the President of the United States designating that country or possession as an economically less developed country for purposes of Subpart F. I.R.C. Section 955(c).

Subpart F Income. "Subpart F income" is the sum of—

(1) The income derived from the insurance of United States risks and

(2) The foreign base period income. I.R.C. Section 952(a). "Foreign base period income" is the foreign personal holding company income, foreign base company sales income, and foreign base company services income for the taxable year, with reductions that take into account deductions (including taxes) properly allocable to such income. I.R.C. Section 954(a), (b)(5).

In determining Subpart F income, there are excluded those items of income effectively connected with the conduct by the foreign corporation of a trade or business within the United States.

Taxability. If a foreign corporation is a controlled foreign corporation for an uninterrupted period of thirty days or more during any taxable year beginning after December 31, 1962, every person—

(1) Who is a United States shareholder at any time during the taxable year and

(2) Who owns stock in the corporation on the last day, in that year, on which the corporation is a controlled foreign corporation,

must include in his gross income for his taxable year in which or with which the corporation's taxable year ends, the sum of—

(a) Except as provided in Section 963 (dealing with minimum distributions to domestic corporations), the shareholder's *pro rata* share of the corporation's Subpart F income for that taxable year of the corporation,

(b) The shareholder's *pro rata* share of the corporation's previously excluded Subpart F income withdrawn from investment in less developed countries for that taxable year of the corporation, and

(c) The shareholder's *pro rata* share of the corporation's increase in earnings invested in United States property for that taxable year of the corporation (but only to the extent this share is not excluded from the shareholder's gross income for his taxable year under Section 959(a)(2), which deals with the exclusion from gross income of previously taxed earnings and profits. Regulations Section 1.951–1(a).

A United States shareholder who, for his taxable year, is a qualified shareholder of a foreign investment company with respect to which an election under Section 1247 is in effect (election to distribute income currently) is not required to include such amounts in gross income under Section 951, nor is a United States shareholder who is subject to tax under Section 551(b) (foreign personal holding company). I.R.C. Section 951(c), (d). Sections 1247 and 551 are discussed later in this chapter.

A United States shareholder of a controlled foreign corporation must include in his gross income his *pro rata* share of the corporation's increase for any taxable year in earnings invested in United States property; but only .o the extent this share is not excludible from his gross income under Section 959, to be discussed later in this chapter. The amount of a controlled foreign corporation's earnings invested at the close of its taxable year in United States property is the aggregate amount of this property held, directly or indirectly, by the corporation at the close of its taxable year to the extent that this amount would have constituted a dividend if it had been distributed on that closing day. I.R.C. Section 956(a). "United States property" means tangible property located in the United States, stock of a domestic corporation, an obligation of a United States person, or any right to use patents, copyrights, inventions, secret formulae and the like in the United States. I.R.C. Section 956(b). But the term does not include:

(1) Obligations of the United States, money, or deposits with persons carrying on the banking business.

(2) Property located in the United States which is purchased in the United States for export to, or use in, foreign countries.

(3) Any obligation of a United States person arising in connection with the sale or processing of property if the amount did not exceed what would be required were the transaction between unrelated parties.

(4) Any aircraft, vehicles, or containers used in the transportation of persons or property in foreign commerce and used predominately outside the United States.

(5) An amount of assets of an insurance company equivalent to the unearned premiums or reserves ordinary and necessary for the proper conduct of its insurance business.

(6) An amount of assets of the controlled foreign corporation equal to the earnings and profits accumulated after December 31, 1962 and excluded from Subpart F income under Section 952(b). I.R.C. Section 956(b).

The rules for constructive ownership of stock in the case of a controlled foreign corporation are the same as for foreign investment companies. This will be discussed later in this chapter under Section 1247.

Section 959 provides that amounts taxed as Subpart F income or as previously excluded Subpart F income withdrawn from investments in less developed countries are not taxed again as increases in earnings invested in United States property. Section 959 also provides an exclusion whereby none of the amounts so taxed is taxed again when actually distributed, directly or indirectly through a chain of ownership (constructive ownership of stock) to United States shareholders or to such shareholders' successors in interest. The exclusion also applies to amounts taxed to United States shareholders as income of one controlled foreign corporation and later distributed to another controlled foreign corporation in such a chain of ownership where these amounts would otherwise again be included in the income of these shareholders or their successors in interest as Subpart F income of the controlled foreign corporation to which they are distributed. Section 959 also provides rules for the allocation of distributions to earnings and profits and for the non-dividend treatment of actual distributions which are excluded from gross income.

Earnings And Profits. The earnings and profits for a taxable year of a foreign corporation attributable to amounts which are, or have been, included in the gross income of a United States shareholder will not, when these amounts are distributed to him directly or through the constructive ownership rules, be again included in his gross income. I.R.C. Section 959(a)(1).

Earnings and profits attributable to amounts which are, or have been, included in the gross income of a United States shareholder as previously excluded Subpart F income withdrawn from investment in less developed countries may be invested in United States property without being again included in this shareholder's income. The first amounts deemed invested in United States property, moreover, are amounts previously included in the gross income of a United States shareholder under Section 951(a), Regulations Section 1.959–1(c).

The earnings and profits for a taxable year of a controlled foreign corporation attributable to amounts which are, or have been, included in the gross income of a United States shareholder under Section 951(a) will not, when distributed in a situation where the constructive ownership rules apply, be also included in the gross income of another controlled foreign corporation for purposes of stock attribution to the other controlled foreign corporation with respect to this United States shareholder. I.R.C. Section 959(b).

The source of the earnings and profits from which distributions are made by a foreign corporation as between earnings and profits attributable to increases in earnings invested in United States property, previously taxed Subpart F income withdrawn from investment in less developed countries, and other amounts is determined in accordance with Section 959(c). Distributions are considered first attributable to amounts in this sequence:

(1) Earnings and profits attributable to amounts included in gross income of a United States shareholder as his *pro rata* share of the corporation's increase in earnings invested in United States property for that year.

(2) Earnings and profits attributable to his *pro rata* share of the corporation's Subpart F income.

(3) Other earnings and profits. I.R.C. Section 959(c).

Except as provided in Section 960(a)(3) (taxes paid by foreign corporation and not previously deemed paid by domestic corporation), any distribution excluded from gross income under Section 959(c) will be treated as a distribution which is not a dividend. I.R.C. Section 959(d).

Special Rules For Foreign Tax Credit. A domestic corporation owning stock in a controlled foreign corporation must include in its gross income the income of this foreign corporation, whether or not the latter is one or more links removed in a change of ownership. Section 960 provides rules for treating foreign taxes paid by controlled foreign corporations on income which is included in the gross income of domestic corporations under Section 951(a) as having been paid by such domestic corporations.

Section 960(a) applies to a domestic corporation which includes in gross income under Section 951(a) an amount attributable to earnings and profits of a foreign corporation at least 10% of the voting stock of which is directly owned by the domestic corporation, or of a foreign corporation at least 50% of the voting stock of which is owned by a foreign corporation at least 10% of the voting stock of which in turn is owned directly by the domestic corporation. If the directly owned corporation is a less developed country corporation, then the domestic corporation is deemed to have paid the same proportion of the income, war profits, and excess profits taxes paid (or deemed paid) by the controlled foreign corporation to a foreign country or possession of the United States for the taxable year which the amount of the earnings and profits of the foreign corporation so included in gross income of the domestic corporation bears to the sum of the entire earnings and profits of the foreign corporation for that taxable year and the total amount of the income, war profits, and excess profits taxes paid by the foreign corporation.

If the directly-owned corporation is not a less developed country corporation, then the domestic corporation is deemed to have paid the same proportion of the total income, war profits, and excess profits taxes paid by the controlled foreign corporation to a foreign country or possession of the United States for its taxable year which the amount of the earnings and profits of the foreign corporation included in gross income of the domestic corporation bears to the entire earnings and profits of the foreign corporation for that taxable year. The taxes so deemed paid by the domestic corporation if the directly-owned corporation is not a less developed country corporation are included in the gross income of the domestic corporation.

A foreign corporation at least 10% of the voting stock of which is owned by a domestic corporation is termed a "first-tier" corporation. A foreign corporation at least 50% of the voting stock of which is owned by a first-tier corporation is termed a "second-tier" corporation. Regulations Section 1.960–1(b). Taxes paid by such corporations are discussed in Regulations Section 1.960–1 and Section 1.960–2.

Adjustments To Basis Of Stock In Controlled Foreign Corporations And Of Other Property. The basis of a United States shareholder's stock in a controlled foreign corporation will be increased, as of the last day in the taxable year of this corporation on which it is a controlled foreign corporation, by the amount required to be included with respect to this stock in the shareholder's gross income under Section 951(a) for his taxable year in which or with which the corporation's taxable year ends. This rule also applies to property by reason of which he is considered as owning stock in a controlled foreign corporation: that is, an interest in a foreign partnership or a beneficial interest in a foreign estate or trust. In the case of a United States shareholder who elects under Section 962 to be subject to tax at corporate rates, the amount of the increase in basis may not exceed the amount of United States tax paid in accordance with this election in the shareholder's gross income under Section 951(a) for that year. I.R.C. Section 961(a).

Similarly, the adjusted basis of such stock with respect to which a United States person receives an amount which is excluded from gross income under Section 959(a) must be reduced as of the time he receives this excluded amount, by the sum of the amount so excluded and any income, war profits, or excess profits taxes imposed by any foreign country or possession of the United States on or with respect to the earnings and profits attributable to this excluded amount when the earnings and profits actually were distributed directly or indirectly through a change of ownership. I.R.C. Section 961(b).

To the extent that an amount excluded from gross income under Section 959(a) exceeds the adjusted basis of the stock or other property with respect to which it is received, the amount is treated as a gain from the sale or exchange of property.

Election By Individuals To Be Subject To Tax At Corporate Rates. An individual United States shareholder may elect to have the provisions of Section 962 apply for his taxable year. If so, Federal income tax on all amounts included in his gross income for that year under Section 951(a) will (in lieu of the amount otherwise determined) be an amount equal to what a domestic corporation would have paid. But the surtax exemption will not exceed an amount which bears the same ratio to $25,000 as the amounts included in his gross income under Section 951(a) for the taxable year bear to his *pro rata* share of the earnings and profits for the taxable year of all controlled foreign corporations with respect to which he includes any amount in his gross income under Section 951(a) for that year. I.R.C. Section 962(a), (c).

The election is made by filing a statement to that effect with the shareholder's tax return. The election is binding and may be revoked only with the Commissioner's approval. I.R.C. Section 962(b).

Receipt Of Minimum Distributions By Domestic Corporations. A corporate United States shareholder may exclude from its gross income the Subpart F income of a controlled foreign corporation if for the taxable year the shareholder elects this exclusion and, where necessary, receives a distribution of the earnings and profits of the foreign corporation sufficient to bring the aggregate United States and foreign income taxes on the pretax earnings and profits of that corporation to a percentage level approaching the United States tax rate for that year on the income of a domestic corporation. The election to secure an exclusion under Section 963 may be made with respect to a "single first-tier corporation" or a "chain" or "group" of controlled foreign corporations. Regulations Section 1.963–1(a).

The manner in which the amount of the minimum distribution for any taxable year is to be determined is set forth in Regulations Section 1.963–2. The distributions counting toward a minimum distribution are set forth in

Regulations Section 1.963–3. Regulations Section 1.963–4 sets forth the requirement with respect to a minimum distribution from a chain or group that the overall United States and foreign income tax must equal either 90% of the United States corporate tax rate applied against the consolidated pre-tax and pre-distribution earnings and profits or, with the application of the special rules set forth in that section, the total United States and foreign income taxes which would have been incurred in respect of a *pro rata* minimum distribution from the chain or group. Regulations Section 1.963–5 provides rules for applying Section 963 in certain cases in which the rate of foreign income tax incurred by a foreign corporation varies with the amount of distributions it makes for the taxable year. Regulations Section 1.963–6 outlines the deficiency distribution procedure that may be followed if for reasonable cause a corporate United States shareholder fails to receive a complete minimum distribution for a taxable year for which it elects the exclusion.

The election is effective only for the taxable year for which made. Regulations Section 1.963–1(c)(3).

Miscellaneous Provisions. No part of the earnings and profits of a controlled foreign corporation will be included in earnings and profits if it is established to the satisfaction of the Commissioner of Internal Revenue that there could not have been a distribution because of blocked foreign income imposed under the laws of any foreign country. I.R.C. Section 964(b).

Elaborate records and accounts must be retained by United States shareholders. See I.R.C. Section 964(c).

If a controlled foreign corporation is an export trade corporation for any year, the Subpart F income of that corporation may, under certain conditions, be reduced by so much of the corporation's export trade income as constitutes foreign base company income. I.R.C. Sections 970 to 972.

Gain On Foreign Investment Company Stock

Gain on the sale or exchange of a foreign corporation is treated as ordinary income to the extent of the taxpayer's ratable share of the corporation's earnings and profits accumulated after December 31, 1962, if this corporation was a foreign investment company at any time during the period when the taxpayer held the stock. This treatment also applies to a distribution which, under Section 302 (redemptions) or Section 331 (complete liquidations) is treated as an exchange of stock. I.R.C. Section 1246(a). This rule applies whether or not the foreign corporation is within the definition of a foreign investment company at the time of the sale or exchange. But the reference is only to a corporation which was a foreign investment company while the taxpayer held the stock at some time during a taxable year beginning after December 31, 1962.

A foreign corporation is a foreign investment company if either of these tests is satisfied for any taxable year beginning after December 31, 1962:

(1) If the foreign corporation is registered under the Investment Company Act of 1940 either as a management company or as a unit investment trust.

(2) If the foreign corporation is engaged (or holds itself out as being engaged) primarily in the business of investing, re-investing, or trading in securities at a time when more than 50% of the total combined voting power of all classes of stock entitled to vote (or of the total value of shares of all classes of stock) was held, directly or indirectly, by United States persons as defined. I.R.C. Section 1246(b). Specific limitations in the statutory language of (1) exclude from foreign investment company treatment certain foreign corporations such as, for example, brokers, banks, and small loan companies.

"Securities" for this purpose includes stock, treasury stock, bonds, evidences of indebtedness, certificates of interest or participation in any profit-sharing agreement, collateral trust certificates, certificates of deposit for securities, and fractional undivided interests in oil, gas, or other mineral rights.

Stock in a foreign corporation, the basis of which (in the hands of the taxpayer selling or exchanging this stock) is determined by reference to the basis (in the hands of the taxpayer or of any other person) of stock in a foreign investment company will be treated as stock of a foreign investment company. The stock which is to be treated will be considered to be held by the taxpayer throughout the period during which the foreign investment company stock was held in addition to the period during which the stock of the foreign corporation was held. I.R.C. Section 1246(c)

This example illustrates Subsection (c): A person owning stock in a foreign investment company transfers the stock to F, a foreign corporation which he controls, in a transaction which would be tax-free under Section 351 (transfer to a controlled corporation), if the use of a foreign corporation is approved by the Secretary of the Treasury under Section 367, which is stipulated to be the case here. The stock of F Corporation received in exchange for the foreign investment company stock will be considered stock of a foreign investment company. If the stock of F Corporation is later transferred by gift, the donee will also treat this stock as stock of the foreign investment company and the holding period of the donee will include the period during which the donor held the stock in the foreign investment company and F Corporation.

Trust certificates of a trust to which Section 677 (relating to income for the benefit of a grantor) applies, and stock in a domestic corporation, will be treated as stock of a foreign investment company to the extent that such trust or corporation has an investment in stock in a foreign investment company. Thus, the taxpayer is deemed to be holding stock of the foreign investment company. The trust certificates or stock are treated as held by the taxpayer throughout the holding period for which the trust or domestic corporation held stock in a foreign investment company, but limited to the period during which he held the trust certificates or stock in the domestic corporation. This stock is deemed to be held by him in the same proportion that the actual investment in stock in a foreign investment company by the trust or domestic corporation bears to the total assets of the trust or domestic corporation. I.R.C. Section 1246(d).

Where stock in a foreign investment company is acquired from a decedent dying after December 31, 1962, the basis of this stock in the hands of the beneficiary under Section 1014 is reduced by the decedent's ratable share of the company's earnings and profits accumulated in taxable years beginning after December 31, 1962. But in no case is the basis to be reduced below the adjusted basis of the stock in the hands of the decedent immediately before his death, regardless of the decedent's ratable share of the earnings. The holding period of the decedent is tacked on to that of the person acquiring the stock. If the executor uses the alternate valuation date, the date the stock is so valued will be considered the date of the decedent's death. Thus, the basis determined at such later date will be reduced by the decedent's ratable share of the earnings and profits accumulated during the period preceding the date of his death and the earnings and profits accumulated during the period between such date and the date of alternate valuation. I.R.C. Section 1246(e)(1).

If foreign investment company stock acquired from a decedent is sold or exchanged at a gain which is subject to ordinary income treatment under Section 1246(a), the taxpayer is allowed a deduction from gross income for the taxable year of the sale or exchange equal to that portion of the decedent's estate tax deemed paid which is attributable to the excess of (A), the value at which such stock was taken into account for purposes of determining the value of the decedent's gross estate, over (B), the value at which it would have been taken into account if this value had been reduced by the amount representing the reduction described in Section 1246(e)(1), above. I.R.C. Section 1246(e)(2).

The taxpayer's ratable share of the accumulated earnings and profits of the foreign investment company includes only his ratable share of the earnings and profits accumulated for the period during which he held stock in the company (excluding any portion of that period occurring in a taxable year of the corporation beginning before January 1, 1963). This determination will exclude the taxpayer's share of undistributed earnings and profits which previously had been taxed to him under Section 951 (relating to amounts included in gross income of United States persons) or under Section 551 (relating to foreign personal holding income taxed to United States shareholders); but such exclusions refer only to income previously included in the taxpayer's income. I.R.C. Section 1246(a)(2).

In the case of entities holding foreign investment company stock under a certificate of trust, the holding period includes the time during which the trust or corporation held the stock of foreign investment companies. I.R.C. Section 1223(10).

Election By Foreign Investment Companies To Distribute Income Currently. The rule as to ordinary income treatment upon gain on disposition of foreign investment company stock (Section 1246) does not apply with respect to "qualified shareholders" of such a company during any taxable year to which the company makes the following election. The election must be made on or before December 31, 1962, with respect to each taxable year beginning after that date. The company's election is:

(1) To distribute to its shareholders 90% or more or what its taxable income would be if it were a domestic corporation;

(2) To designate in a written notice mailed to its shareholders within 45 days after the close of its taxable year the *pro rata* amount of the excess (determined as if the company were a domestic corporation) of the net long-term capital gain over the net short-term capital loss of the taxable year; and also the portion thereof which is being distributed; and

(3) To provide such information as the Commissioner of Internal Revenue deems appropriate. I.R.C. Section 1247(a)(1).

This election permanently terminates as of the close of the taxable year preceding the first taxable year in which any of the following occurs:

(1) The company fails to comply with one of the requirements, unless for a reasonable cause.

(2) The company is a foreign personal holding company.

(3) The company ceases to be a registered foreign investment company. I.R.C. Section 1247(b).

The term "qualified shareholder" means any holder of a registered foreign investment company, who is a United States person (that is, a United States citizen, resident, estate, or trust, or a domestic corporation or partnership). But a United States person will not be treated as a qualified shareholder for a taxable year if in his return for that year (or any previous one) he did not include, in computing his long-term capital gains, his *pro rata* amount of the undistributed portion of the excess capital gains which the company designated for its taxable year ending within or with such taxable year of the shareholder. I.R.C. Section 1247(c).

For any taxable year of the company for which an election is in effect, a qualified shareholder must include in his return in computing his long-term capital gains—

(1) For his taxable year in which received, his *pro rata* amount of the undistributed portion of the excess capital gains for such taxable year of the company and

(2) For his taxable year in which or with which the taxable year of the company ends, his *pro rata* amount of the undistributed portion of the excess capital gains for such taxable year of the company. I.R.C. Section 1247(d).

For purposes of determining whether the purchaser or seller of a share of foreign investment company stock is the shareholder at the close of the company's taxable year who is required to include an amount of undistributed excess capital gains in gross income, the amount of the undistributed excess capital gains will be treated in the same manner as a cash dividend payable to shareholders of record at the close of the company's taxable year. Regulations Section 1.1247–3(b)(3).

A qualified shareholder, who computes his long-term capital gains for a taxable year by including (in respect of each share of stock which he owns in a foreign investment company) the *pro rata* amount of the undistributed portion of the excess capital gains which was designated by the company for its taxable year ending with or within such taxable year, will, as of the day following the close of that taxable year of the company, increase the adjusted basis of each share by this *pro rata* amount. Regulations Section 1.1247–3(c)(2).

If a qualified shareholder of a foreign investment company which has made the election treats any amount as long-term capital gain but he actually holds the share for six months or less, then any loss on the sale or exchange of this share will be treated as short-term capital loss. I.R.C. Section 1247(i).

Gain From Certain Sales Or Exchanges Of Stock In Certain Foreign Corporations. Section 1248(a) refers to a situation where a United States person (as previously defined in this chapter) sells or exchanges stock in a foreign corporation or receives a distribution from a foreign corporation which is treated as an exchange of stock under Section 302 (redemptions) or Section 331 (liquidations). If such a person is deemed to own 10% or more of the total combined voting power of all classes of stock entitled to vote at any time during the 5-year period ending on the date of the sale or exchange when this company was a "controlled foreign corporation," then the gain recognized on the sale or exchange of the stock will be treated as a dividend, to the extent of the earnings and profits of the foreign corporation attributable to such stock which were accumulated in taxable years of the foreign corporation beginning after December 31, 1962 and during the period(s) the stock was held by that person while the foreign corporation was a controlled foreign corporation.

The term "controlled foreign corporation" means any foreign corporation of which more than 50% of the total combined voting power of all classes of stock entitled to vote is deemed to be owned by special constructive ownership rules by United States shareholders on any day during the taxable year of that foreign corporation. I.R.C. Section 957(a). The constructive ownership rules of Section 318(a) apply here, with these exceptions:

(1) Stock owned by a non-resident alien individual (other than a foreign trust or foreign estate) will not be considered as owned by a citizen or by a resident alien individual.

(2) If a partnership, estate, trust, or corporation owns, directly or indirectly, more than 50% of the total combined voting power of all classes entitled to vote of a corporation, it will be considered as owning all of the voting stock.

(3) The phrase "10%" is substituted for "50%" in Section 318(a)-(2)(C), which provides that if such percentage of the stock of a corporation is owned by or for a person, he will be deemed to own whatever proportion of the corporation's holdings his stock ownership in that corporation indicate.

(4) Section 318(a)(3)(a), (B), and (C) will not be applied so as to consider a United States person as owning stock which is owned by a person who is not a United States citizen. I.R.C. Section 958(b). These provisions refer to attribution, respectively, to partners and estates, to trusts, and to corporations.

In the case of an individual, if the foreign corporation stock sold or exchanged is a capital asset that has been held for more than six months, the tax attributable to the amount included in his gross income as a dividend will not be greater than a tax equal to the sum of—

(1) the excess of the United States taxes which would have been paid by the foreign corporation over the foreign income taxes which actually were paid, plus

(2) an amount equal to the dividend minus the amount in (1), above, multiplied by the 25% capital gains tax rate. I.R.C. Section 1248(b).

Section 1248(a) applies to a sale or exchange of stock in a foreign corporation only if gain is recognized in whole or in part upon such sale or exchange. Thus, if a United States person exchanges stock in a foreign corporation and if under Sections 332, 351, 354, 355, or 361 (dealing with corporate reorganizations), no gain is recognized as a result of a determination that under Section 367 (which deals exclusively with foreign corporations) the exchange is not in pursuance of a plan having tax avoidance as one of its principal purposes, then no amount is includible in the gross income of that person as a dividend. Regulations Section 1.1248–1(c).

The following items are excluded from the earnings and profits of a foreign corporation:

(1) Amounts included in gross income under Section 951 (dealing with controlled foreign corporations).

(2) Gain from the sale or exchange of property in pursuance of a plan of complete liquidation, where Section 337(a) would apply if this were a domestic corporation.

(3) Earnings and profits accumulated by a foreign corporation while it was a less developed country corporation (as defined in Section 902(d)), if the stock sold or exchanged was owned for a continuous period of at least ten years, ending with the date of the sale or exchange, by the United States person who sold or exchanged the stock.

(4) Any item includible in gross income of the foreign corporation—

    (a) for any taxable year beginning before January 1, 1967 as income derived from sources within the United States of a foreign corporation engaged in trade or business within the United States, or

    (b) for any taxable year beginning after December 31, 1966, as income effectively connected with the conduct by the corporation of a trade or business within the United States.

(5) Amounts included in gross income under Section 1247 (election as to gain on foreign investment company stock). I.R.C. Section 1248(d).

The exclusion applies in any applicable taxable year in which the controlled foreign corporation is a less developed country corporation, and there is no requirement that the controlled foreign corporation be a less developed country corporation for all taxable years during which it is a controlled foreign corporation for the exclusion to apply. Revenue Ruling 68–187, I.R.B. 1968–16, 24.

The earnings and profits of a foreign corporation for this purpose will be determined in a manner substantially similar to the method employed in the case of a domestic corporation. I.R.C. Section 1248(c)(1). Special rules apply in the case of blocks of stock. See Regulations Section 1.1248–2 and –3. Special rules also apply where the foreign corporation (referred to as a "first-tier" corporation) has an interest in a foreign subsidiary (referred to as a "lower-tier" corporation). See Regulations Section 1.1248-3(f). Specialized treatment is afforded where the lower-tier corporation is a "less developed country" corporation as defined in Section 902(d). See Regulations Section 1.1248–3(g).

Personal Holding Companies

The regular personal holding company tax applied to United States corporations may apply to a foreign corporation which is not a foreign personal holding company. But personal holding company status does not apply in the case of a foreign corporation (other than one with income from personal service contracts), if all of its stock outstanding during the last half of the taxable year is owned by non-resident alien individuals, whether directly or indirectly through foreign estates, foreign trusts, foreign partnerships, or other foreign corporations. I.R.C. Section 542(c)(7).

Foreign Personal Holding Companies

In the case of a foreign personal holding company, the corporation itself is not taxed, for the corporation in fact may not be within the reach of United States taxes. But shareholders who are individual citizens or residents of the United States, domestic corporations, domestic partnerships, and certain estates and trusts may be the subject of the tax.

Unless it is a tax-exempt organization or a banking institution as described in Section 552(b)(2), any foreign corporation will be deemed to be a foreign personal holding company if it meets both the gross income and the stock ownership requirements.

To meet the gross income requirement, it is necessary that either of the following percentages of gross income of the corporation for the taxable year be foreign personal holding company income (to be defined below):

(1) 60% or more; or

(2) 50% or more if the foreign corporation has been classified as a foreign personal holding company for any prior taxable year, unless—

    (a) A taxable year has intervened since the last taxable year for which it was so classified, during no part of which the specified stock ownership requirement exists; or

(b) Three consecutive years have intervened since the last taxable year for which it was so classified, during each of which its foreign personal holding company income was less than 50% of its gross income.

To meet the stock ownership requirement, it is necessary that at some time in the taxable year more than 50% in value of the outstanding stock be owned, directly or indirectly, by or for not more than five individuals who are citizens or residents of the United States (referred to as "United States group"). The stock attribution rules are presented below. I.R.C. Section 552(a), (b).

If a corporation falls into the category of foreign personal holding company, the undistributed foreign personal holding company income is included only in the gross income of the United States shareholders who were shareholders in the company on the last day of its taxable year on which a United States group existed with respect to the company. The United States shareholders must include in their gross income their distributive shares of that proportion of the undistributed foreign personal holding company income for the taxable year of the company which is equal in ratio to that which the portion of the taxable year up to and including the last day on which the United States group with respect to the company existed bears to the entire taxable year. The amount which each United States shareholder must return is that amount which he would have received as a dividend if the above-specified portion of the undistributed foreign personal holding company income had in fact been distributed by the foreign personal holding company as a dividend on the last day of its taxable year on which the required United States group existed. The assumed distribution of the required portion of the undistributed foreign personal holding company income must be returned as a dividend by the United States shareholders for their respective years in which or with which the taxable year of the foreign personal holding company ends. I.R.C. Section 551(a), (b).

The amount which the United States shareholder must thus include in his gross income will be treated as having been re-invested by him as a contribution to the corporation's capital. I.R.C. Section 551(f).

Foreign personal holding company income means:

(1) Dividends, interest, royalties, and annuities.

(2) Gains from the sale or exchange of stock or securities, except in the case of regular dealers in such items.

(3) Gains from commodities transactions.

(4) Income from estates and trusts.

(5) Income from personal service contracts.

(6) Amounts reecived for use of corporation property by the shareholders under specified circumstances.

(7) Income from rents, unless constituting 50% or more of the gross income. I.R.C. Section 553(a).

As to the stock attribution rules, stock owned, directly or indirectly, by or for a corporation, partnership, estate, or trust is considered as being owned proportionately by its shareholders, partners, or beneficiaries. An individual is considered as owning the stock owned, directly or indirectly, by or for his family or his partner. For this purpose, "family" includes only his brothers and sisters, spouse, ancestors, and lineal descendants. If any person has an option to acquire stock, he will be considered to own this stock. I.R.C. Section 554.

Federal Estate Tax

The Federal estate tax rates range from 3% to 77%. The estate of a non-resident alien is taxed only on the transfer of property situated or deemed to be situated in the United States at the time of his death. No marital deduction is allowed with respect to the estate of a non-resident alien. No credit is allowed for foreign death taxes paid; and the expenses, losses, etc., are generally limited to the same proportion of these expenses which the alien's gross estate situated within the United States is of his entire gross estate. Tax rates of a non-resident alien range from 5% to 25%.

The estate of a citizen or resident of the United States is entitled to a $60,000 exemption. The estate of a non-resident not a citizen of the United States is allowed to deduct a $30,000 exemption in computing the taxable estate. In the case of decedents who were residents of United States possessions at the time of death and were citizens solely by reason of being a citizen of the possession, or by reason of birth or residence in the possession, the exemption is the greater of $30,000 or the proportion of the $60,000 exemption granted to United States citizens which the value of that part of the decedent's gross estate which is situated in the United States bears to the value of his entire gross estate. I.R.C. Section 2106(a)(3).

For purposes of the tax imposed on the estates of non-residents not citizens of the United States, all debt obligations (including bonds) of a United States person, the United States, a state or political subdivision thereof, or of the District of Columbia owned and held by a non-resident not a citizen are deemed to be property situated within the United States. An exception to this rule is provided for debt obligations which have derived less than 20% of their gross income from United States sources for the three years prior to the non-resident's death. In such cases, these debt obligations are considered as having a foreign situs. For this purpose, United States currency is not considered a debt obligation of the United States. I.R.C. Section 2104(c).

United States bank deposits, accounts with mutual savings banks, building and loan associations, etc., and amounts held on deposit by insurance companies are, in general, deemed to be property not within the United States (and therefore not includible in the gross estate of a non-resident not a citizen of the United States), with respect to estates of decedents dying after November 13, 1966 and before January 1, 1973. In the case of estates of decedents who are non-residents not citizens of the United States and who die after December 31, 1972, these deposits, accounts, and amounts will be includible in gross estate for purposes of the Federal estate tax. I.R.C. Section 2105(b).

Federal Gift Tax

In the case of a non-resident not a citizen of the United States, the Federal gift tax applies only if the property is situated in the United States. I.R.C. Section 2511(a).

In the case of intangible property transferred by a non-resident alien, the gift tax does not apply, except in the case of an expatriate as defined in Section 2511(b).

Expatriates

Literature is full of rootless persons, ranging from the Wandering Jew to the Flying Dutchman to the United States contribution, Edward Everett Hale's *The Man Without A Country*. But a new dimension to expatriates has been created by the tax laws.

As has been mentioned previously, a 30% income tax rate (lower, if special treaties so provide) rather than progressive tax rates applies to the income of non-resident alien individuals which is not effectively connected with the conduct of a trade or business within the United States. I.R.C. Section 871. Similarly, the Federal estate tax rates for non-resident aliens are less than for citizens or residents of the United States. I.R.C. Section 2101(a). And gifts of intangible property by non-resident aliens are not subject to the Federal gift tax. I.R.C. Section 2501(a)(2).

These favorable tax features for non-resident alien individuals might encourage some individuals to surrender their United States citizenship and to move abroad, particularly if the persons are retired or if, by reason of inherited or other wealth, they are not engaged in business. By so doing, an expatriate could avoid the graduated tax rates on his United States investment income and could avoid some estate and gift taxes. The Foreign Investors Tax Act of 1966 sought to come to grips with this situation.

Section 877 taxes both income effectively connected with the conduct of a United States business and any other United States source income of an expatriate at regular income tax rates, if he lost his citizenship within ten years of the taxable year in question (and after March 8, 1965), where one of the principal purposes of the expatriation was the avoidance of Federal income, estate, or gift taxes. But this treatment does not apply if it results in a smaller United States tax bill than otherwise would be imposed.

In addition to imposing this tax on both the expatriate's United States source income not effectively connected with the conduct of a United States trade or business and his income that is "effectively connected," regardless of its source, Section 877 contains special rules to be used in determining his United States source income. These rules provide that gains from the sale or exchange of property (other than stock or debt obligations) located in the United States, and gains on the sale or exchange of stock of a domestic corporation or debt obligations of United States persons or of the United States, a state or political subdivision, or the District of Columbia are to be treated as income from sources within the United States regardless of where the sale or exchange occurs or title is transferred. Deductions are allowed only to the extent they are properly allocable to the gross income of the expatriate, determined under the above-described provisions (except that the capital loss carryover provision does not apply).

Section 877 contains a special rule with respect to the burden of proving the existence or non-existence of Federal tax avoidance as one of the principal purposes of the expatriation. The Secretary of the Treasury or his delegate must first establish that it is reasonable to believe that the expatriate's loss of United States citizenship would (but for the application of these special provisions) result in a substantial reduction in his taxes based on the expatriate's probable income for the taxable year. If this is established, then the expatriate must carry the burden of proving that the loss of citizenship did not have, for one of its principal purposes, the avoidance of Federal income, estate, or gift taxes. Section 877, however, excepts persons whose loss of citizenship occurs under circumstances where it is unlikely that tax avoidance was a principal purpose. The Senate Finance Committee Report accompanying this measure stated that "this provision does not apply where the person acquired dual citizenship at birth and loses his U.S. citizenship by residing, for a certain period, in the foreign country of which he is also a citizen by birth."

This treatment applies for taxable years beginning after December 31, 1966.

Section 877 is an income tax provision. A new Section 2107 imposes the regular Federal estate tax rates on the United States estate of a non-resident alien dying within ten years after losing United States citizenship if one of the principal purposes of the loss of citizenship was the avoidance of Federal income, estate, or gift taxes. Section 2107 specifies, if certain stock ownership tests are met, that the value of an expatriate's gross United States estate is to include the same proportion of the value of the stock holdings of the expatriate in a foreign corporation as its property having a United States situs bears to all property. The ownership tests that must be met for this provision to apply are:

(1) The decedent must have owned at the time of his death 10% or more of the voting power of all classes of stock of the foreign corporation. Ownership for this test includes direct ownership and indirect ownership through another foreign corporation, or through a foreign partnership, trust, or estate.

(2) The decedent must have owned, at the time of his death, more than 50% of the total voting power of all classes of stock of the foreign corporation. Ownership for purposes of this test is ownership as described in (1), above, plus ownership attributed to the expatriate under the attribution rules of Section 318. (In general, these rules attribute to an individual ownership of stock held by members of his family, as well as by partnerships, trusts, estates, or corporations in which he has certain interests.)

In addition, in determining whether the ownership tests are met, and in determining the portion of the United States situs property owned by the foreign corporation that must be included in computing the value of his gross estate, the expatriate is treated as owning the stock of a foreign corporation(at the time of his death) which he transferred during his life but which under Federal estate tax law generally is not effective in excluding property from a gross estate. These transfers are:

(1) Transfers in contemplation of death. I.R.C. Section 2035.

(2) Transfers with retained life estate. I.R.C. Section 2036.

(3) Transfers taking effect at death. I.R.C. Section 2037.

(4) Revocable transfers. I.R.C. Section 2038.

In computing the estate tax under this provision, the expatriate's estate is allowed the credits for state death taxes, gift tax, and tax on prior transfers.

Section 2107 does not apply to the transfer of the estate of a decedent whose loss of United States citizenship resulted from the application of Sections 301(b), 350, or 355 of the Immigration and Nationality Act.

For Federal gift tax purposes, Section 2501(a)(3) provides for an exception to the rule that gifts of intangible property by non-resident aliens are not subject to the Federal gift tax. This rule does not apply to gifts by donors who within the ten years immediately before the gift became expatriates of the United States with a principal purpose of avoiding Federal income, estate, or gift taxes. This rule applies with respect to the calendar year 1967 and all calendar years thereafter.

Interest On Certain Governmental Obligations

Interest received on and after March 1, 1913 on bonds, notes, and certificates of indebtedness of the United States while beneficially owned by a non-resident alien individual, or a foreign corporation, partnership, or association not engaged in business in the United States, is exempt from Federal income tax. This exemption applies only to bonds, notes, and certificates that were issued before March 1, 1941. Interest derived by a non-resident alien individual, or by a foreign corporation, partnership, or association on such instruments issued on or after March 1, 1941 are not exempt except in respect of any obligations which the Federal Maritime Board and Maritime Commission (formerly the United States Maritime Commission) or the Federal Housing Administration has, before March 1, 1941, contracted to issue at a future date. Regulations Section 1.103–6.

Interest Equalization Tax

The interest equalization tax is imposed on United States persons with respect to the purchase of foreign securities. In the case of debt, the tax rate varies with the period of time to maturity. In the case of stock, the tax rate is 15%. The tax is designed to increase capital costs in the United States for foreigners by about 1% per year. I.R.C. Section 4914.

Chapter 16

Sundry Considerations

Compensation

If stock is transferred by an employer to an employee for an amount less than fair market value, regardless of whether the transfer is in the form of a sale or an exchange, the difference between the amount paid for the stock and the amount of its fair market value is in the nature of compensation and must be included in the employee's gross income. In computing the gain or loss from the subsequent sale of this stock, its basis is the amount paid for the property, increased by the amount of this difference included in gross income. T.D. 5507, 1946–1 CB 18.

Ordinarily, a bargain sale of stock to an employee is regarded as compensation to the extent of the bargain. But such was not the case where the employee did not know that he was getting a bargain. *James M. Hunley,* T.C. Memo. 1966–66, filed March 30, 1966.

The discharge by a corporation of its salary obligations to shareholder-employees by the issuance of the corporation's stock to them equal in value to the salary obligations was deemed to be the payment of consideration for services; and income was realized in an amount equal to the fair market value of the stock received. *Commissioner v. Fender Sales, Inc. et al.,* 338 F.2d 924 (9th Cir., 1964). Where stock, equal in fair market value to salary obligations owed, was issued by a corporation in payment of these obligations to its shareholder-employees, they had to report this as income, notwithstanding the fact that the employees' proportionate interest in the corporation had not changed as a result of the issuance of the stock. Revenue Ruling 67–402, I.R.B. 1967–46, 13.

Shares received for services by an employee were not regarded as compensation where the stock was encumbered with various major restrictions. Nor did the subsequent lifting of these restrictions constitute taxable income in the absence of any understanding that the restrictions were to be lifted. *Robert Lehman,* 17 T.C. 652 (1951). Stock in a taxpayer's employer company was issued to him under an agreement restricting the use and sale of these shares. It was held that these shares had no fair market value upon receipt that could be charged to him as income. The stock could not be sold for a year, although it could be pledged. The stock could be re-sold to the company at cost if the corporation so desired, were employment to terminate within one year of the original agreement. Any sale within two years would be subject to the employe's first refusal at the current bid price in the market. The employee had no pre-emptive rights. It was stipulated that a purchaser could not be found for the stock with its contractual restrictions. *Harold H. Kuchman et al.,* 18 T.C. 154 (1952).

Stock given to an employee under restrictions set by the California Corporation Commissioner was not income until the restrictions were lifted. *Daniel H. Deutsch et al.,* T.C. Memo. 1967–142, filed June 28, 1967.

The fact that an employee happens to be a shareholder of a corporation may influence the Federal income tax treatment of a transaction. Thus, a bonus-type contract which is reasonable in the case of an employee who is not a stockholder may be deemed to be unreasonable if made with a large stockholder, for the incentive of the bonus presumably would not be needed to call forth the shareholder's best efforts. *Irby Construction Co. v. United States,* 290 F.2d 824 (Ct. Cl., 1961). Similarly, where compensation of employee-stockholders is geared to the amount of shares owned, an individual has the burden of proof in establishing that the payment was not a dividend. *Northlich, Stolley, Inc. v. United States,* 368 F.2d 272 (Ct. Cl., 1966).

Where a corporation purchased the minority stock interest of an individual who had an employment contract with the company (which then was cancelled), the corporation could not deduct any part of the purchase price as compensation. The contract made no reference to anything except acquisition of shares and hence was regarded as a capital transaction. *The Coca-Cola Company v. Commissioner,* 369 F.2d 913 (8th Cir., 1966).

Contributions

Contributions to approved charitable organizations in the form of appreciated-value securities create several income tax advantages to the donor, in addition to the personal satisfaction of aiding a worthy cause:

(1) There is no tax upon the appreciation.

(2) There is a charitable deduction within the limits set by Section 170 of the Code.

(3) If the securities pay dividends or interest, future gross income is reduced.

(4) In addition, for estate tax purposes, ultimate gross estate is reduced by any gift which is not made in contemplation of death. See Chapter 13.

"The law with respect to gifts of appreciated property is well established. A gift of appreciated property does not result in income to the donor so long as he gives the property away absolutely and parts with title thereto before the property gives rise to income by way of a sale." *The Humacid Co.,* 42 T.C. 894 (1964).

If donative intent can be shown, a bargain sale of securities to a charitable organization will beget a charitable deduction to the extent of the bargain. Regulations Section 1.1001–1(e). "The fact that the petitioners chose to sell their securities to the Fund at their cost and thereby avoid the payment of a tax upon the appreciation in value of such securities which would have resulted had they sold such securities to third parties, does not, in our opinion, militate against the tax-exempt status of the Fund or against the deductibility of the contributions made." *William Waller et al.,* 39 T.C. 665 (1963).

A contribution of stock to a charity is not made merely by giving instructions to the transfer agent that the shares be transferred. Thus, where such instructions were given in one year but the stock was not transferred on the books of the transfer agent until the following year, the contribution was deemed to have been made in the latter year. *Jack Winston Londen et al.,* 45 T.C. 106 (1965). No deduction was allowed in the year of a letter of gift, where the certificates remained in a broker's custody until the following year. *William B. Neville et al.,* T.C. Memo. 1967–95, filed May 3, 1967. Nor was a gift of securities recognized for tax purposes where the donor merely made a verbal assignment. Transfer must be effected on a formal assignment of the certificate or by the stock transfer agent, or by access to the place where a bearer certificate is located. There must be constructive or symbolic delivery, "a delivery as perfect as the nature of the property and surroundings of the parties reasonably permitted." *Lunsford Richardson,* 39 B.T.A. 927 (1939), *aff'd,* 126 F.2d 562 (2d Cir., 1942).

In order to get a charitable deduction, stock must have ascertainable value. Where a gift of non-voting stock of a closely-held corporation was made to a charitable foundation, value was found in the absence of legal conditions, powers, or restrictions that would make it doubtful if the foundation ever would receive or keep the donated property. Overlapping control did not make the value unascertainable. *Richard P. Makoff et al.,* T.C. Memo. 1967–13, filed January 30, 1967. A gift of a corporation's non-voting stock to a charity by persons who held the voting stock resulted in a valid contribution for tax purposes. The transferors had no right of recapture of the assets so transferred nor to strip the corporation and its shares of value. The charity acquired a substantial proprietary interest in the corporation. *Henry Pullman et al.,* T.C. Memo. 1964–218, filed August 18, 1964.

A charitable deduction was allowed where stock was transferred in trust for charitable purposes. Although the donors were the officers and directors of the corporation the shares of which were transferred, the value of the stock to the charity was not dependent upon their whim; for if the corporation did not pay dividends, the accumulated earnings tax could have penalized not only the corporation but the directors. Also, noted the court, "it will be presumed that a trustee will efface personal interests and faithfully and honestly perform his duties to his *cestui que trust.*" Thus, it was reasonable to assume that the charity would share in the corporation's demonstrated earning power. *United States v. Gates, Jr. et al.,* 376 F.2d 65 (10th Cir., 1967).

Where stock is contributed to a charity and, shortly thereafter, these shares are redeemed by the corporation which had issued them, the reality of the contribution for tax purposes is not affected if the charity was not obligated as a condition of the gift to have the shares redeemed and if the charity was not prevented from selling the shares elsewhere. *Richard P. Makoff et al.,* T.C. Memo. 1967–13, filed January 10, 1967. A gift of appreciated-value property of undeterminable worth and marketability to a charitable organization is valid, even if accompanied by an offer to buy back the property at a stipulated figure, provided the donee is an independent party, there is no pre-arrangement or legal commitment for the sale back, and the donee could decline to sell the property to the donor or his nominee. *Sheppard et al. v. United States,* 361 F.2d 972 (Ct. Cl., 1966).

After a corporation had filed notice of contemplated liquidation, a shareholder donated his stock to a charitable organization and claimed a charitable deduction. The Internal Revenue Service sought to tax the liquidating dividends subsequently received by the charity to the shareholder, on the ground that this was an anticipatory assignment of income. The court disagreed. Although it was unlikely that the liquidation would be repudiated prior to its finality, such an abandonment was entirely possible, and thus there was a contribution of stock rather than an assignment of a right to liquidating dividends. *Jacobs v. United States,* D.C., S.D. Ohio, 1966.

A corporation transferred shares to a charitable organization, under a "gentlemen's agreement" that the corporation could re-acquire the shares one month later at market value. The stock actually was transferred on the books. Evidence indicated that the donor sought to obtain a stepped-up basis for the stock. The transfer and re-purchase of the stock by the corporation was disregarded by the Internal Revenue Service. The amount paid to re-acquire the stock was the charitable contribution. The stock upon re-acquisition had the same basis as before the transfer. Revenue Ruling 67–178, I.R.B. 1967–24, 6.

An individual gave bonds to a charity, which immediately sold them at face to a buyer unrelated to the donor. Upon the basis of this sale, the donor claimed a deduction in the amount of face value. Actually, the obligor corporation had been losing money for four years and was virtually a shell; the buyer admittedly wanted to show his faith in the donor, to whom he felt he could look for ultimate repayment. The charitable deduction was disallowed as a gift of property of no value. *E. S. Dillard et al.,* T.C. Memo. 1961–30, filed January 31, 1961.

A taxpayer who donated Section 306 stock (see Chapter 8) to a charitable foundation did not "realize" income upon the disposition of this stock, where there was no pre-arrangement for the sale by the foundation of the preferred stock which it received or for the redemption by the corporation of any of its preferred stock. Nor would the donor realize taxable income upon a subsequent sale by the charity of this stock. Revenue Ruling 57–328, 1957–2 CB 229.

Where an individual purchased bonds at a premium and donated these bonds to tax-exempt organizations, he could amortize the bond premium (see Chapter 9) even though he had made the purchase without an investment purpose. *Humphreys et al. v. Commissioner,* 301 F.2d 33 (6th Cir., 1962).

The transfer of the donor's promissory note to a foundation was not deductible where, under the law of the state where the donor resided, the note was not enforceable. Said the court: "The word 'contribution' is not defined in the statute, but we think it is clear that whatever is meant it would at least require some right to be relinquished or some obligation incurred by the contributor." *Norman Petty et al.,* 40 T.C. 521 (1963).

Where a pledge to a charitable organization is satisfied by a donation of appreciated-value property, the donor has no taxable income therefrom. Revenue Ruling 55–410, 1955–1 CB 297.

Transferee Liability

Under certain circumstances, the transferee of property is responsible (within limits) for any unpaid Federal taxes of the transferor. A common example of this is the shareholder of a corporation which, after a transfer, is no longer possessed of sufficient assets to pay Federal taxes. "The liability, at law or in equity, of a transferee of property of any person liable in respect of any other tax, in any case where the liability of the transferee arises on the liquidation of a corporation or partnership, or a corporate reorganization within the meaning of section 368(a) [see Chapter 8], shall be assessed against such transferee and paid and collected in the same manner and subject to the same provisions and limitations as in the case of the tax with respect to which such liability is incurred. . . ." Regulations Section 301.6901–1(a)(2). "[T]he term 'transferee' includes . . . the shareholder of a dissolved corporation, . . . the successor of a corporation, a party to a reorganization as defined in Section 368(a), and all other classes of distributees." Regulations Section 301.6901–1(a)(3).

The imposition of transferee liability "generally requires proof [by the Commissioner of Internal Revenue] (1) that the assets were transferred by the corporation to the transferee without adequate consideration, (2) that the corporation was insolvent or that the transfer left the corporation insolvent, (3) that the assets had value and what the value was on the date of the transfer, and (4) that [the Commissioner] has made every reasonable effort to collect the sums due from the transferor." *Samuel Napsky et al.,* T.C. Memo. 1965–284, filed October 27, 1965.

In the case of the Federal gift tax (unlike the Federal income and estate taxes), transferee liability does not depend upon the insolvency of the donor. Regulations Section 301.6901–1(b).

"The interpretative gloss on this provision indicates that in order to discharge this burden the Commissioner must establish that it would be bootless to proceed further against the taxpayer-transferor; that there was a gratuitous transfer to the alleged transferee. . . ." *Kreps v. Commissioner,* 351 F.2d 1 (2d Cir., 1965). When a corporation has been dissolved and all its assets distributed, it is not necessary that the Commissioner first proceed against the transferor corporation for Federal tax deficiencies, inasmuch as such proceedings would be useless. *United States v. Fairall,* 16 F.2d 328 (D.C., S.D.N.Y., 1926). But where adequate provisions have been made for the payment of the corporation's debts, the Commissioner may not assert transferee liability against the stockholders without first proceeding against the trust fund provided. *William A. Moorhead,* 22 B.T.A. 858 (1931).

"[W]e must first decide whether the question of insolvency is to be dealt with in the bankruptcy or in the equity sense of the term. . . . [T]he transferee liability provisions of the Code are limited in their application to cases in which the taxpayer-transferor suffers from more than mere illiquidity. This suggests that we should import to the transferee provisions of the Code the bankruptcy sense of insolvency." *Kreps v. Commissioner,* 351 F.2d 1 (2d Cir., 1965). The Commissioner may prove that the transfer was one of a series in liquidation which resulted in the transferor's insolvency. *Samuel Napsky et al.,* T.C. Memo. 1965–284, filed October 27, 1965.

Where a stockholder receives a liquidating dividend that has a value in excess of the tax liability asserted against the corporation, he incurs transferee liability. *Ford v. United States,* . . . F. Supp. . . . (D.C., W.D. Ky., 1967). But the liability of each transferee is limited to the value of the transferred property which he receives. *Phillips et al. v. Commissioner,* 283 U.S. 589 (1931). The Government need not pursue its claims against all of the stockholders if the full amount of the transferor's tax liability may be satisfied by the assertion of transferee liability against one or some of the transferees. *Boyd W. Morgan Estate et al.,* T.C. Memo., Docket Nos. 12070–1, entered June 2, 1949.

The statute of limitations is extended for one year in the case of each transferee, with a maximum of three years if transferees in turn have transferees. I.R.C. Section 6901(c).

Although the Commissioner has the burden of proof to show that the transferee is in fact the type of transferee described in Section 6901, he does not have to prove that the transferor really was liable for the taxes. *B. S. Sharp,* 35 T.C. 1168 (1961).

Where a dissolving corporation made a request for a prompt assessment, the Internal Revenue Service could still proceed against a transferee after the 18-month limitation period applicable to prompt assessment requests, inasmuch as the statute of limitations for a transferee is one year after the period of limitations against the transferor. *Drew et al. v. Commissioner,* 340 F.2d 365 (Ct. Cl., 1965).

Defense Of Title To Stock

Ordinarily, defense of title (for example, title to stock) is a non-deductible capital expenditure. But where the suit was completely without merit, and unjustified, an individual was permitted to deduct such an expenditure. *Samuel Galewitz et al.,* 50 T.C. 104 (1968).

Insider Profits

Section 16(b) of the Securities Exchange Act of 1934 provides, in part, that for the purpose of preventing the unfair use of information which may have been obtained by an officer, director, or beneficial owner of more than 10% of the stock of a corporation, any profit realized by him from any purchase or sale, or any purchase and sale of an equity security of the corporation within any period of less than six months, will inure to and be recoverable by the corporation. A deduction for a payment to a corporation by an officer or director thereof, as a result of this law, of the amount of profits derived in dealings in the stock of the corporation will not be denied for income tax purposes on the ground that it frustrates sharply defined public policy. "The income tax significance of the capital stock dealings giving rise to the payment determines whether it is deductible as an ordinary loss or as a capital loss." Revenue Ruling 61–115, 1961–1 CB 46.

Where a corporate president reported long-term capital gain upon his own tax return on a sale of stock in one year and, four years later, he was obliged to restore a portion of his profits to the company, he could not re-open his return of the earlier year so as to claim a capital loss carryover. *Eugene H. Walet, Jr. et al.,* 31 T.C. 461 (1958), *aff'd on other issues,* 272 F.2d 694 (5th Cir., 1960).

Payments received by a corporation pursuant to the "insider profits" provision are taxable to the corporation. *General American Investors Co., Inc. v. Commissioner,* 348 U.S. 434 (1955).

Transfers To Avoid Tax

There is a Federal excise tax upon transfers of stock or securities by:
(1) a citizen or resident of the United States.
(2) a domestic corporation or partnership, or
(3) a trust which is not a foreign trust,
to a foreign corporation as paid-in surplus or as a contribution to capital. Similarly covered is a transfer to a foreign trust or a foreign partnership.

The tax is 27½% of the amount of the excess of (1) the value of the stock or securities over (2) its adjusted basis for determining gain in the hands of the transferor. I.R.C. Section 1491.

The tax does not apply:

(1) If the transferee is a tax-exempt organization.

(2) "If before the transaction it has been established to the satisfaction of the Secretary [of the Treasury] or his delegate that such transfer is not in pursuance of a plan having as one of its principal purposes the avoidance of Federal income taxes." I.R.C. Section 1492.

The tax is payable by the transferor at the time of the transfer without assessment or notice or demand. I.R.C. Section 1494.

Stock Options

Gain derived by an employee from the exercise of a stock option granted by his employer is ordinary rather than capital, if the option had been granted as a form of compensation. *Commissioner v. LoBue,* 351 U.S. 243 (1956).

In the case of a restricted stock option, an employee, if he meets all of the terms and conditions of the statute, has no income until he disposes of the option; and then, depending upon the circumstances, a portion of his gain will be taxed upon a capital basis. I.R.C. Section 421.

Comparable rules apply to qualified stock options, employee stock option purchase plans, and restricted stock options. I.R.C. Sections 422–424.

In order to obtain the favored treatment for qualified stock options, an optionee, immediately after the option is granted, may not own stock possessing more than 5% to 10% (depending upon the equity capital of the employer corporation) of the total combined voting power or value of all classes of stock of the employer corporation or of its parent or subsidiary corporations. I.R.C. Section 422(b)(7). Any stock in his employer corporation held by an employee in his capacity as trustee of a voting trust is not included in this determination except to the extent that he has a beneficial interest in this stock. Revenue Ruling 67–237, I.R.B. 1967–30, 6.

The exercise of a qualified stock option may beget capital gain treatment. But if the employee accepts an offer from his employer to tender his option contract for cancellation, in return for a specified sum "as additional compensation," ordinary income results. *Dugan et al. v. United States,* 234 F. Supp. 7 (D.C., S.D. N.Y., 1964).

The transfer of a restricted stock option back to one's employer corporation results in ordinary income. *Rank et al. v. United States,* 345 F.2d 337 (5th Cir., 1965).

In the case of a non-qualified stock option, if an employee receives an option to purchase stock from his employer corporation, he realizes taxable income by way of compensation on the date he receives the stock to the extent of the difference between the fair market value of the stock when it is received and the price paid therefor. If he transfers the option for consideration in an arm's length transaction, he realizes taxable income by way of compensation on the date he receives the consideration to the extent of the value of the consideration. I.T. 3795, 1946–1 CB 15.

Brokerage Commissions

Brokerage commissions paid in the purchase of stocks are not deductible as business expenses but are added to the cost basis of such securities. *Helvering v. Winmill,* 305 U.S. 79 (1938).

Commissions paid in selling securities are not business expense but are an offset against the selling price. *Spreckels v. Helvering,* 315 U.S. 626 (1942).

Expenses By Stockholders

Expenditures which a stockholder makes on behalf of his corporation are not his ordinary and necessary expenses but those of the corporation. *Jacob M. Kaplan et al.,* 21 T.C. 134 (1953). They are not deductible by him but may constitute contributions to the capital of the corporation and hence be an additional cost of his investment in the corporation. *Jean U. Koree,* 40 T.C. 961 (1963).

Expenses By Investors

Expenses of obtaining guidance on the tax consequences of a transaction are deductible if incurred for the production of income. *Higgins v. Commissioner,* 43 F.2d 654 (1st Cir., 1944). Therefore, an investor or his advisor may deduct the cost of this book.

Appendix 1

Identification of Commingled Securities

Verbatim Presentation Of Revenue Ruling 64–160, 1964–1 CB (Part 1) 306.

The following instructions are provided in amplifications of the stock identification requirements of section 1.1236–1(d)(1)(ii) of the regulations:

1. Section 1.1236–1(d)(1)(ii) of the regulations is applicable only to those security dealers who, in the buying and selling of stocks, participate in certain approved methods of clearing stock transactions. In general, such clearing methods are those conducted by a clearing company which involve a deposit of stocks of participating dealers and brokers in depository accounts held in nominee name on behalf of each participating dealer and broker and which effect, between participating dealers and brokers, transfers of title to such stocks while eliminating insofar as possible, physical delivery of stock certificates and utilizing bookkeeping methods to maintain net deposit balances for each stock with respect to which a participating dealer or broker has an interest. Participating or nonparticipating dealers having possession at any time of stocks held for investment which are identified by certificate numbers imprinted on stock certificates may deposit such stock certificates in a depository arrangement conducted by a clearing company. For each date of purchase of each different stock, such dealers shall, as a means of identification, use the separate serial number imprinted on an instruction form furnished by the clearing company in place of the certificate numbers imprinted on the stock certificates that were deposited.

2. Each dealer must maintain in his records, for each stock owned by him in which he is a dealer, two separate accounts, one for shares held for investment purposes and the other for shares held for sale to customers. However, with respect to shares in a depository arrangement, the specific identification of stock by certificate number, as required in section 1.1236–1(d)(1)(ii) of the regulations will not be required.

3. The clearing company which performs the clearing function and which

maintains the clearing facilities for participating dealers must, in addition to other such accounts as it may maintain for each participating dealer, maintain in its records separate investment identification accounts for each such dealer. Such account is to reflect a dealer's position with respect to each stock held for investment. In addition, the clearing company shall render periodic statements to the dealer. Such statements shall indicate the dealer's position with respect to each stock held for investment purposes at the beginning of each day on which changes in such position take place, and the dealer's position with respect to each stock held for investment at the end of such day. Such statements shall be reconciled by the dealer with his accounts and the statements, plus any adjusting entries, shall be retained by the dealer.

4. Each investment account, maintained by a dealer, must disclose the name or identifying symbol of the stock, the date of purchase and the purchase price of each lot of stock and in addition the serial number as imprinted on the instruction form furnished by the clearing company. Such instruction form shall request the clearing company to make an entry in its bookkeeping records to cover the delivery of shares out of the dealer's general account, maintained by the clearing company with respect to such dealer, and the receipt of such shares in the dealer's investment identification account. Such entry on the records of the clearing company must disclose the name or identifying symbol of the stock, the date of purchase and the serial number imprinted on the instruction form. With respect to sales, each investment account maintained by a dealer must disclose the name or identifying symbol of the stock, the date of sale, and the sale price and must refer to the serial number of the instruction form previously used to enter such stock in the dealer's investment identification account on the books of the clearing company. In connection with such sale the dealer, on an instruction form furnished by the clearing company, shall request the clearing company to make an entry in its records to cover a decrease of shares in the investment account and an increase of shares in the general account. This procedure is required solely because of the operation of the clearance system. The entry must disclose the name or the identifying symbol of the stock, the date of the previous purchase and the serial number printed on the instruction form previously used to enter such stock on the records of the clearing company.

5. Separate investment accounts shall be maintained by each participating dealer to reflect purchases and sales of stocks made on behalf of any partner or office-shareholder of such participating dealer. In connection with such transactions, the dealer shall use similar serially numbered instruction forms to request the clearing company to make entries of the same data as that required by paragraph 4 above. The clearing company may make such entries in the investment identification account maintained by it for such dealer provided an appropriate designation, such as "PO," is used in the records of the clearing company to indicate that such entries relate to partner's or officer-shareholder's investments. Such designation shall be so maintained in the records of the clearing company until the entry is eliminated as a result of appropriate instructions from the dealer to the clearing company.

6. Each instruction relating to an investment identification account from a dealer to the clearing company must reflect any information necessary for the maintenance of accounts required herein of the clearing company. Copies of such instructions shall be retained by the dealer and the clearing company. All changes resulting from the dealer's instructions must be reflected in each participating dealer's investment identification account maintained in the records of the clearing company.

7. Each participating dealer, which acts as a clearing agent for other dealers not participating in the clearing operation, must maintain in its books a separate omnibus investment account for each such nonparticipating dealer including its partners or officer-shareholders. In addition, each such nonparticipating dealer shall maintain in its books the same type of accounts required of participating dealers. The clearing company shall maintain for each participating dealer, acting as clearing agent for other dealers not participating in the clearing operation, a separate omnibus investment identification account to reflect the entries resulting from instructions with respect to each nonparticipating dealer, including its partners or officer-shareholders, for which each participating dealer acts. An appropriate numerical designation shall be used to indicate that an account relates to a particular nonparticipating dealer's investment account similarly identified on the books of the participating dealer acting as clearing agent. A separate serially numbered instruction form is to be used by the participating dealer for each nonparticipating dealer investment account entity (nonparticipating dealer's own investment account or investment accounts of its partners or officer-shareholders) on the books of the nonparticipating dealer whenever more than one such entity has transactions in the same security on the same day. The allocation of serial numbers on such instruction forms among the nonparticipating dealer's investment account entities shall be required, however, only on the latter's records.

8. Participating dealers that have investment stocks on deposit in the depository arrangement, in either their investment identification account or an omnibus investment identification account, may make a withdrawal thereof by instructing the clearing company to deliver stock certificates. The certificate numbers imprinted on such stock certificates shall be used as a means of identification in place of the serial number that appeared on the instruction form which resulted in the original entry in such investment identification account or omnibus investment identification account maintained by the clearing company.

9. For purposes of this Revenue Ruling the term "stock" includes only stock listed or traded on a national security exchange registered with the Securities and Exchange Commission and stock rights and warrants so listed and traded thereon.

Nothing contained in this ruling shall be construed as a determination that stocks accounted for in an investment account are capital assets. In addition, in the case of securities dealers who are specialists in specific stocks on a national securities exchange, nothing in this ruling shall be construed as a determination that stocks in which they specialize are capital assets, although accounted for in an investment account.

Appendix 2

Valuation of Closely-Held Stock

Verbatim Presentation of Revenue Ruling 59–60, 1959–1 CB 237.

SECTION 1. PURPOSE.

The purpose of this Revenue Ruling is to outline and review in general the approach, methods and factors to be considered in valuing shares of the capital stock of closely held corporations for estate tax and gift tax purposes. The methods discussed herein will apply likewise to the valuation of corporate stock on which market quotations are either unavailable or are of such scarcity that they do not reflect the fair market value.

SEC. 2. BACKGROUND AND DEFINITIONS.

.01 All valuations must be made in accordance with the applicable provisions of the Internal Revenue Code of 1954 and the Federal Estate Tax and Gift Tax Regulations. Sections 2031 (a), 2032 and 2512(a) of the 1954 Code (sections 811 and 1005 of the 1939 Code) require that the property to be included in the gross estate, or made the subject of a gift, shall be taxed on the basis of the value of the property at the time of death of the decedent, the alternate date if so elected, or the date of gift.

.02 Section 20.2031–1(b) of the Estate Tax Regulations (section 81.10 of the Estate Tax Regulations 105) and section 25.2512–1, of the Gift Tax Regulations (section 86.19 of Gift Tax Regulations 108) define fair market value, in effect, as the price at which the property would change hands between a willing seller when the former is not under any compulsion to buy and the latter is not under any compulsion to sell, both parties having reasonable knowledge of relevant facts. Court decisions frequently state in addition that the hypothetical buyer and seller are assumed to be able, as well as willing, to trade and to be well informed about the property and concerning the market for such property.

.03 Closely held corporations are those corporations the shares of which are owned by a relatively limited number of stockholders. Often the entire stock issue is held by one family. The result of this situation is that little, if any, trading in the shares takes place. There is, therefore, no established market for the stock and such sales as occur at irregular intervals seldom reflect all of the elements of a representative transaction as defined by the term "fair market value."

SEC. 3.   APPROACH TO VALUATION.

.01 A determination of fair market value, being a question of fact, will depend upon the circumstances in each case. No formula can be devised that will be generally applicable to the multitude of different valuation issues arising in estate and gift tax cases. Often, an appraiser will find wide differences of opinion as to the fair market value of a particular stock. In resolving such differences, he should maintain a reasonable attitude in recognition of the fact that valuation is not an exact science. A sound valuation will be based upon all the relevant facts, but the elements of common sense, informed judgment and reasonableness must enter into the process of weighing those facts and determining their aggregate significance.

.02 The fair market value of specific shares of stock will vary as general economic conditions change from "normal" to "boom" or "depression," that is, according to the degree of optimism or pessimism with which the investing public regards the future at the required date of appraisal. Uncertainty as to the stability or continuity of the future income from a property decreases its value by increasing the risk of loss of earnings and value in the future. The value of shares of stock of a company with very uncertain future prospects is highly speculative. The appraiser must exercise his judgment as to the degree of risk attaching to the business of the corporation which issued the stock, but that judgment must be related to all of the other factors affecting value.

.03 Valuation of securities is, in essence, a prophecy as to the future and must be based on facts available at the required date of appraisal. As a generalization, the prices of stocks which are traded in volume in a free and active market by informed persons best reflect the consensus of the investing public as to what the future holds for the corporations and industries represented. When a stock is closely held, is traded infrequently, or is traded in an erratic market, some other measure of value must be used. In many instances, the next best measure may be found in the prices at which the stocks of companies engaged in the same or a similar line of business are selling in a free and open market.

SEC. 4.   FACTORS TO CONSIDER.

.01 It is advisable to emphasize that in the valuation of the stock of closely held corporations or the stock of corporations where market quotations are either lacking or too scarce to be recognized, all available financial data, as well as all relevant factors affecting the fair market value, should be considered. The following factors, although not all-inclusive are fundamental and require careful analysis in each case:

(a) The nature of the business and the history of the enterprise from its inception.

(b) The economic outlook in general and the condition and outlook of the specific industry in particular.

(c) The book value of the stock and the financial condition of the business.

(d) The earning capacity of the company.

(e) The dividend-paying capacity.

(f) Whether or not the enterprise has goodwill or other intangible value.

(g) Sales of the stock and the size of the block of stock to be valued.

(h) The market price of stocks of corporations engaged in the same or a similar line of business having their stocks actively traded in a free and open market, either on an exchange or over-the-counter.

.02 The following is a brief discussion of each of the foregoing factors:

(a) The history of a corporate enterprise will show its past stability or instability, its growth or lack of growth, the diversity or lack of diversity of its operations, and other facts needed to form an opinion of the degree of risk involved in the business. For an enterprise which changed its form of organization but carried on the same or closely similar operations of its predecessor, the history of the former enterprise should be considered. The detail to be considered should increase with approach to the required date of appraisal, since recent events are of greatest help in predicting the future; but a study of gross and net income, and of dividends covering a long prior period, is highly desirable. The history to be studied should include, but need not be limited to, the nature of the business, its products or services, its operating and investment assets, capital structure, plant facilities, sales records and management, all of which should be considered as of the date of the appraisal, with due regard for recent significant changes. Events of the past that are unlikely to recur in the future should be discounted, since value has a close relation to future expectancy.

(b) A sound appraisal of a closely held stock must consider current and prospective economic conditions as of the date of appraisal, both in the national economy and in the industry or industries with which the corporation is allied. It is important to know that the company is more or less successful than its competitors in the same industry, or that it is maintaining a stable position with respect to competitors. Equal or even greater significance may attach to the ability of the industry with which the company is allied to compete with other industries. Prospective competition which has not been a factor in prior years should be given careful attention. For example, high profits due to the novelty of its product and the lack of competition often lead to increasing competition. The public's appraisal of the future prospects of competitive industries or of competitors within an industry may be indicated by price trends in the markets for commodities and for securities. The loss of the manager of a so-called "one-man" business may have a depressing effect upon the value of the stock of such business, particularly if there is a lack of trained personnel capable of succeeding to the management of the enterprise. In valuing the stock of this type of business, therefore, the effect of the loss of the manager on the future expectancy of the business, and the absence of management-succession potentialities are pertinent factors to be taken into consideration. On the other hand, there may be factors which offset, in whole or in part, the loss of the manager's services. For instance, the nature of the business and of its assets may be such that they will not be impaired by the loss of the manager. Furthermore, the loss may be adequately covered by life insurance, or competent management might be employed on the basis of the consideration paid for the former manager's services. These, or other offsetting factors, if found to exist, should be carefully weighed against the loss of the manager's services in valuing the stock of the enterprise.

(c) Balance sheets should be obtained, preferably in the form of comparative annual statements for two or more years immediately preceding the date of appraisal, together with a balance sheet at the end of the month preceding that date, if corporate accounting will permit. Any balance sheet descriptions that are not self-explanatory, and balance sheet items comprehending diverse assets or liabilities, should be clarified in essential detail by supporting supplemental schedules. These statements usually will disclose to the appraiser (1) liquid position (ratio of current assets to current liabilities); (2) gross and net book value of principal classes of fixed assets; (3) working capital; (4) long-term indebtedness; (5) capital structure; and (6) net worth. Consideration also should be given to any assets not essential to the operation of the business, such as investments in securities, real estate, etc. In general, such nonoperating assets will command a lower rate of return than do the operating assets, although in exceptional cases the reverse may be true. In computing the book value per share of stock, assets of the investment type should be revalued on the basis of their market price and the book value adjusted accordingly. Comparison of the company's balance sheets over several years may reveal, among other facts, such developments as the acquisition of additional production facilities or subsidiary companies, improvement in financial position, and details as to recapitalizations and other changes in the capital structure of the corporation. If the corporation has more than one class of stock outstanding, the charter or certificate of incorporation should be examined to ascertain the explicit rights and privileges of the various stock issues including: (1) voting powers, (2) preference as to dividends, and (3) preference as to assets in the event of liquidation.

(d) Detailed profit-and-loss statements should be obtained and considered for a representative period immediately prior to the required date of appraisal, preferably five or more years. Such statements should show (1) gross income by principal items; (2) principal deductions from gross income including major prior items of operating expenses, interest and other expense on each item of long-term debt, depreciation and depletion if such deductions are made, officers' salaries, in total if they appear to be reasonable or in detail if they seem to be excessive, contributions (whether or not deductible for tax purposes) that the nature of its business and its community position require the corporation to make, and taxes by principal items, including income and excess profits taxes; (3) net income available for dividends; (4) rates and amounts of dividends paid on each class of stock; (5) remaining amount carried to surplus; and (6) adjustments to, and reconciliation with, surplus as stated on the balance sheet. With profit and loss statements of this character available, the appraiser should be able to separate recurrent from nonrecurrent items of income and expense, to distinguish between operating income and investment income, and to ascertain whether or not any line of business in which the company is engaged is operated consistently at a loss and might be abandoned with benefit to the company. The percentage of earnings retained for business expansion should be noted when dividend-paying capacity is considered. Potential future income is a major factor in many valuations of closely-held stocks, and all information concerning past income which will be helpful in predicting the future should be secured. Prior earnings records usually are the most reliable guide as to the future expectancy, but resort to arbitrary five-or-ten-year averages without regard to current trends or future prospects will not produce a realistic valuation. If, for instance, a record of progressively increasing or decreasing net income is found, then greater weight may be accorded the most recent years' profits in estimating earning power. It will be helpful, in judging risk and the extent to which a business is a marginal operator, to consider deductions from income and net income in terms of percentage of sales. Major categories of cost and expense to be so analyzed include the consumption of raw materials and supplies in the case of manufacturers, processors and fabricators; the cost of purchased merchandise in the case of merchants; utility services; insurance; taxes; depletion or depreciation; and interest.

(c) Primary consideration should be given to the dividend-paying capacity of the company rather than to dividends actually paid in the past. Recognition must be given to the necessity of retaining a reasonable portion of profits in a company to meet competition. Dividend-paying capacity is a factor that must be considered in an appraisal, but dividends actually paid in the past may not have any relation to dividend-paying capacity. Specifically, the dividends paid by a closely held family company may be measured by the income needs of the stockholders or by their desire to avoid taxes on dividend receipts, instead of by the ability of the company to pay dividends. Where an actual or effective controlling interest in a corporation is to be valued, the dividend factor is not a material element, since the payment of such dividends is discretionary with the controlling stockholders. The individual or group in control can substitute salaries and bonuses for dividends, thus reducing net income and understating the dividend-paying capacity of the company. It follows, therefore, that dividends are less reliable criteria of fair market value than other applicable factors.

(f) In the final analysis, goodwill is based upon earning capacity. The presence of goodwill and its value, therefore, rests upon the excess of net earnings over and above a fair return on the net tangible assets. While the element of goodwill may be based primarily on earnings, such factors as the prestige and renown of the business, the ownership of a trade or brand name, and a record of successful operation over a prolonged period in a particular locality, also may furnish support for the inclusion of intangible value. In some instances it may not be possible to make a separate appraisal of the tangible and intangible assets of the business. The enterprise has a value as an entity. Whatever intangible value there is, which is supportable by the facts, may be measured by the amount by which the appraised value of the tangible assets exceeds the net book value of such assets.

(g) Sales of stock of a closely held corporation should be carefully investigated to determine whether they represent transactions at arm's length. Forced or distress sales do not ordinarily reflect fair market value nor do isolated sales in small amounts necessarily control as the measure of value. This is especially true in the valuation of a controlling interest in a corporation. Since, in the case of closely held stocks, no prevailing market prices are available, there is no basis for making an adjustment for blockage. It follows, therefore, that such stocks should be valued upon a consideration of all the evidence affecting the fair market value. The size of the block of stock itself is a relevant factor to be considered. Although it is true that a minority interest in an unlisted corporation's stock is more difficult to sell than a similar block of listed stock, it is equally true that control of a corporation, either actual or in effect, representing as it does an added element of value, may justify a higher value for a specific block of stock.

(h) Section 2031(b) of the Code states, in effect, that in valuing unlisted securities the value of stock or securities of corporations engaged in the same or a similar line of business which are listed on an exchange should be taken into consideration along with all other factors. An important consideration is that the corporations to be used for comparisons have capital stocks which are actively traded by the public. In accordance with section 2031(b) of the Code, stocks listed on an exchange are to be considered first. However, if sufficient comparable companies whose stocks are listed on an exchange cannot be found, other comparable companies which have stocks actively traded in on the over-the-counter market also may be used. The essential factor is that whether the stocks are sold on an exchange or over-the-counter there is evidence of an active, free public market for the stock as of the valuation date. In selecting corporations for comparative purposes, care should be taken to use only comparable companies. Although the only restrictive requirement as to comparable corporations specified in the statute is that their lines of business be the same or similar, yet it is obvious that consideration must be given to other relevant factors in order that the most valid comparison possible will be obtained. For illustration, a corporation having one or more issues of preferred stock, bonds or debentures in addition to its common stock should not be considered to be directly comparable to one having only common stock outstanding. In like manner, a company with a declining business and decreasing markets is not comparable to one with a record of current progress and market expansion.

SEC. 5. WEIGHT TO BE ACCORDED VARIOUS FACTORS.

The valuation of closely held corporate stock entails the consideration of all relevant factors as stated in section 4. Depending upon the circumstances in each case, certain factors may carry more weight than others because of the nature of the company's business. To illustrate:

(a) Earnings may be the most important criterion of value in some cases whereas asset value will receive primary consideration in others. In general, the appraiser will accord primary consideration to earnings when valuing stocks of companies which sell products or services to the public; conversely, in the investment or holding type of company, the appraiser may accord the greatest weight to the assets underlying the security to be valued.

(b) The value of the stock of a closely held investment or real estate holding company, whether or not family owned, is closely related to the value of the assets underlying the stock. For companies of this type the appraiser should determine the fair market values of the assets of the company. Operating expenses of such a company and the cost of liquidating it, if any, merit consideration when appraising the relative values of the stock and the underlying assets. The market values of the underlying assets give due weight to potential earnings and dividends of the particular items of property underlying the stock, capitalized at rates deemed proper by the investing public at the date of appraisal. A current appraisal by the investing public should be superior to the retrospective opinion of an individual. For these reasons, adjusted net worth should be accorded greater weight in valuing the stock of a closely held investment or real estate holding company, whether or not family owned, than any of the other customary yardsticks of appraisal, such as earnings and dividend paying capacity.

SEC. 6. CAPITALIZATION RATES.

In the application of certain fundamental valuation factors, such as earnings and dividends, it is necessary to capitalize the average or current results at some appropriate rate. A determination of the proper capitalization rate presents one of the most difficult problems in valuation. That there is no ready or simple solution will become apparent by a cursory check of the rates of return and dividend yields in terms of selling prices of corporate shares listed on the major exchanges of the country. Wide variations will be found even for companies in the same industry. Moreover, the ratio will fluctuate from year to year depending upon economic conditions. Thus, no standard tables of capitalization rates applicable to closely held corporations can be formulated. Among the more important factors to be taken into consideration in deciding upon a capitalization rate in a particular case are: (1) the nature of the business; (2) the risk involved; and (3) the stability or irregularity of earnings.

SEC. 7. AVERAGE OF FACTORS.

Because valuations cannot be made on the basis of a prescribed formula, there is no means whereby the various applicable factors in a particular case can be assigned mathematical weights in deriving the fair market value. For this reason, no useful purpose is served by taking an average of several factors (for example, book value, capitalized earnings and capitalized dividends) and basing the valuation on the result. Such a process excludes active consideration of other pertinent factors, and the end result cannot be supported by a realistic application of the significant facts in the case except by mere chance.

SEC. 8. RESTRICTIVE AGREEMENTS.

Frequently, in the valuation of closely held stock for estate and gift tax purposes, it will be found that the stock is subject to an agreement restricting its sale or transfer. Where shares of stock were acquired by a decedent subject to an option reserved by the issuing corporation to repurchase at a certain price, the option price is usually accepted as the fair market value for estate tax purposes. See Rev. Rul. 54–76, C.B. 1954–1, 194. However, in such case the option price is not determinative of fair market value for gift tax purposes. Where the option, or buy and sell agreement, is the result of voluntary action by the stockholders and is binding during the life as well as the death of the stockholders, such agreement may or not, depending upon the circumstances of each case, fix the value for estate tax purposes. However, such agreement is a factor to be considered, with other relevant factors, in determining fair market value. When the stockholder is free to dispose of his shares during life and the option is to become effective only upon his death, the fair market value is not limited to the option price. It is always necessary to consider the relationship of the parties, the relative number of shares held by the decedent, and other material facts, to determine whether the agreement represents a bona fide business agreement or is a device to pass the decedent's shares to the natural objects of his bounty for less than an adequate and full consideration in money or money's worth.

Table of Cases Cited

Index

DATE DUE

MAR 8 '79	MAR 7 '79		
GAYLORD			PRINTED IN U.S.A.